ow to Do erything with

with

Microsoft PowerPoint® 2007

Ellen Finkelstein

New York   Chicago   San Francisco   Lisbon
London   Madrid   Mexico City   Milan   New Delhi
San Juan   Seoul   Singapore   Sydney   Toronto

The **McGraw·Hill** Companies

McGraw-Hill books are available at special quantity discounts to use as premiums and sales promotions, or for use in corporate training programs. For more information, please write to the Director of Special Sales, Professional Publishing, McGraw-Hill, Two Penn Plaza, New York, NY 10121-2298. Or contact your local bookstore.

How to Do Everything with Microsoft® Office PowerPoint® 2007

234567890 FGR FGR 01987

ISBN: 978-0-07-226339-8
MHID: 0-07-226339-3

Sponsoring Editor Roger Stewart	**Proofreader** Amy Rodriguez	**Art Director, Cover** Jeff Weeks
Editorial Supervisor Janet Walden	**Indexer** Robert Swanson	**Cover Designer** Pattie Lee
Project Manager Rajni Pisharody	**Production Supervisor** George Anderson	**Cover Illustration** Tom Willis
Acquisitions Coordinator Carly Stapleton	**Composition** International Typesetting and Composition	
Technical Editor Geetesh Bajaj	**Illustration** International Typesetting and Composition	
Copy Editor Bill McManus		

*To MMY, who taught me how to dive deep within and find the foundation
of happiness and success within myself.*

About the Author

Ellen Finkelstein has written several computer books on AutoCAD, PowerPoint, and Flash, such as *How to Do Everything with PowerPoint 2003*. She writes numerous articles on AutoCAD and PowerPoint, and maintains a web site of AutoCAD and PowerPoint tips and tutorials at www.ellenfinkelstein.com, where you can sign up for her free monthly PowerPoint Tips Newsletter or read her PowerPoint Tips Blog.

About the Technical Editor

Geetesh Bajaj, based in India, is a Microsoft PowerPoint MVP (Most Valuable Professional). He runs the Indezine.com and Ppted.com sites that contain extensive PowerPoint-related content including reviews, tutorials, and a biweekly PowerPoint e-zine. He's also the author of his own book on PowerPoint, *Cutting Edge PowerPoint for Dummies*.

Contents

Acknowledgments xiii
Introduction xiii

PART I   **Create a Presentation**

CHAPTER 1   **Get Started with Presentations** **3**
Get Your Message Across 4
Open a Presentation 6
    Start PowerPoint 6
    Create a New Presentation 6
    Open an Existing Presentation 8
View a Presentation 13
    Look at the Screen 13
    Use the Ribbon, Office Button, and Quick Access Toolbar 15
    Use the Appropriate View 16
    Move Around a Presentation 20
Get Help When You Need It 20
Save a Presentation 22
    Use Save and Publish Options 26
    Save So You Can Find It Fast Next Time 26
    Back Up Your Presentations 27
Summary 27

CHAPTER 2   **Create Your First Presentation** **29**
Create Your Presentation 30
    Choose a Template or Theme 30
    Choose a Background Style 35
    Start from Scratch 36
    Start a New Presentation from an Existing One 36
    Lay Out a Slide 37
    Add Slides 39
    Complete the Presentation Structure 40

Structure a Presentation from an Outline   40
    Understand Outlines   40
    Create an Outline in PowerPoint   43
    Import an Outline   47
Add Text to a Presentation   48
    Use Text Placeholders   49
    Create Text Boxes   52
    Place Text in Shapes   53
    Use WordArt   55
Eliminate Spelling Errors and Discover Synonyms   58
    Check Spelling   58
    Find Synonyms   59
Complete a Presentation: Tutorial   60
    Develop the Framework   60
    Add Slides   63
    Add a Chart   64
    Move a Slide   65
    Add Animation   66
    View the Slide Show   67
Summary   67

CHAPTER 3   Edit Text **69**
Edit for Clarity   70
    Move and Copy Text   71
    Use the Clipboard Task Pane   72
    Edit Placeholder Text   72
    Edit Text in Shapes and Text Boxes   77
    Edit WordArt Text   79
    Add Symbols   79
    Use AutoCorrect   80
    Act on Data with Smart Tags   83
Choose Text with Style   85
    Use the Right Font for the Message   85
    Make a Font Bigger or Smaller   86
Add, Delete, and Rearrange Slides   97
    Work in Slide Sorter View   97
    Import Slides from Other Presentations   98
    Keep a Slide Library   101
Summary   102

CHAPTER 4   Format Bullets and Paragraphs **103**
Create a Bulleted List   104
    Choose a Bullet Type   104
    Set Bullet Size and Color   106

Use an Image as a Bullet 107
Create Numbered Lists 110
Work with Paragraphs 111
Understand Paragraph Formatting 112
Use the Ruler 114
Indent Text 115
Set Tabs 119
Align Text 120
Create Columns 122
Set Line Spacing 122
Summary 124

PART II   Add Multimedia Elements to Your Presentation

CHAPTER 5   Add Art and Graphic Objects **129**
Create an Impact with Graphics 130
Use Clip Art 131
Find Art in the Clip Art Task Pane 131
Create Your Own Clip Art Collection 134
Finding Additional Clip Art and Photos 137
Insert Picture Files 138
Create a Photo Album 139
Edit Images and Drawing Objects 141
Select Objects 141
Move Objects 142
Duplicate Objects 142
Delete Objects 142
Resize Objects 143
Rotate and Flip Objects 145
Group and Ungroup Objects 146
Reorder Objects 148
Substitute Pictures or Shapes 149
Recolor Graphics 150
Manage Pictures 153
Format a Picture 155
Edit Graphic Files 158
Create Drawing Objects 160
Draw Lines, Arrows, and Curves 161
Create Flowcharts and Process Diagrams 165
Insert Shapes 166
Save Drawing Objects for Later Use 168
Edit Points 169
Edit Connectors 170

Lay Out Your Slides with Precision 171
    Use the Rulers 171
    Use Guides 171
    Snap to the Grid and to Objects 172
    Specify an Exact Location 173
    Constrain Shape and Direction 174
    Nudge Objects 174
    Align and Distribute Objects 175
Tips on Design and Layout 176
    Make Text Simple and Consistent 176
    Follow a Simple Plan 177
    Consider Color and Rhythm 177
    Relate Graphics to Content 178
Summary 178

CHAPTER 6   **Work with Colors, Borders, Fills, and 3-D Effects** **179**
Work with Theme Colors 180
    Choose Theme Colors 181
    Create Your Own Set of Theme Colors 182
Change Backgrounds 185
    Create Solid Backgrounds 188
    Create Gradient Backgrounds 188
    Create Picture Backgrounds 192
Use Shape Styles 197
Format Outlines 198
Work with Fills 199
    Change Fill Color 200
    Create Background-Matching,
        Transparent, and Rotating Fills 201
Add Special Effects 202
    Reflect Your Objects 202
    Add a Glow 203
    Add Soft Edges 204
Create 3-D Effects 205
    Create Shadows 205
    Create 3-D Shapes 208
Summary 215

CHAPTER 7   **Coordinate Presentations with Slide Masters,**
             Layouts, and Themes **217**
Format the Slide Master 218
    Enter Slide Master View 219
    Manage Slide Masters 220

Change the Background and Theme Properties 222
Format Headings and Bulleted Text 223
Add Repeating Objects and Animation 224
Add a Footer 225
Insert a Slide Master Component 227
Make Exceptions to the Master Formatting 228
Apply a Master to a Slide 229
Create Custom Layouts 229
Format the Handout Master 230
Enter Handout Master View 231
Customize the Handout Master 232
Format the Notes Master 233
Enter Notes Master View 233
Customize the Notes Master 234
Set Page Size 234
Save Custom Themes 235
Create Your Own Templates 236
Summary 237

CHAPTER 8   **Incorporate Graphs, Tables, and Diagrams** **239**
Present Data Simply 240
Add Graphs to a Slide 241
Choose the Right Chart Type 242
Enter Data on the Spreadsheet 249
Link to a Chart 251
Insert a Spreadsheet as an Object 252
Format a Chart 252
Insert a Chart from Microsoft Excel 262
Present Data in a Table 262
Create a Table 263
Import a Table 264
Format a Table 265
Work with Diagrams 267
Format a Diagram 270
Summary 272

CHAPTER 9   **Add Animation to a Presentation** **273**
Create Professional Animation 274
Animate Text and Objects 274
Use Preset Animation for Quick Results 275
Use Custom Animation for Maximum Control 276
Animate Charts and Diagrams 287
Add Animated GIF Files 290
Add Flash Animation to a Slide 290

Transition from Slide to Slide 293
    Use Transitions Wisely 293
    Choose the Ideal Transition Style 293
Summary 296

CHAPTER 10   **Use Multimedia** **297**
Create a Mood with Sounds and Music 298
Insert Sound or Music Files 298
    Specify Play Settings 300
    Add a CD Soundtrack 303
Show Movies with Video Clips 304
Record Narration 307
Summary 310

PART III   **Manage and Convey a Presentation**

CHAPTER 11   **Interact with Others** **313**
Add Flexibility with Hyperlinks 314
    Hyperlink to Another Slide in Your Presentation 315
    Hyperlink to a Slide in Another Presentation 316
    Hyperlink to Another File or a Web Page 317
    Hyperlink to a New File 318
    Create an E-mail from a Slide 319
    Edit Hyperlinks 320
Use Action Buttons to Control Navigation 320
    Navigate Within a Presentation 320
    Use Action Settings 323
Copy Data 324
    Use the Clipboard and Drag-and-Drop 325
    Import and Export Files 325
    Insert OLE Objects 327
    Link Objects 328
    Manage Files 329
Collaborate with Others 329
    Share and Send a Presentation 329
    Review a Presentation 331
Protect a Presentation 332
Summary 336

CHAPTER 12   **Display a Presentation on a Web Site** **339**
Show Presentations on the Web 340
    Use PowerPoint to Create Web Pages 340
    Create a Viewer-Controlled Presentation for the Web 342

Publish a Presentation to the Web 344
Test Your Web Site 350
Summary 351

CHAPTER 13   **Customize PowerPoint** **353**
Customize PowerPoint's Options 354
Set Popular Options 354
Set Spelling and AutoCorrect Options 356
Specify Save Options 359
Set Advanced Options 361
Set Security Options 363
Find Resources 364
Customize the Quick Access Toolbar 365
Work with Macros 368
Understand the Object Model 369
Use Methods and Properties 371
Use VBA in Your Presentations 372
Use a Macro 378
Manage Macros 379
Summary 384

CHAPTER 14   **Prepare to Deliver Your Presentation** **385**
Decide on the Best Slide Format 386
Print Handouts 386
Use 35mm Slides 386
Use Overhead Transparencies 387
Present Directly from a Computer 388
Run a Presentation on an Autorun CD 388
Choose the Best Equipment 390
Time Your Presentation 395
Set the Timing 395
Use Timing When You Present 397
Set Slide Show Parameters 398
Prepare Your Notes 401
Create Slide Show Variations 402
Create a Custom Show 402
Edit a Custom Show 404
Use a Custom Show 404
Summary 406

CHAPTER 15   **Present Your Slide Show** **407**
Print and Use Handouts 408
Send the Presentation to Microsoft Word 410

Use PowerPoint Viewer 412
    Present a Slide Show with PowerPoint Viewer 412
Practice Professional Presentation Skills 414
    Set up the Room and Check Your Equipment 414
    Speak in Front of a Group 415
    Cope with Disasters 416
    Be Prepared When Using Computer Projection 417
Control Your Presentation 418
    Mark Slides as You Present 421
    Use Hyperlinks and Action Buttons 423
Summary 423

Index **425**

Acknowledgments

The creation of any book is a group enterprise, and this book is no exception. You would not be reading it without the contributions of many people. Some of the important contributions, such as the design, layout, production, and printing of the book, were made by people whose names I don't know, but I thank them anyway.

First, I'd like to thank Margie McAneny, my original acquisitions editor, who offered me the opportunity to write this book. Margie was intimately involved with the book and answered my many questions patiently. Recently, Rogert Stewart took her place and he's been very supportive as we figured out Microsoft Office 2007 together. Agatha Kim, and then Carly Stapleton, acquisitions coordinators both, monitored the submissions of the manuscript, including keeping track of zillions of figures and illustrations (and the difference between them), and handed them over safely for the editorial process. Then Rajni Pisharody picked up the process as Project Manager. I don't know how you do it, but I'm glad you do. Geetesh Bajaj, a PowerPoint MVP (which means he knows a whole lot about PowerPoint), was once again my cheerful and competent technical editor. He came up with many ideas, which were incorporated into the book. Thanks, Geetesh!

Many people contributed presentations for this book. These presentations gave me real-world material to show you in the book's figures and illustrations, and I greatly appreciate them.

Last, but certainly not least, I must thank my family for supporting me while I wrote. My husband, Evan, shopped, did countless washes, and dragged me away from the computer when I needed a break. My kids, Yeshayah and Eliyah, managed to put up with my being endlessly in front of the computer. I love you!

Introduction

Microsoft PowerPoint 2007 is a presentation program, which means that it helps you create presentations that you develop and show on your computer. Presentations are like slide shows, but no physical slides are necessary. While almost all computer users are familiar with word processing programs and many know what a spreadsheet is all about, many computer users have never used a presentation program.

All that is changing. The use of presentation programs is increasing geometrically. While design professionals once created most presentations, presentation programs such as PowerPoint have now made it easy for anyone to create an attractive, effective presentation in a few minutes. There are enough special features—such as clip art, sound files, and animation effects—to help you create a professional-looking presentation if you want to invest a little more time.

PowerPoint is the most popular presentation program available. In fact, *a PowerPoint* has become a generic term to mean any electronic presentation. PowerPoint 2007, an integral part of the Microsoft Office 2007 suite, has been updated to provide greater ease of use and a number of new features. Here is a partial list:

- A completely redesigned interface that does away with menus and toolbars and used a tabbed *ribbon* along the top of the screen instead.

- Customizable slide layouts and a new system of slide masters based on layouts

- Better gradients, as well as new effects, including reflections, glows, and soft edges

- *Themes*, which coordinate design, fonts, colors, and effects

- Galleries, which provide a quick way to format text and shapes—and you can see the result on your object before you commit to a format

- SmartArt graphics, which are diagrams that you can create from scratch or by simply converting existing slide text

- More text effects and formats as well as the ability to apply WordArt effects to any text

- Better integration between Microsoft Excel and PowerPoint for creating charts; easier chart formatting

- Presenter view that lets you see all the slides while your audience sees only the slide you want them to see

  - New compressed XML format that generally results in smaller file sizes

  - Ability to save files in Adobe Acrobat PDF format (with an add-in)

  - Protection features that prevent changes and remove personal information

On the other hand, a few features have been removed. These include the AutoContent Wizard, the macro recorder, the broadcast feature for displaying a presentation to multiple people over the Web or an Intranet, the Send for Review command, summary slides, the title master, and the Speaker Notes box.

Whether you're a new PowerPoint user or are trying to hone your existing skills, you'll find all you need in this book about all of PowerPoint's features and how to use them to get professional results.

What's Special about this Book

How to Do Everything with Microsoft Office PowerPoint 2007 covers all the features you need to make using PowerPoint easy and productive, and then goes further to explain how to make your presentations truly professional. It includes tips, shortcuts, and notes to give you the extra edge you need to create presentations that communicate. Special How To and Did You Know boxes add information beyond the usual content of a book on PowerPoint.

I have designed this book to include not only the specific features of PowerPoint 2007, but also a great deal of information about designing and presenting slide shows that deliver the message effectively. You will see information on the use of color, laying out a slide, rehearsing, and many other topics that directly affect the success of your presentation.

Who Needs this Book

I have written this book for beginning and intermediate users who are familiar with Microsoft Windows. If you are just starting to use PowerPoint, *How to Do Everything with Microsoft Office PowerPoint 2007* explains the basics of presentation programs and brings you through the creation of your first complete presentation by Chapter 2. If you have already used PowerPoint but want to expand your skills, this book provides you with everything you need to know about PowerPoint and about creating presentations.

This book starts out with the basics and then presents the rest of PowerPoint's many features systematically and comprehensively. If you read it from cover to cover, it will bring you to an intermediate-to-advanced level of knowledge and skill.

How this Book Is Organized

The overall organization of *How to Do Everything with Microsoft Office PowerPoint 2007* is from simple to complex, from wholeness to specifics, and from start to finish.

Chapters 1 through 4 provide you with the basics you need to use PowerPoint. By Chapter 2, you have created your first complete presentation. Chapter 2 also demonstrates how to choose a theme and start a presentation from scratch. Chapters 3 and 4 explain how to edit a presentation as well as format bullets and paragraphs.

Chapters 5 through 10 describe how to add graphics, tables, and charts to a slide, including how to work with colors, borders, fills, and 3-D effects. I explain how to include repeating elements and how to make sure that all the slides in a presentation have a unified appearance. Finally, I discuss animation, slide transition effects, and multimedia—the use of sound and video.

Chapters 11 through 15 bring your presentation out of PowerPoint and into the rest of the world where it must inevitably go. I explain how to incorporate data from other applications, develop a presentation collaboratively, display a presentation on the Internet, and customize PowerPoint. I end the book with two chapters detailing the actual presentation process, including how to time and rehearse your presentation, use projection equipment, and actually deliver your slide show.

How to Use this Book

If you are a beginner, you should start from the beginning and read until you have enough information to create your presentation. Try out the features as you read. If you need to create a specific presentation, start creating it from the very first chapter. As you continue reading, you can improve and refine your presentation, using the chapters that cover the features you need.

If you have used PowerPoint before but want to improve your skills and increase your knowledge, scan the Note icons throughout the book because many of them highlight new features. You can then go directly to the chapters that contain the topics you need.

How to Contact the Author

Please contact me at ellen@ellenfinkelstein.com if you have a question about the material in the book or find any errors. However, note that I can't provide technical support for PowerPoint. Also, I welcome you to visit my web site at www.ellenfinkelstein.com. Supporting presentations and files for this book are at www.ellenfinkelstein.com/htde_pp2007.html. While you're there, please sign up for the free monthly PowerPoint Tips Newsletter.

Have Fun!

PowerPoint is great fun to use! However you use this book, whether you're in business, education, or government, enjoy the process and the satisfaction you will get from creating effective, professional presentations.

Part I

Create a Presentation

Chapter 1

Get Started with Presentations

How to …

- Get your message across
- Open a presentation
- View a presentation
- Get help when you need it
- Save a presentation

Microsoft PowerPoint is all about effective communication. PowerPoint gives you the tools you need to create a professional-quality presentation. You don't need to spend big bucks for a graphic artist or a slide bureau to create presentations for you. You can do it yourself. This book provides extensive coverage of PowerPoint features to help you create your own presentations, whether you are a beginner or an advanced user.

Get Your Message Across

Microsoft PowerPoint 2007 is a presentation program. A presentation program creates slide shows, which you can then show on a projection screen or directly from your computer. A PowerPoint file is called a *presentation*, and the individual unit of a presentation is a *slide*. Each slide is equivalent to a page, as pictured in Figure 1-1.

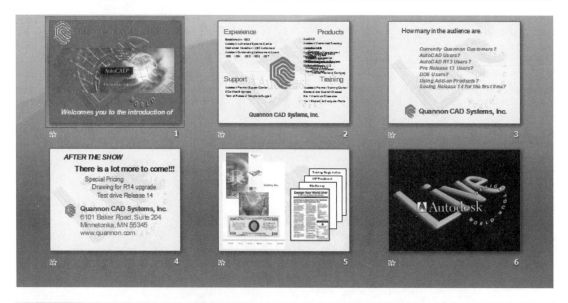

FIGURE 1-1   A PowerPoint presentation consists of a series of slides.

> **NOTE** *While a PowerPoint file is called a presentation, in general use, the word presentation means your oral delivery in front of an audience. Remember that the PowerPoint slides don't replace your words, unless you use the file as a self-running presentation. You are the presentation! (I explain how to let your PowerPoint presentation run itself in Chapter 15.)*

PowerPoint 2007 is light-years ahead of the individual 35mm slides or overhead transparencies of yesteryear. For example, you can

- Add graphics, sound, music, animations, and short video clips to maximize your impact.
- Instantly make changes (as in any computer document).
- Animate text or other objects to emphasize your point.
- Create transition effects from one slide to another.
- Change the color scheme or background for an entire presentation or for a single slide.
- Add graphs (charts), tables, and diagrams to make your point visually and clearly.
- Create interactive or automatically looping slide shows—ideal when presenting at conventions, in a kiosk, or in a classroom.
- Save your presentation in HTML format and publish it on the Internet or an intranet.
- Create an autorun CD of your presentation that can play on systems that do not have PowerPoint installed.

The purpose of a presentation is to communicate. Of course, you can also communicate with your word processing documents. Even spreadsheets communicate something from their numbers. But in a presentation, the process of conveying the message is the point. You use words, art, shapes, color, sound, and special effects to maximize the effectiveness of your message. It's called *multimedia*, and it's a hot, growing field. You may have never used multimedia tools before, but with PowerPoint, you easily get professional results. And with a little practice, you will soon be creating exciting, compelling presentations.

Because it is now so easy to create great presentations, the number of PowerPoint users is in the millions. PowerPoint presentations are everywhere, but customers, managers, and peers expect an ever-higher level of professionalism in the quality of the presentations they see.

In order to communicate effectively, you need to manage three elements:

- **Content** Decide on your primary message, organize points that support your message, and express your ideas clearly. Add content that documents your points. Part I of this book provides introductory concepts and explains how to add text (that is, content) to your slides.
- **Design** Create a design that enhances your message. Overdoing the special effects distracts the audience. Part II covers design.
- **Delivery** Practice delivering your presentation so that your slides add to your message without turning the audience's attention away from you. Part III shows you how to manage and deliver a presentation.

The Impact of Multimedia

Why use multimedia? Scientific research shows that visual aids and the use of color significantly increase the amount of material your audience understands and remembers. Moreover, presentations that include visual aids and other multimedia effects have been shown to be more effective in convincing an audience to take the course of action suggested by the presenter. On the other hand, images that are distracting or irrelevant can reduce learning. For full details on how to add multimedia elements, see Chapter 10.

Open a Presentation

Before you start creating slides, you need to learn the fundamentals of working with PowerPoint. Although the skills you learn in this section don't show up on your slides, they make your life a lot easier—and make creating your presentation a lot smoother. In this section, I show you how to start PowerPoint and open a new or existing presentation file.

Start PowerPoint

The first step is to launch PowerPoint. An easy way to open PowerPoint is to double-click a desktop shortcut. If you don't already have a desktop shortcut for PowerPoint, here's how to create one:

1. Go to Start | All Programs | Microsoft Office and highlight Microsoft PowerPoint (without clicking it).

2. Right-click Microsoft PowerPoint, and choose Copy.

3. Right-click on the desktop and choose Paste.

Of course, if you don't like shortcuts, you can open the PowerPoint icon by selecting Start | All Programs | Microsoft Office | PowerPoint 2007.

Create a New Presentation

To start a brand-new presentation, click the Office button, shown here. You can find it at the upper-left corner of the application window. This button displays a menu that provides functions related to your presentation file; for example, you can open, save, print, and convert files from this menu.

Then, click New to open the New Presentation dialog box, shown in Figure 1-2.
The New Presentation dialog box offers the following ways to start a new presentation:

■ To start a new blank presentation from scratch, click the Blank Presentation button and then click Create (or double-click the Blank Presentation button).

■ To start a new presentation based on an existing presentation, click New from existing in the left pane. The New from existing dialog box opens, which is just like the Open dialog

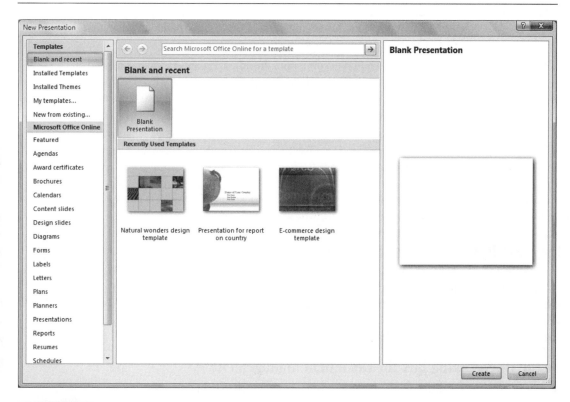

FIGURE 1-2   The New Presentation dialog box lets you create a new presentation in several ways.

box (shown in Figure 1-3 in the next section). This method is equivalent to opening an existing presentation, clicking the Office button, and choosing Save As.

■ To start a presentation based on a template that you have saved, click My Templates in the left pane. The New Presentation dialog box opens, showing only templates that you have saved in the Templates folder. Choose one and click OK.

NOTE   *A template includes graphics, text formatting, and perhaps standardized text. A template can also include animation. By default, in Windows Vista templates that you create are saved in c:\Users\[username]\AppData\Roaming\Microsoft\Templates. I explain how to use a template in Chapter 2. I show you how to create your own templates at the end of Chapter 7.*

■ To use a template that you have used recently, choose it from the Recently Used Templates area.

- To use one of the templates that comes with PowerPoint, click Installed Templates in the left pane. You see a preview of any thumbnail that you click. Choose the template that you want and click Create.

- To use a theme that comes with PowerPoint, click Installed Themes in the left pane. You see a preview of any thumbnail that you click. Choose the theme that you want and click Create. Themes are a new feature for PowerPoint 2007. They are similar to templates but have several differences. I discuss themes in Chapters 2 and 7.

- To choose one of the templates that Microsoft stores on its web site, click a category from the Microsoft Office Online list, choose one of the templates, and click Create. Sometimes there are subtopics to choose from.

All the options for starting a presentation are covered in detail in Chapter 2, where you learn how to create a new presentation.

Open an Existing Presentation

Often you want to work on an existing presentation. Opening a presentation is easy—just click the Office button. If you've opened the presentation recently, you can quickly choose it from the Recent Documents list. Otherwise, choose Open to display the Open dialog box, shown in Figure 1-3 with the Large Icons view. (Use the Views drop-down list in the dialog box to change the type of view.) Locate your presentation, select it, and click Open.

Use the Open Dialog Box for Document Management

The Open dialog box is different in Windows Vista and Windows XP. In either version of Windows, you can use the dialog box to easily find documents.

- **Windows XP**   Down the left side of the Open dialog box are five buttons that can help you find presentations and supporting files more quickly. Together, these buttons are called the My Places bar. Each button represents a folder and you can add folders that you use a lot to help you find presentations more easily. To do so, close the Open dialog box and click the Office button, then choose Save As. In the Save As dialog box, click the Save In drop-down list and choose the desired folder. (You can also choose a drive or Internet location.) Right-click a blank area of the My Places bar and choose Add [folder name]. You can also use the shortcut menu to move or delete items.

- **Windows Vista**   On the upper-left side of the Open dialog box is a list of Favorite Links. Below that is a list of folders. (If you don't see the folders, click the Up arrow next to the word Folders in the left pane.) You can add folders to the Favorite Links list to make presentations easier to access. To do so, use the Folders list to navigate to the drive containing the folder (or to the folder above a subfolder). When you see the folder in the right-hand pane, drag it to the Favorite Links pane.

FIGURE 1-3 Use the Open dialog box to find existing presentations. Here you see the Open dialog box as it appears in Windows Vista.

TIP

To change the order of a link in Windows Vista, drag a link up or down with the right *mouse button.*

Use the Open Options

You have some hidden options for opening a presentation. Two of them are especially useful if you are working on a networked computer. To use the Open options, click the drop-down arrow

Compatibility Mode

When you open a presentation in 97-2003 format, PowerPoint uses Compatibility Mode to maintain its integrity. You also go into Compatibility Mode if you save a document in 97-2003 format. You know that you're in Compatibility Mode because those words appear after the presentation's name in the title bar. In order to maintain compatibility, PowerPoint suppresses new and updated features so that even after you save the presentation, you (or someone else) can reopen the presentation successfully in an earlier version of PowerPoint.

next to the Open button, located in the lower-right corner of the Open dialog box. Choose one the following:

- **Open Read-Only** This option opens a presentation but doesn't allow you to make any changes. However, you can click the Office button and choose Save As to save the presentation under another name or in another location. Use this option when you are working on a network and someone else is currently working on the same presentation.

- **Open as Copy** This option creates a duplicate of the presentation in the same folder as the original and opens the duplicate. You can then make any changes you need.

- **Open in Browser** With this option, you can open a presentation saved in HTML format in your web browser.

- **Open and Repair** Use this option to repair a file that you're having difficulty opening. PowerPoint tries to repair any errors so that you can successfully open the presentation.

- **Show Previous Versions** Previous versions are files created using the Back Up Files Wizard in Windows, or saved automatically as part of a restore point (*shadow copies*). Use this option is you can't open the original file and need to find a duplicate.

The Open dialog box contains some useful options. For example, you can right-click any file and use the shortcut menu to print a presentation and display properties.

When you right-click a file and choose the Properties option, the Properties dialog box opens, displaying some useful information about the presentation, as shown in Figure 1-4. For example, you can find the date the file was created and last modified. The Details tab shows you the number of slides, paragraphs, words, bytes, and more.

You may want to map a network drive (give it a drive letter, such as Z:) that contains presentations for easier access. To do so, click the Tools button in the Open dialog box and choose Map Network Drive.

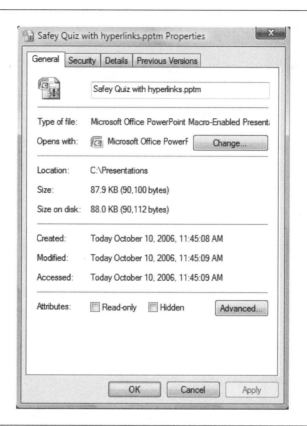

FIGURE 1-4   The Properties dialog box provides you with a great deal of information about the presentation.

Customize the Default File Location

If you often work from one folder, you may wish to make it the default folder for the Open and Save dialog boxes. No longer will you have to navigate to your presentations and other files on your hard disk or network each and every time you want to open them. Whenever you want to open or save a presentation, your preferred folder will be active in the dialog box.

To set the default folder, click the Office button, then click the PowerPoint Options button to open the PowerPoint Options dialog box. Choose the Save item, shown in Figure 1-5. In the Default File Location text box, type the path for the default folder you want. For example, type **c:\presentations**. Click OK.

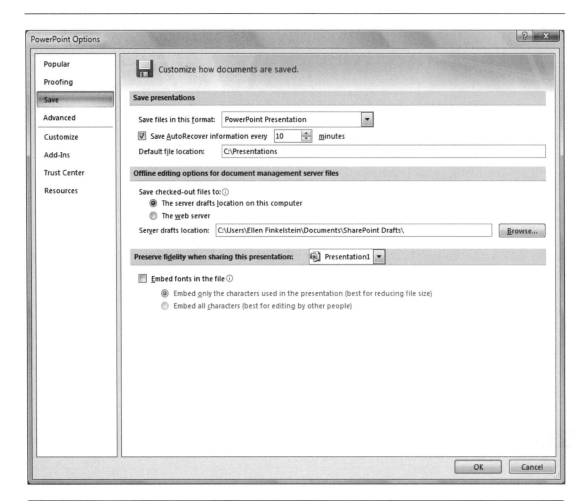

FIGURE 1-5 Customize the default location for saving and opening presentations.

Use a Presentation from the Author's Companion Web Site

If you would like to practice the skills in this chapter but don't have a presentation to work with, you can download a sample presentation from my web site at www.ellenfinkelstein.com/htde_pp2007.html. Quarterly Sales Report.pptx is a simple presentation that you can easily work with. (See Chapter 2 for the steps to create a similar presentation.)

View a Presentation

Understanding PowerPoint's window and views helps you accomplish all your tasks more quickly. PowerPoint 2007 (and all of Office 2007) uses a completely new user interface, so if you're upgrading from PowerPoint 2003 or earlier, you'll need to get used to the changes.

Look at the Screen

Figure 1-6 shows the PowerPoint screen and its elements in Normal view. The following list describes the elements in this figure:

- The Office button provides access to file-related tools, such as those to save, print, open, and share files.

- The Quick Access toolbar provides buttons for commands that you use often.

- The title bar tells you that you are in PowerPoint and displays the name of your presentation. It also tells you if you are in Compatibility Mode. (For more information on Compatibility Mode, see the "Did You Know?" box earlier in this chapter.)

- The tabs provide access to the ribbon. The tabs are similar to the menu bar in previous versions of PowerPoint. As you click each tab, the ribbon changes to display tools applicable for that tab. The new ribbon contains most of PowerPoint's tools.

- The Minimize button reduces the application window to a button on the Windows taskbar.

- The Maximize button fills the entire screen with the application window.

- The Close button closes all presentations if you have more than one presentation open. If you have only one presentation open, the Close button also closes PowerPoint.

TIP   *To close just the presentation, and not PowerPoint, when you have only one presentation open, click the Office button and choose Close from the menu. You can also press* CTRL-F4.

- The Help button opens the PowerPoint Help window, where you can search for answers to your questions by entering search keywords.

- The Slide pane shows the current slide.

- The scroll bar lets you move backward and forward through your presentation.

- The Previous Slide button allows you to move to the previous slide.

- The Next Slide button allows you to move to the next slide.

- The Notes pane shows speaker notes that you have created. You can print these out to use when you deliver your presentation, or to use as handouts to provide your audience with a more complete version of your oral presentation.

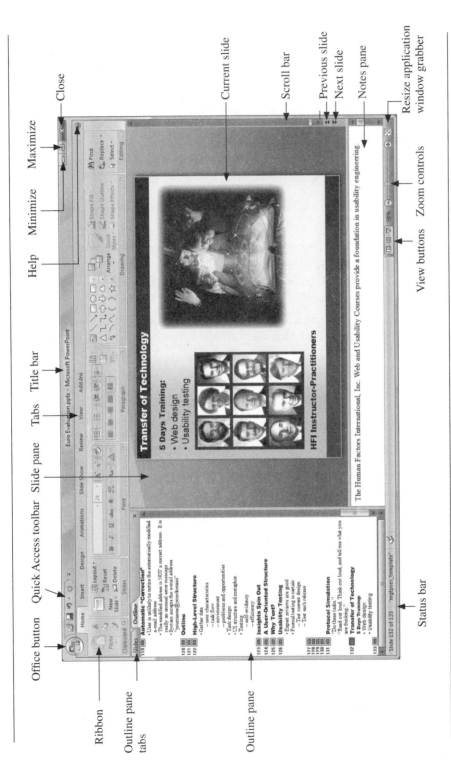

FIGURE 1-6 The PowerPoint screen offers tools to create and edit presentations.

- The status bar tells you which number slide is displayed, as well as the total number of slides, such as Slide 24 of 31. The status bar also displays the name of the *template*, or background.

- View buttons let you change views. Views are covered later in this chapter in the "Use the Appropriate View" section.

- Zoom controls make it easy to zoom in and out in the Slide pane or quickly fit the slide to the size of the Slide pane.

- The resize application window grabber lets you drag the corner of the window to resize it to your needs.

- The current slide is the main attraction in Normal view.

- The Outline pane shows text on your slides or slide thumbnails.

- The Outline pane tabs (Slides and Outline) let you switch between viewing an outline of your text and slide thumbnails.

Use the Ribbon, Office Button, and Quick Access Toolbar

The new PowerPoint interface includes a wide *ribbon* along the top, the Office button, and a Quick Access toolbar for commonly used commands.

The Ribbon

The ribbon has tabs; when you click each tab, the ribbon changes to show tools related to that tab. When you select certain types of objects on a slide, one or more new tabs appear that allow you to set options for those objects.

The ribbon is divided into *groups*. For example, the Home tab's ribbon contains Clipboard, Slides, Font, Paragraph, Drawing, and Editing sections. Sometimes a button or arrow on the ribbon opens a dialog box or pane. Except for the Editing and Slides sections, each of the sections on the Home tab's ribbon contains a small arrow, called a *dialog box launcher*, that opens a dialog box or pane. For example, clicking the Font section's dialog box launcher opens the Font dialog box. Most of these dialog boxes are similar to those from previous versions, so they allow you to use a familiar work flow.

TIP *You can collapse the ribbon to a menu-type bar by double-clicking the current tab. Double-click again to expand the ribbon. Press ALT to display badges that show you keyboard shortcuts for the tabs as well as items on the tab.*

The Office Button

The Office button displays a menu that is similar to the File menu in previous versions of Office. You can display this menu by pressing ALT-F. The items on this menu are discussed elsewhere in this chapter and the book, as appropriate.

Although you can use ALT-F to open the Office button's menu and then press the keyboard shortcuts for the items, the CTRL shortcuts of previous editions, such as CTRL-O to open a file, still work.

The Quick Access Toolbar

The Quick Access toolbar, at the upper-left corner of your screen, lets you quickly execute often-used commands. By default, this toolbar contains Save, Undo, Redo, and Print buttons. This toolbar is the only item on the interface that you can customize. For instructions, see Chapter 13. For example, you might want to add the Open button to this toolbar.

Use the Appropriate View

PowerPoint offers four ways to view a presentation. You choose a view based on what you are doing. Using the appropriate view provides the frictionless flow you need to get your work done.

Most commonly, you change views using the three buttons at the bottom of your screen, on the status bar. The view buttons are shown here:

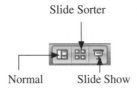

To enter the fourth view, Notes Page view, you need to use the View tab. Then click the Notes Page button in the Presentation Views group of the ribbon. If you want, you can choose the other three views on the ribbon.

 *The New Window feature displays your presentation in a new window. The advantage is that you can look at your presentation in different views at the same time. To open a new window, click the View tab. In the Window group, click the New Window button.*

Use Normal View

Normal view, shown in Figure 1-6, combines a large view of an individual slide, speaker notes beneath the slide, and your choice of an outline of the text of the presentation or thumbnail images of the slides along the left side of the screen. Each section of the view is called a *pane*. Each pane has a scroll bar if it cannot display all the material, so that you can scroll to any part of the presentation.

 *Text that you place in a text box is not included in the text outline. It is treated as a graphic object. However, all text that you type into PowerPoint's default title and text placeholders is included in the text outline. See Chapter 2 for details.*

Use Normal view when you are creating or editing a slide, organizing and writing text, designing a slide's layout, or creating notes for the presenter to refer to when showing the presentation—which is most of the time!

TIP *You can resize any of the panes in Normal view. Place the mouse over a pane border, then click and drag in either direction. For example, if you are working with the outline, make the Outline pane wider.*

Use Slide Sorter View

Slide Sorter view is quite different from Normal view. In Slide Sorter view, shown in Figure 1-7, you see a miniature view of all the slides at once. Slide Sorter view is great when adding, deleting, and changing the order of your slides. You can also add timing and transition effects from one slide to the next. In addition, you can select multiple slides and apply the same options or formatting to all of them.

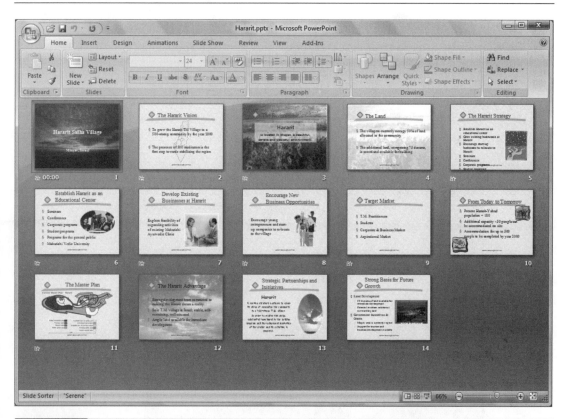

FIGURE 1-7   Slide Sorter view is best for rearranging slides or adding timing and transition effects.

TIP *To quickly switch from Slider Sorter view to Normal view, double-click any slide.*

For details on adding, deleting, and moving slides, see Chapter 3. Transitions and animation are covered in Chapter 9, and timing is explained in Chapter 15.

Use Slide Show View

Slide Show view lets you look at your presentation as you would see it during an actual show. As you can see in Figure 1-8, the slide takes up the entire screen.

Here's where you get to see the results of all your labor! Use Slide Show view to evaluate the results of your work and rehearse what you are going to say. Of course, you also use Slide Show view when you actually deliver your presentation in front of an audience. Preparing for a presentation is the subject of Chapter 14, and Chapter 15 covers the presenting process, but here are the basic techniques for moving around in Slide Show view. It is important to know these techniques because there are no menus, toolbars, or other obvious navigation tools.

- Press ESC to leave Slide Show view and return to your last view (Normal or Slide Sorter).
- Click the mouse to move to the next slide (or the next animation effect). When you click the last slide, you see a black screen. Click again to automatically return to your last view.
- Click the icons at the lower-left corner or right-click to open the pop-up menu. These menus let you navigate to other slides, mark on the slide (temporarily) with an electronic pen as you present, change how the pointer looks and works, black out the slide, and end the show.

FIGURE 1-8 You use Slide Show view when you deliver your presentation.

Use Notes Page View

To enter Notes Page view, click the Notes Page button in the Presentation Views group of the View ribbon. Each Notes page contains one slide and the speaker's notes for that slide. You type notes in the Notes pane while in Normal view. Figure 1-9 shows a slide in Notes Page view. Notes are designed to support you as you present; it's helpful to print out notes to use for reference while presenting. Printed Notes pages also provide an excellent handout that includes a fuller copy of your spoken words. (Chapter 15 provides details on printing notes and handouts.) However, you can also use the Notes pane to write notes to yourself as you create your presentation, or to include comments on the presentation for colleagues or clients. Use your imagination and you'll find many uses for notes in your presentations.

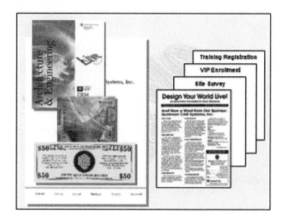

Describe the contents of each attendee's package of materials:

Includes the white Quannon Folder containing:

- The Autodesk Program (Architectural for AM, Mechanical PM)
- 3D Studio Viz demo CD ROM
- Quannon Bucks for special discounts. Get it stamped for double savings
- Design Your World Newsletter
- A survey of opinions (submit to be eligible for the AutoCAD drawing)
- VIP enrollment Form
- Training Registration Form for R14 Training

FIGURE 1-9   Notes Page view provides helpful text when you present.

Move Around a Presentation

Quick navigation through a presentation is always the hallmark of a pro. And why waste time? Here are some techniques for finding your way around in Normal or Slide Sorter view:

■ To move to a different slide, simply click the slide if it is visible, either in Slide Sorter view or on the Slides tab of the Outline pane. You can also click the slide number on the Outline tab of the Outline pane.

■ Use the scroll bar in any pane. For example, to scroll through slides, use the Slide pane scroll bar. As you drag the scroll bar, a tooltip tells you which slide you're up to. Stop when you reach the one you want.

■ Use the Previous Slide and Next Slide buttons. (See Figure 1-6 earlier in this chapter.)

■ Press CTRL-HOME to move to the beginning of the presentation and CTRL-END to move to the end of the presentation.

■ In Normal view, you can use the PAGE UP and PAGE DOWN keys to quickly move to the previous and next slides. Similarly, in Slide Sorter view, use the arrow keys to move between slides.

Get Help When You Need It

No matter how familiar you are with PowerPoint, you will use the Help feature at some time or other. Just click the Help button (shown in Figure 1-6) or press F1 to open the Help window, shown in Figure 1-10.

Type a question in the Search text box and press ENTER or click the Search button. The Help window has the following buttons that aid you in using its features:

■ **Back**   Displays the previous screen

■ **Forward**   Redisplays the screen you saw before you used the Back button

■ **Stop**   Stops searching

■ **Refresh**   Refreshes the screen

■ **Home**   Displays the main Help screen

■ **Print**   Prints the currently displayed Help screen

■ **Change Font Size**   Changes the size of the text in the Help window

■ **Show Table of Contents**   Displays the table of contents so that you can look for Help by topic

■ **Keep on Top/Not on Top**   Pins the Help window on top or lets it go behind other windows

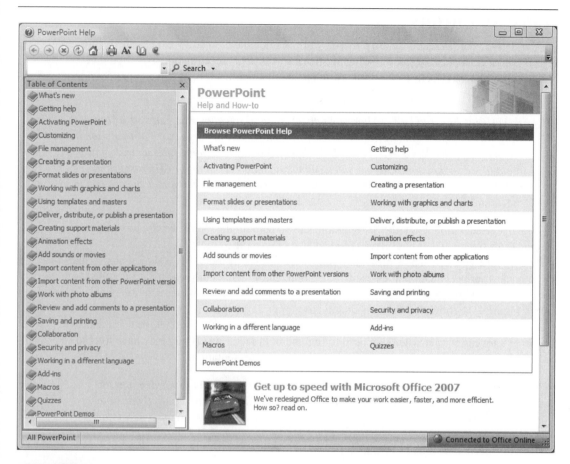

FIGURE 1-10   The Help window provides information about how to use PowerPoint's features.

When you enter some words and search, you get a list of related topics. Click the topic that seems most helpful, and its Help window opens. You can scroll down to see more topics. To see more than the first 25 topics, click the next page number or the Next button at the bottom of the list.

NOTE   *To ensure that you get the latest help from Microsoft's online database, click the Connection Status button at the bottom of the Help window and choose Show Content from the Internet.*

At the bottom of the list of topics is a "Can't Find It?" heading, where you can find a link that offers search tips and other links to possible sources of information on the topic.

To close Help, click its Close button at the upper-right corner of the Help window.

Save a Presentation

You should save your presentation often as you work. As you have no doubt experienced, your computer system can crash or freeze—often destroying your most recent work. You should be especially careful to save before you print, switch to another application, or leave your computer to take a break.

PowerPoint 2007 (and all of Microsoft Office) contains a feature that helps save your work when your computer crashes. When you open PowerPoint again, the presentation is automatically displayed in a special Document Recovery task pane. After a crash, you'll probably see a dialog box asking you to submit an automatic report to Microsoft; this report helps Microsoft analyze the causes of crashes so that it can improve the product in the future.

To save a presentation, click the Save button, shown here, in the Quick Access toolbar, or click the Office button and choose Save. You can also press CTRL-S.

The first time you save a new presentation, PowerPoint opens the Save As dialog box so that you can name your presentation and specify a location. Until then, your presentation is called Presentation1 (or a higher number if you have created more than one new presentation in a session). Figure 1-11 shows the Save As dialog box.

Organizing your presentations and related files such as graphic files, sounds, movies, and so on makes it a lot easier later when you need to find them. In fact, PowerPoint may have trouble locating related files if they are not in the same folder as the presentation.

While image files and certain small found files are generally incorporated into the PowerPoint file, other types of media and document files may be inserted into your presentation using a link. If you think that you'll use such files, create a new folder for your presentation and save it there. Place all the associated files in the same folder and insert them into your presentation from that folder.

The following steps explain how to save a presentation for the first time using the Save As dialog box:

1. Navigate to the desired folder.
2. Type the presentation's name in the File Name text box.
3. To save your presentation in another format, click the Save as Type drop-down arrow to choose the preferred type of document.
4. Click Save.

PowerPoint 2007 (as well as all of Office) uses a different file format from PowerPoint 2003 and earlier versions. However, you can easily save your presentation in the PowerPoint 97-2003 file format so that you can share the file with colleagues who have not yet upgraded.

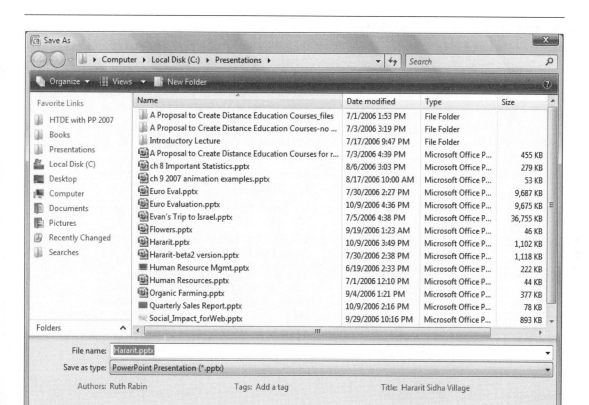

FIGURE 1-11   The Save As dialog box lets you specify a filename and location.

The most common file formats are available by clicking the Office button, choosing Save As and using the submenu that appears. For more options, choose Other Formats to open the Save As dialog box. The Save as Type drop-down list offers all the available options for saving presentations, as explained in Table 1-1.

NOTE   *You can save in two other formats, PDF and XPS, using a free add-in. Both formats maintain the presentation's formatting and make it easy to share presentations with people who don't have PowerPoint. PDF is a popular graphic format from Adobe. Viewing a PDF file requires a free viewer, available at www.adobe.com. XPS is a similar graphic format from Microsoft and also requires a free viewer if you're using Windows XP. (Windows Vista includes the viewer.) After you install the add-in, you can choose Save As from the Office button menu and choose PDF or XPS. You can get the add-in from microsoft.com/downloads. For information on the XPS viewer, go to www. microsoft.com/whdc/xps/viewxps.mspx.*

File Format Option	File Extension	Description
PowerPoint Presentation	.pptx	The default PowerPoint 2007 presentation format, which is a zipped (compressed) format of an XML file.
PowerPoint Macro-Enabled Presentation	.pptm	Use for presentations that contain macros using Visual Basic for Applications (VBA) code. (For more information, see Chapter 13.)
PowerPoint 97-2003 Presentation	.ppt	The format for PowerPoint 97-2002 (XP), and 2003.
PowerPoint Template	.potx	A template that you can use as a basis for new presentations.
PowerPoint Macro-Enabled Template	.potm	A template that includes macros using VBA code.
PowerPoint 97-2003 Template	.pot	A template compatible with PowerPoint 97 through 2003.
Office Theme	.thmx	A set of styles that includes a color theme, font theme, and effect theme. It can also include graphics. For more information, see Chapters 2 and 7.
PowerPoint Show	.ppsx	A presentation that automatically opens in Slide Show view when you double-click it from Windows Explorer. If you open it from within PowerPoint, it opens normally.
PowerPoint Macro-Enabled Show	.ppsm	A PowerPoint show that includes VBA macros.
PowerPoint 97-2003 Show	.pps	A PowerPoint show compatible with PowerPoint 97 through 2003.
PowerPoint Add-In	.ppam	A third-party or supplemental addition to PowerPoint. It may include custom commands and/or VBA code.
PowerPoint 97-2003 Add-In	.ppa	An add-in compatible with PowerPoint 97 through 2003.
PowerPoint XML Presentation	.xml	A presentation in XML format. You can open it in a text editor or in PowerPoint. XML is a structured, text-based format.
Single File Web Page	.mht or .mhtml	An entire presentation saved in one file, including all supporting files, such as images and sounds. It is viewable in some browsers.
Web Page	.htm or .html	A format that lets you display your presentation in a web browser. All supporting files are in one folder. Use this format to post a presentation on a web site or edit it in an HTML editor.

TABLE 1-1 File Format Options for Saving Presentations

File Format Option	File Extension	Description
GIF (Graphics Interchange Format)	.gif	Saves one or more slides as a GIF file—a common graphics format used on web pages. This format supports transparent backgrounds.
JPEG (Joint Photographic Experts Group)	.jpg	Saves one or more slides as a JPEG file. JPEG (also called JPG) is a graphics format used on web pages. This format is best for photographs and detailed images.
PNG (Portable Network Graphics)	.png	Saves one or more slides as a PNG file. PNG is a graphics format sometimes used on web pages. It compresses and downloads well, supports transparency, and is good for photographs and detailed images.
TIFF (Tagged Image File Format)	.tif or .tiff	Turns one or more slides into a bitmap graphic that you can import into other applications. Scanned images are typically in TIFF format.
Device Independent Bitmap	.bmp	Turns one or more slides into a bitmap graphic that you can import into other applications.
WMF (Windows Metafile Format)	.wmf	Turns one or more slides into a graphic that you can import into other applications. WMF is a vector format and resizes well.
Enhanced Windows Metafile	.emf	Turns one or more slides into a graphic that you can import into other applications. EMF is an enhanced vector format that resizes well.
Outline/Rich Text Format	.rtf	Saves just the text of your presentation with most of its formatting so you can import it into a word processing (or other) application.

TABLE 1-1   File Format Options for Saving Presentations (*continued*)

To convert an older presentation (97-2003) to 2007 format, click the Office button and choose Convert. If a dialog box opens, explaining the conversion process, click OK. The Save As dialog box opens. Click Save and confirm to replace the older presentation file. (You can give the presentation a different name if you want to keep the older version.)

You also use the Save As dialog box (click the Office button and choose Save As) any time you want to save a copy of a presentation under a new name or in a new location. If your presentation is a read-only file, meaning that you cannot make changes to it, you also use Save As to save the file under a new name.

After the first save, click Save on the Quick Access toolbar to save additional changes. (You can also click the Office button and choose Save or press CTRL-S.) PowerPoint saves only the changes you made since your last save.

If you save a presentation file that was created in an earlier version of PowerPoint, you enter Compatibility Mode. Compatibility Mode suppresses certain new features of PowerPoint so that you can again open the presentation in an earlier version. This feature helps you work with others who don't have PowerPoint 2007 but who need to open the file.

Use Save and Publish Options

The Save As dialog box offers several options that are either completely new or new for this dialog box. Many of these options were available in the Options dialog box in previous versions of PowerPoint. Some options vary depending on the file type you are saving. To access these options, shown here, click the Tools button in the Save As dialog box.

I cover most of these options in Chapter 13, because they apply to PowerPoint as a whole. Web options are covered in Chapter 12. Here I explain two options available from the Tools menu in the Save As dialog box that apply to saving individual presentations:

| Map Network Drive... |
| Save Options... |
| General Options... |
| Web Options... |
| Compress Pictures... |

- **Add a password**   To password-protect a presentation, choose Tools | General Options to open the General Options dialog box. Here you can add a password for opening and modifying the presentation file.

- **Compress pictures**   To compress images when you save, choose Tools | Compress Pictures. This helps reduce the size of the file. I discuss this option further in Chapter 5.

Save So You Can Find It Fast Next Time

As you probably know, good file organization is definitely an advantage when you need to find your presentations, graphic files, text files, sounds, etc. The following tips provide efficient ways to find your presentations.

Save a Presentation to Its Own Subfolder in the My Documents Folder

You can use the My Documents folder to store files you use often. (For example, you might use your company's logo for every presentation you create.) By creating a subfolder under the My Documents folder, you can keep all files related to that presentation together, avoiding problems down the line.

Customize Where and How a Presentation Is Saved

By default, when you first save a presentation, the Save As dialog box opens with the Documents or My Documents folder (depending on your version of Windows) displayed in the Save In box. If you change the location, the presentation is, of course, saved in your chosen location each time you click the Save button. The next time you start a new presentation in the same session (without closing PowerPoint), the Save As dialog box displays the last location you chose.

If you want the Save As dialog box to open with another folder of your choice, you can change the default file location, as explained in the section "Customize the Default File Location," earlier in this chapter.

You can also specify a default file format for saving presentations. By default, PowerPoint saves your files as PowerPoint 2007 presentations. However, you can save your presentations in an earlier format. From the Save As dialog box, choose Tools | Save Options to open the PowerPoint Options dialog box. In the Save Files in This Format drop-down list, choose the file format you want. If all of your presentations include VBA macros, choose PowerPoint Macro-Enabled Presentation. (If you want to enable macros in just the current presentation, choose PowerPoint Macro-Enabled Presentation (.pptm) from the Save as Type drop-down list in the Save As dialog box.)

Back Up Your Presentations

No discussion of saving would be complete without explaining the importance of backing up, or *archiving*, your work. If you care about your work, back it up. Remember that PowerPoint files can get fairly large, although files in the new format are smaller than those from previous versions of PowerPoint. Here are a few options:

- Tape drives are fairly inexpensive and are large enough to back up an entire hard disk.
- If you have a lot of presentations, a read/write CD-ROM drive lets you save your presentations to a CD-RW.
- Optical drives have a long life and resist accidental erasure. Use them for long-term archiving, perhaps offsite.
- External portable hard drives ranging from 80 to several hundred gigabytes in storage allow quick and affordable backup. Some external hard drives are network compatible and allow you to back up to a network drive.
- If you have broadband access, web storage can serve as a secondary backup.

The main point is not to walk away from your computer at the end of a day without backing up your day's work.

Summary

In this chapter, you learned the basics of PowerPoint: how to open a PowerPoint presentation, organize and find your presentations, view presentations effectively, move around a presentation, get help, and save a presentation. In the next chapter, you get started with actually creating PowerPoint presentations.

Chapter 2

Create Your First Presentation

How to...

- Choose a template, start from scratch, or use an existing presentation
- Choose a theme
- Choose a background style
- Choose a slide layout
- Add slides
- Write or import a text outline
- Use placeholders for text
- Place text in text boxes and shapes
- Create fancy text effects with WordArt
- Eliminate spelling and style errors
- Create a summary slide
- Complete a presentation: tutorial

After learning some basics of PowerPoint in Chapter 1, you are now ready to create a great presentation. Creating a presentation in PowerPoint involves a combination of preparing the text content and adding visual appeal. In this chapter, I explain how to structure the content of a presentation. You can also complete the quick tutorial at the end of the chapter to get a feel for the process of creating an entire presentation.

Create Your Presentation

You can create a presentation in PowerPoint using any one of three methods. Your choice should depend on how independently you want to work and whether you have reusable content. As I explained in Chapter 1, the New Presentation dialog box offers you these three options. Refer to Figure 1-2 and its corresponding text in Chapter 1 for an explanation of this dialog box. The following sections explain these methods in more detail.

Choose a Template or Theme

If you want to start with some formatting and perhaps a background, you might start with a template or theme. Templates and themes provide text styles, some graphics, and other settings. Themes are new for PowerPoint 2007.

Choose a Template

A common way to start a presentation is to choose a template. Use a template when you want to use pre-existing design elements (and perhaps text) as a basis for your presentation. A template is a file that contains one or both of the following:

- **Slide master**   Functions as a blueprint for the entire presentation or all slides that use that slide master. A slide master includes one or more *layouts* that position the components of a slide. You can also add a background, text, text and object placeholders (for your own text, pictures, and so on), text formatting, and animation to a slide master.

- **Theme**   Includes design variations that work well together—theme colors, theme fonts, and theme line and fill effects. A theme can also include backgrounds and graphics.

NOTE   *A few templates on Microsoft's web site also include boilerplate text that you can use as a guide for organizing your own content.*

Did you know?

The Importance of Templates and Themes

Templates provide backgrounds, formatting, and layouts for your slides. A *background* comprises both a background color, pattern, or image and design elements that appear on every slide. The template also includes other features such as theme colors, bullet design, specific fonts, and font sizes. You can also add text animation to the template. Using a template creates a unified look for your entire presentation.

The truth is that if you hire outside professionals to make a slide show for you, they always create a background design from scratch. However, you can often find an appropriate design template that will give your presentation a professional look. PowerPoint 2007 offers many new templates, if you use the Microsoft Office Online options. Your choice of template has a powerful effect on the impact of your presentation. Even when you use a template, you have plenty of flexibility. You can still change the background of any slide (or choose no background at all) and create master slides that override the template settings. Some people like to create presentations with no background (a white background), but they still use templates to format and coordinate text styles and layouts.

Themes, new for PowerPoint 2007, are like templates, except that they don't contain any content, you can use them in Word and Excel, and it's easier to apply a theme from within a presentation file. You can create your own theme that contains a background, with theme colors, fonts, and line and fill effects. You can save a theme as a theme file, which you then can apply to other presentations, or across other applications in Microsoft Office, for a unified look.

Chapters 5, 6, and 7 are packed with helpful information and tips on graphic layout, color, and visual effects that can help you decide the best template or theme to use. Refer to Chapter 7 for details on creating your own templates, themes, slide masters, and layouts.

Remember from Chapter 1 that you can choose a template in the New Presentation dialog box by clicking the My Templates button, the Installed Templates button, or one of the categories in the Microsoft Office Online list. When you find the template that you want, select it and click Create. (If you choose a template from the Microsoft Office Online list, click Download.) Figure 2-1 shows the available templates when you choose the Design Slides item in the Microsoft Office Online section of the New Presentation dialog box and then choose the Business category. Because these templates are online, they may change, so you may see different choices.

Your new presentation appears on the screen with the template and one slide displayed. If the template includes boilerplate text, you may see a number of slide thumbnails in the Outline pane. Usually, the first slide is appropriate for entering the title of the presentation. Figure 2-2 shows the new presentation using the template shown in Figure 2-1. You're now ready to add more slides, text, images, and more.

You can apply a template after you open a presentation by using the procedure for applying a theme, which I explain in the next section.

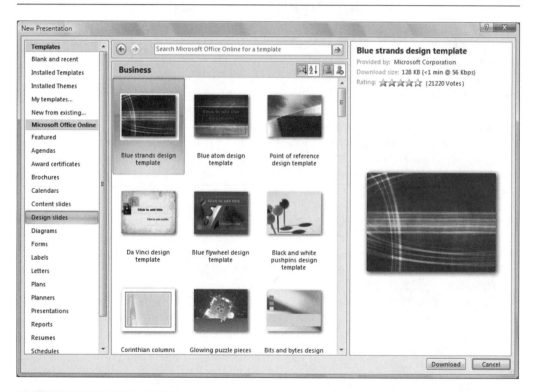

FIGURE 2-1 You can find templates with designs appropriate for several categories.

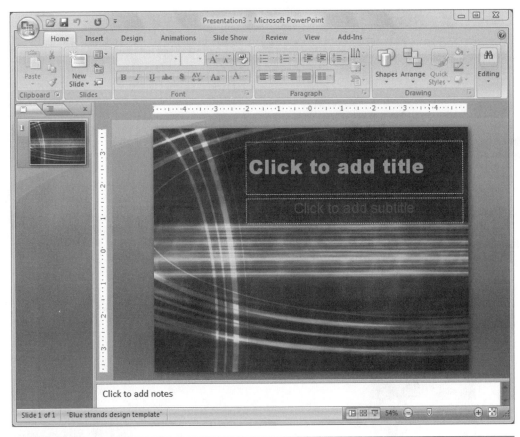

FIGURE 2-2 When you choose a template, the presentation opens with one or more slides and the template already applied.

Choose a Theme

A new feature of PowerPoint 2007 (and most of Office 2007) is *themes*. A theme includes a set of colors (theme colors), related fonts (theme fonts), and line and fill effects (theme effects). The purpose of a theme is to create a set of variations that visually work well together. When you create a new presentation, you may want to choose a theme. However, you can choose a theme at any time, even after you have added all the text. Furthermore, you can use a template file (which has a .potx or .potm file extension) as a theme.

NOTE   *You can create your own themes. I explain how to create a custom theme in Chapter 7.*

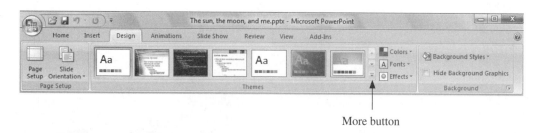

More button

FIGURE 2-3 The ribbon's Design tab lets you choose a theme.

To choose a theme, click the ribbon's Design tab, shown in Figure 2-3. The Design tab offers a collection of tools related to your presentation's design.

To choose a theme, you can click one of the themes that you see on the ribbon, but PowerPoint offers many more themes. To display them, click the More button (shown in Figure 2-3).

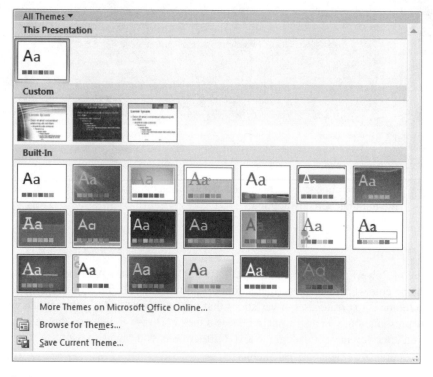

The theme thumbnails give you an idea of the background and the font, but to see what the theme really looks like, hover the mouse cursor over any theme. You see the theme on your slide so that you can quickly decide if you like it or not. In this way, you can try out many themes without committing to one. When you find one that you like, click it to apply it to the entire presentation.

TIP   *The theme appears as it would look on the current slide. Themes may look different on different slide layouts. Before selecting a theme, you may want to add a couple of slides with different layouts and see how the theme looks on those slides. I explain how to add slides and specify layouts later in this chapter.*

You don't have to apply a theme to all the slides in a presentation. To apply it to the current slide (or all selected slides), right-click the theme's thumbnail and choose Apply to Selected Slides. You can also choose Apply to Matching Slides to apply the theme to all slides using the same slide master as the current slide. (I cover slide masters in Chapter 7.)

NOTE   *You can right-click a theme and choose Set as Default Theme. This becomes the theme for all new presentations.*

You can apply themes that you have created to your presentation or to selected slides. In fact, you can use template files or even other presentation files as themes. On the Design tab, click the More button in the Themes group and choose Browse for Themes. In the Choose Theme or Themed Document dialog box, navigate to the file you want to use and click Open.

Choose a Background Style

If you don't want to use the background graphics of a template, you can still choose a background that uses the colors of your theme. You may do this to create a variety of background colors in your presentation that work well together or to apply a different background to the entire presentation. You can choose a background style at any time while you are working on a presentation.

Background styles are simple backgrounds using the presentation's theme colors. You have a choice of different intensities and treatments, but they're all simple. Nevertheless, they're quite good looking; you can't go wrong with one of these styles. To use a background style, click the Background Styles button in the Background group of the Design tab to display the Background Styles gallery, shown next. Hover the mouse cursor over a style to see how it looks on a slide.

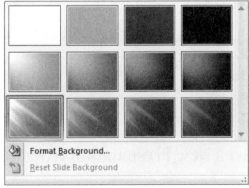

Click a style to apply it to all the slides in a presentation. To change the background of the current slide (or all selected slides), right-click the thumbnail and choose Apply to Selected Slides. If you have more than one slide master, you can also choose Apply to Matching Slides to apply the background style to all slides using the same slide master as the current slide. (I cover slide masters in Chapter 7.)

A great feature of the background styles is related to the fact that the two left columns are lighter and the two right columns are darker. PowerPoint knows to use dark text to contrast with any option in the two left columns and to use light text for the two right columns. Therefore, you don't need to worry about changing the color of the text if you change the background.

 You can create a custom background for any slide or slides. I explain how to customize a slide background in Chapter 6.

Start from Scratch

The second method of creating a new presentation is to start with a blank presentation. Choose Blank Presentation from the New Presentation dialog box.

The main reason to start with a blank presentation is to create your own background design rather than use one of PowerPoint's templates or themes. You can save the result as a template or theme, as I explain in Chapter 7. Remember that you can apply a theme or template at any time, as explained previously in the "Choose a Theme" section of this chapter.

The blank presentation comes with a number of default settings, such as the size of the title text, the type of bullets, and the theme colors. You can change these settings if you want to customize the blank presentation template for your own needs. You might also want to add actual content, such as your company's logo or a copyright statement. These changes will affect all future presentations that you create using the Blank Presentation option.

 *To avoid losing the default settings, first open a blank presentation and save it as blank-old.pptx (or something similar). Then, if you want to revert to the original blank presentation, you can delete your blank.pptx file and rename blank-old.ppt to blank.pptx.*

Here's how:

1. Create any presentation with the settings and/or content that you want.
2. Choose File | Save As.
3. In the Save as Type drop-down list, choose PowerPoint Template.
4. In the File Name box, change the file name to **Blank.pptx**.
5. Click Save.

Start a New Presentation from an Existing One

The third way to start a new presentation is to base it on an existing presentation. Use this method when you want to create a presentation that resembles an existing one. Follow these steps:

1. Click New from Existing in the New Presentation dialog box.
2. In the New from Existing Presentation dialog box, choose the presentation you want to use as the basis for your new presentation.
3. Click Create New.

2

You now have a new, unnamed presentation that is an exact duplicate of the original presentation. Save the presentation to name it.

Lay Out a Slide

Once you choose a template or start a blank presentation, PowerPoint displays one slide on the screen, usually a title slide, containing space for you to enter the title of the presentation. You can either design this slide with its current layout or change the layout. Also, for each new slide you create, you need to choose a layout. A *layout* specifies how the text, graphics, or other elements are positioned on the slide. PowerPoint comes with a number of preset layouts that you can use. Layouts are extremely helpful for creating slides. Picking the right one is essential for designing a legible slide that communicates instantly.

NOTE   *A new feature of PowerPoint 2007 is the ability to create and save your own custom layouts. Chapter 7 explains this procedure.*

Whether you are changing the layout of an existing slide or creating a new slide, you specify the layout for the current slide by choosing the Home tab of the ribbon and choosing Layout from the Slides group. The Layout gallery opens, as shown here:

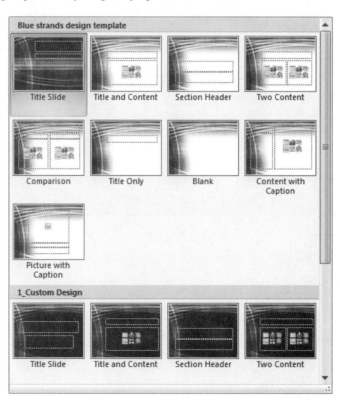

 *Right-click the slide and choose Layout on the shortcut menu.*

The Layout gallery offers the following choices:

- **Title Slide**   Use this layout for the first slide of your presentation. It includes a heading and a subheading. The subheading could be an explanation of the heading or your name, for example.
- **Title and Content**   This layout, shown in Figure 2-4, includes a title and a place to add content. It's the default layout. The content can be text, a table, a chart (graph), clip art,

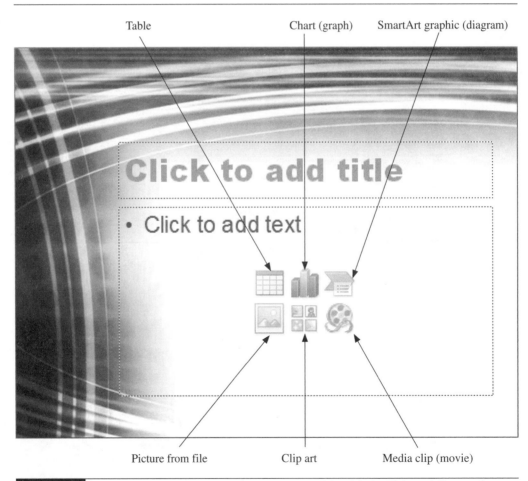

FIGURE 2-4   You can add several types of content on a slide with the Title and Content layout.

an image, a diagram, or a movie. To add text, click the placeholder and start typing. To add one of the other content items, click the appropriate icon. Notice the two dotted rectangles. These are called *placeholders*, and they hold the place for text and other objects on your slide. Later in this chapter, in the "Add Text to a Presentation" section, I discuss how to use the placeholders to add text.

- ■ **Section Header** Use this layout for the first slide in a new section of your presentation. Like the Title Slide layout, it has room for a title and a subtitle.

- ■ **Two Content** This layout has a title and two separate content components. You might use this layout when you want to include text next to an image, table, chart, or diagram. You can also include two images, or an image and a table, for example. The possibilities are many.

- ■ **Comparison** Use this layout when you want to compare concepts, images, or anything else that you display on the slide. This layout includes a title and two side-by-side content areas, each with a subtitle area.

- ■ **Title Only** As its name implies, this layout has only a heading, giving you lots of flexibility to do anything you want on your slide. For example, this layout is great for a large photograph of your product.

- ■ **Blank** Use this layout if you like to work from scratch. This option is useful for a photograph that covers the entire slide.

- ■ **Content with Caption** This layout provides a large content area and a separate area for a small heading and descriptive text. You could use this layout if you want to insert an image and add a caption to it.

- ■ **Picture with Caption** This layout is similar to the Content with Caption layout, but you can only insert an image.

Remember, when you start a new presentation, you can change the layout of the first slide that automatically appears. As you add each slide to a presentation, choose a layout before adding content to the slide.

Add Slides

Most templates include only one slide. If you start with a blank presentation, you have just one slide. You'll soon want to add some more slides. To create a new slide, click New Slide in the Slides group of the Home tab of the ribbon. The new slide uses the layout of the current slide and appears right after it (which is not necessarily at the end of the presentation). However, if the current slide uses the Title Slide layout, the new slide takes on the default Title and Content layout.

If you click the down arrow on the New Slide button, you can immediately choose a layout for the new slide.

Complete the Presentation Structure

Once you have a layout for your first slide, you can complete the structure of the entire presentation in one of two ways:

■ Work in the Slide pane and enter text in the text placeholder(s), if any. Then, add a new slide and complete the text for the new slide. Continue in this way until you have completed your presentation. You can add graphics and animation as you work or complete the text first and go back to work on the artistic parts.

■ Work on the outline tab of the Outline pane (sometimes called the Thumbnail pane, because it can show thumbnails of your slides), and create a text outline for the entire presentation. PowerPoint automatically creates new slides for you. Continue until you have completed your presentation. You can adjust the layout later, if necessary. Of course, you will want to add graphics, animation, and so on.

The next few sections explain how to create outlines in the Outline pane and enter text in placeholders. In the "Import an Outline" section, later in this chapter, I explain how to import an outline that you create in Word or another application.

Structure a Presentation from an Outline

It would be nice to create a presentation without having to type text in the text placeholders on each individual slide. You can. In fact, the quickest way to create a complete presentation is to type an outline of your text on the Outline tab of the Outline pane. Working with the Outline pane is ideal for creating the text of your presentation because you can see most of the text at a glance. This strategy lets you view the flow of ideas from slide to slide. You can easily rearrange text by moving it from one slide to another.

When you type your outline, PowerPoint automatically creates new slides for you as you work. You immediately see the results in the Slide pane at the right of your screen. When you have finished typing your outline, you have a complete presentation. All you need to do is refine it; for example, you probably want to add images, charts, and so on.

Text that you type in the Outline pane is placed in text placeholders. Figure 2-5 shows an outline in the Outline pane. Note that the Outline pane has been expanded by dragging to the right the divider between the Outline pane and the Slide pane. Working with the Outline pane can help you to organize and structure your entire presentation.

Understand Outlines

An outline has *levels* of text, as shown in Figure 2-6. The level determines whether text becomes the title of a slide or *body text* (so called because it makes up the body of the text on a slide). You can create up to five levels of body text. Each level of text is indented more than the previous one and generally uses a smaller type size. You can use bullets to set off each item of body text, but you don't have to. (Chapter 4 explains how to format bullets and how to get rid of them, too.)

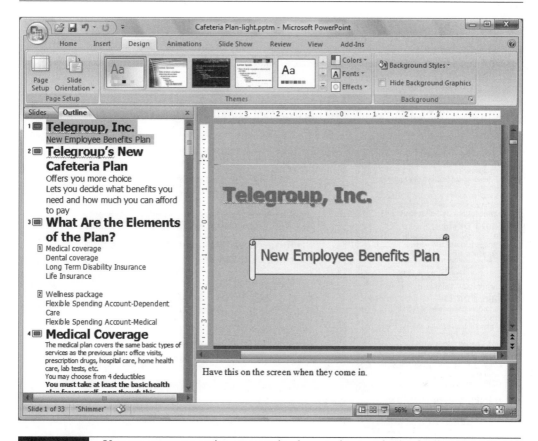

2

FIGURE 2-5   You can create an entire presentation by entering text in the Outline pane.

NOTE   *Try to avoid using several levels of body text. Too many levels can make the flow of ideas confusing.*

Once you know the special terms that apply to the outlining function, you will feel right at home working with outlines. They are listed and explained here:

■ **Promote**   To make text one level higher. For example, second-level body text becomes first-level body text; first-level body text becomes a slide title. To promote selected text, right-click it in the Outline pane and choose Promote from the shortcut menu.

SHORTCUT   *Select body text and press SHIFT-TAB to promote it.*

Slide number and icon   Slide title

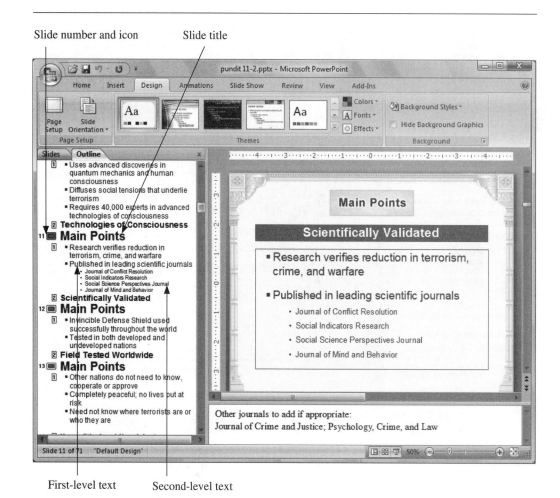

First-level text   Second-level text

FIGURE 2-6   An outline has various levels of text.

■ **Demote**   To make text one level lower. For example, a slide title becomes first-level body text, and first-level body text becomes second-level body text. To demote selected text, right-click it in the Outline pane and choose Demote from the shortcut menu.

SHORTCUT   *Select body text and press TAB to demote it.*

- **Move Up**   To move selected text above the previous text. To move selected text up, right-click it and choose Move Up.
- **Move Down**   To move selected text below the following text. To move selected text down, right-click it and choose Move Down.

 Select the text and drag it up or down to the desired location.

- **Collapse**   To hide all text lower than the slide title, for one slide only. Collapsing text lets you see more of your presentation so you can assess its overall structure. You can collapse text for one slide or for the entire presentation (Collapse All). To collapse the text on a slide, right-click the slide in the Outline pane and choose Collapse | Collapse. To collapse the entire presentation, right-click anywhere in the Outline pane and choose Collapse | Collapse All.
- **Expand**   To display all the levels of text, for one slide only. You can expand text for one slide or for the entire presentation (Expand All). To expand the text on a slide, right-click the slide in the Outline pane and choose Expand | Expand. To expand the entire presentation, right-click anywhere in the Outline pane and choose Expand | Expand All.
- **Show Text Formatting**   To display the font and other text formatting in the Outline pane. To toggle between showing and not showing the text formatting, right-click anywhere in the Outline pane and choose Show Text Formatting from the shortcut menu.

Create an Outline in PowerPoint

To create a presentation by typing an outline within PowerPoint, follow these steps:

1. Start a new presentation using a template, a theme, or a blank presentation.

2. If you would like a slide layout for the entire presentation other than the default Title and Content layout, choose the layout you want from the Layout gallery on the Home tab of the ribbon.

3. Click the Outline tab of the Outline pane.

4. Type the title of the first slide and press ENTER. PowerPoint creates a second slide automatically.

5. If you want body text on a slide, press ENTER after typing the slide's title. Then type the body text. Because it appears as title text on the following slide, select the text, right-click it, and choose Demote (or press SHIFT-TAB). The text returns to the previous slide.

 On a slide that uses the Title Slide layout, if you click Demote, you create a subtitle.

6. Continue to type body text.

7. To create second-level body text, type it as first-level body text, and then demote it, as described in Step 5.

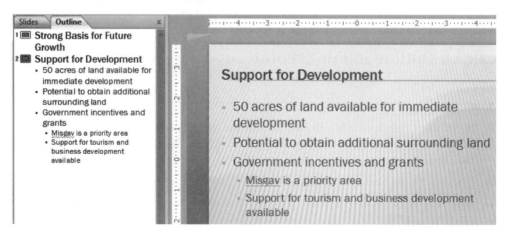

8. To return to a higher level of body text (from second level to first level, for example), select the text, right-click, and choose Promote on the shortcut menu.

9. When you have finished typing the body text for the slide, press ENTER and click Promote until PowerPoint starts a new slide, as shown here:

10. If you want a different layout for the next slide, choose it from the Slide Layout task pane.

If you see that you will have too many bulleted items to fit on a slide, you may be able to fit them in two columns, as shown next. Right-click the slide and, from the Layout item on the shortcut menu, choose a layout with more than one text placeholder, such as Two Content or Comparison. PowerPoint places a number 1 in a small box next to the text in the first column. Press CTRL-ENTER to move to the second column of text and continue typing. If you have already completed the text, select the text on the slide and drag it to the second column. Text in the second column is marked with a number 2 in a box, as shown here.

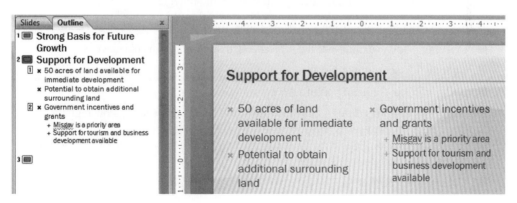

Chapter 3 covers techniques for editing existing outline text.

How to ... Develop an Outline

You should spend a lot of time and thought in creating your outline. It structures the content of your presentation—what you are going to say—and is the first and most important step in creating a presentation.

First decide the objective of your presentation, whether it's selling a product or service, explaining a program, motivating subordinates, or training employees. Then narrow your objective, such as training supervisors how to interview prospective employees.

Get as much information as possible about your audience. What do they already know? Why are they coming to the presentation? What do they want to gain? Then research your topic, always keeping in mind the objective of your presentation and the type of audience.

Next, decide on the structure of the body of the presentation. Let's say you are recommending a strategy for reducing costs in the Human Resources department. Your structure might be the following:

1. State the objective.

2. Explain the present situation.

3. List the possible strategies.

4. Analyze the advantages and disadvantages of each strategy.

5. Recommend one or more strategies.

6. Offer action steps for implementing the strategy or strategies.

Then, place your structure inside a broader framework:

- **Opening**   Tell your audience the subject and, if appropriate, the objective of your talk.

- **Agenda**   If appropriate, list the key areas you plan on covering.

- **Body**   This is the main part of your presentation.

- **Examples and anecdotes**   Give examples, tell anecdotes (such as how high the unnecessary paper used in the department would reach if stacked up), and include pictures, charts, or video clips to add supporting information and interest. These can be integrated into the body of the presentation.

- **Conclusion**   Repeat the key areas you covered, including next steps to take.

Now write the outline, pouring the results of your research into the structure you want to use. When you are done, format the outline as explained in the preceding section, "Prepare the Outline." Use level 1 headings for main topics, the slides. Use level 2 headings for subtopics, the slide content.

Edit and rewrite the outline until you are happy with it. You may want to run it by a colleague or your boss. Leave out anything that might be unclear or unnecessary. Of course, you can always change your text later.

Import an Outline

You may prefer importing an outline created in a word processing program, such as Microsoft Word, over creating the outline in PowerPoint. You may choose this option for several reasons:

- You can work faster in a word processing program.
- You need to collaborate with others who don't have or know PowerPoint in order to create the text for the presentation.
- You receive text for a presentation already created in a word processing program from a client, supervisor, or colleague.

Any time you have text already saved as a word processing document, import the text. There's no need to duplicate the effort of typing it.

Prepare the Outline

Before importing the text, you should review it so that you get the results you want. Most word processing programs have a feature called *styles,* which helps you organize the formatting of your paragraphs. For example, in Microsoft Word, heading styles are used for headings. The Normal style is often used for the body of a paragraph. PowerPoint uses these styles, if they exist in your outline, to organize your text into a complete presentation. By creating the appropriate styles, you can determine exactly how your text will be organized on the slides of your presentation. Figure 2-7 shows an example. Here's how it works:

- Heading 1 style becomes the slide title.
- Heading 2 style becomes first-level body text.
- Heading 3 style becomes second-level body text, and so on.

If you can't use styles, you can simply use tabs. Text at the left margin becomes a slide title. Use a tab at the beginning of a line to create first-level body text. A line of text with two tabs becomes second-level body text. Using this technique, you can even create an outline in Notepad or another text-only editor.

 Be sure that there are no blank lines in your outline, because they are imported as blank slides.

The "Edit Placeholder Text" section in Chapter 3 explains how to insert all or part of an outline into an existing presentation.

Use the Outline

Once you have created and formatted your outline, you can create the presentation. Here are the steps:

1. From PowerPoint, choose File | Open.
2. In the Open dialog box, choose All Outlines from the Files of Type drop-down list.
3. Navigate to your outline and double-click the document that contains your outline.

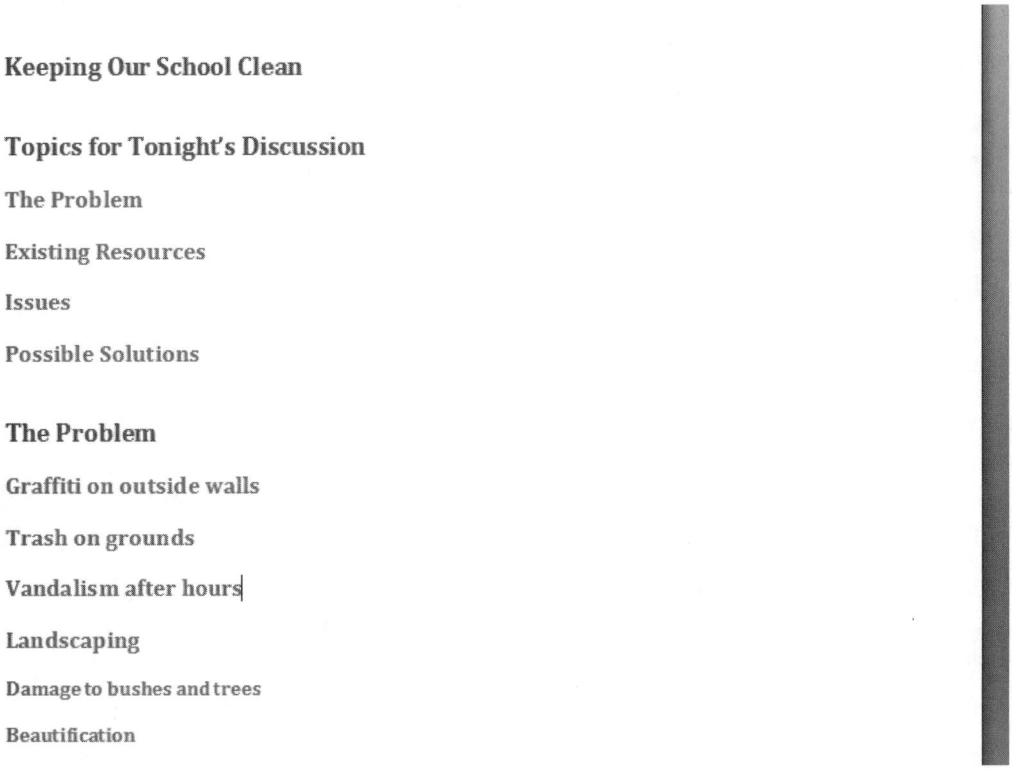

Keeping Our School Clean

Topics for Tonight's Discussion

The Problem

Existing Resources

Issues

Possible Solutions

The Problem

Graffiti on outside walls

Trash on grounds

Vandalism after hours

Landscaping

Damage to bushes and trees

Beautification

FIGURE 2-7 This outline in Microsoft Word (shown in part) contains content for three slides.

PowerPoint creates the presentation. You could then apply a theme and a background style. Figure 2-8 shows the results. After that, you can add clip art, charts, and other design features.

Add Text to a Presentation

In the previous section, you learned how to add text to a presentation by creating an outline. However, you may want to add text directly on the slide or add additional text to an existing slide. Text needs to be very clear—both visually and in content. In this section, you learn how to create professional-looking text.

Before you start to write, you need to decide what kind of presentation you want to create. Is your main goal to provide information or tell a story? In that case, your text is very important, and you may want to use body text in text placeholders. Or suppose you really want to create an impression, a mood. Perhaps you want to excite sales reps about a new product feature but

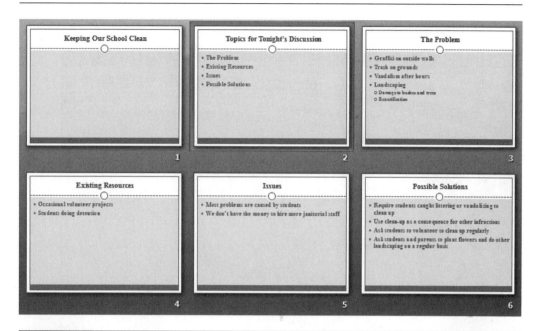

FIGURE 2-8   The outline has been imported into PowerPoint and now includes a theme.

will follow up with all the details on paper or your company's intranet. In this case, text is less important than graphics, color, and animation. You may not use any body text at all. Instead, you may use text boxes and shapes. This book shows both types of presentations so that you can see various possibilities. Once you know the goal of your presentation, you can choose the type of text that meets your needs.

Use Text Placeholders

The easiest way to add text is to click a text placeholder. Several layouts contain text placeholders. You can always recognize a text placeholder because it says Click to Add Text. Placeholders for slide titles, which are also text placeholders, say Click to Add Title. When you click inside a text placeholder, an I-beam cursor appears, showing where the text will appear, as you can see in Figure 2-9. All you need to do is start typing. The dotted border changes to a dashed border and displays *handles*, which you can drag to resize the text box. You can also move the entire text box by clicking the border and dragging.

NOTE   *Content placeholders can also contain other types of content. For example, to insert an image, click the image icon.*

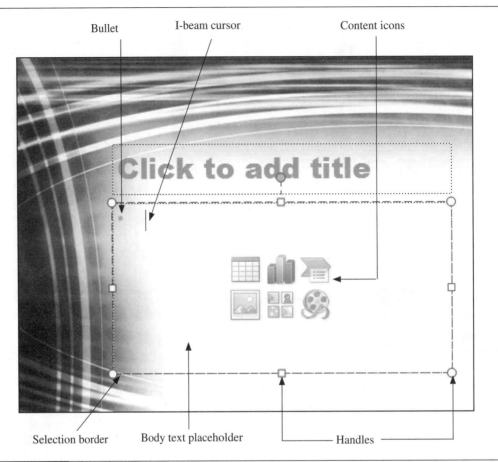

Bullet   I-beam cursor   Content icons

Selection border   Body text placeholder   Handles

FIGURE 2-9 To add text to a text placeholder, click inside it and start typing.

The beauty of text placeholders is that PowerPoint formats the text appropriately for the placeholder. For example, a title is usually centered and uses a larger font. If text has bullets, it is properly aligned to the right of the bullet and uses a smaller font. The slide master controls this formatting, although you can change it. As a result, you get perfectly formatted text every time, for professional results.

To start a new paragraph in the body text area, press ENTER. PowerPoint automatically creates a new paragraph—and another bullet if your text has bullets—so you can continue typing.

NOTE   *Only text that you type in a text placeholder is displayed on the Outline tab of the Outline pane. Other types of text, such as text in text boxes or WordArt, do not appear in the Outline pane.*

The text in the text placeholder telling you to click to add text never appears on the slide during a presentation, even if you never add any text. The same is true of the dotted placeholder border. Therefore, if you insert a slide with a text placeholder and never place any text in it, at presentation you will have a blank slide that includes only the content or design from the template, theme, or background style. Of course, if you don't need the text placeholder, you should probably delete it, or perhaps change to a layout that contains only the text placeholders you need.

Figure 2-10 shows a slide with a title, bulleted text in a text placeholder, and some art. Using the text placeholder makes it very easy to create a slide like this.

Chapters 3 and 4 explain how to customize your text to look any way you want. Chapter 7 explains how slide masters and themes control text formatting for the entire presentation.

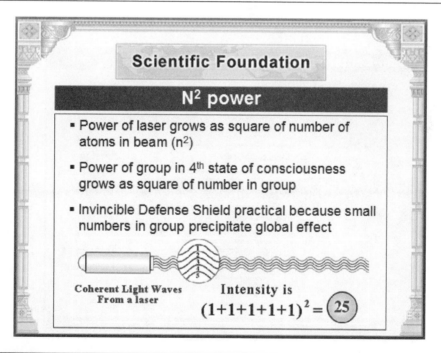

FIGURE 2-10   A slide with a title, bulleted text in a text placeholder, and some art.

Create Text Boxes

A common way to add additional text to a slide is to create a text box. Use a text box when you want to place text anywhere on the slide. For example, you can use a text box to create a caption for a graphic or to emphasize an important message. A text box is an *object*, which means that when you click it, you can move and resize it. You can format the text in a text box in whatever way you wish, but this text does not appear in the Outline pane.

NOTE *Two of the slide layouts, Content with Caption and Picture with Caption, include text boxes for this purpose.*

Figure 2-11 shows an example of text in a text box. This slide uses text boxes to create *callouts* (or labels) that point to the graphic at the center of the slide.

Like most objects in a PowerPoint presentation, a text box has its own properties, including a border, a background color or fill effect, and the text. The text boxes shown in Figure 2-11 do not have a visible border. A visible border is useful when you want to emphasize text, but on this slide, it would distract from the message. The fill has also been eliminated so that the text looks like it has been written directly on the slide. Chapter 6 explains how to format borders and fills.

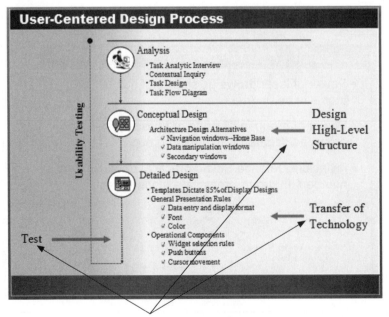

This text is in a text box.

FIGURE 2-11   Use a text box when you want to place text anywhere on a slide.

To create a text box, follow these steps:

1. Click the Text Box button on the Text group of the Insert tab.

2. Click and drag to create the text box. PowerPoint pays attention only to the width of the box you specify, not its length. Don't worry! The box now looks like a text placeholder.

3. Start typing to add the text. When you type enough text to get to the right side of the text box, PowerPoint automatically wraps the text to the next line. The box's length expands as you add text.

4. Click anywhere else on the slide to remove the selection border and handles.

To create the effect shown in Figure 2-11, create the text box using the steps just explained. The text box's formatting depends on the template and theme you are using. If it has a border and a fill, you may want to remove them. To remove the border and fill, right-click the text box and choose Format Shape from the shortcut menu. In the Format Shape dialog box, click the Fill item and choose No Fill. Click the Line item and choose No Line. The text box becomes completely invisible—all you see is the text. Click Close.

Place Text in Shapes

PowerPoint includes a large number of shapes that you can add to a slide. You can use these shapes in many ways, but one way is to place and emphasize text. To insert a shape, click the Insert tab and use the Shapes button in the Illustrations group to display the entire gallery of shapes. Click a shape and then drag the shape on a slide. To place text in a shape, click the shape (if it isn't already selected) and start typing. Click outside the shape to remove the selection border and handles. Figure 2-12 shows an example of text in several arrow shapes. Here, the shapes indicate a process and also emphasize the text. For more thorough information on shapes, see Chapter 5.

Text that you type in a shape is attached to that shape. You can move or rotate the shape, and the text follows suit. Like text boxes, shapes have a border and a fill color or effect. However, you rarely eliminate the border (unless you add a shadow or 3-D effect) because the shape is then not apparent. As you can see on the slide, the distinctive shape and contrasting background color of the shape help to make the text jump out from the rest of the slide.

To create the arrow shape you see in Figure 2-12, choose the Pentagon arrow from the Block Arrows section of the Shapes gallery. On the slide, drag out the shape so that it is slightly wider than it is tall. To change the border, right-click and choose Format Shape. Choose Line and then choose No Line. To change the fill, choose Fill, then Gradient Fill. (I explain the gradient fill controls in Chapter 5.) With the shape still selected, type the text. The text appears in the default font and size. Chapter 3 explains how to change the font and font size.

You can use shapes in place of text placeholders. In the slide shown in Figure 2-13, all the text is in shapes. The formatting of the shapes you see here is repeated often throughout the presentation, for a unified appearance. This slide is part of a distance education course on Human Resource Management.

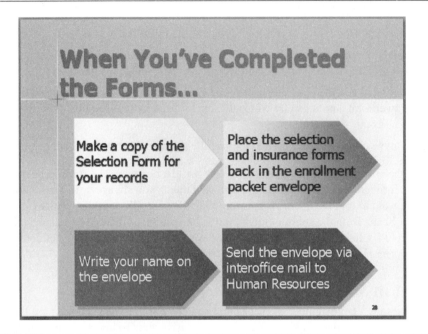

FIGURE 2-12 Text in a shape stands out.

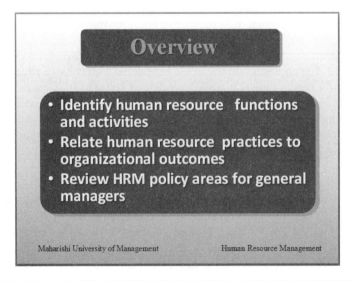

FIGURE 2-13 For a bolder appearance, you can use shapes as replacements for text placeholders.

Use WordArt

WordArt creates fancy text effects. It is ideal for text that you want to stand out. Figure 2-14 shows an example of WordArt text. Although WordArt is a powerful tool and adds a new dimension to your presentation, use it sparingly for maximum effect, and be careful that the words are still legible!

To create WordArt text, click the Insert tab and click the WordArt button in the Text group. The WordArt gallery opens, as shown here. To choose a style, click one of the boxes.

You now see the WordArt on your screen in a selected object, as you see here. Start typing to replace Your Text Here. Press ENTER whenever you want to start a new line. To control the width of the lines, manually resize the WordArt text box. When you're done, click outside the text box to deselect it.

FIGURE 2-14 WordArt creates a powerful impression.

Your WordArt now appears on your slide. You can move and resize the WordArt object as needed.

Edit WordArt Text

To edit any WordArt object, click to select it. When you place or select a WordArt object, the Format tab appears on the ribbon. Click this tab to display tools that help you format the WordArt. In the WordArt Styles group, shown here, click the Quick Styles button to display the same gallery you see when you insert WordArt. You can pass the mouse cursor over any box to see the change in your WordArt. When you find a style that you like, click to choose it. In this way, you can easily try out many WordArt variations.

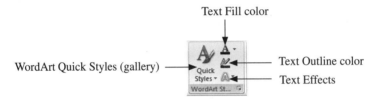

The WordArt gallery makes it easy to choose a predesigned text effect. However, you have total control over all these effects, using the WordArt Styles group of the Format tab. A WordArt effect is made up of these properties:

■ **Text Fill color** To specify the fill color of the text, click the down arrow to the right of the Text Fill button. This displays a range of theme and standard colors. You can also choose More Fill Colors, Picture, Gradient, and Texture for more fill options.

■ **Text Outline color** "Outline" refers the outline around the edges of the letters and the line type can be continuous, dashed, etc. Click the arrow to the right of the Text Outline button to choose from theme and standard colors. You can also choose More Fill Colors, Weight (thickness), or Dashes.

■ **Text Effects** You can apply shadow, reflection, glow, bevel, 3-D rotation, and transform effects to WordArt. Except for the Transform effects, these effects apply to all shapes; I cover these effects in detail in Chapter 6, which covers borders, colors, fills, and 3-D effects. The transform effects, shown in Figure 2-15, allow you to create a shape for the entire text. Figure 2-16 shows some WordArt that uses a transform effect.

NOTE *Many WordArt objects also display one or more pink diamonds when selected. Point and drag on the diamond to change the special characteristics of the WordArt's shape. A boundary appears to help you see the changes as you drag, as shown in Figure 2-16. Each diamond does something different, so you need to experiment.*

2

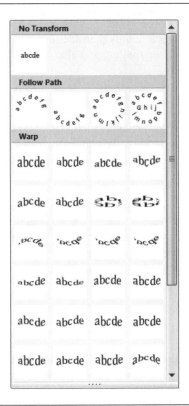

FIGURE 2-15 Transform effects are unique to WordArt and allow you to create many interesting shapes for the WordArt text object.

FIGURE 2-16 You can use transform effects to create various shapes and drag the pink diamonds to adjust parameters of the shape.

Eliminate Spelling Errors and Discover Synonyms

Nothing screams *"unprofessional!"* more loudly than spelling errors in a presentation. PowerPoint not only lets you check your spelling, but also lets you find synonyms so you can use the appropriate word.

Check Spelling

When you type a word that is not in PowerPoint's dictionary, you see a wavy line beneath it, appearing both in the outline and on the slide. To correct the word, right-click it to open the shortcut menu, as shown here, which offers a correct spelling at the top. Click the word you want (there may be several) to correct the spelling.

Words are often underlined inappropriately. For example, names of people and companies are often underlined because they are not in the dictionary. If you use these words frequently, you can choose Add to Dictionary on the shortcut menu and they will never appear underlined again. If the words appear only in this presentation, click Ignore All and they will no longer be underlined in the presentation.

The shortcut menu is enough for most needs, but if you want more detail, click Spelling on the shortcut menu to open the Spelling dialog box, shown next. Note that the dialog box offers more options than the shortcut menu.

The Spelling dialog box lists the misspelled word and suggested alternatives. The Change To box displays the first alternative. You can choose any one of the suggested words or type another possibility in the Change To text box. The dialog box also contains the following options:

- ■ **Ignore**   Ignores only the current instance of the word. This button changes and can appear as a Start or a Resume button, so you can start or resume a spell check.

- ■ **Ignore All**   Ignores all instances of the word in the presentation.

- ■ **Change**   Choose a word from the Suggestions list and click Change to change the current word to the suggested word.

- ■ **Change All**   Changes all instances of the current word to the suggested word.

- ■ **Add**   Adds the word to the dictionary.

- ■ **Suggest**   Suggests possible words. This is done automatically by default.

- ■ **AutoCorrect**   Adds the incorrect and corrected words to the AutoCorrect list. Chapter 13 explains the AutoCorrect feature in detail.

NOTE   *PowerPoint now checks the spelling of WordArt and data that you import, such as Microsoft Excel spreadsheet data.*

If you misspelled a word but the result is actually another legitimate word, the spell checker will not find it. Therefore, always proofread your presentation carefully and never depend on the spell checker to catch all your errors.

You can customize some options that specify how spell check works. For more information, see Chapter 13.

CAUTION   *PowerPoint no longer checks for style; that is, consistency of punctuation and case, or the amount of text on a slide. Check over your presentation to make sure that you use periods consistently, your titles and body use case (upper- and lowercase) consistently, and that you don't put too much text on a slide to be readable. Also, unlike Word, PowerPoint has no grammar checker, so you need to make sure that your grammar is correct!*

Find Synonyms

If you're at a loss for words, you can find synonyms by using the thesaurus. The easiest way to find a synonym is to right-click any word and choose Synonyms from the menu. Pass the cursor over the right arrow to display a list of synonyms, as shown in Figure 2-17. At the bottom of the synonym list, you can choose Thesaurus to display the Research task pane where you can find more options.

In the "Set Spelling" and "Autoformat Options" section of Chapter 13, I explain how to set Options that pertain to spelling.

FIGURE 2-17   You can find synonyms by right-clicking any word and choosing Synonyms from the shortcut menu.

Complete a Presentation: Tutorial

In this section, you create a short presentation to get an overview of the entire process. Throughout the tutorial, I refer you to the chapters that explain the feature in more detail. While the presentation is very simple, it contains many of the features you need to use when creating a presentation.

Develop the Framework

First you develop the framework for the presentation, which includes choosing a theme and adding a logo to the slide master.

1. Open PowerPoint. You see a new presentation with one slide on the screen.

2. Click the Design tab of the ribbon.

3. Click the More (down) button to the right of the Themes group and choose any of the templates. The illustrations here show the Trek theme. The theme's graphics appear on the first slide.

NOTE *If you don't have a title slide on your screen, as shown here, right-click the edge of the slide and choose Layout from the shortcut menu. Choose the first layout, Title Slide.*

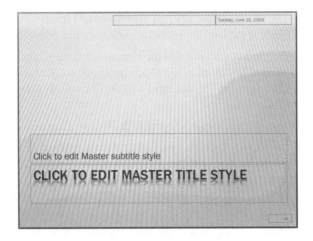

4. To add a logo on all the slides, press SHIFT and click the Normal view button at the lower-right corner of the screen (or click Slide Master from the ribbon's View tab). The slide master view opens, as shown here. For more information, see Chapter 7.

5. Click the Insert tab. (Notice that your tabs are slightly different in Slide Master view.) Click the Shapes button in the Illustrations group of the ribbon to expand the Shapes gallery. In the Basic Shapes group, click the sun shape. Now click near the lower-right corner of the slide master to place the sun.

6. With the sun still selected, press SHIFT and drag any corner handle to enlarge the sun until it is about an inch in diameter. (The size will depend on your screen resolution but need not be exact for this tutorial.) If necessary, drag the sun so it is not too near the edge of the slide. (You can use the arrow keys on your keyboard for more control when you move the sun.) Chapter 5 explains more about adding art and graphic objects.

7. With the sun still selected, make sure that the Format tab is displayed and click the arrow to the right of the Shape Fill button in the Shape Styles group. Choose the yellow color in the Standard Colors section. The sun turns yellow. Chapter 6 explains how to work with color schemes and fills.

8. With the sun still selected, type **The Natural Gift**. This text has a couple of problems.

9. The text wraps to several lines. To fix this, right-click the sun and choose Format Shape. In the Format Shape dialog box, click the Text Box option. Uncheck the Wrap Text in Shape check box and click Close.

10. The text is too light. Select the text you just typed. In the WordArt Styles group of the Format tab, click the down arrow next to the Text Fill button (even though you're not using WordArt). Choose a dark color in the theme colors. Click outside the text to see the results.

11. Again select the text. Click the Home tab. Click Bold in the Font group. The logo should look like the one shown here. You will read about formatting text in Chapter 3.

12. Click the sun logo's border to select it (the border should be solid, not dashed) and choose Copy in the Clipboard group of the Home tab to copy it to the clipboard.

13. In the Outline pane, you see several masters. Only the title slide master displays the logo. Click the Title and Content layout to display it in the Slide pane. Click the Paste button on the ribbon to paste the logo onto the master. It will now appear on all the slides in the presentation that use the Title and Content layout.

14. Click the Slide Master tab and click the Close Master View button in the Close group of the ribbon to return to your first slide. You can see that your logo appears on the slide.

NOTE *To add a logo, you would more likely insert an existing file by choosing Insert | Picture | From File. I explain how to insert images in Chapter 5.*

Add Slides

Once the framework is completed, you start to add slides to the presentation. You can either work on the slides in the Slide pane or add text in the Outline pane.

1. Click the text placeholder that says Click to Add Title. Type **Quarterly Sales Report**. Because the slide master formats titles to be in all uppercase letters, the title appears all in capitals. You also see a slight reflection effect. Chapter 6 covers reflection, shadow, glow, and other effects.

2. Click the text placeholder that says Click to Add Subtitle. Type **2nd Quarter, 2006**. Click outside the textbox to deselect the text and see how it looks.

3. Click Save on the Quick Access toolbar. Keep the suggested title of Quarterly Sales Report. Navigate to the desired location and click Save.

4. Click New Slide on the Home tab. A new slide, using the Title and Content layout, appears.

5. Click the text placeholder that says Click to Add Title. Type **Overall Sales Up**.

6. Click the text placeholder that says Click to Add Text. Type **Total sales were up 6% from last quarter** and press ENTER. A new bullet appears.

7. Type **Gifts were up 15%** and press ENTER.

8. Type **Office supplies were down 14%**. Don't press ENTER. Your slide should look like the slide shown here:

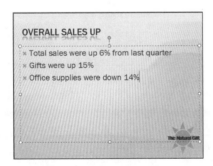

9. Click the Outline tab of the Outline (Thumbnail) pane. Place the cursor on the last line of the text and press ENTER.

10. Right-click the new bullet and choose Promote from the shortcut menu (or press SHIFT-TAB) to start a new slide. The new slide appears in the Slide pane.

11. On the Outline pane, type **Our Competitors** and press ENTER. A new slide appears.

12. Right-click the text area to the right of the new slide's icon and choose Demote from the shortcut menu (or press TAB). The new slide disappears and the cursor is now beneath the previous slide's title.

13. Type **Our market share for gifts increased slightly** and press ENTER. A new bullet appears.

14. Type **Our market share for office supplies decreased slightly** but do not press ENTER.

Add a Chart

After creating some slides, you add a chart showing the details of the quarterly sales in graphic form. Charts and graphs are covered in Chapter 8.

 If you don't have Microsoft Excel installed, you will see Microsoft Graph instead.

Click New Slide on the Home tab. The new slide uses the Title and Content layout.

1. The middle of the slide displays six small icons. Click the top middle icon to insert a chart.

2. In the Create Chart dialog box, choose the Line category from the list of chart types. Then choose the first image, the Line subtype. Click OK.

3. A new Microsoft Excel spreadsheet opens, titled Chart in Microsoft Office PowerPoint. Enter your data for the chart, as shown in Figure 2-18. If you know how to create totals in Excel, you can use formulas for the last row; otherwise, just enter the numbers as shown.

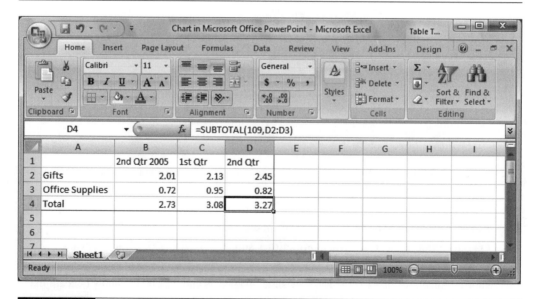

FIGURE 2-18   You enter the data for the PowerPoint chart in Excel.

To delete the fifth row, click the number 5 (the row header), and click Delete | Delete Sheet Rows in the Cells group of the Home tab.

NOTE *You can drag the bar between the column heads to resize the columns of the datasheet.*

2

4. Click the PowerPoint button on the Windows taskbar. Notice the new Chart Tools tab on the ribbon. Your chart has been automatically updated. However, unfortunately, the chart put the type of product on the X axis, instead of on the Y axis.

5. To fix this problem, click the Switch Row/Column button in the Data group of the ribbon.

6. Click the chart if it isn't selected. Then, for each of the three lines in the chart, do the following:

   a. Click the line to select it. (If you have difficulty selecting the line, click the edge of the chart and try again.)

   b. Click the Format tab in the Chart Tools group of the ribbon. In the Shape Styles group, click the down arrow to the right of the Shape Outline button.

   c. Choose Weight | 6 pt. to create a wide line.

7. Click the title of the slide and type **Comparative Sales**.

8. Click anywhere outside the slide to deselect any objects and see the result, shown here:

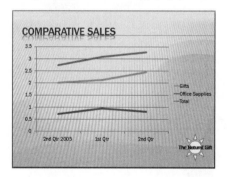

Move a Slide

Here you move a slide to a new position. You can add, delete, or move slides whenever necessary. Chapter 3 covers editing text and slides.

1. Click the Slide Sorter view button at the lower-right corner of your screen.

2. Click Slide 3 (Our Competitors) and drag it to the right of the last slide (slide 4).

Add Animation

Presenters often animate body text so that they can control when each line appears. Here you add an animation scheme to the entire presentation. Animation is explained in Chapter 9.

1. Double-click the second slide to return to Normal view. Click the Animations tab.

2. Click inside the text placeholder that contains the three lines of text. In the Animations group, click the Animations drop-down list and choose By 1st Level Paragraphs under the Fade item.

3. Select slide 4 and repeat step 2 for the text placeholder on that slide.

4. From the Transitions to This Slide group, click the Fade Smoothly transition. At the right, click Apply to All.

Before going on, resave the presentation.

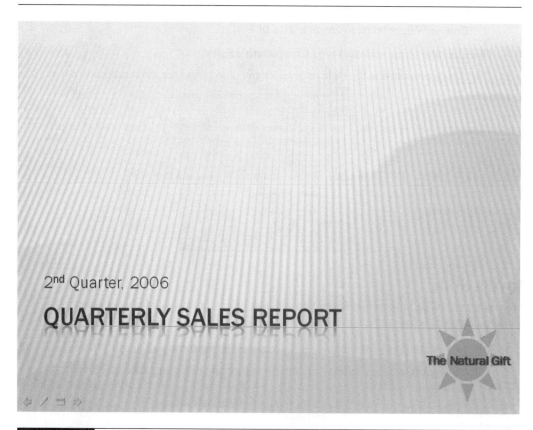

FIGURE 2-19 The first slide of the presentation.

View the Slide Show

Our simple presentation is complete and now is the time to view the results of your work. Chapter 15 covers techniques for delivering a presentation.

1. Click the first slide and click the Slide Show button at the lower-right corner of the screen. You see the first slide displayed full screen as shown in Figure 2-19. Click once anywhere on the screen to move to the second slide.

2. On the second slide, click to display each of the lines of text.

3. Continue to click the mouse button until you have seen the entire slide show. At the end is a black screen.

4. Click once more to leave Slide Show view and return to Normal view.

5. Exit the presentation. Close the Excel worksheet.

Congratulations! You have completed the entire presentation. This overview gives you a firm basis to go deeper into PowerPoint's features, which are covered throughout this book.

Summary

In this chapter, you learned how to create a presentation by choosing a template, by starting with a blank presentation, and by using an existing presentation. You learned how to choose a theme and a background style. The chapter also explained how to choose a layout for your slides. You saw how to add text to a text placeholder, a text box, and a shape. In addition, you learned how to create special text effects with WordArt. This chapter covered creating a text outline from within PowerPoint as well as importing an outline. Once you have created an initial draft of a presentation, you should check the spelling—this chapter explained how. You also learned how to find synonyms. Finally, you created a complete presentation as an overview of the entire process that is developed throughout this book.

In the following chapter, you move on to the next step: editing a presentation.

Chapter 3

Edit Text

How to...

- Move and copy text
- Use the clipboard
- Expand one slide into two
- Edit placeholder text
- Edit text in shapes and text boxes
- Edit WordArt text
- Add symbols to your text
- Use AutoCorrect to automate text changes
- Use the right font for the message
- Make the font bigger or smaller
- Work in Slide Sorter view
- Import slides from other presentations
- Keep a slide library

Once you have created your presentation, you will find that it needs to be edited, just like any other document. Editing a presentation is somewhat different from editing a word processing document, although there are many common elements as well. The differences occur because of the graphical nature of a slide. In this chapter, you learn about editing text as well as your presentation as a whole.

Edit for Clarity

Your main concern when editing text is clarity. Text on a slide is quite different from text in a word processing document. The body text on a slide is often not in full sentences, yet it needs to be clear, nonetheless. Try reading the text on each slide aloud to see if it makes sense. When you deliver the presentation, you expand on the text and explain each item fully. A recent trend (popularized by Cliff Atkinson in his book, *Beyond Bullet Points*) is to use one full sentence on a slide (usually in the title placeholder) rather than phrases. You may find that this style makes your text more meaningful.

A second reason to edit text is aesthetic. If you created your presentation using an outline, you need to run through each slide to see how the text fits on the slide. Text may need to be cut. You may even want to add text for a balanced look.

The basic techniques for editing text are the same in all Windows programs:

- ■ To add text, place the cursor where you want the new text to appear and start typing.
- ■ To edit text, select the text you want to change and type the new text that you want.
- ■ To delete text, select it and press DELETE.

I cover changing fonts in the "Choose Text with Style" section, later in this chapter. Formatting bullets and paragraphs is covered in Chapter 4.

Move and Copy Text

Within a presentation, you can often move selected text by dragging it on the Outline tab of the Outline pane to the new location. Hold down CTRL to copy the text instead of moving it. However, if you can't see both the source and destination locations on the screen at one time, you should use the clipboard. Use the Cut, Copy, and Paste commands in the Clipboard group of the Home tab.

Use CTRL-X to move text and CTRL-C to copy text. Then, place the cursor in the desired location and use CTRL-V to paste the text.

A new feature allows you to select separated chunks of text before copying or cutting them to the clipboard. For example, you may want to select the first and third lines of text on a slide. To do so, select the first chunk of text and then press CTRL as you select additional chunks of text. You can then cut or copy the text to the clipboard.

To copy text from another presentation or document, you can use the clipboard as well. Follow these steps:

1. Open the file that contains the source text.
2. Select the text.
3. Copy the text to the clipboard.
4. Move to the desired destination in the presentation and place the cursor where you want the text to appear.
5. Paste the text from the clipboard.

You can also use drag-and-drop to move or copy text from one file to another. It's more fun but requires more dexterity than using the clipboard. Here's how:

1. Open both files. (It may help to close other, unnecessary files.)
2. From the View tab's Window group, choose Arrange All. You see both your presentation and the other document on your screen. Make sure you can see both the source and destination locations in each window.

3. Click in the source document and select the text you want to move or copy.

4. To move the text, point to it and drag it to the desired location in your presentation. To copy the text, hold down CTRL as you drag.

Later in this chapter, in the section "Import Slides from Other Presentations," I explain how to copy slides from other presentations.

Use the Clipboard Task Pane

Office includes a Clipboard task pane that lets you place up to 24 items on the clipboard at once. To display the Clipboard task pane, click the launcher arrow at the lower-right corner of the Clipboard group of the ribbon's Home tab.

 *You can collect multiple items when the Clipboard task pane is not displayed by opening the task pane manually, clicking the Options button, and choosing Collect Without Showing Office Clipboard, shown here. From then on, multiple items are invisibly collected on the clipboard, even when the task pane is not displayed.*

Once the Clipboard task pane, shown next, is displayed, you simply copy a second item to the clipboard in the usual manner. You can then paste either item into your presentation. Each additional piece of data that you copy to the clipboard (up to 24 items) is added as a separate item. To paste an item from the Clipboard task pane, place your cursor wherever you want the item to appear and then click the item on the task pane.

SHORTCUT *You can use the Paste All button on the Clipboard task pane to collect text from several places and paste it all in a new location.*

Edit Placeholder Text

Because placeholder text appears in the outline, you can edit it either in the outline or directly on the slide. Editing placeholder text on the outline may be more familiar to you because it is quite similar to editing text in a word processor. If all you want to do is simple text editing, do it in the Outline pane.

However, you may want to edit text directly on the slide for several reasons:

- The text is larger and therefore easier to see. You can more clearly see the results of your text attributes, such as color, shadow, font, and font style (such as bold or italic text).

- The slide may contain a graphic, and you may need to see how the text fits with the graphic. For example, you may want to edit your text because it covers the graphic.

- You may be performing several editing functions at once, such as changing the placeholder's background color along with editing the text. Because you must change the placeholder's background color directly on the slide, it is easy to continue your work right on the slide.

When you edit placeholder text on the slide, two objects are involved—the placeholder and the text inside the placeholder. When you click any text in the placeholder, PowerPoint places the cursor where you clicked. The placeholder gets a selection border and handles to show you that it is selected. You can also drag to select the text you want to edit, which automatically selects the placeholder as well. You also see a blue selection block around the text. You are now in Edit Text mode, shown in Figure 3-1. Although the placeholder is selected, your changes affect only the text within it.

The new Mini toolbar, shown here, appears near selected text to simplify the process of editing text. At first, this toolbar is semitransparent, but if you pass your cursor over it, the toolbar becomes opaque so you can easily see the buttons on it. (You can also right-click any text to display the Mini toolbar.) Here you can change the font and its properties, indent and align text, format bullets, and use the Format Painter.

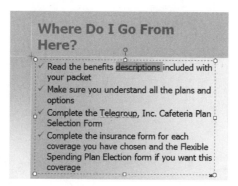

FIGURE 3-1   Editing text in a placeholder

If your slide's text is bulleted, you can delete an entire bulleted item by placing the cursor over the bullet. The cursor changes to a cross with arrows. Click to select the entire bulleted item, and then press DELETE. *This technique works only when the placeholder is already selected.*

If you backspace to delete the text in a bulleted item, or select only the words in an item, you may be left with just the bullet. With the cursor next to the bullet, press BACKSPACE twice to delete the bullet and the empty line. If your slide's text isn't bulleted, press BACKSPACE once. To add body text, place the cursor after the previous item and press ENTER. You can then type the text.

In Chapter 2, I explained how to import an outline. You can also insert an outline into an existing presentation as part of the editing process. Follow these steps:

1. On the Home tab, click the New Slide button's drop-down arrow to display the layouts.

2. At the bottom of the list, choose Slides from Outline.

3. In the Insert Outline dialog box, shown in Figure 3-2, locate your outline and select it. Notice that the Files of Type drop-down list is already set to All Outlines.

4. Click Insert.

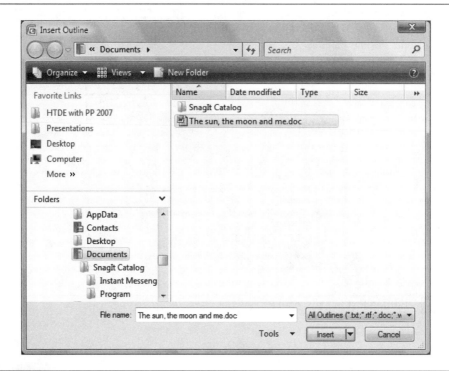

FIGURE 3-2   Use the Insert Outline dialog box to insert an outline into an existing presentation.

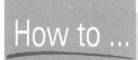

Expand One Slide into Two

If you just can't make the text fit properly on a slide, try splitting the text onto two slides. If the text is in a text placeholder, you can accomplish this task easily on the Outline tab of the Outline pane, as follows:

1. In the Outline pane, position the insertion point at the end of the last bulleted item that you want to appear on the first slide.

2. Press ENTER.

3. In the Outline pane, right-click and choose Promote (or press SHIFT-TAB) until a New Slide icon appears. You can also click Decrease List Level in the Paragraph group of the Home tab.

4. Type a title for the new slide. You may have to adjust the bulleted text to get it to the proper level.

NOTE   *Another way to fit in more text is to divide it up into side-by-side placeholders, using the 2-Content or Comparison layout. In addition, you can now divide text into columns. For more information about columns, see the section "Create Columns" in Chapter 4.*

Work with Placeholders

Once you click a placeholder, you enter Edit Text mode. Any time you press DELETE, text is deleted. In this case, how do you delete the placeholder itself? The answer is not very obvious. Here are the steps:

1. Click the border of the placeholder to exit Edit Text mode. Note that the border changes from dashed to solid.

SHORTCUT   *Another way to exit Edit Text mode is to press ESC.*

2. Press DELETE to see the Click to Add Text message.

Click the border again and press DELETE a second time.

NOTE   *If you want to delete all the placeholders, you can choose the Blank layout and then delete the existing placeholders.*

Here are some other things you can do with placeholders:

- **Duplicate the placeholder**   First exit Edit Text mode. With the placeholder selected, click the Home tab and then click the drop-down arrow on the Paste button in the Clipboard group. From the menu, choose Duplicate. You now have twin placeholders. Move the new placeholder so it doesn't overlap the first one.

SHORTCUT   *Press CTRL-D to duplicate a placeholder.*

- **Cut (or copy) and paste a placeholder to a new slide**   Again, you need to exit Edit Text mode. Then press CTRL-X to cut or CTRL-C to copy. Move to the new slide and press CTRL-V to paste the placeholder.
- **Move a placeholder**   Select the placeholder and place the cursor anywhere over the selection border until you see the crossed-arrows cursor. Then click and drag the placeholder to its new position.
- **Resize a placeholder**   Drag one of the placeholder's handles, and the placeholder grows or shrinks in the direction you drag.

In Chapter 5, I explain how to position and resize any object on a slide more precisely. See the section "Lay Out Your Slides with Precision."

Find and Replace Text

You can search for text throughout the entire presentation. You can also specify replacement text. The Find dialog box now finds WordArt text. You are probably already familiar with the Find and Replace feature of your word processor. To find text, click Find in the Editing group of the Home tab (or press CTRL-F). The Find dialog box shown here is displayed.

Select Match Case to find *Governor* but not *governor*, for example. Select Find Whole Words Only to find *and* but not *sand*. Click Find Next to continue to search for other instances of the search term.

NOTE   *If you display the Outline tab of the Outline pane, PowerPoint highlights placeholder text only in the Outline pane but displays the equivalent slide so that you can work on either the outline or the slide. But, PowerPoint highlights text in text boxes, WordArt, and Shapes on the slide, because that text doesn't appear in the outline. On the other hand, if you display the Slides tab of the Outline pane, PowerPoint highlights placeholder text on the slide.*

You can go directly to the Replace dialog box by clicking Replace in the Find dialog box. Otherwise, choose Replace in the Editing group of the Home tab or press CTRL-H. Click the Replace button to replace the selection, or click Replace All to replace all instances of the text.

Change Text Case

For a professional look, pay attention to proper use and consistency of *case*, that is, capitalization. For example, you may want your slide title to use title case and your body text to use sentence case. When you want to make changes, the Change Case command can help you quickly change the case of text. Just select the text and, on the Home tab, in the Font group, choose the Change Case button. Here are your options:

- **Sentence case**   Starts with an uppercase letter. All the rest of the letters are lowercase, and the sentence ends with a period.

When changing text to sentence case, PowerPoint also changes proper nouns to lowercase. For example, "We Go To School On Monday" becomes "We go to school on monday." You need to manually correct any such mistakes.

- **lowercase**   Contains all lowercase letters.
- **UPPERCASE**   Contains all uppercase letters.
- **Capitalize Each Word**   Capitalizes the first letter of each word. But you'll still need to review the results—if you don't want short words such as *with*, *and*, and *a* capitalized.
- **tOGGLE cASE**   Reverses the case of each letter.

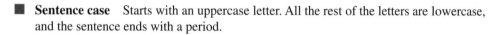

Select the text and press SHIFT-3 to cycle through the case choices, except for Sentence case.

Traditionally, titles were either all uppercase or in *title case*, meaning that each word was capitalized. However, studies have shown that uppercase text is harder to read, so in recent years many people have opted to use sentence case for slide titles, for a more informal look or because they want the title to be a complete sentence. You can use any style you want, but always keep legibility and consistency foremost.

Edit Text in Shapes and Text Boxes

Editing text in shapes and text boxes is very similar to editing placeholder text. When you select the text, you are also selecting the object that contains the text, and a selection border and handles appear around the object.

When you place text in a text box, the text box expands as you type. The text box similarly adjusts when you edit text. If you delete enough text, the text box will shrink accordingly.

If you add text to a shape, by default the text wraps to fit within the boundaries of the shape. You can change this behavior if you want. Right-click the shape and choose Format Shape from the shortcut menu. In the Format Shape dialog box, click the Text Box category, as shown in Figure 3-3. Then, uncheck the Wrap Text in Shape check box.

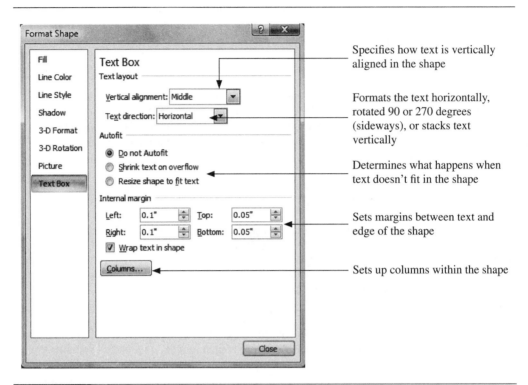

Specifies how text is vertically aligned in the shape

Formats the text horizontally, rotated 90 or 270 degrees (sideways), or stacks text vertically

Determines what happens when text doesn't fit in the shape

Sets margins between text and edge of the shape

Sets up columns within the shape

FIGURE 3-3 Use the Text Box category of the Format Shape dialog box to specify how text fits in a shape.

The Text Box tab of the Format Shape dialog box lets you format all the qualities of any shape, placeholder, or text box that pertain to text. These settings are the key to good-looking text in shapes and text boxes.

To fit more text on a shape or in a text box with no visible border, reduce all four internal margins to zero. On the other hand, when you have a visible border, increasing these margins can sometimes improve legibility.

A new feature allows you to stack text vertically. Choose Stacked from the Text Direction drop-down list. You also need to uncheck the Wrap Text in Shape check box. You see an example on the left of this slide:

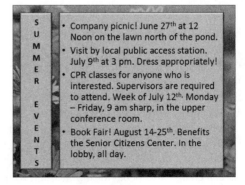

3

Did you know?

Uses for Shapes, Text Boxes, and WordArt

Text used in conjunction with shapes or WordArt can help make your point—if you don't get carried away. For example, to show that sales went up 15 percent, put the text **15%** on the shape of an arrow pointing diagonally upward at about 15 degrees. Here are some guidelines:

- Use shapes to organize your text for the audience. For example, if you set up two columns and three rows of text, in which direction are readers supposed to look first—down the first column or across the first row? You can place shapes behind groups of text that you want readers to consider all at once. Another organizational technique is to add section names or numbers on color-coded shapes to the sections of your presentation.

- When you place text in multiple shapes and text boxes, make sure these objects are aligned with each other to avoid a chaotic effect. Chapter 5 explains how to perfectly align objects.

- Don't put too many shapes with text on a slide. Sometimes simple text is easier to follow.

- WordArt is great fun, but use it sparingly. Use WordArt for short phrases that are separate from the rest of the text, such as "See you there!" or "Don't forget!"

- Remember, too many effects make your text less readable, so use common sense.

Edit WordArt Text

To edit WordArt text, select the WordArt object. The cursor is placed where you clicked, as shown here. You can simply start typing to add text, click to move the cursor, or select some text. You edit the WordArt directly on the slide.

When you select WordArt, the Format tab appears. You can use the WordArt Styles group to edit any feature of the WordArt object in the same way you created it. (See Chapter 2 for a discussion of how to create WordArt.)

Add Symbols

Symbols are text characters that don't exist on your keyboard. To insert a symbol into new or existing text, you need to be in a selected text placeholder, text box, shape, or WordArt object. Click the Insert tab and, in the Text group, click the Symbol button. PowerPoint opens the Symbol dialog box, shown on the next page.

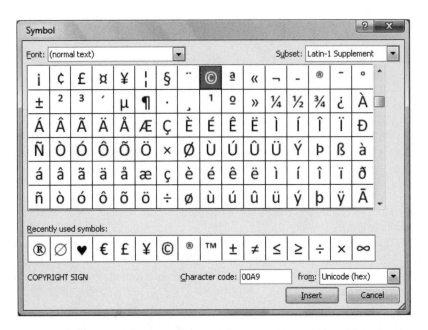

First, choose a font from the Font drop-down list. The default is Normal Text. Choose the symbol you want and then click Insert to insert the symbol. The dialog box stays open so you can insert other symbols. Click Close to close the dialog box.

Besides choosing technical symbols such as the degree symbol (°), the diameter symbol (ø), and the plus-minus symbol (±), you can find arrows, check marks, stars, and other more whimsical symbols. You may especially want to check the Symbol and Wingding fonts.

If you need to create complex equations, use the Equation Editor. Display the Insert tab and choose Object in the Text group. In the Insert Object dialog box, choose Microsoft Equation 3.0 and click OK.

Use AutoCorrect

AutoCorrect is a feature that automatically corrects misspelled words. You can also use AutoCorrect as a shortcut for typing long, difficult words or phrases. To set up AutoCorrect, click the Office button and click PowerPoint Options. Choose the Proofing category and click the AutoCorrect Options button to open the AutoCorrect dialog box, with the AutoCorrect tab on top, as shown in Figure 3-4. Settings you make in the AutoCorrect dialog box also apply to Microsoft Word and Excel.

AutoCorrect does not apply to text in hyperlinks, so check this text carefully. Chapter 11 explains how to use hyperlinks in a presentation.

3

FIGURE 3-4   The AutoCorrect dialog box settings determine how PowerPoint corrects text as you type.

Use the first five check boxes in the middle of the dialog box to correct common typing errors:

- **Correct TWo INitial CApitals**   Changes the second uppercase letter to lowercase.

- **Capitalize First Letter of Sentences**   Changes a lowercase letter to uppercase when PowerPoint thinks you have started a new sentence, usually after a period. See the following discussion regarding exceptions for this setting.

- **Capitalize Names of Days**   Capitalizes Monday, Tuesday, and so on.

- **Capitalize First Letter of Table Cells**   Changes a lowercase letter to uppercase when it is the first letter in a table cell. See the following discussion regarding exceptions for this setting.

- **Correct Accidental Use of cAPS LOCK Key**   Reverses the case of letters when PowerPoint notices one lowercase letter followed by several uppercase letters.

The last check box, Replace Text as You Type, lets you add your own AutoCorrections. Type the incorrect spelling in the Replace box, type the correct spelling in the With box, and click Add. To delete an item, choose it and click Delete.

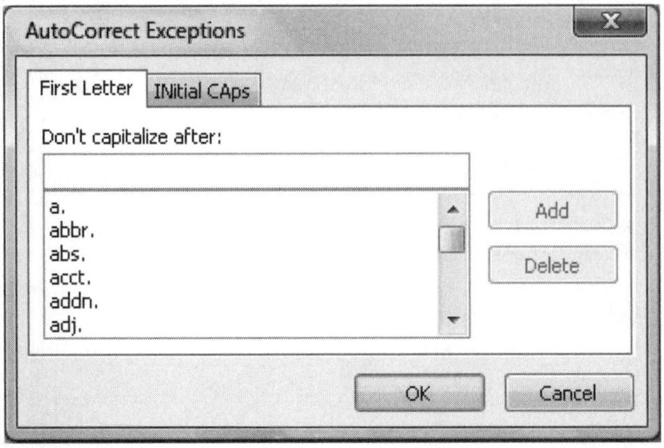

FIGURE 3-5   Use the AutoCorrect Exceptions dialog box to fine-tune the AutoCorrect feature.

*Use AutoCorrect to help you type long or difficult phrases. For example, type **hrd** in the Replace box and **Human Resources Department** in the With box. Then, every time you type "hrd" and press the SPACEBAR or ENTER, PowerPoint replaces those three letters with the full version. Be sure to use a shortcut that you won't type in any other situation.*

Click Exceptions to open the AutoCorrect Exceptions dialog box, shown in Figure 3-5. The First Letter tab specifies exceptions to the Capitalize First Letter of Sentences setting. Because PowerPoint bases its concept of a sentence on anything after a period, you may find that it incorrectly capitalizes words after an abbreviation that you follow with a period. By adding abbreviations that you commonly use, you can avoid this problem.

The INitial CAps tab fine-tunes the Correct TWo INitial CApitals setting. If you type words where the first two letters should be capitalized, add them to this list.

Whenever the AutoCorrect feature changes text, the AutoCorrect Options button appears as a small rectangle near that text when you point to it, as shown here: We look forward

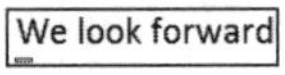

Point to the rectangle and it changes to display a drop-down arrow. Click the arrow and it opens a menu, as shown here:

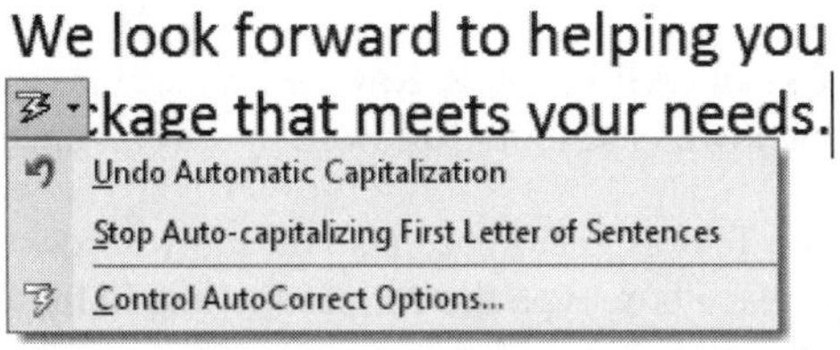

The AutoCorrect Options menu offers the following choices:

- **Undo Automatic Capitalization**   Choosing this option allows you to undo the change. The exact wording varies according to the correction that was made.
- **Stop Auto-capitalizing First Letter of Sentences**   Choosing this option changes the setting in the AutoCorrect dialog box. The exact wording depends on the type of correction.
- **Control AutoCorrect Options**   Choosing this option displays the AutoCorrect dialog box so you can change the settings.

Normally, the AutoCorrect Options button is available whenever you pass the cursor over any text that has been corrected using the AutoCorrect feature. You can disable the button by unchecking the Show AutoCorrect Options Buttons check box (refer to Figure 3-4) in the AutoCorrect dialog box.

Act on Data with Smart Tags

Smart tags help you take actions on certain types of data and labels. For example, you can use this feature to send an e-mail message to a person by clicking the person's name or to set up an appointment by clicking a date. Smart tags help integrate PowerPoint with other Microsoft Office programs, especially Outlook.

Smart tags are marked by a purple dotted underline. When you place the cursor over the text, the Smart Tag Actions button appears. Here you see a date marked as a smart tag, along with its Smart Tag Actions button. Note that this underline is not always easily visible against a dark background. Of course, smart tags do not appear in Slide Show view.

Setting Smart Tag Options

Smart tags are off by default. To activate smart tags, click the Microsoft Office (File) button, click PowerPoint Options, and then choose the Proofing category. Click the AutoCorrect Options button and click the Smart Tags tab, shown in Figure 3-6.

To activate smart tags, check the Label Text with Smart Tags check box in the AutoCorrect dialog box. You can also specify which types of data PowerPoint recognizes. From the list, check the smart tag types you want PowerPoint to use.

To check the presentation for smart tags, click Check Presentation. This procedure sometimes reveals smart tags that were not marked.

> NOTE   *Click More Smart Tags to go to Microsoft's web site and view a list of companies that provide a variety of solutions using smart tags.*

Check Embed Smart Tags in This Presentation if you may need to move the presentation or give it to someone else. Embedding smart tags increases the size of the presentation file. Click OK to close the AutoCorrect dialog box.

FIGURE 3-6 Use the Smart Tags tab of the AutoCorrect dialog box to specify smart tag settings.

Using Smart Tags

To use a smart tag, place the mouse cursor over a smart tag until the Smart Tag Actions button appears. Click the button to display the action list and choose one of the actions. In the following illustration you see the list for a date:

For example, if you choose Show My Calendar, Microsoft Outlook opens with the calendar on the date in the smart tag. You can then see if your schedule is clear or add a reminder.

Choose Text with Style

Part of editing text is formatting it. Because of the graphical nature of PowerPoint, you probably spend more time considering how your fonts look than you would in Word or Excel. The font type determines the shape of the letters in a font. You can also change the font size of any font. You can apply a font *style*, such as bold or italic, and change the spacing between the letters. Finally, you can add certain effects to your text, such as underlining, a shadow, or a glow.

Use the Right Font for the Message

PowerPoint offers you a wide choice of fonts. Your choice affects the impact of your message on the audience. For guidelines on choosing the right font, see "Make Text Count" later in this chapter.

Understand Font Types

Sans-serif fonts have no extraneous lines and are good for titles and text that you want to stand out. They are considered most readable for on-screen reading. The most common sans-serif font in Windows is Arial, which comes in several variants. Some examples of common sans-serif fonts are shown here:

Serif fonts have small extra lines at the ends of letters. They are considered most readable for paragraph text and seem more formal. Newspapers usually use serif fonts. Times New Roman is the most common serif font in Windows. Some examples of serif fonts are shown in the next illustration:

Change Fonts and Create Theme Fonts

When you select text, its font appears in the Font drop-down list in the Font group of the Home tab. To change a text's font, select the text and choose a new font from the drop-down list.

Serif Fonts

- Book Antiqua
- Bookman Old Style
- Courier New
- Garamond
- Georgia
- Goudy Old Style
- Lucida Bright
- Times New Roman

TIP
To remove any formatting that you've added to a font, select the text and choose Remove All Formatting in the Font group of the Home tab. The text reverts to the default formatting.

To replace a font throughout an entire presentation, you need to create new theme fonts. Theme fonts consist of one font for slide titles and another font (or the same one) for body text. You can save the theme fonts and use them in other presentations. Follow these steps:

1. Display the Design tab.
2. In the Themes group, click the Fonts button. You see the Fonts gallery. Notice that the font sets have the same name as the built-in themes; each theme has its own set of fonts.
3. At the bottom of the Built-In Fonts gallery, choose Create New Theme Fonts.
4. In the Create New Theme Fonts dialog box, use the Heading Font drop-down list to choose a new font for slide titles.
5. Use the Body Font drop-down list to choose a new font for body text.
6. In the Name text box, enter a name for the theme fonts.
7. Click Save.

Even new slides use the new fonts you have chosen. The slide master fonts also change. If you save a custom theme, the theme fonts become part of that theme and you can then use them in other presentations. In Chapter 7, I explain how to work with the slide master and to save themes.

To change the font for WordArt text, select the text and choose a new font from the Font drop-down list in the Font group of the Home tab.

Make a Font Bigger or Smaller

Changing the font size is as easy as changing the font—select the text and choose a new size from the Font Size drop-down list in the Font group of the Home tab.

TIP
If you don't care exactly which size you choose but just want to make your text a little bigger or smaller, use the Increase Font Size and Decrease Font Size buttons in the Font group of the Home tab, shown here. Your text quickly goes to the next setting on the Font Size drop-down list, either smaller or larger, according to which button you click.

SHORTCUT
To increase font size, press CTRL-SHIFT->. To decrease font size, press CTRL-SHIFT-<.

As you have no doubt discovered, typical font sizes are much larger on slides than in word processing documents. Fonts are usually measured in points. A *point* is 1/72 of an inch.

While 10- or 12-point text is typical in a word processing document, it is much too small for a slide. In general, you should never use text that is less than 18 points—and then only in a pinch.

3

You will find that 24- to 44-point text is appropriate for most bulleted text, and your slide title should be larger than your body text.

A presentation meant for the Web or a computer monitor can use smaller text than a presentation shown on a screen in front of an audience.

As mentioned earlier, in the section "Use the Right Font for the Message," the default font size is stored in the slide master that comes with the design template. However, if you type more text than can fit in a placeholder, by default, PowerPoint resizes your text to fit into the placeholder. You can turn this feature off by clicking the Office button and clicking PowerPoint Options. Choose the Proofing category, click the AutoCorrect Options button to open the AutoCorrect dialog box, and then click the AutoFormat As You Type tab. Uncheck AutoFit Title Text to Text Placeholder and AutoFit Body Text to Text Placeholder. Click OK twice to return to your slide.

Change Font Spacing

You can change the spacing between letters to stretch out a heading or to squeeze text into a tight space. Of course, always make sure that your text is still easy to read. To change the spacing between letters, select the text. In the Font group of the Home tab, click the Character Spacing button and choose one of the options from Very Tight to Very Loose. For even more control, click More Spacing to open the Character Spacing tab of the Font dialog box where you can specify the number of points between letters. Click OK when you're done.

Kerning is a new feature for PowerPoint 2007. Kerning selectively adjusts spacing between certain letters, based on their shape, to give a more even appearance. For example, in the word "VACATION," kerning moves the V and the A closer together. To turn on kerning for an entire presentation, follow these steps:

1. Select any text box or placeholder.
2. Display the Home tab. In the Font group, click the dialog box launcher arrow (to the right of the Font label) to open the Font dialog box.
3. Choose the Character Spacing tab.
4. Check the Kerning for Fonts check box.
5. Enter a number in the Points and Above text box to indicate to which size (or greater) text you want to apply kerning.

Add Font Styles

Add a font style to your text to emphasize it. To format text with a font style, select it and choose Bold, Italic, Underline, or Shadow from the Font group of the Home. However, remember not to sacrifice legibility.

 *You can make text bold or italic from the Mini toolbar that appears when you select text. If you don't see the Mini toolbar, right-click the selected text to display it.*

PowerPoint 2007 adds many new text formatting options. I discuss these in this section and the next section, "Use the Font Dialog Box." As discussed earlier in this chapter, in the "Edit Text in Shapes and Text Boxes," you can now create vertical text.

You can now apply WordArt styles to any text. QuickStyles are combinations of WordArt formatting that you can quickly apply. Follow these steps:

1. Select the text.
2. Click the Format tab that appears.
3. In the WordArt Styles group of the ribbon, click the QuickStyles button to display the Quick Styles gallery:
4. Choose an option in either the Applies to Selected Text section or the Applies to All Text in the Shape section. To remove the WordArt QuickStyle, click the Clear WordArt button in the gallery.

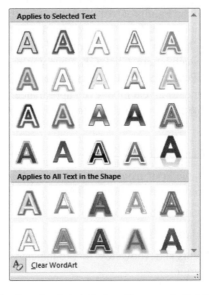

However, you're not limited to the QuickStyles. You can individually specify text fill, text outline, and text effects to create any combination of formatting that you want. Here's how to use these options:

- On the Format tab, in the WordArt Styles group, click the Text Fill button to open the Colors gallery, where you can choose a solid, textured, gradient, or picture fill for the inside of the letters. I discuss fills in detail in Chapter 6.

- Click the Text Outline button to open the Colors gallery, where you can choose an outline color, weight (thickness), and line type (such as dashed).

- Click the Text Effects button to open the Text Effects menu, shown here. This menu opens up a myriad of opportunities for styling your text.

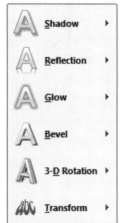

Shadows   Choose the Shadow option of the Text Effects menu to display the Shadows gallery, shown here. You can choose from outside shadows (shadows outside the outline of the letters) and inside shadows. For even more options, click Shadow Options to open the Format Text Effects dialog box, shown in Figure 3-7.

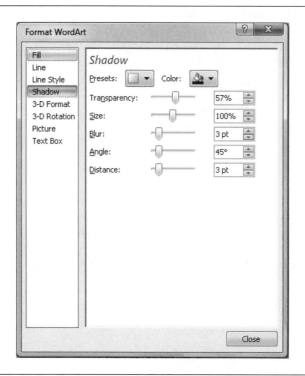

FIGURE 3-7 Choose the Shadow category of the Format Text Effects dialog box to create exacting specifications for shadows of all your text.

In the dialog box's Shadow category, you can choose another color for the shadow. Also, you can make the shadow partially or fully transparent, change its size relative to the size of the object, add a blur (fuzzy) effect for a softer shadow, change its angle relative to the object, and change its distance from the object.

NOTE *Your changes (except for color) are immediately applied to the object. Move the dialog box so that it doesn't obscure the object; then you'll be able to see the results of your choices clearly. Click Close to close the dialog box. If you want to undo the changes, click Undo on the Quick Access toolbar.*

If you just want a simple shadow, use the Shadow button in the Font group of the Home tab. Remember that shadows can make text harder to read, so use them sparingly.

CAUTION *By default, the shadow for text is gray, so it does not show up well on many midrange color backgrounds. Shadows for objects are covered in Chapter 6.*

3

FIGURE 3-8   The picture fill echoes the meaning of the word, the outline sets the text off from the background, and the shadow appears to lift the text slightly off the slide.

Figure 3-8 shows a word that uses a dark-green outline, a picture fill, and a shadow created using the Shadow button on the Home tab. As you can see, you need large text (this is Arial Black, 60-point text) to make this work. Use this type of technique only when it enhances the message and just for one or two words. Because the text is about using images, using a picture fill for the word IMAGES is effective.

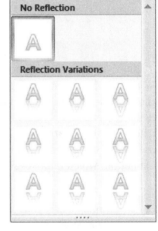

Reflection   A reflection effect mirrors the text. Reflections work best with one line of text; for more than one line, the reflection obscures the next line of text. To add a reflection, choose the Reflection option of the Text Effects menu to open the Reflection gallery, shown here. Choose from one of the reflection options.

Glow   A glow creates a halo of color around the text. Choose the Glow option of the Text Effects menu to display the Glow gallery, shown here, and choose an option. For more color options, click More Glow Colors to open the standard color palette. As with any text effect, use a glow only when appropriate, as it reduces legibility. Be sure that the glow color contrasts with both the text color and the background color.

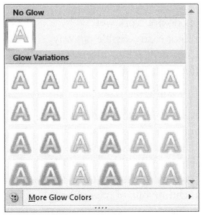

Bevel A bevel is a 3-D effect that adds sharp or curved edges to text to make it appear to rise up from the surface of the slide. Choose the Bevel option of the Text Effects menu to display the Bevel gallery, shown here, and choose one of the bevel treatments:

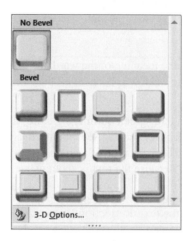

Click 3-D Options to open the Format Text Effects dialog box, with the 3-D Format category displayed, as shown in Figure 3-9. Here you can fine-tune top and bottom bevels, give the object a 3-D depth, add a contour (an outline), specify a material (a surface treatment), and add lighting effects. Click Close when you're done. If you don't like the effect, use the Reset button, which removes 3-D formatting.

 *You don't see the depth unless you also add a 3-D rotation, just as you can't see the height of a box when you are looking straight down at it from the top.*

Most of these advanced effects do not work well with text; they reduce legibility and are not easily visible anyway. I discuss them in more detail in Chapter 6, which discusses shapes, because they are more effective with shapes than with text.

3-D Rotation A 3-D rotation turns the object so that you see it from a different viewpoint. In many cases, you would also add a depth, using the 3-D Format category of the Format Text Effects dialog box (refer to Figure 3-9). Choose the 3-D Rotation option of the Text Effects menu to display the 3-D Rotation gallery, shown here, and choose one of the options:

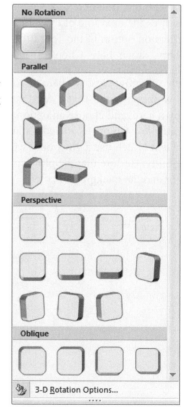

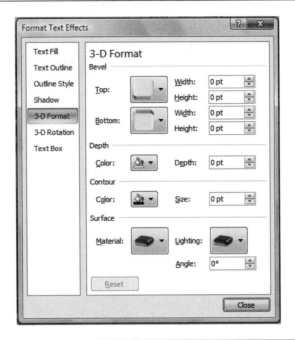

FIGURE 3-9   The 3-D Format category of the Format Text Effects dialog box provides a wealth of controls for formatting 3-D text.

As with the other text effects, you need to use 3-D treatments with care, as they reduce legibility severely. They are meant to turn text into a graphic for a dramatic effect, as shown here:

Transform   The Transform category is unique to text and offers a way to wrap text into different shapes. Previously, this feature was available only for WordArt, but you can now use it for any text.

Choose the Transform option of the Text Effects menu to display the Transform gallery, shown here, and choose one of the options:

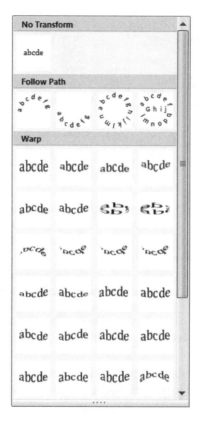

 *Except for the Transform effect, these effects are available for all objects, not just text. Shapes also have a Soft Edges effect that you can apply. I cover effects for objects in Chapter 6.*

Figure 3-10 shows another example of text turned into a graphic, this time using the Circle Transform option. As you can see, the point is not to make the text especially readable, but to create the effect of text going in a circle, because that's what the text is about.

Clear All Formatting

If you've gone overboard with your text formatting and want to remove it all, select the text or the textbox itself. On the Home tab, in the Font group, click the Clear All Formatting button.

Use the Font Dialog Box

The Font dialog box, shown in Figure 3-11, puts most of the settings for formatting text in one place and offers features not available elsewhere.

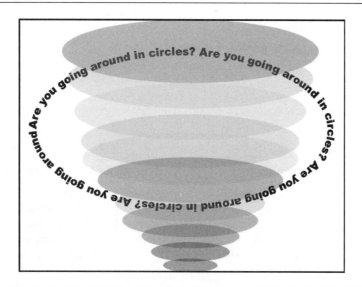

FIGURE 3-10   You can use text effects to turn text into a graphic.

To change existing text, select it and click the Font button in the lower-right corner of the Font group of the Home tab to open the Font dialog box. Choose a font, font style, and font size from the drop-down lists. To change the text's color, click the Font Color drop-down list and choose a color. To choose from a full range of colors, choose More Colors from the drop-down list.

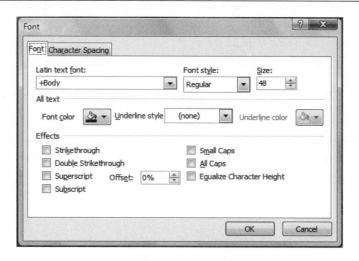

FIGURE 3-11   The Font dialog box contains in one place most of the settings for text formatting.

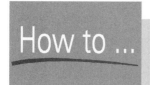 **Make Text Count**

The first rule for making text count is readability. Here are some pointers that will help you ensure your text is legible:

- Shadowed text can make text stand out, but make sure it looks good on your background color. The shadow needs to be subtle and the text needs to be large, or legibility suffers.

- When you place text over a full-color graphic, be sure that the text is readable everywhere on your slide. If the graphic has many colors, some of its areas may blend in too well with your text. A possible solution is to use a semitransparent fill for the text's placeholder or shape. I explain more about shape fills in Chapter 6.

- Be careful about rotated, vertical, and 3-D text—it can be hard to read.

- To get text to stand out, concentrate on the right font, the right size, the right color, and a contrasting background instead of using all capital letters or a very fancy text effect. One of the text styles (bold, italics) or a subtle effect (such as a shadow) can also be effective.

- Don't use more than two fonts on a slide. The effect is chaotic and therefore distracting. A better choice is to limit yourself to one font. Sticking to the theme fonts is a good way to keep fonts clear.

- Associate a font with a type of element. For example, make all your slide titles the same font.

- Keep the font type fairly simple for legibility.

- Have someone else read your presentation, on paper or onscreen, to make sure the flow of ideas is clear. For example, if you set up two columns and three rows of text, in which direction are readers supposed to look first—down the first column or across the first row?

In Chapter 9, I explain how to animate text—another way to emphasize it. You can make text appear when you want it to, as well as have lines you've already presented dim or disappear.

You now have more underlining options. Choose a line type from the Underline Style drop-down list. For example, you can underline text with a dash-dot, wavy, or dotted line. Another new feature is the ability to choose the underline color; choose a color from the Underline Color drop-down list.

From the Effects section, you can choose Strikethrough, Double Strikethrough, Superscript, Subscript, Small Caps, All Caps, and Equalize Character Height. Except for the Superscript and Subscript options, these effects are all new for PowerPoint. Click OK when you're done to close the dialog box.

Copy the Look with Format Painter

You may see text formatting that you like and want to use on other text. Figuring out the exact formatting and changing the text can be time-consuming. Format Painter was designed for just this situation. To format text with Format Painter, follow these steps:

1. Select the text with the formatting you want.

 2. Click Format Painter in the Clipboard group of the Home tab.

3. Select the text you want to format.

> **TIP** *To format several selections of text with the same formatting, double-click Format Painter. You can then select text as many times as you want. Click Format Painter at the end (or press ESC) to stop formatting. You can also use Format Painter with shapes.*

Add, Delete, and Rearrange Slides

Another aspect of editing a presentation involves adding, deleting, and rearranging slides. You do this editing in Slide Sorter view, where you can see most or all of your slides at once. To enter Slide Sorter view, click the small Slide Sorter View button at the bottom-right corner of your screen or choose Slide Sorter from the View tab's Presentation Views group. In Slide Sorter view, you look at the wholeness and flow of your presentation, rather than the details on each slide. (Figure 1-7 in the first chapter shows Slide Sorter view.)

> **TIP** *For simple changes, you can stay in Normal view and work in the Slides (thumbnail) tab of the Outline pane. You can select one or more slides and move, copy, or delete them, for example.*

Work in Slide Sorter View

In Slide Sorter view, you select a slide by clicking it. The selected slide has an orange border. You can drag that slide to any new location. To copy the slide, press CTRL as you drag. You can also move a slide by cutting and pasting. Follow these steps:

1. Select the slide.

2. Press CTRL-X to cut the slide and place it on the clipboard.

3. Click where you want the slide to go, between two other slides. PowerPoint uses a long vertical line to indicate the cursor between the slides.

4. Press CTRL-V to paste the slide.

To duplicate a slide, select the slide and press CTRL-D. The new slide appears after the original slide.

You can delete a selected slide by pressing DELETE. When you move or delete a slide, PowerPoint automatically renumbers all the slides.

To add a new slide, click between two slides. Choose New Slide from the Slides group of the Home tab. The new slide automatically takes on the template or theme of the rest of the presentation.

Import Slides from Other Presentations

You may want to use a slide (or slides) from another presentation. You may even be able to build most of your presentation from slides in other presentations. Because the template is attached to the presentation, not the slide, when you import a slide, it takes on the current template or theme and fits seamlessly into your presentation.

Use the Clipboard to Import Slides

The most common technique for importing a slide is to use the clipboard. Here's how it works:

1. Open the presentation containing the slide or slides you want to use.

2. If you want only one slide, click its icon in the Outline pane. If you want a series of slides, click the first slide's icon, hold down SHIFT, and then click the last slide's icon.

3. Press CTRL-C or click Copy in the Clipboard group of the Home tab to copy the slides to the clipboard.

4. Open your current presentation. If it is already open, click its button on the Windows taskbar to display it. In the Outline pane, click the icon of the slide you want the other slides to follow.

5. Press CTRL-V or click Paste in the Clipboard group of the Home tab. PowerPoint places the new slide (or slides) after the selected slide.

This method of copying slides from one presentation to another is the easiest if you are copying a consecutive group of slides, but if you want to copy several slides that are not together, you can do this more easily in Slide Sorter view:

1. Click the first slide.

2. Press and hold CTRL as you select the rest of the slides you want to copy.

3. Click Copy in the Clipboard group of the Home tab.

4. Put the cursor where you want to place the slides.

5. Click Paste in the Clipboard group of the Home tab.

You may also find it easier to paste slides in Slide Sorter view because the long vertical cursor between the slides makes it clear where your slides will appear. Click between two slides and paste. You can also click before the first slide or after the last one.

Use Drag-and-Drop to Import Slides

You can also use drag-and-drop to copy slides. Drag-and-drop works best when you are copying a small group of slides; otherwise, it is hard to see all the slides without scrolling. Make sure you have only the two presentations open, and follow these steps:

1. From the Window group of the View tab, click Arrange All. You now see both presentations on the screen.

2. Click one presentation and change to Slide Sorter view.

3. Click the other presentation and change to Slide Sorter view.

4. Click the presentation whose slides you want and select them.

5. Press CTRL and click any of the selected slides.

6. Drag the slides to the desired destination in the other presentation. Use the vertical cursor as a guide.

Reuse Slides

PowerPoint offers yet another way to import slides—the Reuse Slides task pane. Use this method when you're not sure which presentation contains the slides you want to import or if you like the interface of this taskpane. First, select the slide that you want to insert the other slide(s) after. Then click the down arrow on the New Slide button on the Home tab's Slides group, and choose Reuse Slides from the bottom of the Layout gallery to open the Reuse Slides task pane, shown in Figure 3-12.

Click Browse to open the presentation that contains the slides you want. If you don't find the slide you want, choose another presentation. Once you see the slide that you want, just click it to import it into your presentation. To import all the slides, right-click any slide and choose Insert All Slides from the shortcut menu.

> **TIP** *If you want the imported slides to look the same as they did in their original presentation, check the Keep Source Formatting check box at the bottom of the task pane.*

Make Adjustments to Imported Slides

By default, new slides take on the template or theme of the current presentation. Even if you want your new slides to take on the template or theme of the current presentation, you may have to make other adjustments. Templates come with a color scheme that includes colors for the slide background, the text, bullets, and fill colors. If you have changed the color of any item in the source slide, such as the text color, the result in the destination slide may not be what you want.

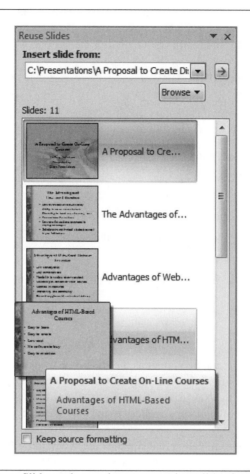

FIGURE 3-12 The Reuse Slides task pane lets you preview slides from other presentations so you can decide which ones you want to import.

You might even find that the text disappears because it is the same color as the background! You can solve this problem by clicking a few times where you expect the text to be until you see handles and a selection border. Whew! You can now select the text and use the Font Color drop-down list in the Font group of the Home tab to change its color.

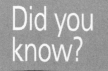

Store a Slide Library Online

Microsoft Office SharePoint Server 2007 is a product that provides a portal for an entire organization, offering content management, search, collaboration, and other features. The feature related to PowerPoint is called PowerPoint Slide Libraries. This new feature provides a centralized location for storing presentations. You can then reuse the slides stored in this location, whether created by you or someone else in your organization.

SharePoint Server is not a free product. For more information, go to http://www.microsoft.com/office/preview/servers/sharepointserver/highlights.mspx.

Keep a Slide Library

Have you ever wondered how professionals find all the neat stuff they put into presentations? One secret is organization. If you reuse slides a lot, you can create a slide library. Here are a few techniques:

- Create a special folder for all the presentations and additional files (sounds, images, movies, etc.) that you may want to reuse.

- Create a special presentation that contains only slides that you use a lot. Give it a name that identifies its purpose, such as Source Slides or Reusable Slides. Place that presentation in an easily accessible location on your computer or network—or in your special folder.

- For each slide that you want to reuse, create a presentation containing that slide alone. Place all such presentations in a folder, perhaps called Source Presentations. Name each presentation in a way that describes the slide it contains.

If you wish, print handouts of these presentations (see Chapter 15 for details) and keep them in a book. Mark the name of the presentations and their locations on the printouts and keep them in a folder or three-ring binder. By leafing through the handouts, you can quickly find the slides you need.

Summary

This chapter showed you how to edit text in a presentation, including moving, copying, changing, and deleting text. It discussed techniques for editing placeholder text, text in shapes and text boxes, and WordArt text. Some special techniques included finding and replacing text, changing text case, and adding symbols.

You learned how to set PowerPoint's editing options to meet your needs and to use AutoCorrect to correct errors as you type, including certain spelling errors. You saw how to use smart tags to quickly act on certain types of data, such as names and dates.

This chapter covered all the ways to work with fonts, including changing the font type, size, and style. I explained the new text effects that allow you to apply WordArt formatting to regular text. The Font dialog box gives you additional control over formatting. You saw how to use Format Painter to copy text formatting.

The second part of the chapter discussed how to add, delete, and rearrange slides, usually in Slide Sorter view. You can also import slides from other presentations, using the clipboard, drag-and-drop, or the Reuse Slides task pane. This chapter ended with some techniques for creating a slide library of slides that you use regularly.

In the next chapter, I explain how to format paragraphs and bullets.

Chapter 4

Format Bullets and Paragraphs

How to...

- Choose and change the bullet type
- Format a bullet's size and color
- Use a picture as a bullet
- Create numbered lists
- Understand paragraph formatting
- Use the ruler to align and indent text
- Work with tabs
- Align paragraph text
- Adjust line spacing

In many presentations, the majority of text is placeholder text. By default, most of the text placeholders are formatted with bullets. The purpose of bullets is to create a list of items. Each item is technically a paragraph of text, even though bulleted text usually consists of short phrases. You can change the formatting of bulleted text to make it more readable or emphasize certain items. You can create bullets from pictures if you want to get really flashy. On the other hand, you might want to eliminate the bullets and work with regular paragraphs. Knowing how to format bullets and paragraphs is essential to creating a professionally designed presentation.

Create a Bulleted List

When you stand up in front of an audience, you talk to the audience. Why do you need text on a slide? The purpose of slide text is to create a visual confirmation of your message. Slide text should be short and to the point. The more quickly the audience grasps the text, the sooner the audience will turn its attention to you and what you are saying.

If your text is not bulleted, you can add bullets by selecting the text and choosing Bullets in the Paragraph group of the Home tab. I explain how to create block text, with no bullets, later in this chapter, in the "Create Paragraphs with No Hanging Indent" section.

Choose a Bullet Type

Each template or theme comes with a default style of bullets for each level of heading on its slide master (except for title text, which creates the title of the slide). Here you see a sample of five levels of bulleted text:

In this illustration, the template uses three different styles of bullets and varies their sizes as well. Another template might use varying colors to distinguish between the heading levels. You can change every feature about any bullet to suit your taste and needs.

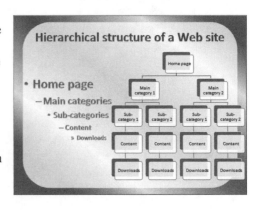

Of course, you don't want your bullets to distract from your text. Use those flashy bullets only when they have a meaningful purpose. For example, if you are selling floral ribbon to florists, you might want to use a picture of a rose as a bullet. In that case, use the rose bullets throughout the presentation. They make the point that you're in the floral business, but they don't distract because they're on every slide and your audience soon knows to ignore them and pay attention to the text. Another good use of an unusual bullet is for occasional use—to draw attention to only one or two items.

To choose a bullet type for an item of text, select the text and click Bullets in the Paragraph group of the Home tab. You can quickly choose common and recently used bullets from the gallery, as shown here. For more options, click Bullets and Numbering at the bottom of the gallery to open the Bullets and Numbering dialog box, shown in Figure 4-1. The Bulleted tab should be active. Any change you make applies to all of the selected text.

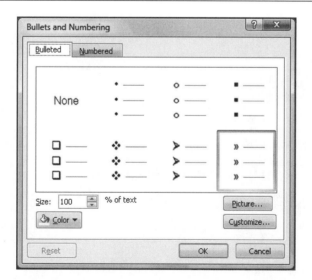

FIGURE 4-1   Use the Bulleted tab of the Bullets and Numbering dialog box to choose and format a bullet for your text.

 *Right-click any bulleted text. From the Mini toolbar, click the down arrow next to the Bullets button and choose Bullets and Numbering.*

In Figure 4-2, you see a slide at the end of a presentation for a graduate class in artificial intelligence. This slide is the bibliography, and the student used file folders as bullets to indicate that each reference is a container of information.

To create a similar effect, select the text and click Customize on the Bulleted tab of the Bullets and Numbering dialog box. Choose a "dingbat" type of font such as Wingdings from the Font drop-down list. Find the dingbat element you prefer (the presenter in the example shown in Figure 4-2 used the open folder), select it, and click OK. Dingbat fonts offer a wide range of small images and symbols.

Set Bullet Size and Color

You change a bullet's size as a percentage of text size. When you change a bullet's size, let consistency be your guide. Generally, a higher-level item, such as a level 2 heading, should not have a smaller bullet than a less important item, such as a level 3 heading. Also, items of the same level should usually have the same size bullet, unless you are making an exception for emphasis. To change a bullet's size, select the bullet item. In the Bullets and Numbering dialog box, change the number in the Size % of Text box, shown in Figure 4-1.

Uma Análise do Fluxo de Comunicação em Organizações Dinâmicas de Agentes

Referências Básicas

Cardozo, E.; Sichman, J.S.; Demazeau, Y. Using the Active Object Model to Implement Multi-Agent Systems. 5th. IEEE Int. Conf. on Tools with Artificial Intelligence. 1993.

Castefranchi, C. Social Power. A Point Missed in Multi-Agent, DAI and HCI. Decentralized A.I. Elsevier Science Publishers B.V. 1990.

Demazeau, Y. From Interactions to collective behavior in agent-based systems. 1st European Conference on Cognitive Science. 1995.

Sichman, J.S. Du Raisonnement Social Chez les Agents: Une Approche Fondée sur la Théorie de la Dépendance. Tese de Doutorado. INP Grenoble. 1995.

Smith, R.G.; Davis, R. Frameworks for Cooperation in Distributed Problem Solving. IEEE Transactions on Systems, Man, and Cybernetics. v.11, n1. 1981.

PCS-EPUSP   20

FIGURE 4-2 This slide is a list of references for a graduate presentation on artificial intelligence.

When you click the Color drop-down list box in the Bullets and Numbering dialog box (see Figure 4-1), you see the choices shown here:

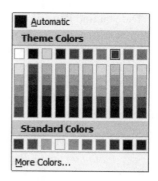

Choose the color you want, and click OK to close the Bullets and Numbering dialog box. Like a bullet's size, a bullet's color should generally be consistent within a heading level unless you are using color for special emphasis. Theme colors are covered in Chapter 6.

Use an Image as a Bullet

For variety, you can use an image as a bullet. Follow these steps:

1. Select the text for which you want to have the new bullets.

2. Click Picture in the Bullets and Numbering dialog box. PowerPoint opens the Picture Bullet dialog box, shown in Figure 4-3.

3. To use one of the bullets displayed, choose it and click OK.

Your new bullet is now in place.

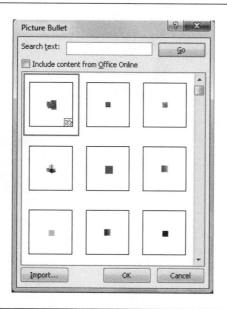

FIGURE 4-3   PowerPoint offers a large selection of images that you can use as bullets.

Did you find PowerPoint's choice of picture bullets boring? What if you want a bullet that is more exciting, or specifically relates to the topic of the text that follows it? Are you selling computers and want to use computers for bullets? You can create your own bullets from any bitmap file. Examples of bitmap file types are .bmp, .tif, .gif, and .jpg files. Windows metafiles (.wmf) work as well.

To use your own bitmap as a bullet, click Import in the Picture Bullet dialog box. The Add Clips to Organizer dialog box opens, shown in Figure 4-4. Choose the image you want and click Add.

NOTE *In the Add Clips to Organizer dialog box, if you don't see previews, click the Views button on the toolbar and choose one of the icon sizes so you can see the images.*

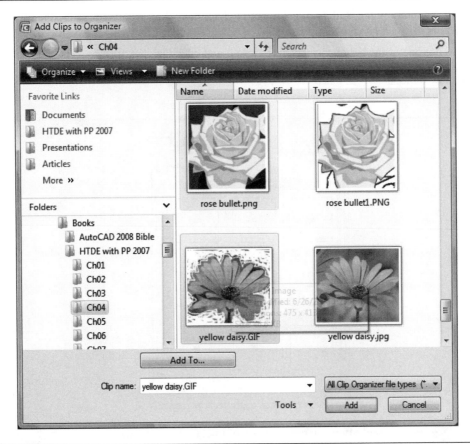

FIGURE 4-4 Use the Add Clips to Organizer dialog box to find image files to use as bullets.

Don't have a field day and use every bullet you can find. Instead, choose one appropriate bullet and use it consistently, as shown in this example:

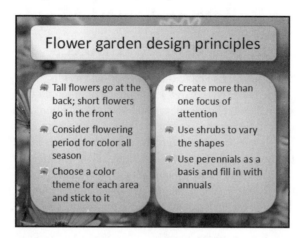

To create bullets from your own images, you usually have to jump through a few hoops. Many images are not suitable for bullets when you first find them. Often, you need to manipulate the graphic file. You may be able to do so right in PowerPoint. First import the image into PowerPoint, by choosing Picture from the Insert tab's Illustrations group. Select the image and click Open. (Refer to Chapter 5 for more information on working with graphic files.) For example, you may want to do the following:

- **Rotate the image**   With the image selected, hover the mouse over the green dot until you see the rotate cursor, then click and drag in the desired direction.

- **Make the background transparent**   With the image selected, click the Picture Tools Format tab. Then choose Recolor from the Picture Tools group. Choose Set Transparent Color and click the background.

- **Adjust the brightness or contrast**   Use the Brightness and Contrast drop-down lists in the Picture Tools group of the ribbon.

- **Crop the image**   Use the Crop button in the Size group of the ribbon and drag in from any of the four sides.

When you are done, you need to save the image as a file, as follows:

1. Right-click the image and choose Save as Picture.

2. In the Save as Picture dialog box, type a name for the image and choose a location.

3. Click Save.

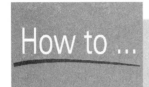

Use Bullets and Numbering in Shapes and Text Boxes

You can create bulleted text in shapes and text boxes. For best results, the text should be left-aligned. To left-align selected text, click Align Left in the Paragraph group of the Home tab.

To add bullets to selected text, click Bullets in the Paragraph group of the Home tab. To add numbering, click Numbering in the same location. To create bullets or numbering as you type, click Bullets or Numbering first and then start typing. Click Bullets or Numbering again when you want to return to regular text. You can use all the features of the Bullets and Numbering dialog box as described earlier, including custom bullets.

When you add bullets to text in shapes and text boxes, the text is not properly indented to set off the bullets. To indent the text, you need to use the Ruler, which I cover later in this chapter, in the "Use the Ruler" section.

In Chapter 8, I explain how to create diagrams using SmartArt. You can add bullets to many SmartArt shapes as well. Click the SmartArt shape to select it. Click the Design tab under the SmartArt Tools category. Then click Add Bullet in the Create Graphic group of the ribbon.

To use the image as a bullet, select the desired text and follow these steps:

1. Click the down arrow next to the Bullets button in the Paragraph group of the Home tab.
2. Click Bullets and Numbering.
3. Click the Picture button.
4. In the Picture Bullet dialog box, click Import.
5. Find the image file, choose it, and click Add.
6. In the Picture Bullet dialog box, click the picture and click OK.

PowerPoint creates the bullets.

You may still need to change the size of the bullet, as explained earlier in this chapter. To change the bullets for an entire presentation, you have to change the slide master. Slide masters are covered in Chapter 7.

Create Numbered Lists

Use a numbered list when your items have a logical sequence. To create a numbered list, select the bulleted items you want to number and click Numbering in the Paragraph group of the Home tab.

FIGURE 4-5 Use the Numbered tab in the Bullets and Numbering dialog box to format numbered text.

PowerPoint automatically restarts numbering for second-level body text. You can change the numbering back to bullets by clicking Bullets in the Paragraph group of the Home tab.

To format the numbering, select the text and click the down arrow next to the Numbering button to display a gallery of common and recently used numbering formats, as shown here.

For more control, click Bullets and Numbering to open the Bullets and Numbering dialog box, with the Numbering tab on top, as shown in Figure 4-5. Here you can change the size and color of the numbers as well as specify the starting number.

Work with Paragraphs

In Chapter 3, I explained how to format the characters in your text—by choosing the fonts, font size, and so on. A different aspect of formatting text involves formatting it as paragraphs. Paragraph formatting includes indentation, columns, tabs, alignment, and line spacing. To lay out text on your slide in a pleasing, legible manner, you need to know about paragraph formatting.

A *paragraph* is any single line of text or multiple lines of text followed by a return. You create a *return character*, which moves text to the next line, when you press ENTER on your keyboard.

TIP   *Occasionally, you may want text to be treated as one paragraph but look like two paragraphs. You can start a new line without using a return by pressing SHIFT-ENTER (instead of just ENTER) at the end of a line. This is called a soft return, or line break. PowerPoint interprets both lines as one paragraph. For example, to create the separate, unbulleted lines after the first bullet, as shown in Figure 4-6, you press SHIFT-ENTER. A soft return is also useful to force titles or slide text to move to the next line when the automatic wrapping creates an awkward break in the text. For example, if a two-line title contains one word on a second line, you can add a soft return earlier in the title; this can create a more pleasing result.*

Understand Paragraph Formatting

Before leaping in, you may want to understand some terms that are commonly used for paragraph formatting:

■ **Margin**   The space between the edge of your working area and your text. In a text placeholder, the margin is the space between the edge of the placeholder and your text. The left margin of a paragraph is the left edge of the text.

FIGURE 4-6   You can create an unnumbered line within a paragraph by pressing SHIFT-ENTER at the end of the line.

- **Indent**   The amount that text is moved to the right of the left margin.

- **First line indent**   An indent for the first line of a paragraph. Subsequent lines are not indented.

- **Hanging indent**   A first line that is indented less than the subsequent lines of a paragraph. The first line "hangs out" from the rest of the paragraph. Bulleted text is formatted as a hanging indent. The bullet is at the left margin and hangs out from the rest of the paragraph, which is indented, as shown in Figure 4-7.

- **Tab**   A place where the cursor stops when you press the TAB key. Tabs are used to align text.

- **Left-aligned**   A paragraph in which the left side of every line is lined up.

- **Centered**   A paragraph in which the center point of every line is lined up.

- **Right-aligned**   A paragraph in which the right side of every line is lined up.

- **Justified**   A paragraph in which both the left and right sides of every line are lined up.

- **Distributed**   A paragraph in which the letters are spaced out to reach from margin to margin.

- **Line spacing**   The spacing between the lines in a paragraph. You can also separately control the spacing before and after paragraphs.

Figure 4-7 shows some examples of paragraph formatting.

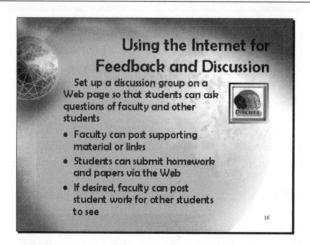

FIGURE 4-7   This slide includes text with right alignment, a first line indent, and a hanging indent.

Use the Ruler

PowerPoint comes with a top ruler and a side ruler that can help you format paragraph text. To view the rulers, check the Ruler check box on the View tab of the ribbon.

The display of the rulers depends on which object you select. If you select any object other than text, the rulers look like this:

This kind of ruler is called a *slide ruler*. It has a zero point at its middle and measures the entire slide. Remember that you see this ruler even if you select the outline of a text placeholder or a shape containing text. You can use this kind of ruler for judging layout and distances for objects. In Chapter 5, I explain how to lay out and align objects on a slide.

If you select text, whether in a text placeholder, a text box, or a shape, the rulers look like those shown in Figure 4-8.

These rulers look like the rulers you see in your word processor. The zero measurement starts from the left or the top and continues from there. The white portion measures only the area of the text. The ruler's length adjusts automatically if you click on another, differently sized placeholder.

PowerPoint has a Paragraph dialog box that you can use to format paragraphs. To access it, click the dialog box launcher arrow at the lower-right corner of the Paragraph group of the Home tab. However, it's much easier to format paragraph text using the top ruler. The side ruler is used mostly to judge size and distance and contains no controls. The top ruler has the following indent controls:

- ■ **First Line Indent marker** Drag to the left or right to control the indentation of the first line. This marker moves independently of the other two markers.

■ **Left Indent marker**   Drag to the left or right to set the left margin of the entire paragraph. This marker is always at the same location as the Hanging Indent marker. When you drag it, the Hanging Indent and First Line Indent markers follow along with it, so that the relationships among them don't change.

■ **Hanging Indent marker**   Drag to the left or right to set the indentation for subsequent lines of a paragraph. This marker is always at the same location as the Left Indent marker. However, when you drag the Hanging Indent marker, the First Line Indent marker does not move, letting you change the relationship between the two.

There's an art to dragging the markers because they are so small. It's easy to inadvertently grab the Left Indent marker (the rectangle) instead of the Hanging Indent marker (the lower triangle), and vice versa. After a little practice, you'll get better at it. Until then, remember the Undo button on the Quick Access toolbar!

Indent Text

The most common use for the ruler is to move bullets and to change the spacing between a bullet and its text. However, you can use the ruler to indent any paragraph text—to the right or to the left.

Move Bullets

While the default distance between the bullets and text is usually acceptable, you may want to move the bullets to the right, closer to the text. If the text is too far from the bullets, it seems disassociated, and your audience may not be sure where one item ends and the next begins.

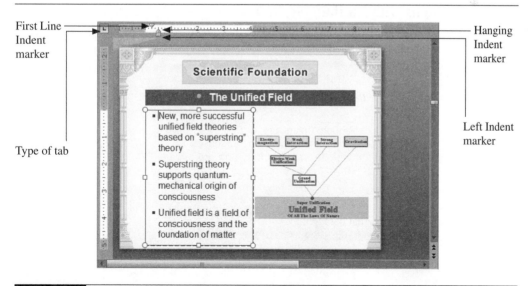

FIGURE 4-8   Use the top ruler to format indentation and set tabs.

In bulleted text, the first line of a paragraph is the line with its bullet. To move a bullet, select the text containing the bullet. You can also select all the text in a placeholder or shape. Then drag the First Line Indent marker to the right. The First Line Indent marker (the upper indent marker) moves independently of the other markers, so the indentation of the rest of the paragraph is unaffected. Therefore, moving the First Line Indent marker to the right brings the bullet closer to the text. While you are dragging the marker, PowerPoint places a dashed guideline from the marker to your text so you can gauge the effect of your dragging. If you have numbered items instead of bullets, you can move the numbers in the same way.

By default, the bullet is already at the left margin, so you can move it only to the right. Once you've moved a bullet to the right, you may want to move it back to the left again. In that case, drag the First Line Indent marker to the left.

Indent Paragraph Text

Instead of moving the bullets, you may want to move the text. The Hanging Indent marker controls the alignment of the text, which controls the indentation of lines in a paragraph after the first line. However, because the text of the first line (after the bullet) also aligns with the subsequent lines, you actually affect the entire paragraph.

To move the text, drag the Hanging Indent marker to the left (toward the bullet) or the right (away from the bullet).

 *Be careful not to drag the rectangular Left Indent marker. It maintains the relationship between the first line and the subsequent lines of a paragraph. Therefore, the indentation of the entire paragraph changes as you drag the rectangular Left Indent marker. As you drag, both the First Line Indent and Hanging Indent markers come along for the ride.*

Create Paragraphs with No Hanging Indent

Sometimes you may want plain block text instead of bulleted text. For example, you might have only one statement to make on a slide, as shown here:

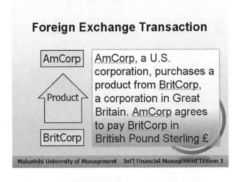

It's easy to remove bullets if you don't want them, but you'll still have a hanging indent unless you change the paragraph formatting. You usually don't want a hanging indent without bullets, but the procedure for getting rid of the hanging indent is not intuitive to many people. Here are the steps to change bulleted text to block paragraphs:

1. Click the text placeholder for which you want to create block paragraphs. This activates Edit Text mode and you see a dashed border.
2. Select all the text in the placeholder.
3. Click Bullets in the Paragraph group of the Home tab to remove the bullets.
4. Drag the Hanging Indent marker (the bottom triangle) to the left until the paragraphs are at the left margin.

Did you know?

Bullets Are Boring!

As a result of some well-publicized criticism and the personal experience of millions of audience members, bulleted text has the reputation for being boring. As soon as people see a slide with nothing but bulleted text, they imagine a long presentation containing nothing but lines and lines of text following bullets, and they tune out quickly.

How can you avoid creating presentations of bulleted text? Remember that your presentation is really what you say, not the PowerPoint slides. Contrary to tradition, the slides don't need to contain a short version of everything you say.

In the section in this chapter, "Create Paragraphs with No Hanging Indent," I explain how to create simple, blocked text. By using this procedure on the slide master (discussed in Chapter 7), you can easily create a presentation that doesn't use bullets. By saving this presentation as a template (also covered in Chapter 7), you can ensure that all of your presentations based on that template have no bullets. What a thought!

What do you put on your slides, if not bulleted text? Here are some possibilities:

- Use the slide title area to enter a complete sentence summarizing your main point, and omit the bulleted text. Instead, add an image, use some text as a graphic, or just leave the title alone on the page. (Don't be afraid!) You can place the title placeholder in the middle of the slide, or even at the bottom.
- Instead of bulleted text, use only three to four words that elicit your message very simply. If you want, you can add an image.
- Use images only, perhaps as metaphors for what you are saying. For example, if you're talking about a difficult project, place an image of an uphill path or a rocky road.

(continued)

For example, here is some text from WebMD.com that I wanted to use in a presentation: "TM was compared with progressive muscle relaxation as a means of controlling stress in older African Americans with high blood pressure. Of the 197 men and women (out of 213) who completed the screening, the reductions in blood pressure in the TM group were significantly greater than those in the progressive muscle relaxation group. TM reduced systolic blood pressure by more than 10 points and diastolic pressure by more than 6 points (compared with a 5 point reduction for systolic and a 3 point fall for diastolic with progressive muscle relaxation). High blood pressure (hypertension) is defined as systolic blood pressure—the top number—averaging 140 mmHg or greater, and/or diastolic blood pressure—the bottom number—averaging 90 mmHg or greater."

(Source: "Treating Hypertension Naturally'" by Carol Sorgen; http://www.webmd.com/content/article/61/71419.)

I could have broken up this content into bulleted text, but instead I created the simple slide that you see here. The rest I explained verbally.

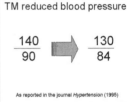

Using fewer words focuses more attention on you, the presenter. Your audience spends less time reading and more time listening.

Change the Margins in a Text Placeholder

In Chapter 3, I briefly mentioned how to change the margins for both text placeholders and objects that contain text. Here I explain the concept more fully.

The *margin* is the space between the text and the edge of the placeholder. If you want to center the text better in the placeholder, you can increase the margins. By default, the margins are .1 inch on the left and right and .05 inch on the top and bottom. These settings might sound like small margins, but they affect the wrapping of the words in the placeholder. Because the borders of the placeholder are usually invisible on your slide, you can reduce the margins to 0 with no problem. However, if you choose to place a visible border around your text, you may wish to increase the margin to avoid the border coming too close to the text. (Chapter 6 covers formatting borders.)

 *You can often fit more on a line by reducing the text margins. The text margins are used when text is wrapped to the next line. The empty space between the text and the placeholder's border is useless when the border is invisible.*

To change the margin between the text and its placeholder, right-click the placeholder and choose Format Shape. In the Format Shape dialog box that opens, click the Text Box category, shown in Figure 4-9. Change any of the numbers in the Internal Margin section and click Close. This technique works for all types of shapes, not just text placeholders.

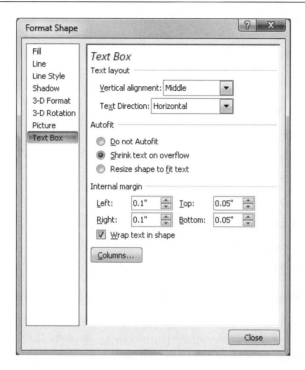

FIGURE 4-9   Use the Text Box category of the Format Shape dialog box to change the margins between the placeholder and the text.

Set Tabs

You probably don't use the TAB key on your keyboard to align text anymore. That was its original purpose, but now that word processors offer tables, which align text more easily, TAB is used mostly to move the cursor from cell to cell in a table. Nevertheless, you may sometimes wish to use a tab to align a small amount of text when a table is not needed. (Tables are covered in Chapter 8.)

NOTE   *In PowerPoint 2007, tabs apply individually to each paragraph, not to the entire placeholder or text box.*

There are four types of tabs, as described in Table 4-1. Each type has its own marker at the left of the ruler.

Tab Position	Icon	Description
Left	⌞	Aligns the left edge of text with the tab.
Center	⌃	Centers the text at the tab.
Right	⌟	Aligns the right edge of text with the tab.
Decimal	⌄	Aligns decimal points with the tab. Figure 4-10 shows an example of text aligned with a decimal tab.

TABLE 4-1 Four Tab Types

To set a tab, follow these steps:

1. Select a text placeholder. Tab markers are not displayed unless a text placeholder is selected.

2. Click the tab button at the left of the top ruler until you see the type of tab you want.

3. Click the bottom edge of the ruler where you want to place the tab.

4. Press TAB before the text that you want to align at the tab.

To remove a tab, select a placeholder and drag the tab marker off the ruler.

NOTE *You can also set tabs in the Tabs dialog box. Click the Paragraph dialog box launcher arrow at the lower-right corner of the Paragraph group of the Home tab to open the Paragraph dialog box and then click the Tabs button there.*

Align Text

Aligning text refers to how the text is lined up in reference to the margins. You can control both horizontal and vertical alignment.

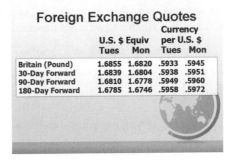

FIGURE 4-10 Use a decimal tab to align numbers that contain decimal points.

Horizontal Alignment

Horizontal alignment includes left, right, and centered text. Bulleted text is left-aligned by default. However, you may sometimes want to use another alignment. For example, it is common to center titles. Text in text boxes or shapes is also often centered. Figure 4-11 shows some examples of various paragraph alignments.

The procedure for aligning text is the same for placeholder text, text in text boxes, and text in shapes, as described here:

- **Left-align**   To left-align text, select the text and click Align Left in the Paragraph group of the Home tab (or press CTRL-L).

- **Center**   To center text, select the text and click Center in the Paragraph group of the Home tab (or press CTRL-E).

- **Right-align**   To right-align text, select the text and click Right Align in the Paragraph group of the Home tab (or press CTRL-R).

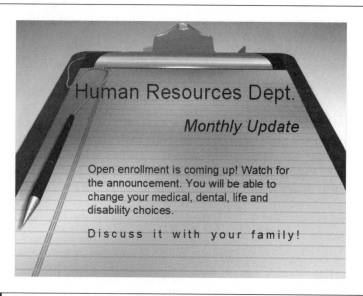

FIGURE 4-11   You can center, right-align, justify, and distribute paragraphs.

- **Justify**   To justify text, select the text and click Justify in the Paragraph group of the Home tab.
- **Distribute**   To distribute text from margin to margin, click the dialog box launcher button at the lower-right corner of the Paragraph group of the Home tab to open the Paragraph dialog box. Choose Distributed from the Alignment drop-down list and click OK.

Align Text Vertically

You can also specify where the text fits vertically in a text box, shape, or placeholder. You use the Text Box category of the Format Shapes dialog box. You can choose from the following vertical alignments:

- Top
- Middle
- Bottom
- Top Centered
- Middle Centered
- Bottom Centered

Vertical alignment can make a big difference in the way text fits into a placeholder, text box, or shape.

TIP   *If you use the Bottom alignment for slide titles, you avoid the shifting of the text that occurs when you create a longer, two-line title. Instead, all the titles align at the bottom point and two-line titles simply add a line on top.*

When working with text in text boxes or shapes, you may want to consider both horizontal and vertical alignment to get the exact result you need.

Create Columns

A new feature allows you to create columns in a text placeholder, text box, or shape. Select either the text or the object itself. On the Home tab, in the Paragraph group, click the Columns button and choose one, two, or three columns. For more control, click More Columns to open the Columns dialog box. Here you can specify the number of columns as well as the spacing between them.

Note that you may not see the columns if the text box is long enough to hold all of the text; resize the box to adjust the flow from one column to the next.

Set Line Spacing

The final aspect of paragraph formatting involves setting how much space you want between lines within a paragraph and between paragraphs.

Set the Spacing within a Paragraph

Would you like to space the lines of text further apart to fill up more space or enhance readability? The solution is to change the line spacing, as shown here, in the right column of text:

To set line spacing within a paragraph, select the text and click the dialog box launcher arrow at the lower-right corner of the Paragraph group of the Home tab. The Paragraph dialog box opens, shown in Figure 4-12. From the Line Spacing drop-down list, choose Single, 1.5 Lines, Double, Exactly, or Multiple. Use the Exactly setting to enter an exact number in points; this is the only way to reduce line spacing to less than single spacing (for when you need to squeeze text a little). Use the Multiple setting to enter any number in terms of line spacing; for example, enter **3** to triple space text.

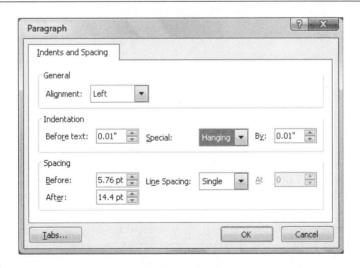

FIGURE 4-12   Use the Paragraph dialog box to set the spacing between lines within a paragraph as well as the spacing between paragraphs.

Set the Spacing between Paragraphs

You can also specify how much space PowerPoint places before and after paragraphs. You may want to increase the spacing between paragraphs to separate them in your audience's awareness or simply to spread them out pleasingly on the slide. Often, lines of bulleted text are too close together and are more legible with space between them. If you want space between lines of bulleted text, use line spacing rather than adding a blank space between the lines and then removing the bullet; you'll get more precise results and the text will flow better if you need to make changes.

To set the spacing between paragraphs, you use the Paragraph dialog box, shown in Figure 4-12. In the Spacing section, you can separately control the spacing before and after a paragraph. You probably don't want to add extra spacing both before and after a paragraph, because the two measurements are added together. Add spacing before *or* after your paragraphs, but not both.

Here you see an example of the effect of increasing the space following a paragraph. Compare the left and right columns. By adding space after the first paragraph, the second paragraph stands out more.

Summary

In this chapter, you learned all about bullets and paragraph text. PowerPoint gives you a great deal of control over bullets. You can choose from various types of bullets, change their size and color, or use no bullets. You can choose a picture bullet or create your own bitmap files and make bullets from them. You can also create bulleted text in text boxes and shapes. You can create numbered lists, too.

To format paragraph text, you use the top ruler. When text is selected, the ruler shows indent markers and tabs. You drag the indent markers to align the text, move the bullets, or move the text relative to the bullets. You can remove the hanging indent automatically created for bulleted text and create blocked text.

You can use tabs to align text. PowerPoint lets you choose from four types of tabs: left, right, centered, and decimal. To add a tab, choose the type of tab you want on the tab button to the left of the ruler and click anywhere on the ruler.

PowerPoint offers five types of horizontal paragraph alignment. You can left- or right-align text, center it, justify it, or distribute it. You can also specify vertical alignment.

A new feature lets you create columns of text in a placeholder, text box, or shape. You can also specify the spacing between the columns.

You can squeeze lines in a paragraph together to fit more on a slide or spread them out to make them more readable, using the Paragraph dialog box. You can also add space before or after a paragraph using the same dialog box.

This chapter ends Part I. Part II explains how to work with art, objects, color, 3-D effects, slide masters, themes, and layouts—all the finishing touches you need to make your presentation look truly professional.

4

Part II

Add Multimedia Elements to Your Presentation

Chapter 5

Add Art and Graphic Objects

How to…

- Find clip art
- Create a clip art collection
- Insert picture files
- Create a photo album
- Edit pictures and objects
- Insert shapes
- Lay out slides with precision

Until now, you have mostly worked with text, but a presentation is much more than words. Without adding appropriate art and graphic objects to your slides, you cannot create the impact needed for an effective presentation. The visual effect of art helps your audience remember and understand your message more quickly and easily. In fact, one of the main differences between amateur and professional presentations is the quantity, quality, and appropriateness of the graphics. It's even possible to create a presentation containing no words, only images. This chapter is all about graphics, including clip art, photos, and shapes.

Create an Impact with Graphics

When your viewers first see a slide, they scan it quickly before focusing on specific elements. They tend to focus first on large, simple shapes. Shapes can include not only the shapes that come with PowerPoint but also lines, rows of bullets, and borders. Viewers tend to next move to shapes and patterns that are more complex. Finally, they focus on the text. You can exploit these viewer tendencies to guide their focus and thereby increase their understanding of your material.

In addition, graphic elements wake up your audience by grabbing their attention. Perhaps from our continual immersion in television and movies, we're used to constantly changing input. A presentation consisting of only text soon becomes boring, and viewers tune out. Offering a changing menu of shapes and pictures keeps your audience engaged. A good guide is that at least half of your slides should include graphics. Note that graphics that are displayed on each slide, such as a company logo, don't count here. The audience learns to ignore repeating graphics—they soon become as boring as the text. You need to create a balance. On one hand, contrast and newness can work wonders. On the other hand, overloading a presentation with graphics or extremely varying styles soon negates the alertness effect. If you vary your presentation to alternate between quiet and active slides while maintaining some continuity of style, your audience will stay tuned in. Here you see a slide on the topic of web page design that uses a strong and meaningful graphic of an eye, a brain, and a hand:

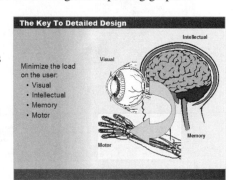

Art has a more subtle effect than simple graphic shapes. The right art can evoke a mood that supports your message. Think of how your audience might react to the following:

- A flag
- A dollar sign
- A happy family
- A pastoral farm scene
- Traders on the floor of the New York Stock Exchange

Each picture has a different effect. Even the manner in which the art is rendered has an effect—a photo makes a different impression than a rough sketch. An example of a photo used to explain an employee benefit feature covering medical costs is shown here:

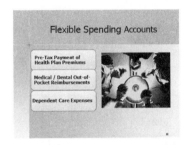

The colors you use are important too. Chapter 6 is all about using colors and other effects.

Use Clip Art

Clip art is ready-made art that you can simply choose and insert onto a slide. The clip art collection and the Clip Organizer are shared by all Microsoft Office applications, such as PowerPoint, Word, Excel, and Publisher. Note that the clip art collection includes photographs as well as drawn art, and even a few sounds and movies. (See Chapter 10 for lots more about sound, music, and video.) You probably have other art available on your computer or network. You can also find clip art and photos on the Internet or buy your own collection, which you can download or get on a CD-ROM or DVD.

Find Art in the Clip Art Task Pane

You find clip art, including photographs, in the Clip Art task pane. You can open this task pane, shown in Figure 5-1, in two ways:

- Choose a slide layout that includes a clip art placeholder. Then click the Clip Art icon to open the Clip Art task pane.
- On the Insert tab of the ribbon, click Clip Art in the Illustrations group.

FIGURE 5-1 The Clip Art task pane helps you search for and insert drawn art and photos.

In the Clip Art task pane, enter one or more keywords in the Search For box and press ENTER or click Go. You can refine your search in two ways. To specify where to look, choose from the following options in the Search In drop-down list:

- **My Collections** Clip art collections that you have created. Creating collections is covered later in this chapter, in the "Create Your Own Clip Art Collection" section.
- **Office Collections** Clip art collections that come with Microsoft Office.
- **Web Collections** Clip art collections available from the Microsoft Office Online collection.

By default, PowerPoint looks in all three locations. To save time and get more precise results, you can uncheck any option that doesn't interest you. Click the plus signs in the drop-down list to expand all the subcategories if you want to limit your search even more.

You can also create a Shared Collection, which is a collection on a shared network that is available to a group of people. If this type of collection exists, you see it on the list as well.

You can also restrict the type of clip art you want to find, in the Results Should Be drop-down list. You can choose Clip Art, Photographs, Movies, and Sounds. If you are interested in only clip art and photographs, uncheck Movies and Sounds. Uncheck everything in the drop-down list except Photographs if that's what you want.

Once you type in your keyword and press ENTER, PowerPoint displays the related clip art in the task pane. Click a piece of art to insert it or drag it onto your slide. For more options, pass your cursor over an item to display a drop-down arrow. Click the arrow to open this shortcut menu:

You can use this menu to do the following:

■ Insert the clip art.

■ Copy the clip art to the clipboard.

■ Delete the clip art from the Clip Organizer (explained in the next section).

■ Copy the clip art to a collection. Collections are discussed in the next section.

■ Move the clip art to a collection of clip art, without leaving a copy in its original location.

■ Edit the keywords for the clip art. Clip art is organized by keywords so that you can search for individual clip art images by typing a keyword.

■ Find similar-style clip art. This option is only available if the clipboard is one in a series of similar clip art images.

■ Preview the clip art and view its properties. Choosing this option opens the Preview/ Properties dialog box, shown next. Properties include filename, file type, resolution, size, location, date created, orientation (portrait or landscape), and keywords, as well as others.

 *Unfortunately, you cannot edit keywords for Office collections, only those for your own collections.*

Create Your Own Clip Art Collection

The Clip Organizer is a convenient place to store clip art that you use regularly—a company logo and a purchased clip art collection are good candidates. You can add this clip art to the Clip Organizer, place it in a category, and give it searchable keywords. You can then use this clip art in any of the Microsoft applications that share the Clip Organizer. Clip Art is organized into *collections*, and collections that you create are called *My Collections*, as opposed to Office Collections and Web Collections.

Because the Clip Organizer is used for other Office programs, you can access it separately to organize images for all the programs. Choose Start | All Programs | Microsoft Office | Microsoft Office Tools | Microsoft Clip Organizer.

To add your own clip art to your collection and organize it, open the Clip Organizer by clicking Organize Clips in the Insert Clip Art task pane. The Clip Organizer is shown in Figure 5-2.

You can click any item of clip art to display the drop-down arrow, which opens the same menu available from the Clip Art task pane. To create a new collection, right-click My Collections and choose New Collection. Then give the collection a name. Select that collection before adding clip art to make sure it goes into that collection.

5

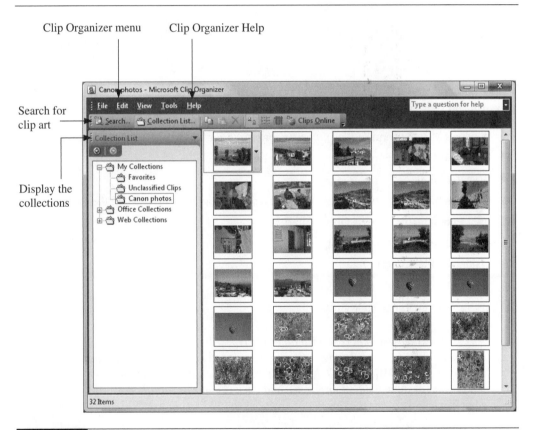

FIGURE 5-2 The Clip Organizer lets you organize clip art into your own collection.

To add graphic files to a collection, choose File | Add Clips to Organizer. You can then choose one of three options:

- **Automatically** Searches your hard disk or folders that you specify and creates collections.
- **On My Own** Lets you specify individual files.
- **From Scanner or Camera** Activates your scanner or digital camera and inserts the resulting file into the Clip Organizer. The dialog box you see here opens:

You can add your own pictures to the Clip Organizer in the following formats:

- Windows Metafile Format (.wmf), a vector format. Vector files look good even when scaled.
- Enhanced Metafile Format (.emf), a vector format.
- Bitmap (.bmp).
- Graphics Interchange Format (.gif), the most common graphics format on the Web.
- Joint Photographic Experts Group (.jpg).
- Portable Network Graphics (.png).
- Macintosh PICT (.pct).
- Tagged Image File Format (.tif).
- Vector Markup Language (.vml).

Special filters let you import several other file types. To install filters, close all open programs, choose Start | Settings | Control Panel, and double-click Add/Remove Programs. Choose Microsoft Office (or Microsoft PowerPoint, if you installed PowerPoint as an individual program), and click Change or Add/Remove (depending on your Windows version). Follow the instructions on the screen.

To specifically search the Microsoft Office online collection, click Clip Art on Office Online at the bottom of the Clip Art task pane. PowerPoint seamlessly transports you to the Clip Art and Media Home web site, where you can find and download picture, music, sound, video, or animation clips. The site includes thousands of high-quality images in various styles and covering various topics, including seasonal graphics. For example, you can click the Templates link and then the Presentations category to find PowerPoint templates.

Finding Additional Clip Art and Photos

It's easy to find images for your presentations. Some are free, and some you have to pay for. You can find individual pieces of clip art or entire collections containing thousands of files. Here are a few sources for clip art I've found:

- **ClipArt.com (http://www.clipart.com)**   Over 2.5 million clip art images, including some photos and lots of fonts. As of this writing, you pay $15.95 per week or $99.95 per year.

- **DigitalJuice (http://www.digitaljuice.com)**   You can purchase a huge selection of PowerPoint backgrounds, photos, and animations.

- **Barry's Clipart Server (http://www.barrysclipart.com/clipart)**   Barry's offers an excellent selection of free clip art collections on a wide variety of topics. You can drag clip art directly onto your slide.

There are a number of excellent sites that specialize in photos. Royalty-free stock photos are photos that you can use for your own purposes, without paying a royalty each time you use one. Sites that charge for these photos usually have a better selection and more professional photos. However, there are some sites that offer a good selection of free stock photos, especially nature photos.

You can search the web site by keyword or choose a category. The web site then displays the applicable clips. Choose the ones you want and follow the instructions to download the clips. PowerPoint automatically places them in the Clip Organizer under Downloaded Clips. (If you see a choice to open an image with the Clip Organizer or save it, choose to open it.)

To drag clip art onto a slide from the Clip Organizer, you can use one of two methods:

- Adjust the size of your browser window so you can see the slide at the same time and drag an image onto a slide.

- Drag the clip art down to the Windows taskbar onto your presentation's button, wait until the presentation appears, and drag onto the slide.

NOTE   *You should carefully check the permission rules for photos. Some are only for noncommercial use. Many allow you to use the photos in any way, as long as you don't redistribute them to others. Some sites offer photos that are in the public domain, which means that you can use them for any purpose sometimes you are requested to include attribution, which may not be appropriate in a PowerPoint presentation.*

Here are some good sites that sell stock photographs:

- **Photos.com (http://photos.com)** Over 200,000 photos for a fixed fee per month or year.

- **iStockphoto (http://www.istockphoto.com)** Over 900,000 images, most costing from $1 to $3, contributed by site members.

- **Shutterstock (http://www.shutterstock.com)** Almost 900,000 photos for a fixed fee per month or year.

- **Fotolia (http://www.fotolia.com)** Over 900,000 photos for $1 to $3 each, depending on the image size.

- **Indezine (http://www.indezine.com/photos)** Photos collected from many excellent sources.

Here are some sites that offer free stock photographs. Some of these are collections of excellent amateur photographers, and you can contribute your photos as well.

- **Stock.xchng (http://www.sxc.hu)** Photographers upload their photos to share. You'll find many high-quality photos, with more than 200,000 available.

- **morgueFile (http://www.morguefile.com)** Offers free image reference material for use in all creative pursuits.

- **Flickr (http://www.flickr.com)** A site that lets people contribute their own images. Many are simply personal photos. Each person can specify the type of licensing, so look for a description of permissions.

- **Unprofound (http://www.unprofound.com)** A small but interesting collection of photos sorted by basic colors instead of the usual categories. This is an interesting concept if you're looking for photos that match your color theme.

To save images from a web site, right-click the image and choose Save Picture As (Internet Explorer) or Save Image As (Mozilla Firefox and Netscape Navigator). Otherwise, follow the instructions on the web site for downloading the images.

Insert Picture Files

You don't need to use the Clip Organizer to insert a picture. You may never want to use a particular graphic again, so there's no point adding it to the Clip Organizer. To insert a picture:

1. From the ribbon's Insert tab, click Picture in the Illustrations group to open the Insert Picture dialog box. You can also click the Picture icon in any content placeholder.

2. Navigate to the file you want to insert.

3. Double-click the file.

> **TIP** *You can link to the file instead of inserting it, or both link to and insert the picture. To use these choices, instead of double-clicking the file, as explained in step 3 in the previous list, click the down arrow to the right of the Insert button. Choose Link to File or Insert and Link. Linking reduces the size of your presentation file, but you need to make sure that you include the image file if you move the presentation or send it to someone else.*

You may need to resize or move both the image and any existing text placeholder.

> **TIP** *You can insert multiple images at once. To insert multiple images, open the Insert Picture dialog box as just described and select all the images you want to insert. Then click Insert. To select a group of files that are together, press SHIFT and click the first file in the group, then press SHIFT and click the last file in the group. To select files that are not together in a group, press CTRL and click the additional files you want to add. They all appear stacked on the same slide, and you can then move them to the desired location.*

Create a Photo Album

You can create a presentation that contains a series of photos with captions, called a photo album. The Photo Album feature automates inserting photos from files, a scanner, or a digital camera into a specially formatted PowerPoint presentation. You can show your friends your summer vacation pictures or publish your album on the Web.

> **TIP** *You can use the photo album feature whenever you want to insert several images at once, and automatically place one on each slide.*

 To create a photo album, display the Insert tab. In the Illustrations group, click Photo Album. The Photo Album dialog box appears, as shown in Figure 5-3.

To create a photo album, follow these steps:

1. Click File/Disk to choose your images. A dialog box opens where you can choose the images you want to add. You can choose one or select a group. Click Open. As you add images, they appear in the Pictures in Album list.

2. You can select any image, rotate it, and adjust its brightness and contrast using the buttons. You can also remove an image and change the order of the images.

3. To add a new slide containing a text box, click New Text Box to add a text slide. When you return to your photo album, you'll see a text box with the words Text Box. Click the words and type a caption or description of a picture. This text box is on its own slide.

4. In the Picture Options section, you can choose to add captions below all the pictures or to make all the pictures black and white.

5. In the Album Layout section, choose a layout. The layout specifies how many images fit on a page.

6. You can also select a frame shape from the Frame Shape drop-down list. For example, in addition to the default rectangle shape, you can choose a rounded rectangle or corner tabs (that look like the tabs you paste into a physical photo album).

7. If you wish, choose a theme or template. Click Browse, choose a theme or template, and click Open.

8. Click Create.

To edit a photo album, again click the Photo Album button. From the drop-down list, choose Edit Photo Album. The Edit Photo Album dialog box is just like the Photo Album dialog box that you use to create the photo album. You should make any adjustments in this dialog box. A photo album contains special formatting and may not function properly if you try to edit it like you would a regular presentation. However, I have had success adding text boxes to slides for captions, deleting individual slides, and reordering them in the usual way.

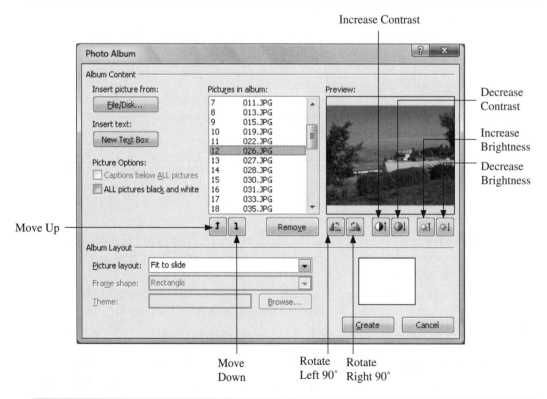

FIGURE 5-3 The Photo Album dialog box contains settings for creating a photo album—a presentation containing a series of images.

Edit Images and Drawing Objects

You may need to edit graphics to get the look you want. PowerPoint offers more options than ever before for editing your images. You may be able to get the results you want right in PowerPoint. The same holds true for drawing objects, also called *shapes*, that you draw in PowerPoint. At some point, you'll probably want to select, delete, resize, and perform other edits on your images and drawing objects. Except where noted, all of the techniques in this major section apply to both graphic images and drawing objects.

Select Objects

The first step in editing any object is to select it. By now, you have had enough experience with PowerPoint to know that you select an object by clicking it. You may have to click an image or shape on its border to select it. A selected object has handles that you can use to resize or reshape the object.

You can choose more than one object at a time. You can then reformat all the objects with one command. Start by selecting the first object. Then, press SHIFT and click a second object. Keep on going until you have selected all the objects that you want to use.

Press SHIFT and click a selected object to deselect an object that you selected in error, without deselecting other objects already selected.

Another way to choose multiple objects is to use a selection box. First click at one corner of the rectangular area you want to enclose. Be careful not to click an object—click only empty space on the slide. Then drag to the opposite corner of the rectangle. PowerPoint displays a blue, transparent rectangle as you drag. Release the mouse button when the rectangle encloses all the objects you want to select. In this situation, too, you can press SHIFT and click any of the selected objects to deselect them. This is a great technique when you want to select all the objects in an area except one or two.

If you have an image or shape that covers the entire slide, it's sometimes difficult to select other objects on top of it. In this situation, first click off of the slide to start the selection rectangle and then drag to the opposite corner of the rectangle. In this way, you don't select the larger object that covers the slide.

To select all the objects on a slide, press CTRL-A. Or, on the Home tab in the Editing group, choose Select | Select All.

Objects are often layered on top of each other. You may find it difficult to select the object you want if it is behind another object. If the slide does not have too many objects, you may find it easier to cycle through all the objects until the object you want is selected. To accomplish this task, first select any object. Then press TAB repeatedly until the object you want is selected.

The Format tab, which appears when you select any graphic object, has a Selection Pane button in the Arrange group of the ribbon. Click this button to display the new Selection and Visibility task pane, which lists all the objects, both images and shapes, on the active slide in the display order from top to bottom. You can use this pane to do the following:

- Click any object in the pane to select it on the slide.
- Press CTRL as you click to select multiple objects.
- Click any object's "eye" icon to hide it. Click the icon again to redisplay the object.
- Click the Up and Down Reorder buttons to move objects forward and backward. (I explain reordering objects later in this chapter.)
- Rename the objects. Click any item and enter a name name. If you plan to animate objects, these new names can be very helpful in manipulating your animations in the Custom Animation task pane. (I discuss animation in Chapter 9.)

Move Objects

You have probably already moved many objects in PowerPoint. Generally, you select the object, move the cursor over the object until you get the four-headed arrow cursor, and then drag the object. In the "Lay Out Your Slides with Precision" section later in this chapter, I explain techniques for positioning objects precisely.

Duplicate Objects

You can duplicate any selected object. From the Home tab, in the Clipboard group, click the Paste button's down arrow and choose Duplicate. PowerPoint creates a copy of the object, slightly overlapping the original. You have no control over the location of the duplicate, but it is selected when it appears, so you can immediately drag it to a new location. You can also copy it to the clipboard and paste it—either on the same slide or another one.

To duplicate a selected object, press CTRL-D.

You can use CTRL-D to insert several equidistant objects. Select the object and press CTRL-D. Drag the duplicate any distance and direction from the original object. The next time you press CTRL-D, the third object will be the same distance and direction from the second object. You can continue to create a row of several equidistant objects in this way.

Delete Objects

To delete an object, select it and press DELETE. Pressing BACKSPACE also deletes any selected object or objects.

When you press CTRL-X (or choose Cut from the Home tab's Clipboard group), the selected object is deleted and moved to the clipboard. You can then paste it on another slide or even in another application.

In Chapter 3, I discussed how text placeholders are in Edit Text mode when you select them. Pressing DELETE just deletes one of the characters of the text. This is true of any shape containing text. To delete any object containing text, click the border and then press DELETE.

Resize Objects

When a graphic appears on your slide, it may be much too big or small. You can quickly resize any selected object using the handles.

To maintain the proportion of the picture or drawing object, click it to select it and then drag one of the corner handles in the desired direction. If the object is so large that you can't even see the handles, use the Zoom control at the lower-left corner of your window to reduce the zoom until you can see the entire object—this is common with inserted images.

Although PowerPoint 2007 does a reasonably good job of keeping images clear, remember that resizing always affects the resolution of bitmap graphics.

When you drag on either the left or right handles, the object becomes wider or narrower. Drag on the top or bottom handles to change the height. The side of the object *opposite* the handle you drag remains fixed. The center and all other sides of the object move as you drag.

TIP

You can also resize an object so that the center remains fixed. To do so, press CTRL while dragging a handle.

Specify an Exact Size

You may want your object to be a certain height or width. Instead of dragging the handles, you can specify the exact size. To do so, select the object and display the Format tab that appears. In the Size group, enter a value in the Height or Width text box (and press ENTER or click anywhere else) or use the arrows to change the value. What happens next depends on whether you are resizing an image or a drawing object:

- For an image, the proportions of the graphic stay the same, so if you double the width, the height doubles automatically. However, as I explain in the next paragraph, you can change the proportions of a graphic.

- For a drawing object, the proportions do not stay the same, so if you double the width, the height remains unchanged.

Click the dialog box launcher arrow at the lower-right corner of the Size group to open the Size and Position dialog box, with the Size tab on top, as shown in Figure 5-4. Here you can specify height and width as well as change the size of an object by scaling it. For example,

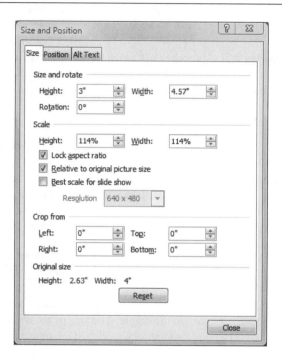

FIGURE 5-4 Use the Size tab of the Size and Position dialog box to exactly specify an image's size.

you can scale an object or object to 75% of its original size—and you can separately control the scale of the height and the width. To change the proportions of an image, and distort its original shape, uncheck the Lock Aspect Ratio check box in the Scale section of the dialog box. Click Close when you're done.

You can rotate the object by an exact angle in this dialog box, with a precision of 1-degree increments. A positive rotation angle rotates the picture clockwise. Use a negative angle to rotate counterclockwise.

In the upcoming "Rotate and Flip Objects" section, I explain how to rotate an image by dragging.

Crop a Graphic

You often want to use only a portion of a graphic, to emphasize the main focus. For example, you may want only an image of a house, without its surrounding or border. Click Crop on the Format tab, in the Size group. The cursor changes to look like the Crop button. The cursor changes again to a T shape as you pass it over the middle of any one of the picture's borders. Then drag inward. The Crop button stays depressed so that you can crop from more than one side. Figure 5-5 shows an example of a graphic before and after cropping. Note that you cannot crop drawing objects.

FIGURE 5-5 By cropping this house's edges, you can create a different look.

Rotate and Flip Objects

You may want to rotate an image or shape to create a different look, or just to slant it slightly. Whatever your reason is, you can easily rotate any object. If you just want to rotate the object 90 degrees left or right, select the image, click the Format tab that appears, and click Rotate in the Arrange group. Then choose Rotate Left 90° or Rotate Right 90° from the drop-down menu. You can continue to click these items to rotate the image to any increment of 90 degrees.

For the ultimate in flexibility, use the green Free Rotate dot at the top of any selected image, as shown here. Place the cursor over the dot and it changes to the Free Rotate shape. Click and drag to rotate the object to any angle you want.

For precise rotation, click More Rotation Options from the Rotate drop-down menu to open the Size and Position dialog box. In the Size and Rotate section of the Size tab, you can set the rotation to any degree.

To mirror an object (called *flipping*), select the object, and display the Format tab that appears. In the Arrange group, choose Rotate. Then choose Flip Horizontal to mirror around a vertical line, or Flip Vertical to mirror around a horizontal line.

To create a symmetrical shape by mirroring an object, copy the object and paste it. Choose Draw | Rotate or Flip. Move the copy next to the original. You can then group the two objects to create a perfectly symmetrical shape.

Here is an example of an image created by copying and flipping.

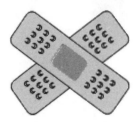

Group and Ungroup Objects

If you want to work with certain objects together more than once, you should group them. Grouped objects act like single objects. You might group individual images that you want to place together, graphics that you create from multiple shapes, or a caption for a graphic image. For example, if you create your own daisy from a circle and several ovals, you would group them to move and resize the flower as one object. In these instances, you want a set of objects to remain together.

Ungroup Objects

Sometimes, you start with grouped objects. For example, some vector-based art can be ungrouped into individual drawing objects. (Drawing objects are discussed fully later in this chapter, in the "Create Drawing Objects" section.) You can manipulate the art in unusual ways using this technique. For example, in Figure 5-6, you see an image of two roses on the left. This picture was first ungrouped. Then the elements in each rose were selected together and grouped. On the right, the roses have been duplicated and moved—something that you can easily do by ungrouping the picture, editing it, and regrouping it.

To ungroup a graphic or any grouped objects, follow these steps:

1. Select the graphic.
2. Click the Format tab that appears.

3. In the Arrange group, click the Group button and then click Ungroup from the drop-down list.

Right-click the graphic and choose Group | Ungroup.

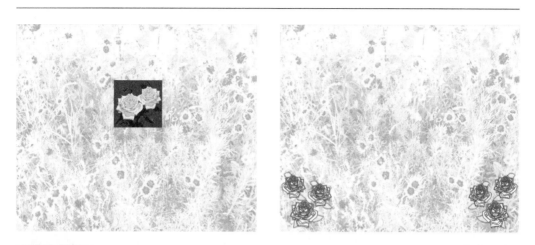

FIGURE 5-6   You can manipulate vector art by ungrouping it and converting it to drawing objects.

Sometimes you need to ungroup the art twice: once into a few larger objects and again into many smaller ones. When you choose Ungroup for inserted clipart, you see the message shown here. Click Yes to convert it to a Microsoft Office drawing.

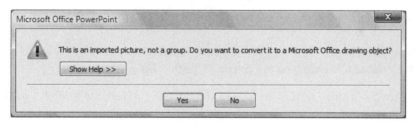

CAUTION   *If you ungroup a picture into individual components, you often have hundreds of tiny pieces that can easily be deleted or moved inadvertently. Don't forget to regroup the picture for easier handling. In Figure 5-6, each rose was regrouped to create two objects. Also, occasionally, you may lose the colors when you ungroup pictures.*

TIP   *Always save your presentation before you start making major changes to a graphic, and then you can have a little fun. If you don't like the results, you can undo all your changes or close the presentation without saving it. Another option is to duplicate the slide and work on the duplicate. If it doesn't work out, just delete the new slide; otherwise, delete the old slide.*

Group Objects

To group selected objects, choose the Format tab that appears and choose Group | Group in the Arrange group. Or right-click any one of the selected objects and choose Group | Group.

 *Select the objects and press* CTRL-G.

When you ungroup objects, PowerPoint still remembers that the objects were part of a group. You can later select one of the objects and choose Group | Regroup in the Arrange group of the Format tab to re-create the original group.

 *If you need to change one object in a group, you don't need to ungroup the objects. First select the group and then click the object. You can then change that object individually.*

Reorder Objects

It is common to have objects that cover one another. You often place objects on a slide in a certain order, only to find that the wrong object is on top. You reorder objects to specify which object appears on top. To reorder an object, select it and click the Format tab that appears. Then choose one of the following in the Arrange group:

 ■ **Bring to Front**   Brings the selected object to the front of any other objects it overlaps.

■ **Send to Back**   Sends the selected object behind any other objects it overlaps.

If you have several layers of overlapping objects, you may not want to move an object all the way to the back or front. Instead, you can do one of the following:

■ Click the down arrow next to the Bring to Front button and choose Bring Forward to bring the selected object one layer toward the front.

■ Click the down arrow next to the Send to Back button and choose Send Backward to send the selected object one layer toward the back.

 *Right-click any selected object and choose Bring to Front or Send to Back. You can also use the submenu to bring the object forward or backward one layer.*

A new feature in PowerPoint 2007 is the Selection and Visibility pane. On the Format tab, choose Selection Pane in the Arrange group to display the Selection and Visibility pane, which lists all the objects on your slide. Click any object and use the up and down arrows at the bottom of the pane to move objects up and down in the display order.

In Figure 5-7, you see a slide containing several layers of pictures. On the right side of the first slide, the pictures are obviously in the wrong order.

Substitute Pictures or Shapes

If you insert a picture but decide that you want a different picture, you can substitute another one. If you have applied formatting to the picture, PowerPoint applies the same formatting to the new picture. To switch to another picture, select the picture, click the Format tab that appears, and choose Change Picture in the Adjust group of the ribbon. The Insert Picture dialog box opens where you select a picture and click Insert.

Would you like to switch shapes? Maybe you think another shape would look more attractive or fit around the text better. It's easy:

1. Select the shape you want to change.

2. Click the Format tab that appears.

3. In the Insert Shapes group, click the down arrow next to the Edit Shape button and choose Change Shape from the drop-down menu.

4. The Shape gallery opens. Choose another shape.

PowerPoint applies the same formatting to the new shape.

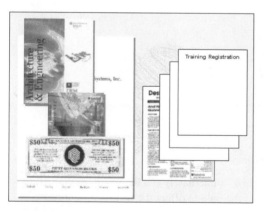
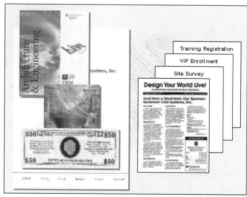

FIGURE 5-7   By reordering the objects on this slide, you can ensure that important information is not obscured. (Courtesy of MasterGraphics, www.masterg.com.)

Recolor Graphics

You can recolor images to match a color theme, to provide more contrast for text, or for any artistic reason. Recoloring pictures can be indispensable when you have a picture that does not look good against the presentation background or if you need a series of color-coordinated images. This section does not apply to shapes. Chapter 6 explains how to format the fills and borders of shapes.

Set the Color Type

You can quickly change an image to grayscale, sepia (brown tones), black and white, or a washout. A washout is also called a *watermark*—a light-toned graphic—and is used as a background behind text. Furthermore, you have many new options for recoloring your image to match any color you want.

 *The recoloring feature has been greatly expanded in PowerPoint 2007, allowing you to adjust bitmap images in ways that previously required a separate application. However, the ability to recolor vector images color by color has been removed.*

When you select a picture and display the Format tab that appears, in the Adjust group, clicking the Recolor button displays the drop-down palette shown here:

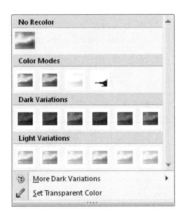

For all the options, pass the cursor over a color tile to immediately see the result on your slide. Then click when you like the result. The top section of the palette offers the following options:

- **No Recolor**   Uses the image type that came with the graphic. This is the default option. You can use this button to restore the original image coloring if you previously changed it.
- **Grayscale**   Changes the graphic to shades of gray. Colors are assigned a shade of gray in relation to their intensity.
- **Sepia**   Changes the graphic to shades of brown.
- **Black and White**   Converts your graphic to black and white, with no shading.

■ **Washout** Creates a light-toned graphic. An example is shown in Figure 5-8. A washout is not transparent, and you may need to move it behind text, as explained earlier in this chapter in the "Reorder Objects" section.

The next row of the Recolor drop-down palette, Dark Variations, offers several dark colors that you can choose. Use these colors when you want to place light text in front of an image. The Light Variations row contains several light colors that you can use if you want to place dark text in front on an image.

Point to More Dark Variations to display the same color palette you see when choosing any color. Here you can choose from any variation in the color theme, standard colors, and recently used colors (not limited to dark colors). You can go even further and choose More Colors to open the Colors dialog box and choose any color you want! I explain the Colors dialog box in more detail in Chapter 6.

5

TIP *If you want the image to appear as a background on every slide, save it as a file (right-click and choose Save as Picture) and place it on the slide master, as explained in Chapter 7.*

Adjust Contrast and Brightness

A washout brightens an image and reduces its contrast. You may want to fine-tune the brightness and contrast on your own. The Brightness and Contrast buttons, in the Adjust group of the Format tab, let you do so.

Increasing contrast makes dark colors darker and light colors lighter. Increase contrast when a graphic is not clear enough. Decreasing contrast makes dark colors lighter and light colors darker. If you continue to decrease a graphic's contrast, you end up with all grays. Decrease contrast when you want a softer effect.

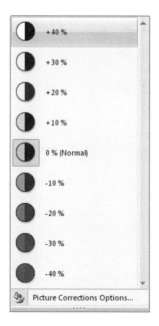

FIGURE 5-8 You can change a graphic to a washout. (Courtesy of U.S. Fish and Wildlife Service. Photo by Craig Blacklock.)

To change the contrast, click the Contrast button to display the choices shown here. To increase the contrast, choose a higher setting; to decrease the contrast, choose a lower setting.

If you want a more extreme setting, choose Picture Correction Options to open the Format Shape dialog box, with the Picture category active, as shown next. Here you have full flexibility to set the contrast (and brightness) to any value from 0% to 100%.

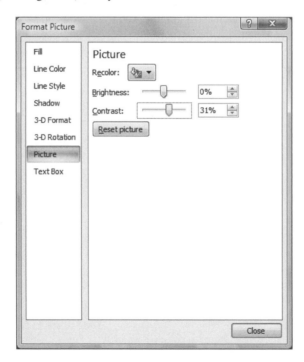

Figure 5-9 shows a graphic before and after adjusting contrast. The contrast was originally very high but the presenter reduced the contrast to get a softer look and clearer details. (Note that this graphic was created using an image-editing program—as a result, there are other special effects that cannot be created in PowerPoint.)

Increasing brightness lightens all the colors in the graphic. You can increase brightness to correct a dark graphic. Decreasing brightness darkens all the colors. You may find that a graphic looks good on paper but is too bright when you shine it on a wall screen with an LCD projector—in that case, decrease its brightness. To change brightness, click the Brightness button to display the same choices that you have for changing contrast. As with contrast, you can click Picture Correction Options to open the Format Shape dialog box and set the brightness to any value from 0% to 100%.

Set Transparent Color

You can create a transparent area on some types of image files. Both GIF and PNG files support transparency, but JPG files don't. The most common reason to set a transparent color is to remove a background around an image. To create a transparent area, follow these steps:

1. Select the image.

2. Click the Format tab that appears.

3. In the Adjust group, choose Recolor to display the recolor options.

4. At the bottom of the list, click Set Transparent Color. When you move your cursor back onto the slide, you see a special cursor, shown here.

5. Click the color in the picture that you want to be transparent.

Manage Pictures

You can compress images to reduce file size, reset a picture to its original format, and switch to another picture. These operations help you manage the pictures in your presentation, but don't apply to shapes.

FIGURE 5-9   You can get a softer, more detailed look by lessening contrast.

Compress Images

Large images in a presentation increase the file size and can result in slow display or even a crash during a slide show. Many people simply insert high-resolution photos, including those taken with a digital camera, but doing so makes presentations large and unwieldy. You can compress the images in a presentation to make the entire presentation smaller, so that it loads more quickly. This functionality is especially important for presentations that you place on the Internet.

The ideal situation is to create the images using a low resolution. Additional adjustments always affect quality. For onscreen presentations, 72 to 150 dots per inch (dpi) is usually fine, unless you're displaying highly detailed or technical images. Printed presentations require a much higher resolution, generally 220 to 600 dpi.

To compress an image, select it and click Compress Pictures in the Adjust group of the Format tab that appears. The Compress Pictures dialog box opens, as shown here:

You can simply click OK to compress all the images in a presentation. To compress only the selected image, check the Apply to Selected Pictures Only check box. For more options, click the Options button to open the Compression Settings dialog box, shown here:

You can specify that PowerPoint compress images whenever you save by checking the first check box. You can also choose to delete cropped areas of pictures. PowerPoint remembers the full image so that you can restore it if you decide you don't like the cropping effect. Then you can choose the amount of compression, from 96 to 220 dpi. Click OK to return to the Compress Pictures dialog box and click OK again to compress the pictures and return to your presentation.

If you don't know the origin of your images, it's not a good idea to compress all of them at once. You may lose details that you need.

Reset a Picture

When you make changes to a picture, PowerPoint remembers the original settings. Click Reset Picture in the Adjust group of the Format tab to return the picture to its original state. However, note that resetting does not reverse compression.

Add Alternate Text for Web Browsers

If you will post the presentation on a web page, you may want to add alternate text for your images. This text has several important uses:

- ■ This text shows up before the image loads or if the image is missing.
- ■ Some people turn off images in their browser if they have a slow connection, so they see this text instead.
- ■ Web search engines use this text to index web sites.
- ■ People with sight disabilities may use a special reader that reads the text out loud; including alternate text helps to make your presentation meaningful to them.

To add alternate text, select the picture. In the Size group of the Format tab that appears, click the dialog box launcher arrow at the lower-right corner to open the Size and Position dialog box. Click the Alt Text tab. Enter the text in the Alternative Text box and click Close.

Format a Picture

You have many options to change the way a picture looks. You can give the picture a new shape, add a border, or apply effects. You can find these effects by selecting any picture and clicking the Format tab of the ribbon.

NOTE   *Many of the formatting options for pictures are new for PowerPoint 2007. You can now easily change their shape, add new effects, and choose from preset picture styles. Drawing objects also have new shape styles, which I cover in Chapter 6.*

Use Picture Styles

Picture styles are a collection of formats that you can quickly apply to any image. To apply one of the preset picture styles, click the More button (down arrow) in the Picture Styles group of the Format tab to display the gallery shown here. Pass your cursor over any style to immediately see its effect on your picture, and click when you find a style you like. As you can see, the styles are combinations of shapes, borders, and special effects that include rotation and reflection.

Figure 5-10 shows a slide with the original, plain picture on the left and again with the first picture style, a reflection, added on the right.

FIGURE 5-10 You can quickly choose a picture style to change the picture's formatting.

The picture was scaled down to make room for the reflection, which evokes the meaning of the text on the slide.

You can create your own picture styles or modify a preset one by using the following drop-down lists in the Picture Styles group of the Format tab:

- **Picture Shape**   Choose from any shape that you can draw in PowerPoint.

- **Picture Border**   Choose a border color from the set of theme colors, or choose More Outline Colors to choose any color. You can also choose a border weight (thickness) and dash (or dot) line type.

- **Picture Effects**   Choose from Preset, Shadow, Reflection, Glow, Soft Edges, Preset, and 3-D Rotation. Most of these options were discussed in Chapter 3 in the context of text effects and apply the same way to pictures. For example, adding soft edges to a picture can create a very gentle, understated effect. The Preset option opens a gallery of preset effects that you can choose.

TIP   *If you add an effect to a picture, you can extract the original picture. Right-click the picture and choose Save as Picture. In the Save as Picture dialog box, click the down arrow next to the Save button and choose Save Original Picture.*

Use the Format Shape Dialog Box

For general graphic editing and to use all the options individually, click the dialog box launcher arrow at the lower-right corner of the Picture Styles group of the Format tab. The Format Shape dialog box opens, shown in Figure 5-11 with the Fill category displayed. I cover this dialog box further in Chapter 6 for creating fills, borders, and 3-D effects.

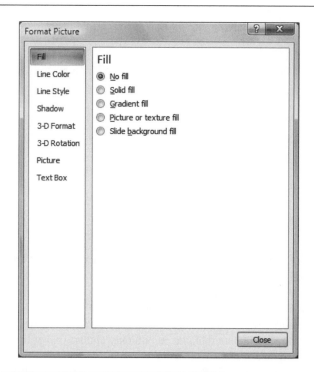

FIGURE 5-11 In the Format Shape dialog box, you can specify many settings for pictures.

SHORTCUT *You can also right-click any picture and choose Format Picture on the shortcut menu.*

Use the Fill category to format fill color. In this instance, *fill color* refers to the background of the image. You won't see a fill for many graphics because the image takes up the entire area; the result depends on the existing background. When you click the Color drop-down arrow, you can choose from Theme Colors, Standard Colors, Recent Colors, or More Colors. (Fill colors and effects are covered in Chapter 6.) You can also set the transparency of the fill.

From this drop-down menu, you can change the fill in the following ways:

- **No Fill** Eliminates any fill.
- **Solid Fill** Creates a solid fill.
- **Gradient Fill** Allows you to specify a gradient of colors. I explain how to create a gradient in Chapter 6.
- **Picture or Texture Fill** Allows you to specify an image or texture.
- **Background** Creates a solid fill that is the same color as the slide background.

Adding a fill may make a graphic look awkward and stilted, as shown here (left). Without the fill (right), the graphic seems to be an integral part of the slide.

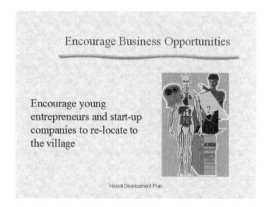 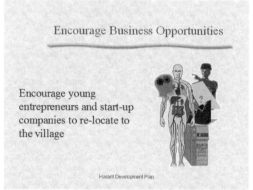

Use the Line category of the Format Shape dialog box to create a border around the image. You can create a solid or gradient border. If you specify a line, you can then use the Line Style category to set the line's width, choose a compound line (such as a double-line), choose a dashed or dotted line, and choose a join type (how corners meet).

Use the Shadow category to give your image a shadow. I discuss shadows in detail in Chapter 6, but it's good to mention here that you can quickly choose one of the preset shadows from the Presets drop-down list.

You can use the 3-D Format and 3-D Rotation categories to create 3-D effects. Again, I discuss these in detail in Chapter 6.

The Picture category lets you change contrast and brightness. I discussed this feature earlier in this chapter, in the "Adjust Contrast and Brightness" section.

The Text Box category applies only to shapes that contain text. I discussed these settings in the "Edit Text in Shapes and Text Boxes" section of Chapter 3.

When you have completed editing your picture, click Close to return to your slide.

You cannot crop, group, or change the fill, border, shadow, or transparency of an animated GIF image in PowerPoint. Use an animated GIF-editing program and then insert the file on the slide again.

Edit Graphic Files

Unfortunately, you may not be able to get the results you want within PowerPoint. When you want a more sophisticated way to edit graphic files, you need to find a graphic-editing program that can do the job and can save the results in a file format that PowerPoint can accept. Fortunately, there are many such programs. Most professionally created presentations include images that have been edited using separate software. The premier example of this type of software is Adobe Photoshop (http://www.adobe.com/products/photoshop/main.html), a high-end graphic-editing program that can create just about any effect you want for a bitmap graphic.

If you don't have Photoshop, other less expensive, simpler alternatives are available, such as the following, that allow you to do almost everything you want:

- **Adobe Photoshop Elements**   As the name says, contains elements of Photoshop (http://www.adobe.com/products/photoshopelwin/).
- **Ulead PhotoImpact**   Image-editing from Ulead (http://www.ulead.com/pi/runme.htm).
- **Microsoft Digital Image**   Image-editing from Microsoft (http://www.microsoft.com/products/imaging/default.mspx).
- **Corel Paint Shop Pro**   Image-editing from Jasc (http://www.corel.com and click the Products link).
- **CorelDRAW and Corel Painter**   Drawing and editing programs from Corel (go to http://www.corel.com and click the Products link).

One more tool for editing bitmaps is Microsoft Paint, which is included with Windows. Paint is a simple program, but it is especially useful for coloring in black-and-white clip art. As long as an area is enclosed, Paint can fill it with color. You can also easily touch up a drawing by adding your own freely drawn lines. To open Paint, choose Start | All Programs | Accessories | Paint.

NOTE   *When you are trying to fill an image with color, Paint works best with BMP files. Right-click any image that you have inserted and choose Save as Picture. Then save it in .bmp format. You can then open it in Paint.*

To fill in an area with color, choose a color from the Color palette at the top of the screen. Click to choose a foreground color and right-click to choose a background color. Then choose the Fill with Color tool. Click in any enclosed area of the picture to fill with the foreground color and right-click to fill with the background color.

TIP   *To add a custom color, choose Options | Edit Colors and click Define Custom Colors in the dialog box. Also, if the Color palette shows only shades of gray, choose Image | Attributes and click the Colors options button.*

Here you see a drawing in its original black-and-white form and after being colored using Paint:

To create the graphic, fill in each area in Paint, using the procedure previously explained. Save the graphic and import it into PowerPoint. With the graphic selected, display the Format tab, choose the Set Transparent Color tool from the Recolor drop-down list of the Adjust group, and click the white background. (Many graphics come in with a white background.) Finally, resize, crop, and place the graphic as desired.

 *Not all formats support transparency. If necessary, save the image in Paint as a GIF file, a format that supports transparency. Note that the GIF format supports a maximum of 256 colors.*

Vector files can usually be edited with success within PowerPoint, but third-party drawing programs may have better tools.

Create Drawing Objects

Microsoft Office has its own drawing tools that you can use to create graphics on your own. While you won't be able to create sophisticated drawings or artwork, you can create some useful shapes to add focus and impact to your slides. In addition, you can manipulate these shapes to create some great effects, such as shadows and 3-D. These tools create *drawing objects* or *shapes.*

You use the Illustrations group of the Insert tab to insert shapes, which you can easily resize and color. Shapes are surprisingly flexible, and there are loads of them. Here you see a slide that makes creative use of shapes: one is a curved arrow that is repeated and rotated to create a circular shape, and the other is a series of squares that have been combined to create a step shape with the number 2 inside, indicating the second slide.

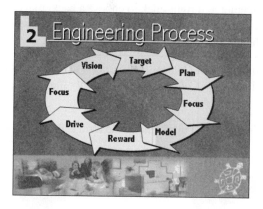

Slide courtesy of Jennifer Rotondo

To insert a shape, click the Shapes button in the Illustrations group of the Insert tab to open the Shapes gallery, shown in Figure 5-12. Click the shape you want to insert it onto the slide using the default size, or drag on the slide to size the shape as you insert it. In the following sections, I provide more details about some of the types of shapes you can use.

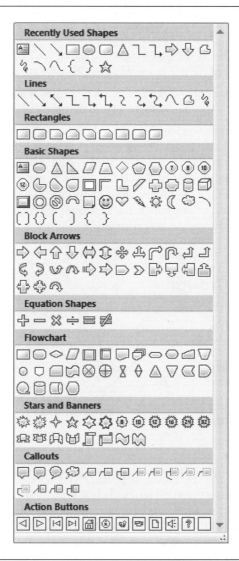

FIGURE 5-12   The Shapes gallery contains all of the shapes that you can insert onto a slide.

Draw Lines, Arrows, and Curves

Use lines and curves to create your own shapes or touch up existing ones. Of course, you use arrows to point to other objects. On the Insert tab, click the Shapes button in the Illustrations group and use the Lines category to find the lines and curves. Each tool works slightly differently—which sometimes leads to a frustrating experience. Here are precise instructions to make it easy:

- To draw a single line, choose the Line tool, move the cursor to your slide, and then click and drag. The end point of the line is where you release the mouse button.

- To draw an arrow, choose one of the arrow tools. Click and drag to create the arrow. The point of the arrow is where you release the mouse button.

- To draw a curved shape, choose the Curve tool. You can create a multi-curved shape. First click at the desired start point. Then move the cursor to either the desired endpoint or to where you want to create a curve that changes the direction of the line, and click. You can continue to click at curve points. Double-click to end the curve. Here you see a curve with two vertices. To create this curve, click at the start point, move the cursor to the first bend point, and click again. Click again at the second bend point and double-click at the end. The arrow was added separately.

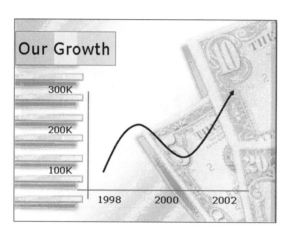

- A *freeform shape* is a multi-segmented shape that can contain both lines and freeform curves. To start, choose the Freeform tool and click at the desired start point. To create a line segment, move the mouse to the desired endpoint and click. You can continue drawing line segments in this way. To draw freeform curves, drag the mouse. The shape follows the cursor, as if you're drawing with a pencil. To end the freeform object, double-click.

- A *scribble* follows the cursor as you drag with the mouse. To draw a scribble, choose the Scribble tool. Click at the desired start point, and drag, drawing as you go. Just release the mouse button to end the scribble.

To close a shape, click near its start point. PowerPoint automatically connects the endpoint to the start point.

To draw several individual lines, right-click one of the line tools and choose Lock Drawing Mode. You can then draw any number of lines, without reclicking the Line button. To stop drawing lines, choose any other button. You can use this technique for any shape. To quickly insert loads of identical shapes in their default size and fill, use the Lock Drawing Mode feature and click as many times as you want on the slide.

Lines, arrows, and connectors have only two handles when selected. When you drag one handle, the other end remains fixed. You can therefore change the endpoint's position freely, so that both the length and angle of the line are changed.

When you press SHIFT and drag, the line's angle is held constant, and you can change only the line's length.

Format Lines

You can control the color, width, line type, and transparency of lines, as well as several other properties. To format a line, select it and display the Format tab that appears. In the Shape Styles group, choose Shape Outline to display the palette shown here:

To change the color, click one of the colors, or choose More Outline Colors to open the Colors dialog box, where you can pick any color or define your own.

To change the line's width, point to Weight and choose one of the widths from the list. To enter a different weight in points, choose More Lines to open the Format Shape dialog box with the Line Style category displayed, as shown in Figure 5-13. Similarly, to create a dashed or dotted line, point to Dashes and choose one of the line types or choose More Lines to open the same dialog box. If the dialog box doesn't cover up the line, you can see it change immediately as you make your choices.

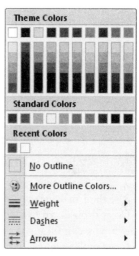

To open the Format Shape dialog box quickly, right-click a line and choose Format Shape. Click the Line Style category.

In the Line Style category, you can format a line as follows:

- **Width**   Enter a width in points in the text box.
- **Compound Type**   You can choose double or triple line types.
- **Dash Type**   You can choose dotted or dashed lines.
- **Cap Type**   Determines the shape of the start point of the arrow.
- **Join Type**   Determines how line segments meet. It only applies if you draw an elbow connector or a freeform shape with multi-segmented shapes.

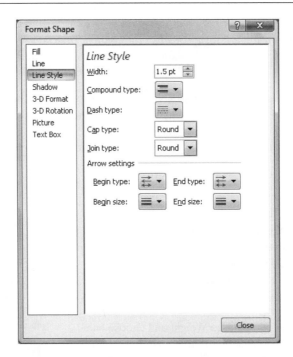

FIGURE 5-13 Use the Line Style category of the Format Shape dialog box to control arrows.

Use the Line category of the Format Shape dialog box to change the color by choosing from the Color drop-down list. You can also change the transparency of the line. If the line is thick enough, you can fill it with a gradient in the same Line category of the dialog box. I discuss gradients in Chapter 6.

Format Arrows

If you don't like the default arrowhead shape, you can change it. To change an arrow type, select the arrow and display the Format tab that appears. In the Shape Styles group, choose Shape Outline | Arrows and choose one of the options. If you want more control over arrow size and shape, choose More Arrows at the bottom of the menu to open the Format Shape dialog box with the Line Style category displayed, as previously shown in Figure 5-13.

Use the Arrows Settings section of the Line Style category to control the part of the arrow that is specific to arrows:

- **Begin Type** Use this drop-down box to create an arrow with an arrowhead at its beginning.
- **Begin Size** If the arrow has an arrowhead at its beginning, use the drop-down list to choose the type and size of the arrow.

■ **End Type**   Choose the type of arrow at the end. (The choices are the same for both the beginning and the end of the arrow.)

■ **End Size**   Choose a size for the arrowhead at the end of the arrow.

You format arrows in much the same way that you format lines. Because an arrow is a combination of a line and an arrowhead, the settings at the top of the Line Style category of the dialog box and in the Line category affect the arrow as well.

Increasing the line weight affects both the arrowhead and the line. Therefore, if you want to make the arrowhead larger, increase the line weight of the entire arrow.

5

Create Flowcharts and Process Diagrams

The Shapes gallery lets you insert a variety of flowchart shapes and connectors. *Connectors* are used in flowcharts and process diagrams to connect shapes. Figure 5-14 shows a simple flowchart.

You can create a variety of preset diagrams, called SmartArt. You can even convert bulleted text to diagrams. These are explained in Chapter 8.

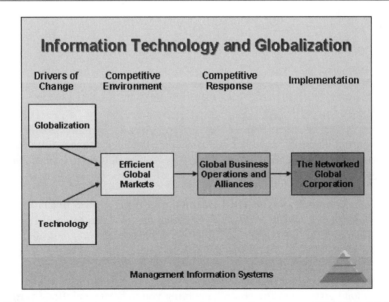

FIGURE 5-14   A flowchart diagram connects shapes with arrow or lines. (Courtesy of Maharishi University of Management, http://www.mum.edu.)

To insert a flowchart shape, choose one of the shapes in the Flowchart section of the Shapes gallery. Then click and drag on the slide to obtain the desired size. Continue until you have all the shapes that you need.

Once you have your shapes in place, you can use the connectors to show how the shapes relate to each other. Choose one of the connectors from the Lines section of the Shapes gallery. Connectors can have no arrows, one arrow, or two arrows and they can have "elbows" or be curved.

When you place the cursor near one of the flowchart shapes, PowerPoint displays small red boxes at appropriate points on the shape. Click, and the connector snaps exactly to one of the boxes. Now drag to the second shape, and the red boxes appear on that shape. Click to snap the end of the connector to one of the boxes.

You can easily edit flowcharts and process diagrams, because connectors know what they are connected to and try to remain stuck to their shapes. If you move one of the flowchart shapes, the connector readjusts its length and direction accordingly.

Insert Shapes

PowerPoint has a generous selection of shapes that you can insert onto your slides. From the Shapes gallery, use the following categories:

- Rectangles
- Basic Shapes
- Block Arrows
- Equation Shapes
- Stars and Banners
- Callouts
- Action Buttons

As you can see from Figure 5-12, earlier in this chapter, the choice ranges from utilitarian to whimsical. I explain how to use action buttons in the "Use Action Buttons to Control Navigation" section in Chapter 11.

To draw a perfect circle, use the Oval tool on the Drawing toolbar and either press SHIFT *as you drag, or click the slide without dragging. Likewise, to draw a perfect square, use the Rectangle tool and either press* SHIFT *or click without dragging. Right-click either tool and choose Lock Drawing Mode to draw several shapes at once.*

Some of the shapes display one or two small yellow diamonds when selected. Dragging this marvelous diamond gives you extra control, enabling you to create an infinite variety of shapes. Initially, the effect of dragging the diamond in a specific direction may not be obvious, so experiment! Figure 5-15 shows some examples of these variations on a theme.

5

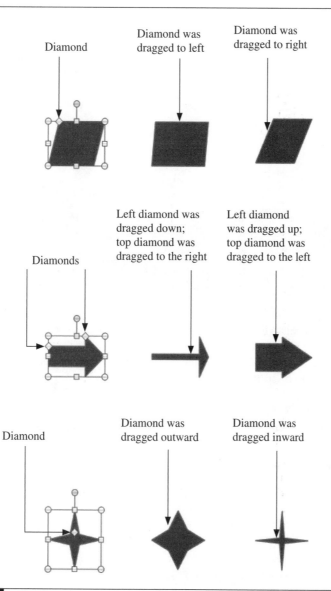

FIGURE 5-15 If a shape has a yellow diamond when selected, you can manipulate the shape's features.

A *callout* is a combination of a text box and a line, which points to an object. Here's an example that uses callouts:

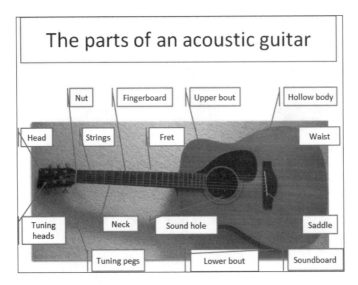

You can see the callout choices in Figure 5-12, earlier in the chapter. As you can see, there is quite a variety. The callouts with a faded box do not display a box—you see only the line and the text.

You probably won't know the right size for the callout until you have typed its text. Therefore, the easiest way to insert a callout is to follow these steps:

1. Choose the callout you want.

2. Click on your slide. PowerPoint inserts the callout using its default size and configuration.

3. Type the text for the callout.

4. Drag on the handles to adjust the size of the callout to fit the text. Alternately, change the size of the text.

5. Move the callout to its desired location.

6. Drag the diamond(s) until the line points to the appropriate spot.

Save Drawing Objects for Later Use

When you create drawing objects, you can add them to the Clip Organizer. If you spent quite a bit of time creating them and might use them again, by all means, place them in the Clip Organizer. Here's how:

1. First create the drawing object or objects.

2. Select the objects.

3. Press CTRL-C, or click Copy in the Clipboard group of the Home tab.

4. In the Illustrations group of the Insert tab, click Clip Art. PowerPoint opens the Insert Clip Art task pane.

5. Click Organize Clips.

6. Choose a category.

7. Press CTRL-V. You may have to scroll down to see the new item.

> **TIP** *Don't forget to add keywords to help you find the drawing object again. Pass the cursor over the object's thumbnail, click the down arrow, and choose Edit Keywords.*

You can also save drawing objects as a separate graphic file. Select a drawing object, right-click it, and choose Save as Picture. Once you have saved it, you can choose Picture in the Insert tab's Illustrations group to insert the picture onto a slide.

> **TIP** *Once you save a drawing object as a picture and re-insert it, you can manipulate it like a picture. For example, you can crop it, change its brightness and contrast, or set a transparent color (if it's a GIF or PNG file).*

Edit Points

Curve, freeform, and scribble objects are created with vertices that are located where you clicked as you created the object. You can edit these vertices to reshape these objects. Select the object and then display the Format tab. In the Insert Shapes group, click Edit Shape | Edit Points (or simply right-click the shape and choose Edit Points). PowerPoint now displays all the vertices, as shown here. You can drag any vertex in any direction. This method is great for making minor corrections in these objects.

When you click on a vertex, you'll see two small handles appear, connected to the vertex by a thin, blue line. If you drag the handles, instead of the vertex, you can create *Bézier curves*, which are mathematically-derived curves, sometimes called *splines*. These curves offer a way to create beautiful shapes that you cannot create in any other way. You can turn a straight line into a curve and change an existing curve's curvature.

 If the vertices are close together, you may not be able to access the handles. Try increasing the zoom. Also, if you click a vertex on a straight line, the handles appear on the line; you can still drag them off the line to turn the line into a curve.

While editing points, you can also do the following:

- **Add a vertex**　Press CTRL and click anywhere on the outline to add a vertex, or right-click and choose Add Point.
- **Delete a vertex**　Press CTRL and click a vertex, or right-click and choose Delete.
- **Straighten a segment**　Right-click along a segment and choose Straight Segment.
- **Convert a straight segment to a curved segment**　Right-click along a segment and choose Curved Segment.
- **Create a corner point**　Right-click a vertex and choose Corner Point to maintain the vertex as a corner.
- **Create a smooth point**　Right-click a vertex and choose Smooth Point to use the vertex as a part of a curve.
- **Create a straight point**　Right-click a vertex and choose Straight Point to maintain the vertex as part of a straight line.

If you want to edit the points of another shape (except a line or arrow), you can easily do so. Just select the shape and click the Format tab that appears. In the Insert Shape group, choose Edit Shape | Convert to Freeform. For example, you can turn a rectangle into a freeform. Then you can edit its points.

Bézier curves take some practice, but the results can be rewarding.

Edit Connectors

Connectors have several unique properties that make them different from lines. First, there are three types of connectors—straight, elbow (angled), and curved. You can change any connector's type by right-clicking it and choosing a different type of connector from the Connector Types item of the shortcut menu.

To disconnect one end of a connector from its object, drag the handle at that end. You can then drag the handle to another object. To move the entire connector, drag its middle, and both ends become "undone."

PowerPoint can automatically reroute connectors so they travel the shortest distance. Right-click a connector and choose Reroute Connectors from the shortcut menu. This command is also available in the Insert Shapes group of the Format tab. Click the down arrow next to the Edit Shape button and choose Reroute Connectors from the shortcut menu.

Lay Out Your Slides with Precision

For those perfectionists who like to lay out a slide precisely, a number of tools are designed especially for you. Actually, precise layout is also a hallmark of good design, so here are a few pointers.

Use the Rulers

The rulers are very helpful when laying out a slide. As you move the cursor, the top and side rulers each show their position with a line. By observing the lines as you point to an object, you can know its position. You can use this information to position other objects. To show the rulers, display the View tab and check the Ruler check box in the Show/Hide group.

5

> **NOTE**   *The rulers as they apply to text are covered in Chapter 4.*

Use Guides

The guides are one of the best tools for placing objects. Guides are fine horizontal and vertical lines that cross the entire slide. To view the guides, follow these steps:

1. Select any object on the current slide.

2. Click the Format tab that appears.

 3. In the Arrange group of the tab, click the arrow next to the Align button and choose Grid Settings. The Grid and Guides dialog box opens, shown in Figure 5-16.

4. Check the Display Drawing Guides on Screen check box.

5. Click OK.

> **SHORTCUT**   *Press ALT-F9 to display (and hide) the guides.*

The default guides appear through the zero mark of each ruler. If you added or moved guides, you see the last guide setup you created.

You can use the guides to measure distances. To do so, drag a guide. The measurement from the guide's start point appears. To properly use guides, you often need more than one in each direction. To add a guide, press CTRL and drag any guide. PowerPoint creates a new guide. Use the measurement to place the new guide precisely, as shown here:

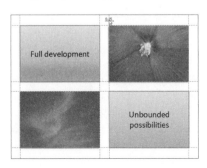

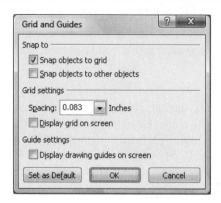

FIGURE 5-16 Use the Grid and Guides dialog box to display guides and specify grid settings.

One reason that guides are so useful is that objects snap to them as you move them. To try this, place a guide and drag any object near the guide. You will see that the object's edge snaps to the guide.

To delete a guide that you have added, drag it to its corresponding ruler. Drag horizontal guides to the top ruler, and vertical guides to the side ruler.

If your slides use an asymmetric layout, the center of the slide is not obvious. Use guides often to make sure that objects are laid out in a balanced way.

Snap to the Grid and to Objects

PowerPoint slides have a grid that you can use to control the placement of objects. By default, the grid is invisible, but you can display it and control its spacing. By default, whenever you draw, resize, or move an object, it *snaps* to this grid. As a result, objects tend to line up easily, without much fuss.

Sometimes you want total control. To temporarily disable the grid snapping, press ALT as you drag or draw an object.

You can also snap one object to another. To set this up, open the Grid and Guides dialog box (see Figure 5-16), as explained in the previous section. Check the Snap Objects to Other Objects check box.

Use the Grid Settings section of the dialog box to set the grid spacing and display the grid. If you like to work this way all the time, click the Set as Default button to keep your settings for other presentations. Click OK when you're done.

Specify an Exact Location

The Position tab of the Size and Position dialog box, shown in Figure 5-17, lets you precisely set the position of an object vertically and horizontally. To open this dialog box, click the dialog box launcher arrow in the Size group of the Format tab and click the Position tab.

You can measure from the top-left corner or the center of the slide. Use the rulers to judge the setting you need. Enter values in the Horizontal and Vertical text boxes and then choose one of the options in the From drop-down list. Click OK when you're done.

> **TIP** *By default, PowerPoint uses inches to measure the position of objects. You can position in millimeters by typing mm after a measurement and by points by typing pt.*

5

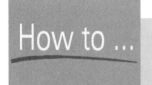

Create a Custom Grid

If the standard grid that PowerPoint provides doesn't suit your needs, you can create your own, with varied spacing and a margin, for instance. One way to create a grid is to draw it on the slide master. (I discuss the slide master in detail in Chapter 7.) Follow these steps:

1. From the View tab, choose Slide Master to display the slide master.

2. Display and set up guides in the arrangement that you want, as explained earlier, in the section "Use Guides."

3. Draw a line along the first guide. (Grids are traditionally light blue, but you can make yours any color that works for you.) By default, the line snaps to the guide.

4. Choose CTRL-D to duplicate the line and drag it to the second guide.

5. Continue to duplicate the last line you've created, as often as necessary.

6. When you've done this in both directions on the slide master, insert a rectangle with no fill to create a margin all around the slide.

7. Select the lines and the rectangle and group them.

Return to your presentation, and you will see the grid on all your slides. You can create a template containing only a slide master with this grid and use it for all your presentations. Or, once you've created this grid, you can copy it from one presentation to another.

When you have finished the presentation, go to the slide master and delete the grid.

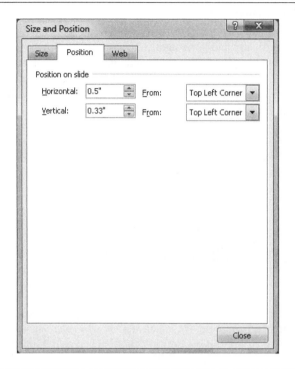

FIGURE 5-17   You can use the Position tab to exactly specify where a shape or image goes.

Constrain Shape and Direction

While drawing lines, you can constrain them to be horizontal, vertical, or diagonal (in increments of 45 degrees) by pressing SHIFT as you draw. You can also press SHIFT to create a circle using the Oval tool or a square using the Rectangle tool. In the "Resize Objects" section earlier in this chapter, I explain how to resize objects proportionally to prevent horizontal and/or vertical distortion.

To constrain the movement of objects to the horizontal or vertical direction, press SHIFT as you drag the object.

Nudge Objects

Do you find it difficult to move objects a very short distance with the mouse? You're not alone. PowerPoint lets you *nudge* objects, which means to move them a short distance. To nudge an object, select it and press the arrow keys (up, down, left, or right) on the keyboard. Each time you press an arrow key, the selected object moves one grid line in that direction.

TIP

If you want super control, press CTRL as you use the appropriate arrow key. PowerPoint moves your object in increments of .02 inch. Remember that you can also press ALT while dragging to disable the grid completely.

TIP

A simple solution for precise positioning is often to increase the zoom. You can make more subtle adjustments in the positioning of objects at a larger zoom percentage.

Align and Distribute Objects

PowerPoint enables you to automatically align objects and distribute them evenly across an area or the entire slide.

To align two or more objects, first decide how you want to align them. If the objects are lined up approximately vertically, you can line them up along their left sides, right sides, or through their center. If the objects are lined up approximately horizontally, you can line them up along their top sides, bottom sides, or through their middle.

To align objects, first select two or more objects. Display the Format tab that appears. Then choose Align in the Arrange group of the ribbon. Choose one of the options on the submenu.

TIP

Choose Align Center to move one or more objects left or right to the center of the slide (halfway between the left and right sides of the slide). This is like centering text. Choose Align Middle to move the object or objects up or down until it's centered between the top and bottom of the slide. This technique is great for centering one object on the slide. By using both Align Center and Align Middle, you can place the object in the exact center (and middle) of the slide.

Here you see objects that need vertical aligning. Notice the position of the "Product" arrow in relation to the rectangles above and below it. On the right you see the result of using the Align Center option.

Another slick trick is to distribute three or more objects equidistant from each other, either horizontally or vertically. This saves you lots of calculations and is often a must for a neat-looking slide. To distribute objects, first choose three or more objects. Then click Align from the Arrange group of the Format tab. From the submenu, choose either Distribute Horizontally or

Distribute Vertically. Here the objects on the left have been redistributed on the right to have an equal amount of space between them.

To arrange objects equal distances from each other in relation to the entire slide, first click Align to Slide on the Align drop-down menu. Then start again—choose Distribute Horizontally or Distribute Vertically.

Tips on Design and Layout

Graphic designers use principles that help to create a slide that looks balanced, easy-to-understand, and professional. The following sections discuss several of these principles.

Make Text Simple and Consistent

Pay a great deal of attention to consistency and legibility of text. As much as possible, stick to the same type family throughout the presentation. For example, you might consider using Arial, Arial Bold, Arial Black, and Arial Narrow. Don't use more than three fonts; one or two are preferable. Include font styles in your counting, because Times Roman regular and Times Roman italic appear as different fonts to your audience. Even different font sizes can sometimes give the impression of a different font. Use common sense and keep it simple.

Consider the old belt and suspenders principle: you don't want to wear both to hold up your trousers—it's either one or the other. You don't need to use red type *and* make it bold. The point comes across clearer if you choose one or the other and give your presentation a more homogeneous look.

The line length of your text should never be more than 45 to 55 characters, including spaces. More than that is difficult for audiences to read. In most cases, the type will be large enough so that this is not a problem. The general principle is to use shorter rather than longer lines of text.

When mixing two different fonts, consider the *x-height* of the font: the height of the lowercase *x* as well as of many lowercase letters, such as *a*, *c*, and *e*. Two fonts may be the same point size but have different x-heights. For example, Garamond has a much smaller x-height than Arial. As a result, the entire font looks smaller and is harder to read. To compensate, you could increase the font size of the Garamond text. Here you see an example of both fonts side by side for comparison.

Follow a Simple Plan

Organize the elements of your slide in advance. Decide which elements are most important and which are least important and design them accordingly. Numbering and footnotes should be least important. If your slide titles are 44 points and bold and body copy is 36 points, create footnotes that are 18 points. Don't forget to stand back and take a look at your slides. If some minor element jumps out at you, adjust it as necessary—remove the bold, make it smaller, or change the color. The titles don't need to be more than 10 points larger than the slide text.

Create a visual theme. A visual theme allows the graphic representation to express the content. For example, if you're giving a lecture on herb gardening, you might want to use natural-looking colors that emphasize the illustrations and photographs—leaf borders, leaf bullets, or pictures of finished recipes that express the theme visually. Match the look of the presentation to your audience and your organization's desired image.

If your slides are busy, with lots of text and graphics, make the background simple. The more contrast you create between your text and your background, the easier your slides are to read. If you use a 3-D or shadow effect, use it as emphasis. It's the belt and suspenders principle again—don't overdo special effects, or they lose their impact. The same principle works for highly saturated colors—use them in small areas for emphasis.

Consider Color and Rhythm

Audiences naturally read from left to right and from top to bottom. Audiences also notice dark or bright areas before light ones. So place and emphasize items with those two principles in mind. If you have a dark background, lighter areas stand out more because of the brightness and contrast.

Use cooler, muted colors for backgrounds, light or dark. Brighter warmer colors are "sweet"—they're hard to look at for a long time. Light text on a dark background looks a little larger than vice versa. But don't be afraid to use lighter backgrounds with dark text—they create a softer look that is appropriate for many messages.

Think about the rhythm of the entire presentation. Like a piece of music, your presentation should have a regular beat without getting boring. For example, your slides could go like this: text, text, image, text. You can also create a rhythm, such as large image, text, text, smaller images, text, text. To give the eye a rest and keep your audience attentive, you need to create variety. You can do this by varying the slide layouts or using your own variations to place objects on a slide.

Finally, do a usability test. You can even learn from a six-year-old's comments on your work. Then do the same with your colleagues at work. These people can point out issues that you missed, such as "This slide is about gardening. Why are the slides red?" Or "This part is too small for me to read." You'll get a lot of useful feedback and bring in an important element of objectivity. Don't be shy—people love to tell you what they think!

Thanks to graphic designer Stuart Friedman for these tips. He can be reached at graphics@iowatelecom.net.

Relate Graphics to Content

The purpose of graphics is not to make a slide pretty, but to enhance understanding. Therefore, choose graphics that contribute to the meaning of the text, rather than just make the slide look good. Help learners to organize and integrate the information that you are presenting; don't just throw the information at them. Dr. Richard E. Mayer, a professor and researcher in the area of educational psychology at the University of California, Santa Barbara, brings out several principles in his book *Multimedia Learning* (Cambridge University Press, 2001) that can be applied to PowerPoint presentation design:

- Words and pictures help people learn better than words alone. Therefore, do add graphics; don't rely solely on text to get your message across.

- Extraneous words or pictures hinder learning. Therefore, eliminate unnecessary words; too much information overloads the audience. Make sure that graphics are meaningful and help the audience understand the words. Design charts that are simple and clear.

- Placing related words and pictures next to each other or presenting them at the same time helps learning. An example would be a text label pointing to an image or chart. Another example would be using a laser pointer to point to an image while explaining it.

- Organize the content with clear outlines and headings. You can help the audience understand the organization by using sections marked by color coding or recognizable icons.

- Use a conversational style rather than a formal style. Don't use overly formal or stilted language, and avoid jargon.

People learn better from animation with spoken text than from animation with printed text. This means that you need to verbally explain what audiences see. So don't forget that the most important part of the presentation is you.

Summary

In this chapter, you learned all about graphics. The first part of the chapter covered how to insert images on your slides. I discussed finding clip art, using the Clip Organizer, creating a photo album, and inserting graphic files. I explained how to edit pictures and drawing objects.

The second part of the chapter covered shapes, including inserting, formatting, and editing them. Finally, I reviewed some special techniques for laying out a slide with precision and provided some design tips.

The next chapter is all about colors, borders, fills, and 3-D effects.

Chapter 6

Work with Colors, Borders, Fills, and 3-D Effects

How to…

- Choose theme colors
- Customize theme colors
- Create gradient, texture, and pattern backgrounds
- Create a picture background
- Use shape styles
- Format fills and outlines
- Add reflections, glows, and soft edges
- Create shadows
- Add 3-D effects

Color is an essential element of a presentation. Different colors send different messages to your audience. By using colors in borders, fills, backgrounds, and the slides as a whole, you can transform a ho-hum presentation into a forceful one. Add special effects, shadows, and 3-D effects to realize the full power of your message.

Work with Theme Colors

Every template and theme includes default theme colors, a set of 12 colors that is automatically applied as follows:

- Four text and background colors (two dark and two light).

The four background and text colors are automatically swapped between dark and light to retain contrast. Therefore, if you use a dark background, you'll have a light text color and vice versa.

- Six accent colors. These are contrasting colors. They show up in shapes, charts, and so on.
- Hyperlink color. The color is applied to hyperlinked text.
- Followed hyperlink color. The color is applied to a hyperlink after it is clicked to show that the hyperlink has been followed. (Hyperlinks are covered in Chapter 11.)

In addition, templates and themes include a number of alternate theme color sets that you can choose. Theme colors ensure that your presentation has a coordinated look—for example, not only should all titles look the same, but the colors should work well with each other.

You don't have to do anything to work with the default theme colors for your template or theme. PowerPoint automatically assigns the appropriate colors to the elements in your presentation based on the theme colors.

Choose Theme Colors

You can imagine that you would not want to use the same theme colors for selling vacation packages to Hawaii as for selling long-term health care insurance. Even the same presentation might use different theme colors for different situations. For example, if a presentation to employees on their employee benefits program is good news, you might use brighter colors, whereas if the new program represented a cutback, you would use softer colors. In fact, a quick way to give a presentation an entirely new look, or to try out different looks, is to change the theme colors.

To choose different theme colors, click the Design tab. In the Themes group, click the Colors drop-down list to display the Theme Colors gallery, shown in Figure 6-1. If you apply a template, presentation file, or custom theme, you may see additional theme colors.

6

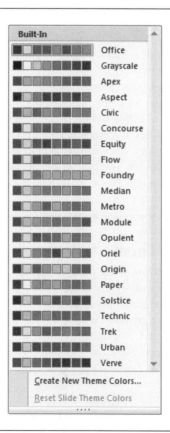

FIGURE 6-1   You can vary the look of your presentation by choosing a different theme color set.

If you open an older presentation, you'll see the colors of its color scheme here. Previous versions of PowerPoint had sets of colors called a color scheme. Also, the hyperlink and followed hyperlink colors do not appear in the theme color sets. However, if you create a new theme color set, as I describe in the next section, you see these two colors and can change them.

A great way to see how the colors look in a larger space is to create a rectangle with a gradient that uses the 10 text, background, and accent colors. As you pass your cursor over the theme colors, the gradient's colors change and you can get a better feel for how the colors look together. I explain how to create gradients later in this chapter, in the "Create Gradient Backgrounds" section.

As you look at the theme colors, you'll see that the colors in each theme are related. One theme might feature blues, greens, and grays—soft colors—while another uses warmer greens, oranges, and browns. One set of theme colors is usually in shades of gray. Each theme color set is designed to create an overall impression that you can apply to your entire presentation.

To choose theme colors, click any set of theme colors to apply it to all the slides in your presentation. To apply it to selected slides, use the Slides tab of the Outline pane to select the slides to which you want to apply the new theme colors. Right-click the set of theme colors you want to use and choose Apply to Selected Slides.

Be consistent with theme colors in your presentation. If you want to use more than one set of theme colors, do so only in a limited way. For example, if you have four sections to your presentation and each presentation has a slide to introduce the new part, use a different set of theme colors only for these section slides and perhaps your overall title slide. The other slides would then all use the basic theme colors. Another option is to use a different theme color for each section of the presentation. Of course, you can fill any shape with any color that you want, as explained later in this chapter—you don't have to limit yourself to the theme colors. However, the value of the theme colors is that they all look good with each other and coordinate all your slides.

Create Your Own Set of Theme Colors

You may think that the themes color choices are pretty ugly, or they simply may not suit your sense of style and design. Fortunately, PowerPoint gives you the flexibility to create any theme colors you can think up. To create a custom set of theme colors, click Create New Theme Colors at the bottom of the Theme Colors gallery. The Create New Theme Colors dialog box opens, shown in Figure 6-2.

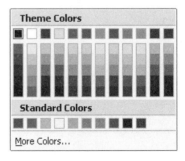

The Create New Theme Colors dialog box shows the 12 colors of the current theme color set. To change a color, click the color you want to change to display the color palette of theme and standard colors, shown here.

Did you know?

Factoring in Lighting and Mood

Conventional wisdom is to use a dark background for presentations shown on a screen and a light background for overheads and printed handouts. The choice actually is more complex. In a dark room, dark backgrounds with light text show up well, but in a light room, a dark background appears faded and the light text does not show up as well. Instead, use dark text against a light background. Also, back in the days when projectors projected a weaker light, people darkened the room during a presentation and avoided very light backgrounds because they were too bright for comfort in the darkness. Today, most projectors are bright enough to allow you to present in a lighted room, so light backgrounds work better.

The purpose of the presentation is another consideration. Yellow or white text against a dark background can appear harsh. When you want a softer impression or perhaps are conveying bad news, use a lighter background. A light green or blue with dark text often works well. However, be sure that the text contrasts sufficiently with the background for good legibility.

6

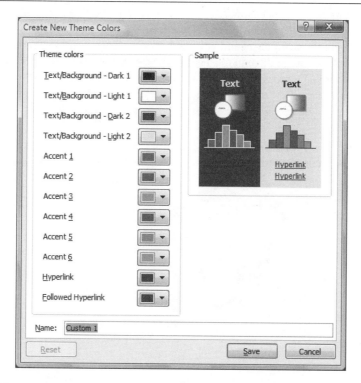

FIGURE 6-2   Use the Create New Theme Colors dialog box to fulfill your own sense of color style.

If you can't find the color you want, click More Colors to open the Colors dialog box, shown in Figure 6-3 with the Standard tab on top. To choose a standard color, choose a hexagon from the Colors palette and click OK to return to the Create New Theme Colors dialog box.

You may not find the color you want on the Standard tab. Many companies have exact specifications for company colors. When it comes to color, the Custom tab, shown in Figure 6-4, is where the fun is.

The simplest way to create a color is to click a color in the main panel. The narrow bar at the right changes the *luminosity*—the brightness; drag it up or down to get the shade you want. The Custom tab also lets you use one of the more formal systems for determining color, RGB or HSL:

- Choose RGB from the Color Model drop-down list to use the red-green-blue (RGB) system, which defines a color by the amount of each primary light color. You can type in a number for each color or use the arrows to change the color by small increments. The numbers must be from 1 to 255; when all three colors are 255, you get white.

- Choose HSL from the Color Model drop-down list to use the hue-saturation-luminosity (HSL) system, which defines a color by hue (the color), saturation (the intensity of the color), and luminosity (the brightness of the color). In the HSL system, you also set all three values at 255 to get white.

Click OK to return to the Create New Theme Colors dialog box. When you've finished changing the theme colors, enter a name in the Name box and click Save. The new theme color set becomes the current theme color set and you can now use it in your presentation. Whenever you need those colors, you'll see them in the Theme Colors section. Even better, PowerPoint also includes several shades and tints of each color, so you have even more choices.

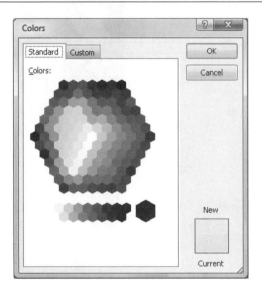

FIGURE 6-3   You have a large choice of colors from the Standard tab of the Colors dialog box.

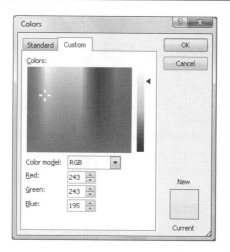

FIGURE 6-4   You can specify any color on the Custom tab.

NOTE   *The Colors dialog box, including the RGB and HSL systems of the Custom Tab, is offered by PowerPoint (and all Microsoft Office applications) whenever you need to choose a color. For example, if you select a rectangle that you inserted on a slide, click the Drawing Tools Format tab, choose Shape Fill, and then choose More Fill Colors, you get the same Colors dialog box. In other words, whenever you need a color, you can use the Colors dialog box.*

Change Backgrounds

Each slide has a background. The background is the bottom-most layer of the slide and is not an object that you can manipulate. You can never place anything behind the background, and it always covers the entire slide. A background can be a solid color, or you can use one of the fill effects discussed in the next four sections. Backgrounds certainly don't have to be dull! Here are some examples:

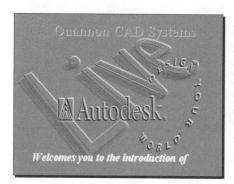

The Effect of Color

Colors elicit emotional responses, so the colors you use are important. However, never sacrifice legibility merely for the sake of a pleasing color combination. Very light backgrounds can cause an uncomfortable glare in a dark room. Similarly, avoid using strong primary colors, such as yellow or red, as backgrounds; they're simply too bright.

Due to the way our eyes work, and because color-perception deficiencies are common, avoid the following color combinations: red/green, brown/green, blue/black, and blue/purple. Here are some pointers about individual colors:

- **Red** Handle with care. It can elicit such emotions as desire and competitiveness. However, it also carries negative connotations, such as financial loss. Red works best as an occasional accent color to make an item stand out.

- **Black** Suggests finality and simplicity. However, in certain circumstances, it is associated with mourning and death.

- **Purple** Can imply immaturity and unimportance.

- **Brown** Connotes uneasiness and passivity.

- **Green** Has positive associations when used as a background color. Researchers believe that it stimulates interaction, which makes greens and teals good colors for trainers, educators, and those whose presentations are intended to generate discussion.

- **Blue** Commonly associated with a calming and conservative effect. However, due to blue's popularity for business presentations, some business audiences now equate blue backgrounds with staleness and unoriginal thinking. When corporations specify blue backgrounds, professional presentation designers typically try to infuse them with some originality and texture.

If you're making a presentation to an international audience, remember that colors have differing connotations in different countries, so do some research.

While background colors help set the emotional tone for your presentation, the colors you use for text, tables, charts, and other graphic elements have a bearing on how well the audience understands and remembers your message. Research has shown that the effective use of selective contrast, known as the *von Restorff effect* (or *isolation effect*), makes audiences remember the outstanding item—and even your entire message—better. An example of this technique is to make certain text larger or brighter than most text or to put it in a shape.

Most experts agree that your theme colors should include one or two bright colors for emphasis—but to preserve the power of these colors, use them with restraint.

On the other hand, there is a trend to create slides with no background. Instead, you use plain white (or off-white, or a very subtle texture) and add images that don't cover the entire slide. Here's an example of this type of slide:

If you don't need many choices and want a quick solution, click the Design tab and then click Background Styles in the Background group. The Background Styles gallery, shown here, opens. The gallery's choices depend on the theme or template you are using.

NOTE *You can, and often do, format the background on the slide master, which I discuss in Chapter 7. The slide master allows you to format the background of the entire presentation in one step, or more than one background for a presentation.*

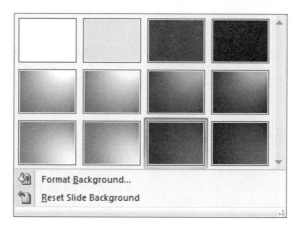

Pass the cursor over one of the backgrounds to see how it looks on the slide. To apply the background to all slides, just click it. To apply the background only to selected slides (you can easily select the slides you want on the Slides tab of the Outline pane of Normal view, or in Slide Sorter view), right-click and choose Apply to Selected Slides. These backgrounds do not affect shapes, images, or text on the slide master. (See Chapter 7 for more on slide masters.) To hide these other objects, check the Hide Background Graphics check box in the Background group of the Design tab.

If you choose one of the lighter background styles in the two left columns, PowerPoint automatically uses dark text for contrast. If you choose one of the darker background styles in the two right columns, PowerPoint uses light text. In this way, your text is always legible.

For more options, in the Background group of the Design tab, choose Format Background from the Background Styles drop-down list to open the Format Background dialog box, shown in Figure 6-5 with the Fill pane displayed.

Right-click the background of the slide (not on any object) and choose Format Background.

You can apply the four background types—solid, gradient, texture, and picture—to the fill of any shape, including a text placeholder. The same principles are applicable to all fillable objects. I discuss fills later in this chapter.

Create Solid Backgrounds

To specify a solid color, choose the Solid Fill option. Then click the Color drop-down arrow to display the theme colors and the standard colors. Click More Colors to open the Colors dialog box, shown in Figures 6-3 and 6-4 and previously discussed in this chapter.

Check the Hide Background Objects check box (see Figure 6-5) to hide any objects on the slide master, such as shapes or images. You may have a presentation that has a great background and a logo on every slide; however, on a slide with a graph, you may want to use a plain color and hide the logo to help the audience focus on the graph. This would be a good slide for which to check the Hide Background Objects check box.

Create Gradient Backgrounds

Choose the Gradient Fill option to specify a gradient. In a *gradient*, the colors vary across the slide. In a one-color gradient, the intensity of the color varies. In a two-color gradient, the background changes from one color to the second. Click the Preset Colors drop-down arrow in the Format Background dialog box to give yourself the choice of a number of preset gradients, with names like Early Sunset, Nightfall, and Desert. These gradients range from soft to exciting; some are quite beautiful.

FIGURE 6-5   The Format Background dialog box offers many ways to create a background for the slides in your presentation. Here you see the dialog box as it looks when you specify a gradient background.

NOTE   *In PowerPoint 2007, you can now have up to ten colors in a gradient, and you have more choices over where the colors change. There are also more types (styles) of gradients.*

To create a gradient background, follow these steps:

1. If you want to apply the background to certain slides, select the slides on the Slides tab of the Outline pane in Normal view (or select the slides in Slide Sorter view).

2. On the Design tab, click Background Styles I Background to open the Format Background dialog box. (Refer to Figure 6-5.)

3. Choose the Gradient Fill option.

4. If you want, choose one of the gradients from the Preset Colors drop-down list and click Close; otherwise, specify the properties of the gradient as described next.

Choose a Gradient Type

PowerPoint offers the following five gradient types, three of which also offer variations. The next step is to decide which gradient type and variation you want.

- **Linear**   The colors are lined up in parallel bars. You can change the angle of the bars by choosing an option from the Direction drop-down list or by specifying an exact angle from the Angle text box.

- **Radial**   The colors radiate out from a circle. The circle's center can be in the middle or at any of four corners. You can choose the location of the gradient's center by choosing an option from the Direction drop-down list.

- **Rectangular**   The colors radiate out from a rectangle. The rectangle's center can be in the middle or at any of four corners. You can choose the location of the rectangle's center by choosing an option from the Direction drop-down list.

- **Path**   The colors radiate out concentrically from a shape. This type offers no options and is not distinguishable from the rectangular gradient type when used on a background or rectangle. It's most visible when you use a star shape.

- **Shade from Title**   The colors radiate from the slide's title placeholder. This gradient is available only for backgrounds, not for shapes.

Figure 6-6 shows a three-color (black, gray, and white) gradient background using four of the five gradient types.

Specify Gradient Colors

You can specify up to ten colors for a gradient. You can also decide where each color starts and its transparency. (Transparency is not applicable for a background, but can be used when you fill a shape.) This gives you lots of options!

Each color is called a *stop*. By default, there are two stops, or the number of stops you most recently created in the current PowerPoint session. To see the number of stops, click the Gradient Stops drop-down list. To add a stop, click Add. To remove a stop, select it and click Remove.

To specify the color, position, and transparency of a stop, select it from the Gradient Stops drop-down list. Then choose a color from the Color drop-down list. See "Create Your Own Set of Theme Colors," earlier in this chapter, for details on choosing colors.

Specify the Stop Position

You can think of a gradient as having a beginning—the 0% point—and an end—the 100% point. If you create a two-color gradient with stops at 0% and 100%, the two colors meet in the middle, as shown on the left in Figure 6-7. If you change Stop 2's position to 50%, the color change is between 0% and 50%, as shown on the right in Figure 6-7.

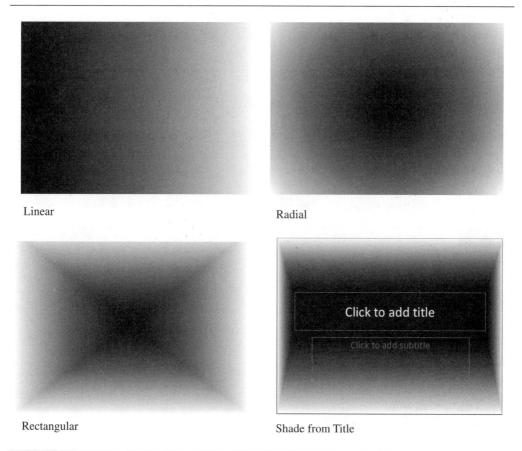

Linear

Radial

Rectangular

Shade from Title

6

FIGURE 6-6   PowerPoint 2007 includes several gradient types.

Stops don't need to be equidistant; you can create interesting effects by bunching them up on one end of the gradient and then spreading them out on the other end, as shown here:

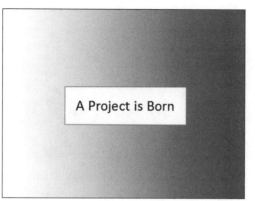 

FIGURE 6-7 You can specify where the colors of a gradient meet by changing their stop position.

This gradient has six stops, as follows:

- Stop 1: White at 0%
- Stop 2: Medium-dark blue at 10%
- Stop 3: Dark blue at 20%
- Stop 4: Light blue at 25%
- Stop 5: White at 80%
- Stop 6: Dark blue at 100%

As you can see, this arrangement allows for light title text and dark body text on the slide. To set the stop positions, choose a stop from the Gradient Stops drop-down list and drag the Stop Position slider. You can also enter a number or use the arrows to change the number. As you change the position, you see the result on your slide (move the dialog box over, if necessary). But remember that unless you plan a gradient carefully, combining light and dark colors may make some of your text illegible.

Click Close to apply the gradient to the selected slide or slides. Click Apply to All to apply the gradient to the entire presentation. If you change your mind after you close the dialog box, click Undo on the Quick Access toolbar to undo the gradient.

Create Picture Backgrounds

Perhaps the most common type of background is a picture. You can use any picture you like, from a file or clip art. You can insert the picture once, which is most common, or tile it to create a texture.

Use a Picture as a Background

When you insert a picture, PowerPoint automatically stretches your picture to cover the entire slide, so you don't need to worry about its size. As with any background, you need to make sure that your text is legible.

You can insert the image on the slide as an object rather than as a background. You have more options for editing the image when it's an object. (See Chapter 5 for more ways to manipulate pictures in PowerPoint.) If you then want to use it as a background, right-click the picture, and choose Save as Picture. Then you can insert it as a background. Many people use third-party software, such as Adobe Photoshop, to create montages with sophisticated effects and then insert those pictures as a background.

Experiment to get the effect you want. A picture can create a sophisticated effect on a slide, so it's worth the effort. Figure 6-8 shows an example of a scenic picture used as a background.

To insert a picture as a background, choose the Picture or Texture Fill option in the Format Background dialog box, as shown in Figure 6-9. Then do one of the following:

- Click File to open the Insert Picture dialog box, where you can choose any picture on your system or network.

- Click Clipboard to paste a picture onto the background. First, you need to copy the image to the clipboard from some other location.

- Click ClipArt to open the Select Picture dialog box. You can scroll down to browse through all the clip art or enter a keyword in the Search Text box and click Go to filter the images. Choose one and click OK.

FIGURE 6-8   Here a beautiful photo is used as a background. To increase legibility, the text placeholder has a partially transparent background.

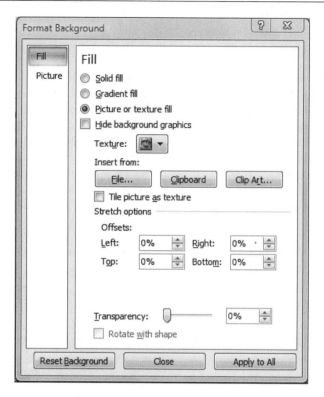

FIGURE 6-9 When you choose Picture or Texture Fill in the Format Background dialog box, you can insert an image as a background.

Some other settings offer ways to get specific results:

- Uncheck the Tile Picture as Texture check box to avoid getting a tiled array. I explain this option in the next section.
- Use the Stretch Options section of the dialog box to move the picture from the edges of the slide. You can use this technique to minimize distorting a picture. However, the default color shows on the rest of the slide where the image no longer appears. Instead, you may want to simply insert the image on the slide at the desired size and location.
- Set the transparency by dragging the Transparency slider.

NOTE *The Rotate with Shape check box applies only to shapes, not to backgrounds.*

A new feature allows you to recolor as well as change the contrast and brightness of the background picture, just as you can for a picture that you insert on a slide. Click the Picture category in the left pane of the dialog box. On the right you can do the following:

- Click the Recolor drop-down list to choose a tint for the picture. (For more information see "Recolor Graphics" in Chapter 5.)
- Change the contrast and brightness. (I explain this feature in "Adjust Contrast and Brightness" in Chapter 5.)
- Click Reset Picture to return it to its original settings.
- Click Reset Background to return to the default background.

When you're done, click Close to apply the picture to the background of the current or selected slides. Click Apply to All to apply the picture to the entire presentation. After closing the dialog box, click Undo on the Quick Access toolbar to undo changes that you don't like.

Create a Texture Background

6

Texture backgrounds can look as if you have placed a physical object with a texture, such as wood, marble, or water droplets, on your slide. Textures are pictures, and you can use your own images, if you like. To use a texture background, click the Textures drop-down arrow in the Format Background dialog box to display the Textures gallery, shown here. Textures generally provide an understated, dignified impression, but make sure that they don't make your text hard to read.

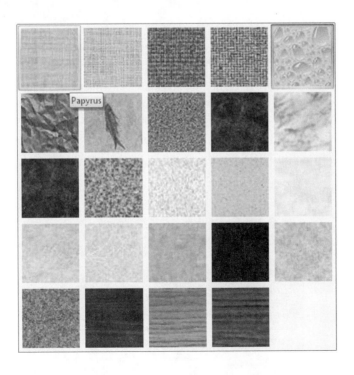

To create your own texture from an image file, click File, Clipboard, or ClipArt, as explained in the previous section. When you use an image, check the Tile Picture as Texture check box to create tiles of the picture. In the Tiling Options section that appears, you can do the following:

- Offset the picture by a specified number of points in the X (horizontal) and Y (vertical) directions.

- Scale the picture in the X and Y directions. To avoid distorting the image, use the same scale in both directions. The smaller the scale, the more tiles PowerPoint creates. Here you see an image inserted as a picture on the left, and tiled at 15% on the right. A very different look!

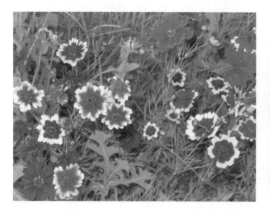 

- Align the drawing from one of eight directions. The Alignment setting determines where PowerPoint starts tiling. The image is cut off at the other end. For example, if you align the image from the top left, it may be cut off at the bottom and right of the slide.

- Create a mirrored effect horizontally, vertically, or both. You can create interesting (and weird) effects by mirroring the images, as shown here. (Don't expect to put any text on a slide like this, though!)

Not all graphic files work as textures. Because of this tiling effect, the best graphics for textures are simple and repetitive, like the samples provided with PowerPoint. After you choose a texture, click Close or Apply to All to return to your presentation.

You can find more than 100 free seamless textures at http://www.ppted.com/001100/back/ htdeppt2007.html.

Use Shape Styles

Once you have your background, you may want to add some shapes, whether geometrical shapes, text boxes, or text placeholders. Chapter 2 explained how to insert text boxes and placeholders, and Chapter 5 explained how to insert shapes. Here I explain how to format them.

You can enhance your shapes by formatting their outlines, fills, and effects. To make this easy, PowerPoint has a number of preset *shape styles,* which are combinations of formatting that you can choose from a gallery. To apply a shape style to any selected objects, display the Format tab that appears and click the More button in the Shape Styles group to display the gallery, shown here:

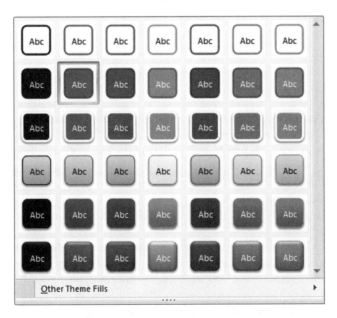

Pass the cursor over any option to see how it looks on your slide. (You may have to move the object so that the gallery doesn't cover it up.) When you find a format that you like, click it to apply it. Choose Other Theme Fills to see the same Background Style options available from the Background group on the Design tab, as explained earlier in this chapter.

Of course, you can individually format outlines, fills, and effects. The sections that follow explain how.

6

Format Outlines

Every theme color set includes a default color for shape outlines, generally the Accent 1 color. An *outline* is the border around a shape, text box, text placeholder, or picture. You can change the outline color or choose not to use an outline at all. For example, by default, text placeholders have no outline.

To format the outline of any object, select it and click the Format tab that appears. In the Shape Styles group, click the Shape Outline button to display the color palette of theme and standard colors, shown here. Choose No Outline to remove an existing outline, and choose More Outline Colors to open the Colors dialog box, explained in detail earlier in this chapter.

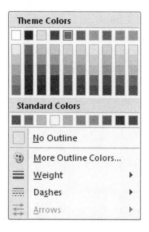

Choose Weight to change the thickness of the outline, and choose Dashes to create a dashed or dotted outline. I discussed these options in the "Format Lines" section of Chapter 5, because the same options apply to lines that you draw. The default thickness of an outline is often too thin to be clearly visible, so try making it thicker if you're not getting the result that you want.

Another way to format the outline of a shape, and find more options, is to click the dialog box launcher arrow in the Shape Styles group of the Format tab (or simply right-click the shape and choose Format Shape). In Figure 6-10, you see the Format Shape dialog box with the Line Color pane displayed.

You can choose No Line to remove an outline, or change the outline's color in the Color drop-down list. The new option is that you can format the outline as a gradient. In most cases, you want a fairly thick line, so that viewers can see the gradient. Here you see a shape with a gradient outline at a 225° angle to create the effect of light coming from the upper-left corner:

> **Annual Results**

You rarely want a border around a picture unless you want to create a picture-frame effect. Text placeholders usually don't have borders, but text boxes can go either way: use a border when you want the text to stand out from the rest of the slide's text. Omitting the outline in a shape creates a subtle effect; on the other hand, an outline can make the shape more powerful.

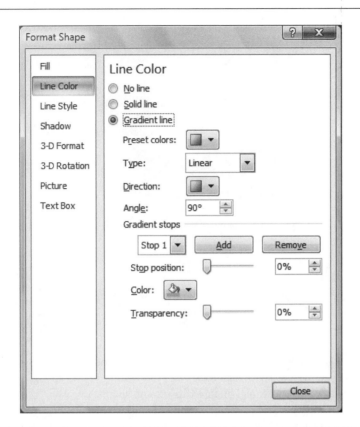

FIGURE 6-10   Use the Line Color pane of the Format Shape dialog box to format the color of outlines.

Figure 6-11 shows some shapes using various outline options. Try out various options to find the effects you like.

Work with Fills

A *fill* is what's inside an enclosed space, such as a shape or a text box. Every theme color set includes a default fill color, usually the Accent 1 color, but you can change any fill. You can also use the same fill effects for object fills as you can for backgrounds—gradients, textures, and pictures.

> **TIP**   *After you format a shape, you may want to make that formatting the default for new shapes that you insert. To do so, right-click the shape and choose Set as Default Shape. Thereafter, any shape that you insert will have the same fill, outline, and effects as the selected shape.*

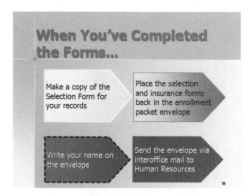

FIGURE 6-11 Each of the arrow shapes has a different outline format. The lower-right arrow shape has no outline.

Change Fill Color

To change the fill color quickly, select the object and display the Format tab that appears. Click the Shape Fill drop-down arrow in the Shape Styles group to display the options shown here:

If you've read this far, you are familiar with these choices. You can choose from theme colors or standard colors, select No Fill, or choose More Fill Colors to open the Colors dialog box.

You can create gradient, texture, and picture fills for any shape. In other words, the same effects that I covered in the "Change Backgrounds" section are available for any fill, as follows:

- Choose Picture to open the Insert Picture dialog box, where you can select a picture file.

- Choose Gradient | More Gradients to open the Format Shape dialog box with the Fill pane displayed. Choose the Gradient Fill option to see the same options shown earlier in Figure 6-5 and discussed in the "Create Gradient Backgrounds" section.

- Choose Texture to display the Texture gallery, discussed in the "Create a Texture Background" section earlier in this chapter.

Here you see a slide containing picture fills:

Create Background-Matching, Transparent, and Rotating Fills

Some additional options are available only in the Format Shape dialog box. Right-click any object and choose Format Shape to open the Format Shape dialog box. In the Fill pane, shown in Figure 6-12, choose the Background option to set the fill to the same color (or effect) as the slide background. Be careful, though. If your background is a solid color and the object has no line, it promptly disappears because you can't distinguish it from the background!

You can use invisible objects in PowerPoint games and quizzes to create invisible hyperlinked buttons. For example, in a quiz, if you want users to click anywhere on a slide to return to the previous slide (to retry answering the question), you can cover the entire slide with an invisible rectangle that is hyperlinked to the previous slide. Chapter 11 explains how to add hyperlinks to objects.

6

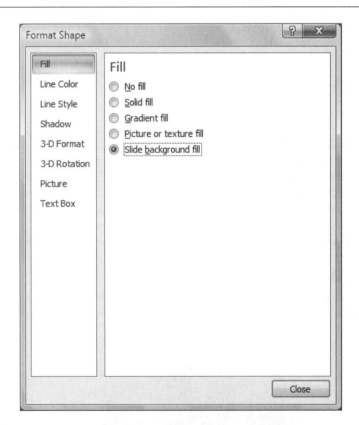

FIGURE 6-12   You can use the Fill pane of the Format Shape dialog box to create a fill that matches your slide's background.

Although backgrounds can be transparent, transparency becomes truly meaningful for shapes. Solid, gradient, picture, and texture fills can be transparent. You can create great effects by layering transparent objects or placing a partially transparent object on a background. Transparency can range from 0% to 100%. Using this feature, you can create a gradient that ranges from no transparency to partial or full transparency.

In the Fill pane of the Format Shape dialog box, drag the Transparency slider bar or type a percentage. As you change the transparency, you can immediately see the result on your slide. (You may have to move the dialog box to see the selected object.) Look back to Figure 6-8 to see a slide that uses a 40% transparent text box over a picture background. The fill makes the text more readable but still lets the picture background show through.

To create an invisible object when your background is not a solid, instead of using the Background option, make the object 100% transparent. In fact, transparency is the most common way to make an object invisible.

For gradient, picture, and texture fills, you can check the Rotate with Shape check box to rotate the fill if you rotate the shape.

Add Special Effects

PowerPoint 2007 has added a number of special effects that allow you to create looks that were difficult, if not impossible, previously. These include reflections, glows, and soft edges. (I discuss shadows, bevels, and 3-D rotation— which are 3-D effects— in the following section, "Create 3-D Effects.") These effects are collectively called *shape effects.*

You can quickly format objects by using theme effects. On the Design tab, click Effects in the Themes group and choose one of the built-in effects. These theme effects create a unified style for all of the objects in your presentation. Although you can customize theme colors (as explained at the beginning of this chapter) and theme fonts (covered in Chapter 3), you cannot customize theme effects.

Reflect Your Objects

The new reflection effects add a full or partial mirroring of your object. Generally, you use reflections for the beautiful effect. Here you see an example of a reflected picture fill:

To add a reflection to an object, select it and click the Format tab that appears. Then choose Shape Effects | Reflection from the Shape Styles group. The Reflection gallery, shown here, opens. The variations are subtle, so try several out to see the differences. As you pass your cursor over an option, you see the result on your slide. Click to apply the one you like.

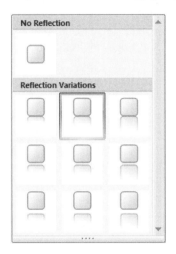

6

To add a reflection to text, select the text and choose Text Effects | Reflection from the WordArt Styles group of the Format tab. Make sure that the text is still legible, especially if you have more than one line of text.

Add a Glow

A *glow* is a fuzzy band of color surrounding a shape. You can create a glow in any color and in four sizes. To add a glow, select the shape and display the Format tab that appears. From the Shape Styles group, choose Shape Effects | Glow to display the Glow gallery, shown here. You can choose More Glow Colors to open the Color palette and choose from theme colors and standard colors, and then you can choose More Colors to open the Colors dialog box and choose any color you want.

Add Soft Edges

Like a glow, a soft edge affects the edge of a shape, but the effect applies inward toward the center of the shape rather than to the outside of the shape. You can choose from six values, measured in points. The larger the Soft Edge value, the more obvious the effect—however, the shape looks smaller.

To add soft edges, select an object and display the Format tab that appears. From the Shape Styles group, choose Shape Effects | Soft Edges to display the Soft Edges gallery, shown here:

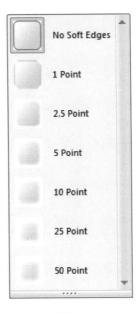

Look at Figure 6-13 to get an idea of the difference between a glow and soft edges. The two ovals started out the same size. The one on the left has the largest glow. The one on the right has 25-point soft edges. (The next smaller size, 10 point, is hard to see.) Notice how much smaller the oval on the right looks.

FIGURE 6-13   The glow and soft edges effects both soften the edges of a shape, but in a different way. The oval on the left has the glow effect; the one on the right has the soft edges effect.

Create 3-D Effects

PowerPoint can create 3-D graphics that include shadows, bevels (edge treatments), 3-D rotation, materials (surface treatments), thickness, elevation, and lighting. A simple 3-D effect is a shadow, which gives the impression that the shape is raised off the slide's surface. True 3-D effects are more complex and actually draw a third dimension. Both shadows and 3-D effects come with loads of options and settings and can quickly improve the quality of your presentation's graphics. But remember not to overuse these effects and be consistent in the effects you choose.

Create Shadows

Shadows create a subtle yet effective 3-D impression. Here you see a slide with several graphics. The ones on the left use shadows and look much more three-dimensional than the newsletters on the right.

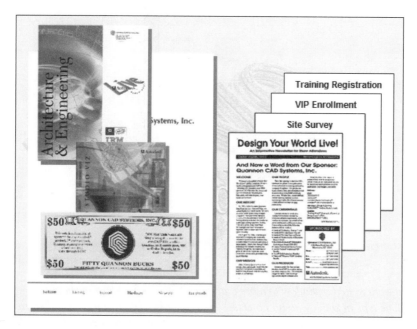

The graphics here were created by scanning the actual documents, inserting them as pictures, and then adding shadow effects, as discussed next.

To create a shadow, select any object (except text) and display the Format tab. From the Shape Styles group, choose Shape Effects | Shadow to display the Shadow gallery, shown next. (To shadow text, click Text Effects | Shadow in the WordArt Styles group of the same tab.) You can pass the cursor over a shadow type to see the effect immediately on your slide (although the gallery often covers up most of the slide). Choose No Shadow to eliminate a shadow you have created previously. Otherwise, choose any of the options. Notice that the options come in groups, Outer, Inner, and Perspective. You may need to try a few shadows out before you find what you like.

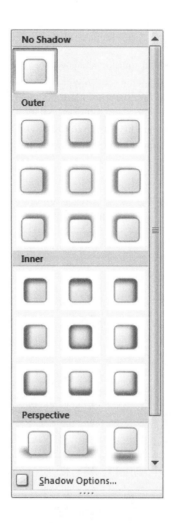

TIP   *If you want to add a shadow to more than one object on a slide, you should generally add the same type of shadow to all objects, so that it looks like the light is coming from the same angle for all the objects. When you create 3-D effects, they should mimic the real world to some extent; otherwise, the effect may be confusing to your audience.*

Some colors and shapes show up a shadow better than others. A shadow that looks great on a rose-colored, rectangular shape may be scarcely noticeable on a green, star shape. Semitransparent fills let the shadow show through, which can create a muddled effect. The color of the shadow is important. Often the shadow's color is too similar to either the object's fill or the slide background. You can change the color of a shadow, as I explain next.

If a shadow doesn't turn out to your satisfaction, you still have a lot more options. On the Shadow gallery, click Shadow Options to display the Format Shape dialog box, with the Shadow pane displayed, as shown in Figure 6-14.

You can click the Presets drop-down arrow to display the same options available from the Shadow gallery. Click the Color drop-down arrow to choose the shadow's color from the selections shown next. Note the shades of gray. Usually shadows are gray and darker than the object, as you have probably noticed in real life. However, other colors can create a fun effect. Remember that to be noticed, the shadow needs to contrast with both the object's fill color and the slide's background. On the other hand, you don't want the shadow effect to distract your audience from the shape. You may want to choose a lighter gray for a

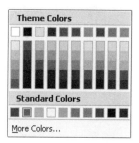

dark background or a darker gray for a light background. Remember that the main purpose of a shadow is to make the shape itself appear to stand out from the surface of the slide.

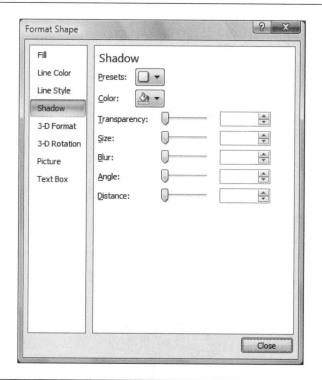

FIGURE 6-14   Use the Shadow pane of the Format Shape dialog box to fine-tune your shadows.

To get exactly the shadow effect you want, you can also specify the following:

- **Transparency**   You can make shadows transparent so that other objects behind the shadow, including the background (if any), show through, as you can see in the cup's shadow shown here:

- **Size**   Generally, shadows are 100% of the size of their object, but you can change that to create the effect of a very close light (and larger shadow), or vice versa.
- **Blur**   A blur creates a soft shadow edge. In the real world, multiple light sources create soft shadows.
- **Angle**   The angle determines the direction of the shadow, and therefore the apparent direction of the light.
- **Distance**   Generally, shadows are attached to their objects and have a 0-point distance from them. You can increase the distance to give the appearance of a detached shadow (like Peter Pan's!). An object that's above a surface would have a detached shadow. Adding a distance makes the shadow stand out much more.

Create 3-D Shapes

You can take a further step and create realistic 3-D shapes. A 3-D shape displays sides and shading like a real three-dimensional object. Here you see a slide with a 3-D shape:

Courtesy of MasterGraphics (http://www.masterg.com).

This is the final slide of the presentation and invites the audience to "test drive" the new software that the company is selling. You could create this 3-D shape by inserting a rectangle, choosing a solid fill color and no outline, and then adding a 3-D depth and rotation, as discussed in this section.

PowerPoint comes with two 3-D shapes, a can (cylinder) and a cube. There's also a beveled rectangle.

You usually start with a 2-D shape that you insert on the slide. (You can also use an imported vector graphic that you have ungrouped. See "Group and Ungroup Objects" in Chapter 5.) When you insert the shape, you're looking at it in a 2-D view. You could say that you're looking at it from the top or the front. If you add a depth, which is the third dimension, you can't see it until you rotate the object in the third dimension. Here you see a 2-D rectangle, and the same rectangle with a depth and 3-D rotation:

Rotate Objects in 3-D

PowerPoint comes with a number of preset rotations. Each 3-D rotation assumes that the viewer is standing in a different position vis-à-vis the object. As with shadows, you don't want to use different 3-D effects on several objects on a slide—it could give your audience vertigo! You can create classy effects using 3-D, but use it with constraint.

You can quickly rotate an object in 3-D space. If you start with the box or cylinder, this is all you need to do. If you start with a 2-D object, you need to add depth as well, as I explain in the "Control 3-D Depth and Contours" section further on in this chapter. To rotate an object in 3-D, follow these steps:

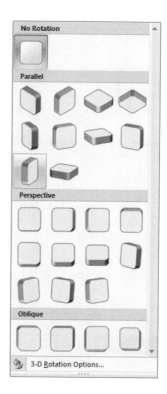

1. Select the object.

2. Click the Format tab that appears.

3. In the Shape Styles group, choose Shape Effects I 3-D Rotation to display the 3-D Rotation gallery:

4. Choose one of the rotation options in the gallery. Note that you can hover the mouse over an option to immediately see the result in the object, although the gallery sometimes obscures the object.

The 3-D Rotation gallery has three sections:

- **Parallel**   Parallel views don't show perspective; parallel lines stay parallel.
- **Perspective**   Perspective views converge parallel lines as they go off into the distance. The typical example is the rails of a railroad track that appear to touch in the distance.
- **Oblique**   Oblique views show two sides of a 3-D object, in a kind of diagonal approach.

For more precise control over the angles of rotation, click 3-D Rotation Options to open the Format Shape dialog box with the 3-D Rotation pane displayed, as shown in Figure 6-15.

 *Right-click the object and choose Format Shape. Click the 3-D Rotation option.*

To quickly apply one of the preset rotations, click the Presets drop-down list. These are the same options that you see in the 3-D Rotation gallery.

You can separately control the X, Y, and Z rotation of any object. A 0,0,0 rotation means that there is no rotation and you're looking at the object from the top in a 2-D view. To manually change the rotation, use the following controls:

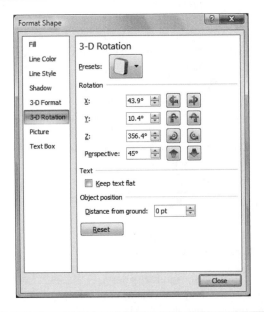

FIGURE 6-15   The 3-D Rotation pane of the Format Shape dialog box lets you fine-tune the rotation of shapes in 3-D.

- **X:**   Rotates the object to the left or right. You can use the Left or Right button to rotate the object several degrees at a time, or enter a value in the X text box. As you increase the number, the right side of the object rotates toward you and the left side rotates away from you.

- **Y:**   Rotates the object up or down. You can use the Up or Down button to rotate the object several degrees at a time, or enter a value in the Y text box. As you increase the number, the top side of the object rotates toward you and the bottom side rotates away from you.

- **Z:**   Rotates the object clockwise or counterclockwise. You can use the Clockwise or Counter-clockwise button to rotate the object several degrees at a time, or enter a value in the Z text box. As you increase the number, you are turning the object counterclockwise. This is like 2-D rotation.

Experiment with these settings so that you can see for yourself how they work. It's easier to understand when you try it out for yourself!

Create 3-D Beveled Edges

A *bevel* is a 3-D effect that controls the edges of objects. PowerPoint 2007 has new bevel settings that can create professional-looking 3-D effects. To add a bevel to an object, select the object. In the Shape Styles group of the Format tab that appears, choose Shape Effects | Bevel to display the Bevel gallery, shown here:

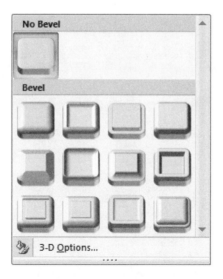

You can hover the mouse over a bevel to immediately see the result in the object; however, you may need to move the object if the Bevel gallery hides it. When you see the bevel you like, click it. (The tooltips even give them fun names like Cool Slant and Art Deco.) The following illustration shows some examples of the donut shape with a depth of 22 points and six different bevel treatments. (I explain how to add depth next.) You can see that the only difference among the objects is the top edge of the donut. As with most 3-D effects, it's a good idea to choose an effect and stick with it throughout the presentation.

You can specify the width and height of any bevel option and you can also create bottom bevels for the bottom edge of 3-D objects. From the Bevel gallery, choose 3-D Options or right-click an object, choose Format Shape, and click the 3-D Format option to open the Format Shape dialog box, with the 3-D Format pane displayed, as shown in Figure 6-16.

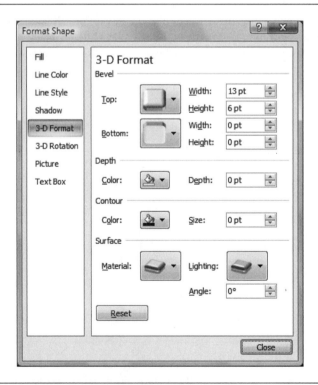

FIGURE 6-16 The 3-D Format pane of the Format Shape dialog box offers numerous settings for specifying how a 3-D object looks.

In the Bevel section, you can choose any bevel style from the Top or Bottom drop-down list. Then you can change the values in the Height and Width boxes. Increasing the height and width makes a bevel more dramatic; some of the bevel types are subtle and not easily noticed at their default values.

Should you create a top or bottom bevel? It depends on the 3-D rotation you are using. Generally, you won't be able to see both clearly, so pick the one that's most visible. Of course, you can always add both, but the effect of the bevel that's at the back side of the object won't be apparent.

Control 3-D Depth and Contours

To create a 3-D object from a 2-D one, you need to add depth. To add depth, follow these steps:

1. Right-click the object and choose Format Shape to open the Format Shape dialog box.
2. Choose the 3-D Format option.
3. In the Depth section, enter a depth value in points. Remember that 72 points equals one inch.
4. To see the effect, remember that you need to rotate the object in 3-D. With the Format Shape dialog box still open, choose the 3-D Rotation category and choose one of the rotations from the Presets drop-down gallery.

You can change the color of the extrusion portion of the 3-D object, the part that shows the object's depth. In the 3-D Format pane, in the Depth section, choose a color from the Color drop-down list. Change the color for dramatic purpose, but note that a markedly different 3-D color is not a realistic effect.

NOTE *Regardless of the 3-D effect, you can fill the front face of the object with any of the PowerPoint fill options mentioned in the section "Change Backgrounds" earlier in this chapter.*

A contour is like an outline, but it outlines all the edges of the 3-D shape that are displayed in its current rotation. In the Contours section, choose a color and the width of the contour in points. A wide contour makes the edges of the shape much clearer.

Figure 6-17 shows the donut shape in several variations.

Specify Material and Lighting

You can choose options that display the surface of your 3-D object to look like it's made of various materials. These options display different types of highlights that seem to vary the shininess, translucency, and lighting. Some materials are meant to look more realistic; others are more stylistic. You can also choose from a number of lighting options that mimic both realistic lighting situations and those that a professional photographer might create. The materials and lighting effects are meant to be used together, because some materials look better with specific types of lighting.

6

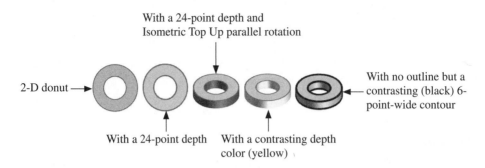

With a 24-point depth and
Isometric Top Up parallel rotation

2-D donut

With no outline but a
contrasting (black) 6-
point-wide contour

With a 24-point depth   With a contrasting depth
color (yellow)

FIGURE 6-17   This 2-D donut passed through several steps in its transformation to a 3-D
donut.

These options might seem complex, but PowerPoint is not like a professional rendering
program where you can specify hundreds of material types and the lighting location of dozens of
lights by x, y, z coordinates accurate to six decimal places. Just try out some options and see what
you like. When you find a combination that suits you, stick with it to create your own object style.

TIP   *You'll see the difference in the effects more clearly when you use a 2-D object with a
depth that also has some curvature to the object, or a rounded bevel added.*

To specify a material, follow these steps:

1. Right-click the object and choose Format Shape.

2. Click the 3-D Format option to display the 3-D Format pane, shown previously
in Figure 6-16.

3. From the Material drop-down list, choose one of the options, shown here, in the
Standard, Special Effect, or Translucent sections:

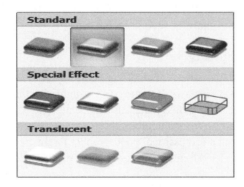

To specify the type of lighting, choose one of the options, shown here, from the Lighting drop-down list:

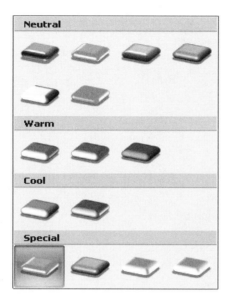

You can also change the angle of the lighting by entering a value in the Angle text box. The angle determines the apparent source of the lights.

TIP   *A good way to get a feel for the angles is to click and hold the up or down arrow to see the light's highlights move around the object.*

Summary

This chapter started off by exploring theme colors and how you can use them to create a uniform look in your presentation. Then I explained how to create any background you want—from plain colors to gradient, textures, and pictures.

I next discussed formatting shapes. You can use shape styles or individually format outlines and fills. Additional effects that you can use are reflections, glows, and soft edges.

The simplest 3-D effects are shadows, which give the impression that an object is raised off the surface of the slide and therefore casts a shadow. The chapter ended with a complete discussion of 3-D objects, including 3-D rotation, bevels, depth, contours, materials, and lighting.

The next chapter explains how to coordinate elements throughout an entire presentation with slide masters, layouts, and themes.

Chapter 7

Coordinate Presentations with Slide Masters, Layouts, and Themes

How to...

- Format and manage slide masters
- Create custom layouts
- Format the handout master
- Format the notes master
- Save custom themes
- Set page size
- Create your own template

The past few chapters have focused a lot on creating a presentation, but PowerPoint has a secret hidden beneath the text and objects you add to each slide. A slide master is a controlling level that's underneath all the slides in your presentation. Layouts define which components a slide contains. A new feature of PowerPoint 2007 is the ability to create your own slide layouts. I've discussed the new themes in previous chapters. You can also save custom themes. In this chapter, you learn how to use masters, layouts, and themes to coordinate and polish the look of an entire presentation.

Format the Slide Master

A slide is made up of three major layers: the background, the slide master, and objects. The background was discussed in Chapter 6; it is a rectangle at the bottom-most layer of each slide. Objects are the top layer; you can easily move, resize, or format them. Objects include shapes (whether drawing objects, text placeholders, or text boxes) graphics, sounds, and movies. The object layer is the default mode of functioning in PowerPoint. When you work on your slide, you most often work on this object layer.

The slide master is between the background and the objects. You need to go into a special Slide Master view to access the slide master. You use slide masters to create uniform features throughout a presentation. You can, and often do, specify a background on the slide master; if you do, the presentation uses this background. In this situation, the slide master controls the background as well.

The slide master includes any text or graphics that you want to appear on every slide. For example, you may want a company's logo on each slide. Although the logo is an object, because you insert it on the slide master, it appears on each slide and you cannot select or manipulate it in any way except from Slide Master view.

In addition, the slide master acts like a template to control most text properties, such as font, font size, color, bullet style, shadows, and special effects. These properties are attached to the text placeholders, which are also on the slide master. However, you can move, resize, and delete the text placeholders as if they were objects on your slide. Of course, because text is on the object layer, you can change these properties directly on each slide. However, to make global changes to the entire presentation, you use the slide master.

NOTE *You can have several slide masters for a presentation. Each slide master controls only those slides that use that slide master.*

You can make changes to a slide master and save the resulting presentation as a template. Then, each time you start a new presentation based on that template, your text is formatted the way you want. Any other changes you made to the slide master, such as inserting a logo, slide numbers, or your name, also appear in the new presentation. PowerPoint templates are saved as .potx or .potm files. (If your template includes macros, which I cover in Chapter 13, you need to use the .potm filename extension.) In the section "Create Your Own Templates" at the end of this chapter, I explain how to use the master to create your own template.

You can also save your changes as a theme. The main differences between a template and a theme are as follows:

- A template provides design information, such as a background and font formatting, but can also contain slides with content. A theme just provides design information. It can't contain slides.

- You can apply a theme to Word and Excel documents; you can't do this with a template. (Note that the backgrounds in themes are unique to PowerPoint; they don't carry over to Word or Excel.)

You don't need to use the slide master to create a presentation. The template or theme may be all you need. You can also make changes to the theme colors and background and quickly apply them to the entire presentation, as explained in Chapter 6.

However, if you decide to use the slide master, you should use it early in the process of creating a presentation. (Because you need to know all about slide formatting to work with slide masters, I waited to explain them until I explained all the essential PowerPoint features.) First, set up the global features you want on the slide master and then make as few exceptions to individual slides as possible. This procedure saves you from making changes to many individual slides. It also ensures a uniform look for the entire presentation.

Enter Slide Master View

To enter Slide Master view, press SHIFT and click the Normal View button, which appears with other view buttons at the bottom-right corner of your screen. You can also click the View tab and choose Slide Master from the Presentation Views group. PowerPoint opens the Slide Master view, shown in Figure 7-1. You can control formatting for your entire presentation from this view.

Note the large number of layouts available on the left. The layout that is active when you enter Slide Master view corresponds to the layout of the current slide. If you immediately enter Slide Master view after creating a new presentation, the layout for a title slide is active because, by default, a new presentation opens with one title slide.

To exit Slide Master view, click the Normal View icon or click Close Master View on the Slide Master tab.

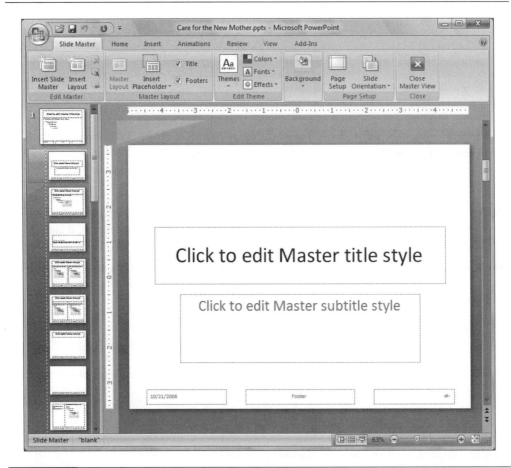

The slide master controls repeating elements and placeholder text formatting for the entire presentation.

Manage Slide Masters

When you enter Slide Master view, the ribbon changes to provide tabs that are useful for formatting the slide master, as shown here:

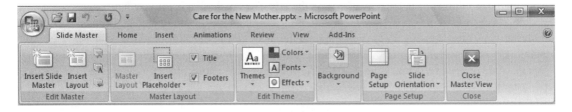

You can add additional slide masters. Each slide master starts with the same layouts. You can add or delete layouts and change the graphics, background, and text formatting. To add a slide master, display the Slide Master tab and choose Insert Slide Master from the Edit Master group. You see the masters displayed at the left, as shown in Figure 7-2. The larger slide represents the master itself, whereas the smaller slides show the individual layouts for that master. Therefore, changes that you make with the larger slide selected affect the entire master; changes that you make with a specific layout selected affect only slides using that layout. For example, you can change the background for just one layout, and only slides using that layout will display that background.

7

FIGURE 7-2   Each slide master contains its own list of layouts.

If you have more than one master, you can delete any additional masters. To delete a master, right-click the master's large slide in the left pane and choose Delete Master. Alternatively, you can select the slide master's large slide and click Delete Slide in the Edit Master group of the Slide Master tab.

Normally, a master is deleted when all slides using the master are deleted or when you choose a new design template and apply it to all the slides in the presentation. You can prevent a master from being automatically deleted by *preserving* it. Select the master you want to preserve in the left pane and click Preserve in the Edit Master group of the Slide Master tab.

You can rename the master. Click the master's large slide in the left pane and choose Rename in the Edit Master group of the Slide Master tab. Type a new name in the Rename Master dialog box and click Rename. You see the change immediately on the status bar.

Adding a template or theme automatically adds a slide master to your presentation. Usually, you add a template or theme from Normal view, on the Design tab, as explained in Chapter 2. However, you have additional options when you add a template or theme in Slide Master view. Follow these steps:

1. Go to Slide Master view. If you want to replace an existing slide master, select it in the left pane.

2. Click Themes in the Edit Theme group of the Slide Master tab. The Themes gallery opens.

3. To use one of the themes from the Themes gallery, right-click it and choose one of the following:

   - **Apply to Selected Slide Master**   Replaces that slide master with the new one
   - **Add as New Slide Master**   Adds a new slide master

4. To use a template or a theme that isn't in the Themes gallery, click Browse for Themes at the bottom of the gallery. In the Choose Theme or Themed Document dialog box, choose a theme, template, or presentation file and click Apply to replace the selected slide master.

If you have more than one slide master and want to make changes that apply to every slide, you need to separately change each slide master. For example, if both slide masters use black text and you want all the text to be navy blue, change the text color in both slide masters.

Change the Background and Theme Properties

Although the background can be considered its own layer, you can format it from the slide master to affect the entire presentation. The relationships between the background, the theme properties, the template, and the slide master can be confusing at first, but make a lot of sense once you understand the concept.

The template or theme contains the settings for the slide master, including the background, color theme, font theme, and effects theme. When you assign a template or theme, PowerPoint always remembers that template or theme and displays its name on the status bar.

PowerPoint continues to remember the template or theme even if you end up changing everything about it—the background, the text properties, and so on. However, as explained earlier, you can rename the slide master if you wish. Because templates and themes are separate files, you can apply them to any presentation, but the slide master applies only to the presentation containing it.

You can change the background from Slide Master view, as follows:

- ■ To change the background of every slide that uses a slide master, select the larger slide in the left pane, right-click it in the main pane, and choose Background. Your change affects every slide that uses that slide master. (See Chapter 6 for instructions on formatting the background.)

- ■ To change the background of a particular layout in a slide master, select that layout in the left (thumbnail) pane, right-click it in the main pane, and choose Background. Your change affects every slide that uses that layout of the slide master.

After changing the background, your presentation may no longer look anything like the original template or theme, but that's okay. If you change the background from Normal view, the background affects only the active slide, unless you choose Apply to All.

However, the theme colors, fonts, and effects control the master, not vice versa. If you change the theme color for text, background, and accents from any slide, for example, the entire presentation is affected. If you view the slide master, you will see that it has been changed to reflect your changes. If you try it the other way around—view the master and change the background, title color, and text color—the changes affect all your slides but the theme colors do not change. If you have a presentation whose slides don't reflect the theme colors, for example, remember that someone could have made changes to either the master or to individual slides that overrode the color theme.

Format Headings and Bulleted Text

At the top of the master, in the area labeled "Click to edit Master title style" (refer to Figure 7-1), you format slide titles. This text not only gives you an instruction, but also shows you the current text properties. Text color, font, size, alignment, case (capitalization), and effects are some of the properties you can change. You make the changes as you would on the object level. The techniques for editing text properties were discussed in Chapter 3.

NOTE *Remember that the first, larger slide shown in the left pane controls the entire master. If you click that slide and change the font color, for example, you change the font color for the entire master, and therefore for every slide that uses that master. On the other hand, if you make a change with a specific layout selected, the change affects only that layout—and therefore only slides that use that layout.*

Below the master's title text is an area for body text, called "Click to edit Master text styles." Here, you specify the formatting for five or more levels of bulleted text. You can format the text, bullets, and the paragraph alignment and indentation. See Chapter 4 for information on formatting bullets and paragraphs. If you like fancy bullets and want to use them throughout your presentation, or if you want to remove the bullets entirely, here's the place.

> **TIP** *The text in the text placeholders changes when you return to Normal view. For example, for the Title and Content layout, the text in the title area changes to "Click to add title." You can edit the text that appears in the master and the text will remain as you edited it when you return to Normal view. This text can then function as instructions for other users. For example, if you would like a content placeholder to be used for a product photo, you could change the text in that placeholder to "Insert product photo here."*

PowerPoint 2007 now offers several new options for formatting text, such as all uppercase text. To create a title that is always uppercase (even if you don't type it that way), select the title placeholder in the master and click the Home tab. Then click the dialog box launcher arrow in the Font group to open the Font dialog box. Choose the All Caps option and click OK.

Add Repeating Objects and Animation

You can add objects to every slide that uses a specific master by adding it to the first, larger layout of that master. A company logo is probably the most common example, as shown in Figure 7-3. To create this effect, open the slide master and display the Insert tab. Click the Picture button to locate and choose the graphic file and click Insert. Then move and resize the graphic as necessary.

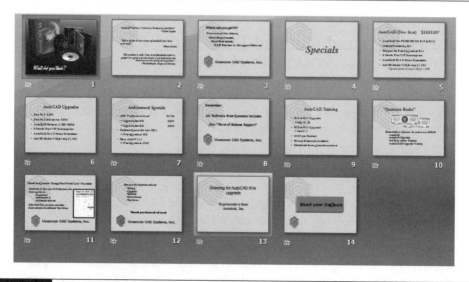

FIGURE 7-3 The light-gray logo is on the slide master, so it appears on every slide except the title slide, which uses a different master.

Remember that on the slide master, you can't see the actual text on each slide. Because the logo will appear on every slide, be careful to place the object where it won't interfere with your text. Then double-check this placement after you have completed the presentation. The easiest way to check is to go to Slide Sorter view, where you can get a bird's-eye view of the entire presentation. If the object collides with text on one or more slides, return to the master and move it to a better location.

> **TIP** *Insert the logo on the slide with the most content. If it fits, press CTRL-X to cut it to the clipboard, open the slide master, and press CTRL-V to paste it onto the master in the same location.*

Because objects that you insert on the slide master are not on the object layer, you cannot select them unless you are in Slide Master view. If you are unable to select an object, try going to Slide Master view.

You can add a shape or image that covers part of the slide or the entire slide. If you do so, right-click it and choose Send to Back so that it doesn't cover the text placeholders.

You can also add animation on the slide master. This animation appears on all slides. For example, if you animate text on the master's main slide, all text in the presentation uses the same animation. (This could get annoying; be careful not to overdo animated text.) You can also add a slide transition to the master; this method automatically applies the transition to all slides using that master. For more information on animation, see Chapter 9.

Add a Footer

The slide master comes with placeholders for the date, a text footer, and the slide number. Many users add the date for documentation purposes. A text footer can specify your name or department without being obtrusive. Slide numbers are especially helpful if you might need to go back and forth in your presentation while you present. Slide numbers are also invaluable in the creation process, while you are still deciding on the order of your slides. You change the location and formatting of these footers directly on the slide master.

> **TIP** *There are no separate headers, but you can move the footer placeholders to the top of the slide master and turn them into headers.*

To add or change the footer's content, use Normal view (not Slide Master view) and click the Insert tab. In the Text group, click the Header & Footer button. PowerPoint opens the Header and Footer dialog box, shown in Figure 7-4 with the Slide tab on top.

To use the Header and Footer dialog box, follow these guidelines:

- Check the Date and Time check box if you want to place the date and time on each slide.

- Choose the type of date and time. The Update Automatically option displays the current date and time. Click the drop-down arrow to choose the format. You can choose a format that includes the time. If you select the Fixed option, slides always display the date that you enter in the text box, rather than the current date. This means that tomorrow, you'll still see today's date. Use a fixed date when you want to document the date a presentation was created.

- Check Slide Number to add a slide number to each slide.
- Check Footer to include a text footer, and then type the footer text in the box.
- Check Don't Show on Title Slide to omit footers on any slide using the Title Slide layout.

Click Apply to All when you are finished making all the settings you want to add the footers to all the slides. Click Apply to add footers only to the selected slide or slides.

If you run a presentation through several revisions and collaborate with others to create the final version, place the date and time in a text box on the first slide, without using the Footer feature. Include instructions to each reviewer to enter the current date and time just before they pass on the presentation. In this way, everyone instantly knows when the presentation was last saved, without having to look at the file information in Windows Explorer—many people do not display these details in Explorer. Don't forget to delete the text box when the presentation is finalized.

You can also show or hide a footer, or a title placeholder, in the slide master. Display the slide master. On the Slide Master tab, check or uncheck the Footers or Title check box in the Master Layout group. This doesn't affect your slides and is just for convenience.

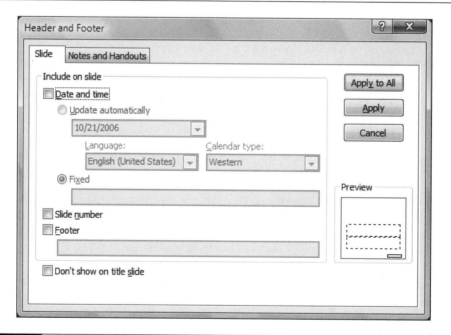

FIGURE 7-4 The Header and Footer dialog box lets you add the date, slide number, and a text footer to all your slides.

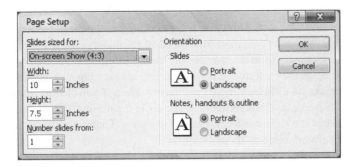

FIGURE 7-5   Use the Page Setup dialog box to change the starting slide number, as well as slide size and orientation.

Occasionally, you may want your slide numbers to start with a number other than one. Perhaps your presentation is the second half of a larger presentation. To change the starting slide number, in either the master or Normal view, display the Design tab and click the Page Setup button in the Page Setup group to display the Page Setup dialog box, shown in Figure 7-5.

Under Number Slides From, type a new starting number or use the arrows to change the starting number. Click OK.

Insert a Slide Master Component

On the slide master, you can delete footers or even title and body text placeholders. If you want to replace them, select the layout in the thumbnail pane and choose Slide Layout in the Master Layout group of the Slide Master tab. The Master Layout dialog box, shown here, opens. You can check any missing layout component to reinsert it on the master. Then click OK.

NOTE   *The Title Master no longer exists in PowerPoint 2007. Instead, you use the Title Slide layout of the master.*

Make Exceptions to the Master Formatting

You aren't locked into the slide master. You may want to make exceptions to the formatting you have created in the slide master. In fact, most of the formatting already covered in this book has had the effect of making exceptions to the master. Any time you reformat bulleted text on a slide, change font color, or change the background for a slide, you are creating an exception to the master.

Any change you make on a slide overrides the master. Even if you change the master, your changes remain. That's because although the slide master is the master of the presentation, you, the user, are the master of the slide master. What you say goes. Therefore, if you make changes to a slide, PowerPoint always respects those changes.

The advantage of the slide master is that you can make changes that affect the entire presentation. It is certainly much easier to change text color once than to change it individually on each slide. Moreover, if you need to change the text color again, as long as you made the change on the master, you need change only the master. If you made the change on each slide, guess what? Now you have to go back to each slide and change it individually.

Suppose you want to create a slide without any background graphics. You might want to do this for a great image that will look best taking up the entire slide. Just follow these steps:

1. Display the slide.
2. Click the Design tab.
3. Check Hide Background Graphics in the Background group.

This technique hides all the background graphics from the slide, including the graphics that make up the design template and any graphics you may have added to the master. This all-or-nothing approach may not work in your situation. Let's say you want to see the design template's graphics but not a graphic you added, such as your company's logo. (Perhaps it doesn't fit on one slide.) Here's how to accomplish the task:

1. Display the slide you want to work on.
2. On the Design tab, check Hide Background Graphics in the Background group.
3. Press SHIFT and click the Normal View button to open the slide master.
4. Select the graphics that make up the background design for the design template. Remember that on the slide master, they are objects just like objects you create on a slide. Press SHIFT and click to select additional objects. You might have to select several objects.
5. Press CTRL-C to copy the graphics to the clipboard.
6. Click Normal View to return to Normal view and display the slide you were working on.
7. Press CTRL-V to paste the graphics onto the slide. You now have your background graphics but not any additional objects you added to the master, in this case, your company's logo.

Another option would be to create a custom layout for the slide. I explain how to create custom layouts in the "Create Custom Layouts" section later in this chapter.

TIP *If you change the background on a slide and want to return to the background of the master, right-click the slide and choose Format Background. Click the Reset Background button and click OK.*

Apply a Master to a Slide

When you have completed formatting a slide master, you generally want to apply it to any slides that you have already added. Masters appear along with themes on the Design tab, so you apply a master in the same way that you apply a theme. Select the desired slides and click the More button in the Themes group of the Design tab. At the top, you see the masters in the current presentation, as shown here. Right-click the one you want and choose Apply to Selected Slides.

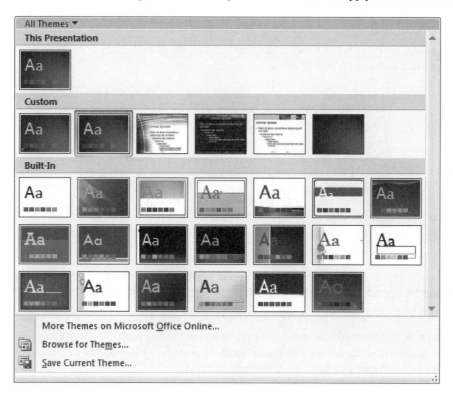

Create Custom Layouts

A *layout* is a set of slide components placed on a slide. In the "Lay Out a Slide" section in Chapter 2, I explain how to use layouts. A new feature for PowerPoint 2007 is the ability to create custom layouts. You can insert any of eight components and then place and size them as you wish. This custom layout becomes part of the master. If you then save the file as a template or theme, any presentation that uses that template or theme can access that custom layout.

Follow these steps to create your own layout:

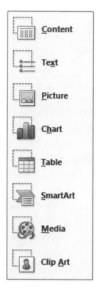

1. On the View tab, click the Slide Master button in the Presentation Views group to display the slide master.

2. On the Slide Master tab, in the Edit Master group, click Insert Layout. You see a new layout in the left pane below the selected layout, as shown in Figure 7-6. The tooltip for the new layout reads 1_Custom Layout Layout: Used by No Slides.

3. In the Master Layout group of the Slide Master tab, click the down arrow of the Insert Placeholder button to display the Placeholder gallery, shown here:

4. Choose a placeholder and drag on the slide master to place and size it.

5. Continue to repeat Steps 3 and 4 until you have all the placeholders you need, as shown in this example:

6. Give the layout a meaningful name. With the layout selected in the left pane, display the Slide Master tab and click the Rename button in the Edit Master group. In the Rename Layout dialog box, enter a name and click Rename.

You can now exit Slide Master view and use the layout for any slide. To use the layout with other presentations, save the file as a template (.potx or .potm) or Office theme (.thmx) file and use that template or theme as a basis for a new presentation.

Format the Handout Master

You can create printed handouts of your presentation to give to your audience to take home or to show your boss during the approval process. Handouts show your slides in groupings of two to nine per page. Handouts are covered in Chapter 15. However, because we are on the topic of masters, you may want to know about the handout master.

The handout master controls the formatting of handouts. You can add art, text, the date, and page numbers to your handout master and they will display on the handouts, in addition to your slides,

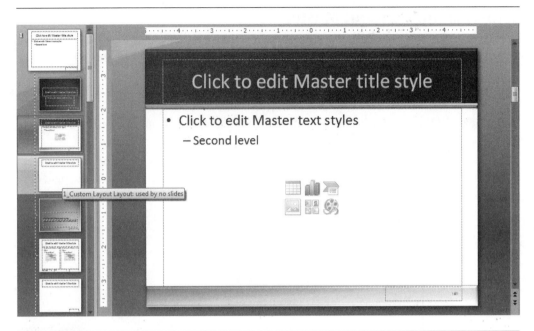

FIGURE 7-6   When you insert a new layout, it starts with just a title text placeholder.

which are automatically included. Settings on the handout master have no effect on your slide master or slides.

Enter Handout Master View

To enter Handout Master view, press SHIFT and click the Slide Sorter View icon at the bottom left of your screen. You can also display the View tab and click the Handout Master in the Presentation Views group. You see a blank handout master, as shown here. By default, the handout master contains a header area for text, a date area, a page number area, and a footer area for text.

Customize the Handout Master

When you open the handout master, PowerPoint changes the ribbon to display tools for formatting the handout master. In the Page Setup group of the Handout Master tab, do the following:

1. Click the Handout Orientation button and choose Portrait or Landscape. This action formats the orientation of the entire page.

2. Click the Slide Orientation button and choose Portrait or Landscape to format the orientation of the slides on the page.

3. Click the Slides Per Page button and choose a layout for the slides on the page, from one to nine slides per page. The three-per-page choice, shown here, prints lines to the right of each slide so the reader can jot down notes. You can also print the outline.

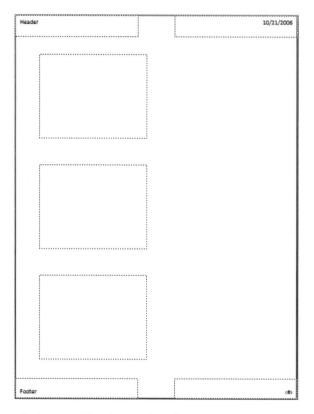

You don't have to limit yourself to the standard format. You can add graphics, text boxes—anything that you can add to a slide. For example, you can create captions for each slide or callouts pointing out features of a slide. You can add your phone number or e-mail address—the possibilities are limitless.

To add a header, footer, the date, or page numbers, display the Insert tab and click the Header and Footer button in the Text group while in Handout Master view. PowerPoint opens the Header and Footer dialog box, with the Notes and Handouts tab on top. This tab is almost the same as the Slide tab, shown previously in Figure 7-4. The only differences are the following:

- You can specify both a header and a footer.

- You must choose Apply to All. You cannot separately format the various pages of the handouts.

Refer to the section "Add a Footer" earlier in the chapter for more information on using this dialog box. When you have finished formatting your handouts, return to your previous view by clicking Close on the Handout Master tab.

You can format a background for the handout master. Handout masters are not saved in templates or themes.

7

Format the Notes Master

As explained in Chapter 1, you can use the Notes pane to create notes to accompany your presentation. You can then print these notes along with an image of each slide. Traditionally, notes are used by the speaker during the actual presentation. For example, notes are a good place to put your jokes so that you won't forget the punch lines. Printed notes contain one slide per page and a large area for text—your notes. However, you can use notes for other purposes, such as to write down ideas for the presentation as you are creating it, or to create and print comments for your supervisor who is reviewing the presentation.

If you will send the presentation to people who missed your live delivery, use the Notes pane to enter your entire talk. In this way, people receiving your presentation can read what you said. Without your notes, people who read just the text on the slides may misinterpret your meaning. On the other hand, be sure to delete any personal notes to yourself that you don't want others to see.

You create the notes by typing in the Notes pane. Chapter 15 contains more information about creating and using notes. The notes master formats these notes.

Enter Notes Master View

To enter Notes Master view, display the View tab and click the Notes Master button (not the Notes Page button) in the Presentation Views group. PowerPoint opens the Notes Master view, as shown in Figure 7-7.

Because the actual notes page includes a picture of a slide on the top and your notes at the bottom, the top of the notes master shows the slide master to represent the actual slides that will be printed. You can only move and resize the slide master. The notes that you enter in the Notes pane for each slide will automatically appear at the bottom.

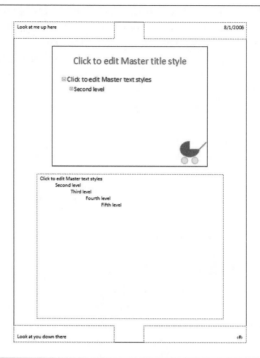

FIGURE 7-7   Notes Master view lets you format the look of your notes when printed.

Customize the Notes Master

Although notes are usually just text, you can add graphics. For example, if you are preparing a presentation for a client, you might send the client your preliminary presentation for review in the form of notes pages. You might want to add your company logo in the notes area. Graphics, headers, and footers don't appear in the Notes pane when you are in Normal view. You see them on the notes master, in Notes Page view, and when you print notes. Printing notes is covered in Chapter 15.

To add a header, footer, the date, or a page number, use the same procedure explained previously for the handout master. When you're done, click the Close Master View button on the Notes Master tab.

Set Page Size

Another way of formatting an entire presentation is to set the page size. Display the Design tab and click the Page Setup button to display the Page Setup dialog box, shown earlier in Figure 7-5. By default, PowerPoint sizes your slides for an onscreen slide show. Slides are 10 inches wide by 7.5 inches high. When you click the Slides Sized For drop-down arrow, you see the choices shown here. You can scroll down for more choices. Once you choose the type of presentation, you can customize the size using the Width and Height text boxes. The 16:9 and 16:10 are new wide-screen options.

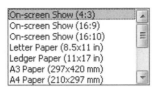

CAUTION

If you want to change the slide size and orientation, do so before you start working on your presentation; otherwise, text and graphics may not fit on each slide as you expect and may be distorted as well.

On the right side of the dialog box, you can set the orientation of the slides separately from the notes, handouts, and outline. By default, slides are in landscape orientation (the width is longer than the height), and everything else is in portrait orientation. Click OK when you're done.

Save Custom Themes

Now that you understand masters, you have the tools to create your own themes from scratch. Remember that a theme includes colors, fonts, and effects as well as a slide master, which contains a background and perhaps graphics. I explained how to change theme fonts in Chapter 3. In Chapter 6, I explained how to customize theme colors and choose theme effects.

NOTE

You can save theme colors and theme fonts. These are separate XML files in subfolders within the Document Themes folder where themes are saved. However, you can only choose from preset theme effects. In the future, you may be able to download new theme effects as well as create your own.

After making so many changes, you probably want to save them so that you can use them again in other presentations. To do so, follow these steps:

1. Open a blank or existing presentation.

2. Make the desired changes to the slide master and layouts, as explained throughout this chapter.

3. Choose theme colors or save custom theme colors, as described in Chapter 6.

4. Choose a theme effects option.

5. Choose theme fonts or save custom theme fonts, as described in Chapter 3.

6. Display the Design tab. In the Themes group, click the More arrow and choose Save Current Theme to open the Save Current Theme dialog box.

7. Enter a name for the theme and click Save.

The theme is saved in a folder reserved for themes, so that you can find it whenever you need a theme.

To apply the theme to any other presentation, whether new or existing, display the Design tab. In the Themes group, click the More arrow and choose the theme from the Custom section of the Themes gallery.

Create Your Own Templates

Like themes, templates include a slide master (including its background, bullet formatting, and layouts), theme colors, theme fonts, and theme effects. The background can include graphics that make up a design. You can even include text and shapes on slides—in other words, you can develop some actual content for your template that you may want to reuse in the future. Once you have created and saved all these components, you can then use that template for other presentations.

Creating your own template is really a must if you create a lot of presentations and want the highest-quality results. Having your own template means that everything is already set to your specifications and you can start to work right away. Here are the steps you need to take:

1. Open a blank or existing presentation.

2. Make the desired changes to the slide master and layouts, as explained throughout this chapter.

3. Choose theme colors or save custom theme colors, as described in Chapter 6.

4. Choose a theme effects option.

5. Choose theme fonts or save custom theme fonts, as described in Chapter 3.

6. Click the Office button and choose Save As to open the Save As dialog box. In the Save as Type drop-down list, choose PowerPoint Template (*.potx).

7. Type a name for the template in the File Name text box and click Save.

To use your template, start a new presentation. Click the Office button and choose New. In the New Presentation dialog box, double-click the My Templates button to choose your template.

If you want the extra professional touch that a graphic artist can provide, you can find a professional who specializes in creating PowerPoint presentations. You can also purchase design templates. Here are four useful sources:

- Ppted: http://www.ppted.com
- PresentationPro: http://www.presentationpro.com
- Digital Juice: http://www.digitaljuice.com
- CrystalGraphics: http://www.crystalgraphics.com

You can find many free backgrounds and templates by searching on the Internet. I offer some on my web site at http://www.ellenfinkelstein.com/portfolio.htm.

Summary

In this chapter, you put together all the knowledge you have learned about creating presentations and put it to use to create slide masters. Slide masters control the overall look of a presentation.

In the slide master, you can change the background, format title and slide text, insert objects and graphics that will appear on every slide, and add footers.

Slide masters contain slide layouts, and you can create your own slide layouts by inserting, placing, and sizing layout components, such as text and clip art placeholders.

This chapter also explained how to use handout masters to format handouts, and notes masters to format notes.

The Page Setup dialog box lets you format the size and orientation of your slides.

Once you can create masters, you have the tools you need to create your own themes and templates. The chapter ended with a description of how to create and save themes and templates.

In the next chapter, you learn how to incorporate graphs, tables, and diagrams into your presentations.

Chapter 8

Incorporate Graphs, Tables, and Diagrams

How to...

- Create a graph
- Import data
- Choose the right chart type
- Format a chart
- Add a table to a slide
- Import a Word table
- Create diagrams

Effective presentations sometimes require more than pictures. Fortunately, PowerPoint lets you add graphs, tables, and diagrams to your slides. You can even convert bulleted text to diagrams. In this chapter, you learn how to present complex data as simply and clearly as possible.

Present Data Simply

The more complex the data you need to present, the more you should plan ways to present that data so that your audience can comprehend it at a glance. While long tables of data are okay for printed reports, they are not effective on slides. A slide is not big enough, and the audience doesn't have enough time to read through lots of numbers. (If you really need to present large amounts of data, provide a printed handout.) You may need to present less data, but you may also be able to find a way to format the data more simply. For example, the table shown next doesn't make the trends immediately obvious:

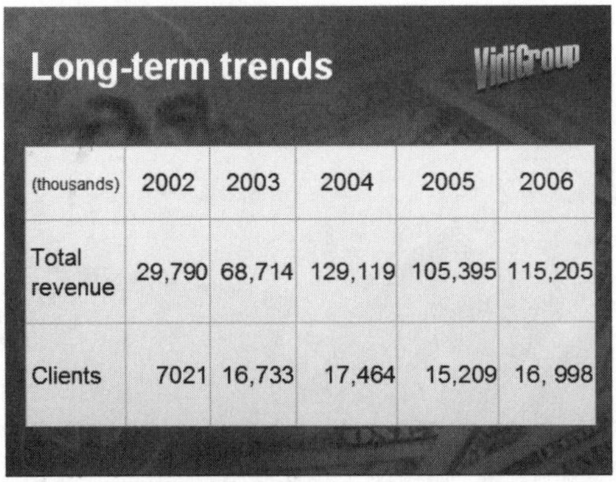

Long-term trends *VidiGroup*

(thousands)	2002	2003	2004	2005	2006
Total revenue	29,790	68,714	129,119	105,395	115,205
Clients	7021	16,733	17,464	15,209	16, 998

Background courtesy of Digital Juice (http://www.digitaljuice.com).

If your point is the growth of the company, you could split the data onto two slides and use the following two charts instead:

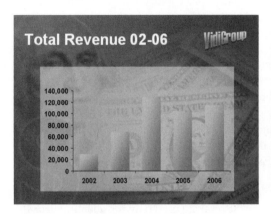 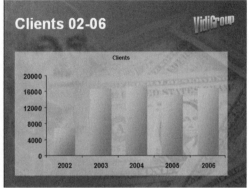

Your audience doesn't see the exact numbers, but the overall message is much clearer. The audience can immediately see the trend.

Add Graphs to a Slide

A graph visually portrays a series of numbers. Graphs are usually more effective than tables when the figures show a trend. Your audience can see the direction of the trend at a glance rather than have to figure out the trend by analyzing the numbers in a table. The most direct way to add a graph to a slide is to use a chart placeholder. In PowerPoint 2007, you automatically switch to a Microsoft Excel spreadsheet (if you have Excel installed) to enter the data for the graph. (If you do not have Excel installed, you use Microsoft Graph, the old graph program used by previous versions of Microsoft Office.) Later in this chapter, in the "Insert a Chart from Microsoft Excel" section, I explain how to import an existing graph from Microsoft Excel.

NOTE   *PowerPoint uses the word* chart *to mean a graph. I use the two words interchangeably in this chapter.*

To create a graph using a chart placeholder, create a new slide with one of the Content layouts. The content icons on these layouts let you choose from a variety of content types, including charts. Then click the Chart icon. Another way to insert a chart is to click Chart in the Insert tab's Illustrations group.

TIP   *If you want, you can create a custom layout for a chart. Use either the content or chart placeholder. I explain how to create custom layouts in Chapter 7.*

Choose the Right Chart Type

As soon as you insert a chart or click a Chart icon in a content placeholder, the Create Chart dialog box opens, as shown in Figure 8-1. This dialog box enables you to choose a chart type. As you can see, you have a wide array of options, but remember that not every chart type is suitable for the type of data you have.

The key to choosing a chart type is to understand your data and the strengths and weaknesses of each chart type. The ideal chart type for your presentation is the one that presents the data most clearly. In the next few sections, I give you the information you need to understand each chart type.

To choose the chart type, choose one of the major chart types from the list at the left of the Create Chart dialog box. Then choose one of the variations on the right. Click OK to open an Excel worksheet for the presentation (if you have Excel installed) or PowerPoint's chart module (if you don't have Excel installed).

You can't always use any chart type you want. Some types of graphs are suitable for data with several rows; others shouldn't have more than one row. Several are used only for scientific data.

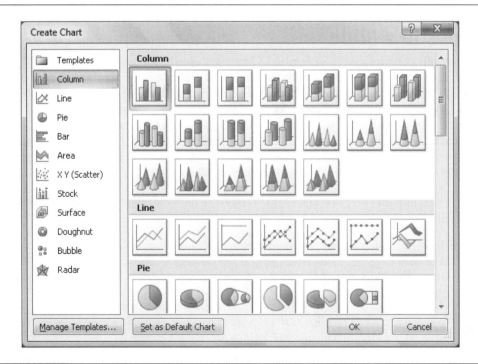

FIGURE 8-1   Your first task is to decide which type of chart you want to use.

If you aren't sure which kind of chart to use, try several to see which one seems to make the point most clearly.

Column

Column graphs are among the most common type of chart. You often see them showing financial data over time, where quarters or years are the column categories in the spreadsheet. On the graph, these time categories are shown across the bottom (on the X axis) and the data for each time category is shown along the left side (on the Y axis). If you are showing data for more than one item (such as several products or locations), you will see as many vertical bars as you have items. Figure 8-2 shows an example of a spreadsheet and its corresponding column chart showing income for both sales and service over four years.

If you want to show the relationship of your data to totals, try one of the stacked column charts. And if you have more than one series and want to show relationships across both categories and series, try the last 3-D Column subtype.

Line

A line graph is similar to a bar graph, but instead of creating bars, a line is drawn from value to value. Line graphs are especially good at showing trends—your audience immediately grasps if the line is going up, down, or remaining flat. However, line graphs are not as visually impressive as column or bar graphs. The 3-D subtype creates ribbons instead of lines.

You can add labels at each data point to make the actual values on the line graph stand out, as shown in the following example. Here you see a line graph using the same spreadsheet used for

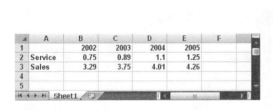
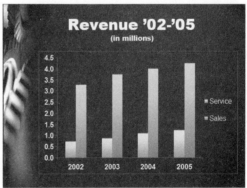

FIGURE 8-2   A simple column graph is the most common type of chart.

the column graph shown previously. For clarity, the lines have been formatted to make them thicker than the default line weight.

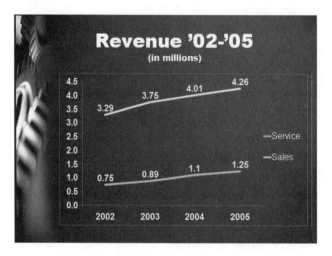

Pie

A pie chart shows which percentage each data value contributes to the whole pie. For this reason, pie charts are suitable for spreadsheets with only one row—that is, one data series. Pie charts are often used for breaking down revenues or expenses. Pie charts look great on slides, but keep the number of items to six or less, if possible. Here you see the spreadsheet and its corresponding pie chart:

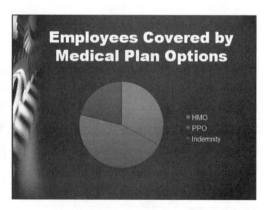

PowerPoint offers some great-looking 3-D pie charts. You can also create exploded pies (messy!) and pie charts that break down one of the chart's components into subcomponents.

Bar

Bar graphs also compare data across categories, but the categories are shown along the left (Y) axis and the data is shown along the bottom (X) axis, as shown next with the Stacked Bar subtype. This graph uses the same spreadsheet as the column graph.

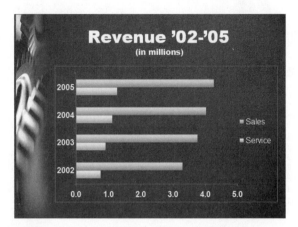

Column and bar graphs are visually impressive and easy to understand. You can use fill effects on the bars—gradients or even images—for a sophisticated look.

Area

An area chart is plotted like a line chart, but the area under the lines is filled in. Because of the fill, an area chart shows up better on a slide. Another advantage of an area chart is that you can use one of the stacked subtypes, which show the relationship of the data series to their total. Here you see a 100 percent stacked area chart, which shows the trend in the percentage that each value contributes across the categories.

In this case, you clearly see how much each of the five employee benefits categories contributes to the total employee benefits cost over the four quarters of the year. Your audience would immediately understand that medical expenses are the largest part of the total cost, with pension expenses (the top area) coming second.

Scatter

A scatter chart (also called an XY chart) is used when both the categories (columns) and the series (rows) are numbers, to draw conclusions about the relationships in the data. It is an effective way to present many data values at once. Here you see a spreadsheet showing average annual salaries based on age and years of college education completed:

	C	D	E	F	G	H	I	J	K
1	1.0	2.0	3.0	4.0	5.0	6.0	7.0	8.0	
2	19.1	20.2	21.0	25.5	25.7	27.9	28.0	30.0	
3	19.3	20.4	21.1	25.7	25.9	28.0	28.5	30.5	
4	20.3	20.5	22.0	26.0	26.1	28.7	29.1	31.0	
5	22.7	23.1	23.2	27.1	27.3	28.9	30.1	32.1	
6	22.8	23.2	24.1	27.5	28.5	29.4	31.2	33.5	
7	23.3	23.4	24.2	28.1	29.2	29.7	32.7	35.0	
8	24.1	24.2	24.3	29.0	30.1	30.5	33.2	36.0	
9	24.2	24.2	24.5	30.1	31.3	32.2	34.1	37.2	
10									

Sheet1

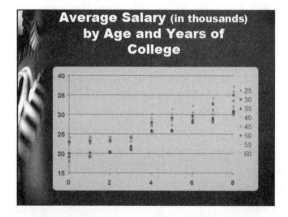

The scatter chart shows years of college education along the X axis and annual salary along the Y axis. Each marker type in the legend indicates a different age. You can clearly see how salary goes up with age and education, including a jump for those with four years of college. (This chart uses dummy data.)

Stock

A stock chart is specifically designed to plot stock prices. The simplest version plots high, low, and closing prices, which must be located in rows in the spreadsheet in that order. The first row can be the names of stocks, sectors, dates, and so forth. Here you see a spreadsheet with dummy data for three sectors and the corresponding stock chart:

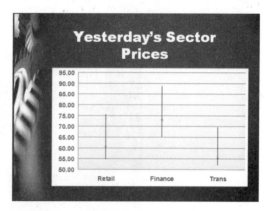

Surface

You can use a surface chart when you have two series (rows). The surface chart plots both series as it would with a line graph and connects lines to create a ribbon-like surface. The topology of the surface shows the combined value of both series. Here you see a surface chart showing quarterly sales of DVDs and CDs. You can see that in the fourth quarter, the combined sales were the highest for the year.

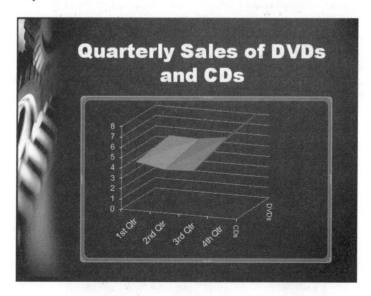

Doughnut

A doughnut chart is like a pie chart, but you can use it for data with more than one series (row). You can also use the exploded doughnut option. Here you see an unexploded doughnut, showing medical plan choices made by employees in two offices:

The point is to show the proportions between the choices, not the total numbers. Because the Chicago office has fewer employees than the New York office, a chart type emphasizing totals, such as a bar chart, would not make the point clearly.

Bubble

A bubble chart lets you plot three series (rows) of data. The first row becomes the horizontal (X) axis, the second row becomes the vertical (Y) axis, and the third row is indicated by the size of the bubbles. In the next example, you see data for four U.S. cities—the X axis is average annual precipitation, the Y axis is temperature, and the size of the bubbles indicates population in thousands. In which city would you rather live? (Try to guess which city is which. The answer is at the end of the chapter.)

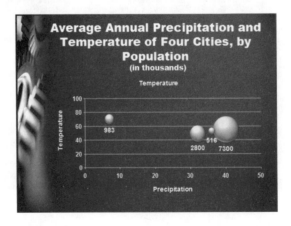

Radar

A radar chart compares the values of several data series. Each category (column) has its own value axis radiating out from the center. Lines connect all the values in a series. A radar chart is usually used for scientific data and may be confusing for a presentation. Here you see a radar chart showing average annual temperature and rainfall for three U.S. cities.

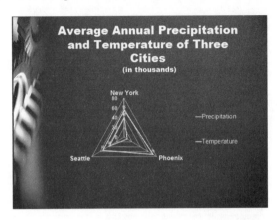

8

To change the chart type of an existing chart, select the chart and choose Change Chart Type from the Type group of the Chart Tools Design tab to open the Change Chart Type dialog box.

Enter Data on the Spreadsheet

Once you choose a chart type, it's time to enter your data. When you click OK in the Create Chart dialog box, if you have Excel installed, Excel automatically opens with the title Chart in Microsoft Office PowerPoint - Microsoft Excel, as shown in Figure 8-3. Where did those numbers come from? The spreadsheet opens with dummy data already filled in.

The Excel spreadsheet is where you insert your data. This data is the basis for your chart. Columns are labeled A, B, C, and so on, and rows are numbered 1, 2, 3, and so on. A cell is one of the rectangles that contains data and is called by its column and row, so that the active cell in Figure 8-3—the one with the black border—is B2.

To enter your own data, you can delete all the dummy data first, by clicking in the top-left corner box (above the column of numbers and to the left of the row of letters) and pressing DELETE. Alternatively, you can simply go from cell to cell and replace the data. Move from left to right across a row by pressing TAB, or click the cursor in any cell to type there.

CAUTION   *You may find that you need to actually delete rows or columns rather than just delete cell contents. You'll know if you need to do this, because you'll see extra items in the legend or extra blank items on the X axis. To delete a row or column in Excel, click its header (the letter or number) and click the Delete button's down arrow in the Cells group of the Home tab. Then choose Delete Sheet Rows or Delete Sheet Columns.*

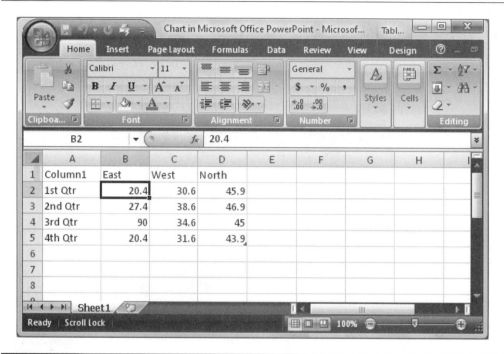

FIGURE 8-3 After you choose a chart type, Excel opens with dummy data already included.

If you need to enlarge the spreadsheet to see more of your data, place the cursor over an edge or corner of the application window and drag outward. You can also drag column dividers to change column widths.

If you already have the data in another Excel worksheet, you don't need to retype it. To get your existing data into the Excel worksheet for your presentation, follow these steps:

1. From the open Excel worksheet, click the Office button and choose Open to open the other worksheet.

2. Select the existing data and copy it to the clipboard

3. Switch back to the spreadsheet for your presentation.

4. Select the dummy data and press DELETE.

5. Place the cursor in cell A1 and paste the data from the clipboard.

However you get the data into the spreadsheet, when you switch back to your PowerPoint window, you see the change in the graph. However, the chart still needs to be formatted for legibility and style.

TIP   *If you have already created the chart in Excel, you can copy it to the clipboard in Excel and paste it onto your slide.*

In most cases, the column headings of the spreadsheet relate to time (such as 1st Qtr and 2nd Qtr) and become the X axis, which is usually the *category* axis. The row headings contain the types of data for each time period and become the Y axis, which is usually the *data* axis. When you start formatting the chart, you will find it helpful to keep these terms in mind.

NOTE   *If you don't have Microsoft Office Excel 2007 installed on your computer, when you create a new chart in PowerPoint, a chart then appears with a datasheet, which is like a spreadsheet. (This is the Microsoft Graph application.) You can then enter your data in the datasheet to create your graph. You can also import data into the datasheet. For example, you may not have Excel on your computer, but you may have an Excel file (in the older .xls format) that someone gave you. To do so, choose Edit | Import File from the datasheet menu to choose the file that contains your data.*

You can keep the Excel worksheet open as you work and switch back and forth between Excel and PowerPoint. When you're done, you should save the Excel worksheet if you might want to use it in Excel at a later time. The current worksheet is only temporary, so you save a copy. Click the Office button and choose Save Copy As to save the file. When you're done with the Excel worksheet, choose Close on the Office button's menu.

NOTE   *After you close the spreadsheet (or datasheet, if you don't have Excel), you can view it at any time by selecting the chart and clicking the Show Data button in the Data group of the Chart Tools Design tab.*

Link to a Chart

Excel can create its own charts, and you may already have a completed chart available in an Excel spreadsheet. In this situation, you may want to link to the existing chart rather than create it in PowerPoint. When you link to the chart, if you change the underlying data in the Excel spreadsheet, the chart in your PowerPoint presentation changes too.

CAUTION   *When you link to an Excel file, that file is separate and does not automatically come along with the presentation. For example, if you send the PowerPoint file to a colleague and then change the Excel data, the colleague's copy of the presentation does not change, because the Excel file is not in the same location. Therefore, if you need updated charts, remember to include the Excel file whenever you send someone the PowerPoint file. To ensure proper linking, it's a good idea to put the Excel file in the same folder as the PowerPoint file before you create the link.*

To link to a chart in an Excel worksheet, follow these steps:

1. Open the Excel worksheet. If you have not already created the chart, do so now, using Excel's tools.

2. Click the border of the chart in Excel and choose Copy in the Clipboard group of the Home tab.

3. Switch to your PowerPoint presentation. If you don't already have a content or chart placeholder on the slide, change the layout to one that includes such a placeholder. (Right-click a blank area of the slide and choose Layout.)

4. Click the border of the placeholder to select it.

5. On the Home tab, click Paste in the Clipboard group. You can also choose Paste | Paste Special for some additional options.

You now see the chart on your slide.

Insert a Spreadsheet as an Object

When you insert, or embed, a spreadsheet as an object, you edit the object by double-clicking it. The menus and toolbars change to those of the original spreadsheet application, which you use to make changes. Here's how to embed a spreadsheet:

1. Display the slide where you want the spreadsheet.

2. Choose Insert | Object.

3. To create a new chart, click Create New and then choose your spreadsheet from the list. For example, choose Microsoft Excel Chart if you have Excel. To insert a chart you've already created, click Create from File and then click Browse. Locate and double-click the file. (If you created a new Excel chart, you see dummy data and a chart, similar to the spreadsheet.)

You can now use your spreadsheet's tools to edit the data and the corresponding chart. When you're done, click anywhere outside the chart to close it.

 *Because you can now link directly to an Excel spreadsheet, you'll usually get better results by linking than by inserting it as an object.*

Format a Chart

Rarely is the default version of the chart acceptable for a slide. Sometimes the labels aren't readable. Perhaps the scale of the axes is not appropriate. The charts you have seen in this chapter were formatted after their initial creation. PowerPoint gives you a great deal of control over the format of a chart, but the options can be bewildering.

Charts have a number of elements that can be formatted individually. Not all charts have every element. For example, only 3-D charts have a floor. Other elements are optional, such as axis titles. The type of formatting available depends on the type of element. Obviously, you can change the font, font size, and font color only for elements that contain text. Table 8-1 describes the most often-used chart elements.

Figure 8-4 shows a 3-D chart and its elements. Knowing these elements helps you know what part of a chart needs formatting.

Element	Description
Category axis	Usually (but not always) the horizontal (X) axis. In the spreadsheet, this axis comes from the column headings.
Value axis	Usually (but not always) the vertical (Y) axis. In the spreadsheet, this axis comes from the values in each row.
Series axis	A third axis (on some 3-D charts), labeled with the names of the data series being plotted. In the spreadsheet, this axis comes from the row headings.
Chart title, if any	A title for the chart.
Axes titles, if any	Titles for the axes.
Data labels, if any	Labels containing the actual values.
Plot area	The area within the axes in a 2-D chart.
Each series of data	Each row of data (there may be several) that is plotted on the graph.
Chart area	The entire chart, including the plot area, the legend, and a chart title, if any.
Floor	In a 3-D chart, the floor that creates the chart's depth.
Walls	In a 3-D chart, the two walls that create two of the three dimensions.
Legend, if any	The labels that indicate the names of the series.
Tick marks	Marks that divide the axes into regular units.
Gridlines	Lines running perpendicular to the value axis from the tick marks, which help the viewer visualize the values plotted on the graph.

TABLE 8-1   Chart Elements

8

NOTE   *You can format chart elements like other drawing objects. For example, you can select one bar or pie section and fill it with a picture. Select the element, right-click, and choose Format Data Point. Click the Fill category and choose the Picture or Texture Fill option. Detailed instructions on filling objects are in Chapter 6.*

As a general guideline, include as few features as possible without sacrificing clarity. For example, titles, gridlines, and a data table often clutter up a chart without providing any additional necessary information. Save the fine details for a printed handout.

When you click a chart to select it, PowerPoint adds three new tabs to the ribbon, all under the Chart Tools heading:

- **Design**   Lets you change the chart type, save the formatting as a template (which I explain later in this chapter), switch rows and columns, edit the data source, display the data (in Excel, if you have it installed), choose a chart layout, and choose a chart style.

- **Layout**   Lets you insert pictures, shapes, or a text box, format labels, axes, and the background, and add analysis features such as a trend line or error bars.

- **Format**   Lets you open a dialog box to format the selected chart element, reset the chart to match a style, change shape styles, change text styles, arrange elements, and specify an exact size for the chart.

You use these tabs to get the exact look you want for your chart.

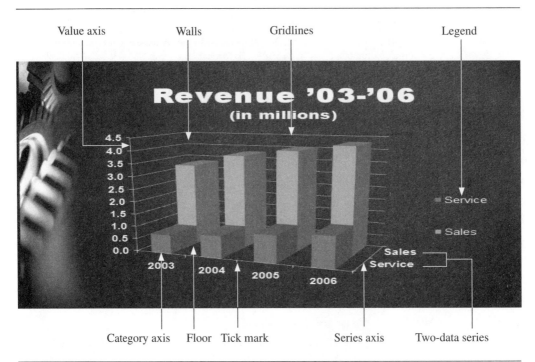

FIGURE 8-4 A chart is made up of many elements, each of which you can format individually.

Choose a Chart Layout and Style

For a quick start, you can choose from a number of preset layouts and styles. A layout specifies where the elements are, especially the title and legend. A layout also specifies certain features, such as data labels, which show the exact value of a data point.

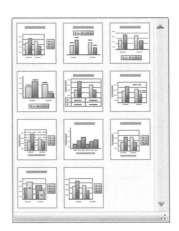

To choose a chart layout, click the chart to select it. Click the Chart Tools Design tab. From the Chart Layouts group, click the More button to display the Chart Layouts gallery, shown here. (The gallery changes depending on the type of chart you created.) Choose various options to see the results and pick the one you like best.

A chart style determines the fills, outlines, and effects of the chart elements, including the text. To choose a chart style, click the More button in the Chart Layouts group to display the Chart Style gallery, displayed here. As you can see, you have lots of options!

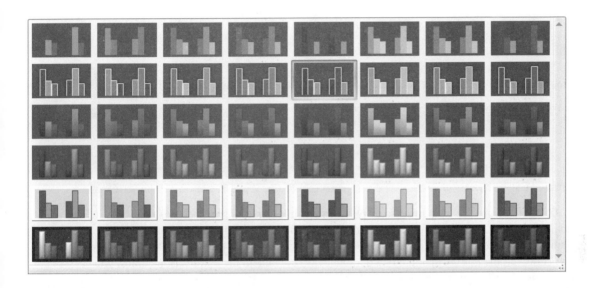

Unfortunately, the text size in all the chart styles is very small, and increasing the text size involves several steps. Therefore, choose a chart style first and then increase the text size. If you increase the text size first and then choose a chart style, all your text becomes small again!

Format Chart Elements

Choosing a chart layout and a chart style is a good way to start, but you usually have to format some chart elements individually. You can use the ribbon's tools for this purpose; furthermore, each element of a chart has its own customized Format dialog box (such as the Format Plot Area dialog box) that fine-tunes that element. To format an element, first make sure that the chart is selected. Then click the element itself to select it. In the chart shown here, the plot area is selected:

As you move the mouse cursor around a chart, tooltips pop up to tell you which object you are passing over.

The first place to go to format a chart element is the Chart Tools Layout tab. As you can see here, you find the element that you want to change in the Labels, Axes, or Background group:

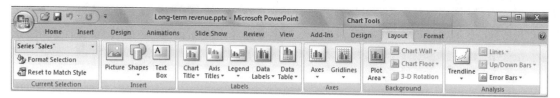

Click an element's down arrow to display some common options. Sometimes there are submenus as well. In most cases, you can also get to a dialog box for more options. In the example shown here, you can click More Plot Area Options to open the Format Plot Area dialog box. However, the Format dialog boxes do not always contain all the options; sometimes, you need to use the ribbon.

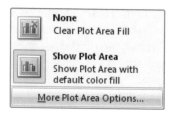

Right-click an element and choose the Format item to open its Format dialog box. For example, if you right-click one of the axes, you can choose Format Axis to open the Format Axis dialog box.

Figure 8-5 shows the Format Axis dialog box. Some of the categories are familiar if you're used to formatting shapes; you can change the fill, the line, the line style, the shadow, and the 3-D format. (For more information on this type of visual formatting, see Chapter 6.) However, the Axis Options pane offers you choices that are very specific to axes. Here are some of the settings you can choose for axes and other chart elements (labeled in Figure 8-4):

- **Axes** You can specify the minimum and maximum numbers as well as the intervals for major and minor units. You have several other options to choose exactly how the axes work and look. The Number pane lets you format exactly how numbers will appear. The Alignment pane aligns the text—great for fitting axis labels into tight spaces.

- **Axes titles** Axes titles are text boxes that you can use to explain what the axes measure. The axes titles are optional. To turn them on, click the Axis Titles button in the Labels group of the Layout tab and choose any one of the options except None.

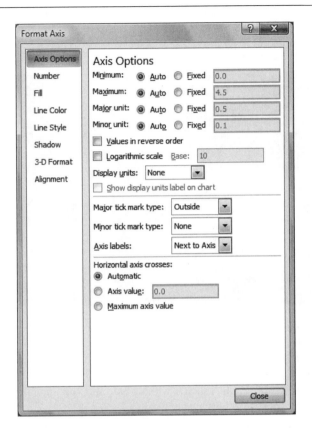

FIGURE 8-5 The Format Axis dialog box is typical of dialog boxes that you use to fine-tune the formatting of chart elements.

You can format the fill, line, line style, shadow, and 3-D format. You can separately specify options for the horizontal and the vertical axis titles.

■ **Data series** The data series is the part of the chart that plots the values, such as the columns, bars, or lines. For certain charts, you can set which axis PowerPoint uses to plot the data series. You can set options for the spacing between the data series (for example, the columns). You will often want to change the color of bars or columns, which you do using the Fill and Line panes. You can also use the Shadow pane to add a shadow.

TIP *Decrease the Gap Width on the Series Options pane of the Format Data Series dialog box to increase the width of the columns or bars. The result is a chart that is clearer and more striking.*

■ **Data labels** Data labels show the exact value of a data series, as you see here. Use data labels when precision is important for your presentation. You can format the fill, line,

line style, shadow, 3-D format, and alignment. The data labels are optional. To turn them on, click the Data Labels button in the Labels group of the Layout tab and choose any of the options except None.

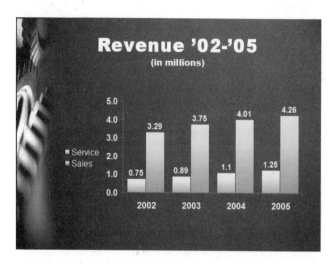

- **Data table**   A data table is a spreadsheet that shows the source data of a data series. Generally, you would not use both a chart and a data table, but if you feel that your audience will want to see the underlying data, you can include it. You can format the fill, line, line style, shadow, and 3-D format, as well as the table borders. The data table is not on by default. To display it, click the Data Table button in the Labels group of the Layout tab and choose any of the options except None.

- **Chart area**   The chart area is the entire area of the chart, including the chart itself, the plot area (that contains the chart), as well as a legend and axes titles, if any. You can format the fill, line, line style, shadow, and 3-D format.

- **Legend**   The legend shows which color (or shape) corresponds to which data series. In addition to the same formatting options as for the chart area, you can choose the placement of the legend. The legend is an optional item and may not appear. To display it, click the Legend button in the Labels group of the Layout tab and choose any one of the options except None.

 *You can simply drag the selected legend to the desired location.*

- **Gridlines**   Gridlines are lines that run horizontally from the Y axis. You can format the line and line style of the gridlines. Choose No Line to turn off gridlines. On the Layout tab, use the Gridlines button's down arrow to choose the type of interval you want for the gridlines.

- **Plot area**   The plot area is the inner area that contains the data series and axes. Only 2-D charts have a plot area. You can format the fill, lines, line style, shadow, and 3-D format (giving it a bevel, for example). You can quickly add or remove the fill using the Plot Area button in the Background group of the Layout tab.

- **Chart wall**   Only 3-D charts have walls. Use the Chart Wall button in the Background group of the Layout tab to add or remove the fill. In the Format Chart Wall dialog box, you can also format the fill, line, line style, 3-D format, and 3-D rotation. (See the 3-D view item in this list for more details about 3-D rotation.)

- **Chart floor**   Only 3-D charts have a floor. Use the Chart Floor button in the Background group of the Layout tab to add or remove the fill. In the Format Chart Floor dialog box, you can also format the fill, line, line style, 3-D format, and 3-D rotation.

- **3-D view**   The 3-D view controls the angle of the entire chart. Often, you can make a 3-D chart clearer by changing its 3-D view. Use the 3-D View button in the Background group of the Layout tab to open the Format Chart Area dialog box with the 3-D Rotation pane displayed, as shown in Figure 8-6.

8

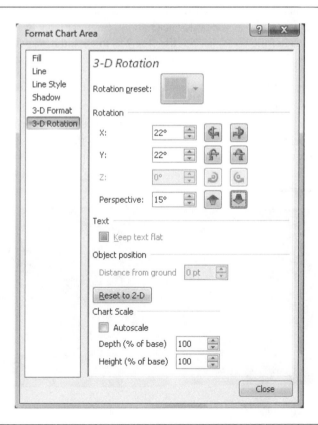

FIGURE 8-6   You can change the rotation of a 3-D chart to precisely control the viewpoint.

You can turn the graph left or right (the X direction) or up or down (the Y direction). You can also change the perspective, making the view angle wider or narrower. To try out the options, move the dialog box off the slide and click the arrows to see the result immediately. At the bottom of the dialog box, you can change the width and length of the floor. The width of the floor may affect the legibility of the labels, so widening it can be helpful. Click Close when you're done.

Depending on the type of chart, you can add statistical features to your graph. You can add trendlines, drop lines (on area or lines charts), high-low lines (on line charts), up-down bars (on line charts), and error bars. You can find these options in the Analysis group of the Chart Tools Layout tab.

Format Text Properties

To change the text in a chart, such as the numbers on the axes or the labels in a legend, click the text and then right-click to display the Mini toolbar. Pass the cursor over this toolbar to make it opaque. You can change fonts, font sizes, font styles, alignment, and text color.

Figure 8-7 shows a chart before and after formatting. The data shown earlier in Figure 8-2 was used. The column chart type was selected. The chart appeared with the Service and Sales items on the X axis, instead of the years, so the first step was to click the Switch Row/Column button in the Data group of the Chart Tools Design tab. The following formatting was done:

- The gridlines were removed to get a cleaner look. To do this, use the Gridlines button in the Axes group of the Layout tab.

- In the Format Data Series dialog box, the gap width was reduced from 150% to 100% in the Series Options pane, which has the effect of widening the columns. At the same time, the overlap was changed to -5%, which created a small gap between the two series. To accomplish this, right-click any of the bars and choose Format Data Series.

FIGURE 8-7   Format your chart to make it simple and clear.

■ A two-color, three-step gradient was added to each of the data series (the two sets of columns). To format the fill, right-click a data series and choose Format Data Series. Choose the Fill option and create a gradient, as explained in Chapter 6.

■ A shadow was added to the columns. Right-click a data series and choose Format Data Series. In the Shadow pane, choose one of the preset shadows or specify your own custom settings. (See Chapter 6 for more information on formatting shadows.)

■ Data labels were added. To add data labels, use the Data Labels button in the Labels group of the Layout tab. Figure 8-7 uses the Outside End option.

■ A shape was added to emphasize important information and rotated slightly.

TIP   *If you don't think your chart conveys the message adequately, feel free to add shapes, such as arrows, or text boxes. You can also animate elements of a chart—see Chapter 9.*

On the other hand, sometimes you want to be dramatic. For example, PowerPoint's chart feature lets you fill columns or bars with a picture that you can tile like a texture. Here you see an example that uses a graphic of a book to indicate book sales:

To create a slide like this, first create a chart. Column and bar charts work best; here a column chart was used. The wider the bars, the better. With the chart selected, right-click one of the columns and choose Format Data Series to open the Format Data Series dialog box. On the Fill pane, choose Picture or Texture Fill. Click the File or Clipart button and choose a picture.

In the bottom section of the dialog box choose one of the three options: Stretch, Stack, or Stack and Scale With (and then enter a number of units per picture).

Save Chart Properties

You can save all your hard work formatting a chart if you think you might use the same formatting in the future. Follow these steps:

1. Select the chart.

2. Display the Chart Tools Design tab.

3. In the Type group, click the Save Template button.

4. In the Save Chart Template dialog box, enter a name for the template. The file is saved with a .crtx filename extension.

5. Click Save.

To use this chart template, when you choose a chart type, click the Templates item instead of one of the preset chart types. Choose your template from the saved templates and click OK. To change the chart type of an existing chart, select the chart and choose Change Chart Type from the Type group of the Chart Tools Design tab. There you can access the template option.

You can save a template and share the template with others to maintain consistent standards across an organization.

Insert a Chart from Microsoft Excel

If you have already created and formatted a chart in Excel, for example, you can paste it onto a slide. Follow these steps:

1. In Excel, click the chart's border.

2. Click Copy in the Clipboard group of the Home tab or press CTRL-C.

3. Switch to PowerPoint and display the appropriate slide.

4. Click paste in the Clipboard group of the Home tab or press CTRL-V.

Present Data in a Table

Using a table is an easy way to present lots of text or to summarize complex information that you want your viewers to remember. Use a table to make your point quickly and succinctly when you are not trying to show relationships or trends, as shown here. Another good use of a table is to supplement a chart with additional details. Show your audience the chart first so they get the main point, and then let them focus in on all the nitty-gritty.

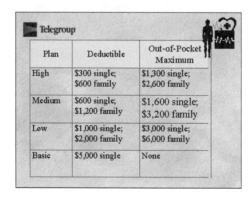

Create Clear Charts

Charts are an essential component of many presentations. However, many charts are unclear and require extensive explanation before the audience can understand them.

You create a chart to make a point. Suppose you're creating a presentation about your company's financial results. You could put a summary of the company's balance sheet into the presentation. However, if what your audience really wants to see is the company's debt-to-equity ratio, which is buried somewhere in the balance sheet, a simple pie chart of the debt-to-equity ratio would be more effective.

Once you determine that the key point is to show the improvement in earnings per share, for example, you can create your chart, perhaps a column chart. But even a simple column chart should be designed to serve a purpose. Choose colors and fills so that the viewer's eye is drawn to improvement rather than to past losses. The border around the chart that PowerPoint creates by default is also unnecessary. Also, 3-D charts are notoriously hard to evaluate—it's difficult to see exactly where the top of the column is. If you wish, add an arrow to guide the viewer's attention to the latest earnings. If there is a recent improvement, add a text box or shape and explain it in a few words. Shadows and shaded fills on the columns enhance visual appeal. Animation (discussed in Chapter 9) can be used to focus the attention of the audience on what the presenter is saying, but don't make the animation too complex.

Here are some basic rules of thumb for charts:

- Guide the attention to your main point. Use an arrow, animation, or a contrasting color to guide the eye.

- Reduce the number of lines or bars. Try to use one data series (line or row of bars) per chart. If necessary, create two charts on separate slides to present all the data.

- Use an axis scale or data points, but not both, unless the exact numbers are important.

- Remove details. Gridlines, footnotes, and other details detract from the message. If many details are necessary, consider a printed handout instead.

A well-designed chart needs very little explanation. The audience gets the idea quickly and can pay more attention to your analysis and follow-up discussion.

Create a Table

The simplest way to create a table is to create a new slide using one of the content layouts. Click the Table icon and PowerPoint opens the Insert Table dialog box. Specify the number of columns and rows you want. When you click OK, PowerPoint creates the table on your slide.

You can create a table on a slide without a table placeholder by clicking the Table button in the Tables group of the Insert tab. A grid appears. Drag down and to the right to fill in the number of columns and rows you want. You can always modify the table later.

Finally, you can draw a table by dragging rows and columns with your mouse. Drawing a table is fun and an excellent way to create a more complex table, varying the size and shape of the columns and rows. Here's how to draw a table on a slide:

1. Choose the Insert tab and click the down arrow of the Table button in the Tables group. Choose Draw Table. The cursor changes to a pencil.

2. Create the outer boundaries of the table by dragging from the top-left corner to the bottom-right corner. (Yes, you can do it from right to left if you want.)

3. Drag across to create rows. You can just drag a little and you see the row already created.

4. Drag vertically to create columns. Once you have created a row, you can create a partial column.

To erase a line, display the Table Tools Design tab and click Eraser in the Draw Borders group. Drag across the line—or just click it—to erase it. To control the border line type and width, use the Pen Style and Pen Weight drop-down lists, also in the Draw Borders group.

Here you see a table created using this method. This table would be difficult to create with the Insert Table button.

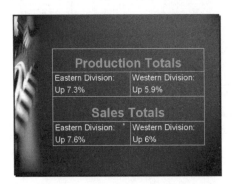

Once you have created a table, click in the first cell and start typing data. Press TAB to move from cell to cell. You can click in any cell to type in that cell. If you press TAB from the bottom-right cell, PowerPoint creates a new row so you can add more data.

In the upcoming section "Format a Table," I explain how to add, delete, split, or merge cells, rows, and/or columns. You can also apply a table style, change font size, center text, make text bold, and so on.

Import a Table

As with charts, you don't have to reinvent the wheel. If you have already created the table in Word, Excel, or Access, for example, you can import it onto your slide. If you wish, you can start in PowerPoint, embed an object from one of those programs (or another program of your choice), and use the toolbars and menus of that program to create the table in PowerPoint. However, note that it's more difficult to make an embedded object appear to be a seamless part of the slide. Remember these points when deciding which program to use:

- Use Word if you feel more comfortable with its formatting tools.
- Use Excel when you want to include calculations, statistical analysis, or sorting and search features.
- If you need the power of a relational database, use Access.

Here's the procedure for importing a table:

1. Choose Insert | Object.
2. To create a new table, choose Create New and choose the type of object from the list.
3. To import an existing table, choose Create from File and type the filename or choose Browse to locate the file.
4. Click OK.
5. When you embed a table from another application into PowerPoint, you need to double-click it to open it. The other application's menus and toolbars appear so you can use them to edit the table. For more information about sharing information between PowerPoint and other applications, see Chapter 11.

8

TIP *To import a table that is part of an existing file, such as a Word document, open the file, select the table, and copy it to the clipboard. Display the slide where you want the table and paste it from the clipboard. This table becomes part of your presentation and you can apply table styles to it or format it using PowerPoint's tools.*

Format a Table

Assuming you have created a table within PowerPoint (or pasted a table into PowerPoint), you now need to format it. The default table that PowerPoint creates, shown here, doesn't stand out at all! The default formatting will vary based on the presentation's theme or template.

A simple way to format a table is to apply a table style. Select the table and click the Table Tools Design tab. In the Table Styles group, click the More button to display the Table Styles gallery, shown here. You can scroll down in the gallery for even more choices. If you move the table to the side so that you can still see it with the gallery open, you can hover the mouse over any choice to immediately see the result in the table. Then click when you see a choice that you like.

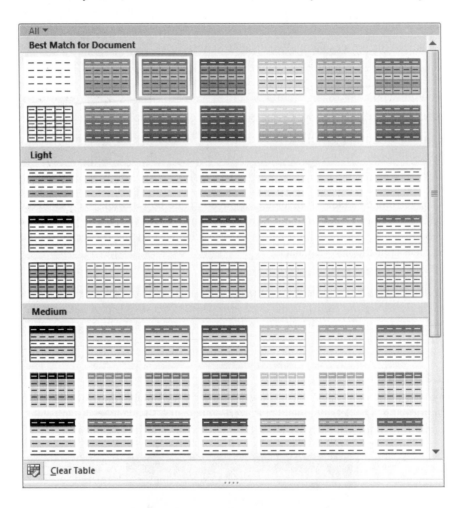

For more control, you can individually format cell shading, borders, and effects by using the buttons to the right of the Table Styles group. These controls are similar to those for shapes, which I described in Chapter 6, but you have fewer options. Table effects are limited to bevels, shadows, and reflections. Bevels create a nice 3-D effect for the table cells.

To format text, select the text that you want to format. Then, right-click the selected text to display the Mini toolbar, where you can change the font, font size, and font color. To change the text direction, alignment (horizontal and vertical), and margins, use the Alignment group of the Layout tab that appears when you select the text in the table.

To add or delete rows and columns, show or hide gridlines, or merge and split cells, you again use the Layout tab. This tab also lets you fine-tune cell and table size.

The following are probably the minimum tasks you need to do to get a professional-looking table:

- Resize and place the table.
- Select the entire table and format the font, font size, and font color.
- Change the borders. If you can't find a table style that you like, use the Borders drop-down list on the Table Tools Design tab. To delete borders, choose No Borders.
- If you wish, use the Shading drop-down list to choose a fill. You can use any of the fill effects discussed in Chapter 6.

The following is the simply formatted chart. The point is clear—we're going up, but can we go higher?

TIP   *You cannot animate a table row-by-row or column-by-column. A solution is to create multiple tables next to each other and animate them as separate objects. See Chapter 9 for more information about animation.*

Work with Diagrams

PowerPoint 2007's diagrams offer a graphic way to display the relationships between elements of a process or organization. You can even convert bulleted text to a diagram, now called a *SmartArt graphic*. This feature has been extensively updated in PowerPoint 2007. The SmartArt feature includes the following types of diagrams:

- **List**   Provides a graphical alternative to bulleted text.
- **Process**   Shows consecutive relationships.
- **Cycle**   Shows a process that takes place in a continuous cycle.
- **Hierarchy**   Shows hierarchical relationships, often those of employees in an organization. Use for organization charts.

- ■ **Relationship** Shows a variety of relationship types, including radial, Venn (overlapping), and diverging.
- ■ **Matrix** Shows the relationship of four items in a quadrant to a whole.
- ■ **Pyramid** Shows relationships where each element is the foundation of the next, or other relationships that you can portray with a pyramid.

Don't forget that you can create your own diagrams using shapes, especially the flowchart and connector shapes.

You can create a SmartArt graphic in three ways:

- ■ Use one of the Content layouts and click the Diagram icon.
- ■ To add a diagram to an existing slide, display the Insert tab and click the SmartArt button in the Illustrations group.
- ■ To convert existing level 1 and level 2 body text, select the placeholder. On the Home tab, in the Paragraph group, click the Convert to SmartArt button. This method can be quite magical, but each diagram type uses its own rules for converting text, so you might have to make some adjustments.

Right-click the placeholder and choose Convert to SmartArt.

If you're not converting existing text, the Choose a SmartArt Graphic dialog box, shown in Figure 8-8, opens. If you're converting existing text, you can choose from the options in the drop-down list that appears when you click the Convert to SmartArt button, or click More SmartArt Graphics to open the dialog box. Choose the type of diagram you want, choose a layout, and click OK. To see a description of a diagram layout, click its image.

You immediately see the diagram and a text pane to its left, as shown here. You can type the text in the text pane or directly in the diagram. If you're converting existing text, the text automatically appears both in the text pane and in the diagram.

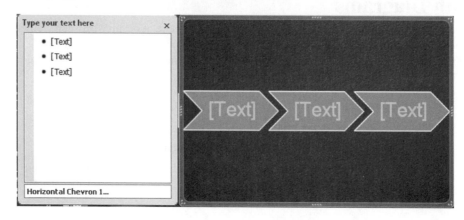

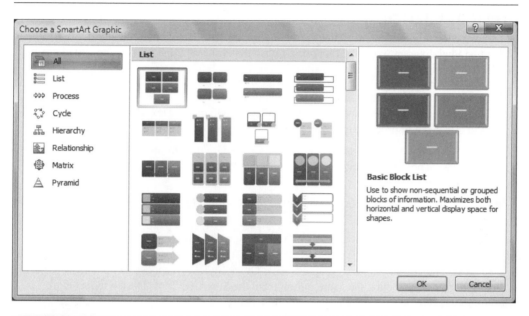

FIGURE 8-8 Using the Choose a SmartArt Graphic dialog box, you choose the type (and subtype) of the diagram that you want to create..

Here you see the result after entering text. The SmartArt graphic uses default formatting. In the next section, I explain how to change the formatting.

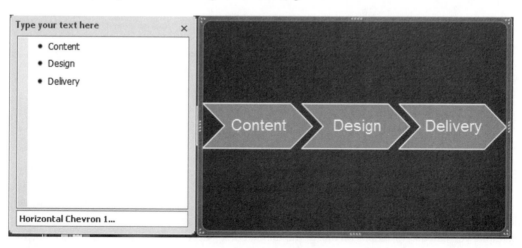

Format a Diagram

You may need to add or delete an element from a diagram. For example, if you start with three shapes in a radial diagram, you may think of a fourth that you want to add. You can add elements to a selected diagram in several ways:

- In the Text pane, use text tools to add another bullet. For example, you can place the cursor after the last item and press ENTER. Press TAB to demote text (from level 1 to level 2) and SHIFT-TAB to promote text.

- On the SmartArt Tools Design tab, use the Create Graphic group's tools to add a bullet or add a shape. The Layout button's drop-down list has special tools to help you format organizational charts.

- Right-click a shape and choose one of the options to add a shape from the shortcut menu.

You can delete shapes by selecting them and pressing DELETE, or by deleting text in the text pane.

Like charts and tables, SmartArt graphics have Quick Styles. To choose a Quick Style, select the SmartArt graphic and click the More button from the SmartArt Tools Design tab's Quick Styles group to open the Quick Styles gallery, shown here:

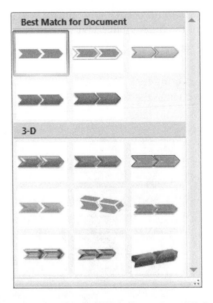

In addition, you can choose from a number of color styles. Click the Change Colors drop-down arrow, also in the Quick Styles group, to display the available color styles, shown here. For example, you can use variations on one of the theme colors' accent colors, or decide on a colorful style that varies the color of each shape.

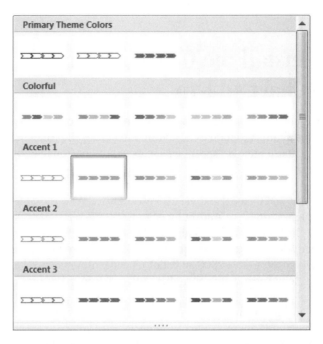

You can switch to another SmartArt graphic in the same category (such as Process), using the Layouts group of the SmartArt Tools Design tab.

For more control over individual settings, use the SmartArt Tools Format tab. The controls on this tab are familiar because they are similar to those that you use to format shapes. I discuss formatting shapes in Chapter 6. You can change the size of the entire graphic on this tab, in the Size group; you can also drag the lower-right corner of a graphic to resize it. Enlarging the entire graphic can help you fit text on the shapes more easily.

You can also select any text and change the font, size, and color. Right-click the selected text to display the Mini toolbar, where you can control the text.

Here you see the formatted diagram using a 3-D Quick Style and one of the colorful color styles:

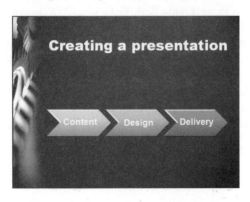

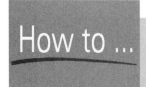

How to ... Install the Organization Chart Add-In

Microsoft's older Organization Chart application still exists but is no longer being updated. You can separately install this program as an add-in. First close all programs.

In Windows XP, choose Start | Control Panel, choose Add or Remove Programs, and then choose Change or Remove Programs. Choose Microsoft Office and click Change. In the next dialog box, click Add or Remove Features and click Continue. Expand the Microsoft Office folder, and then expand the Microsoft Office PowerPoint folder. Click the X button next to Organization Chart Add-In for Microsoft Office Programs and choose Run from My Computer. Click Continue to install the add-in.

In Windows Vista, choose Start | Control Panel and choose Programs, then Installed Programs. Choose Microsoft Office 2007 and click Change. You may need to provide approval to continue. In the next dialog box, click Add or Remove Features and click Continue. Expand the Microsoft Office folder, and then expand the Microsoft Office PowerPoint folder. Click the X button next to Organization Chart Add-In for Microsoft Office Programs and choose Run from My Computer. Click Continue to install the add-in.

To use the application, display the Insert tab. In the Text group, click Object and choose Organization Chart Add-in for Microsoft Office Programs. This program has its own Help system to help you use its simple features.

Summary

In this chapter, you learned how to present complex information clearly using graphs, tables, and the new SmartArt graphics that create diagrams.

PowerPoint lets you create or insert a graph (or chart) to suit your presentation needs. To determine the type of chart, you need to understand the structure of your data and the specific qualities of the types of charts PowerPoint offers. Once you have chosen a chart type, you should format it for maximum simplicity and impact.

Tables add clarity to complex information, and PowerPoint lets you draw a simple or complex table to present information. Tables also need to be well formatted to deliver the message loud and clear.

Diagrams show relationships between elements. The new SmartArt graphics offer many types of diagrams. You can quickly convert existing text to a SmartArt graphic.

In the next chapter, you learn how to animate slides and create electronic transition effects between slides.

In the "Bubble" section, the cities shown in the chart are (from left to right) Phoenix, Chicago, Seattle, and New York.

Chapter 9

Add Animation to a Presentation

How to...

- Animate text and objects
- Add preset animation
- Create custom animation
- Edit animation
- Animate charts and diagrams
- Add animated GIF files
- Add Macromedia Flash animation
- Add transitions from slide to slide

To add the finishing touches to a presentation, you can include two types of animation—within a slide and from slide to slide. Animation on a slide (often called *builds* when applied to text) determines how and when objects on the slide appear. Animation from slide to slide, called *transitions,* specifies how a new slide appears after the previous slide disappears. PowerPoint includes powerful animation effects and features.

Create Professional Animation

For animation to be professional, it has to have a purpose beyond the Wow! effect. Animation can certainly enliven a presentation, but too much animation will distract your audience from your main message. All professional presenters make the same point about animation—pick one or two effects and stick to them. Another good use of animation is to make an important point stand out. These principles apply to both animation on a slide and transitions between slides.

Animate Text and Objects

Animating objects has an additional purpose—to focus your audience's attention on what you're saying. To animate a slide, you need to know what you are going to say while that slide is displayed—and in what order. You then use that order to determine the order in which the objects appear on the slide. Object animation, especially when applied to text, is sometimes called a *build* because the objects build up on the screen, one after another. You can control the following aspects of the animation:

- How the object appears and where (if anywhere) it moves.
- In what grouping the object appears. For example, text most often appears paragraph by paragraph but can appear by the word or even by the letter.
- Whether the animation occurs when you click the mouse or automatically after a preset number of seconds.

- Whether a sound plays during the animation.

- What happens, if anything, after the animation. For example, you can change the color of a previously displayed object when the next object appears or hide it completely.

Use Preset Animation for Quick Results

For a quick solution, PowerPoint offers three animation effects that you can apply to any selected placeholder or object:

- **Fade**   Gradually displays the object, so that it starts out invisible and gradually fades in to its full color.

- **Wipe**   Gradually displays the object from the bottom, so that it appears to be painted on the slide (wiped) upward.

- **Fly In**   Flies the object onto the slide from the bottom.

When you animate placeholder text, all the text in the placeholder is considered one object. However, you can choose to animate it by 1st level paragraphs—that is, bullet by bullet, which is usually what you want. To animate by word or even letter, use custom animation. You add animation (preset or custom) in Normal view.

To add preset animation, follow these steps:

1. Display the slide for which you want animation and select the object or placeholder that you want to animate.

2. Display the Animations tab.

3. In the Animations group, click the Animations drop-down list. If you selected a text placeholder, you see the options shown here on the left; otherwise, you see the options shown on the right:

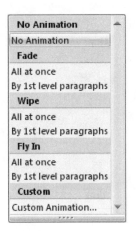

NOTE   *Pass the cursor over each option to see the animation on the slide. Then click the effect you want.*

4. Choose the animation you want from the list. You immediately see the results on the slide.

To see the animation full screen, go into Slide Show view. Click the mouse to see each successive step of the animation.

Figure 9-1 shows the effect of the Fade preset animation on a slide of bulleted text. Each bulleted item sequentially fades in at the click of the mouse. At the end of the process, the entire slide's contents are visible.

Use Custom Animation for Maximum Control

For more control over animation, you need to create your own settings. It's not hard; once you've done it once or twice, you'll be able to get exactly the effects you want.

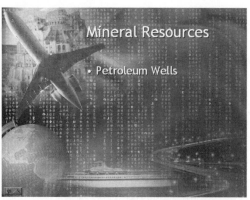
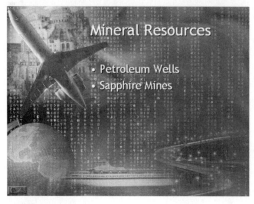
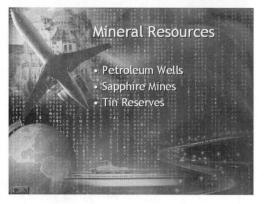

FIGURE 9-1   The Fade preset animation is very simple. Each item fades in, one after the other, as you click your mouse. (Presentation courtesy of Geetesh Bajaj, http://www .indezine.com.)

Don't forget that you can also animate shapes, including text boxes. Because these objects often serve to draw attention anyway, adding animation to them increases the effect.

To specify a custom animation, you must be in Normal view. On the Animations tab, click the Custom Animation button to open the Custom Animation task pane, shown in Figure 9-2.

Add Custom Animation

The first step to adding animation is to select an object on the active slide and click Add Effect in the Custom Animation task pane. You see the menu shown here, which provides you with four basic types of animation:

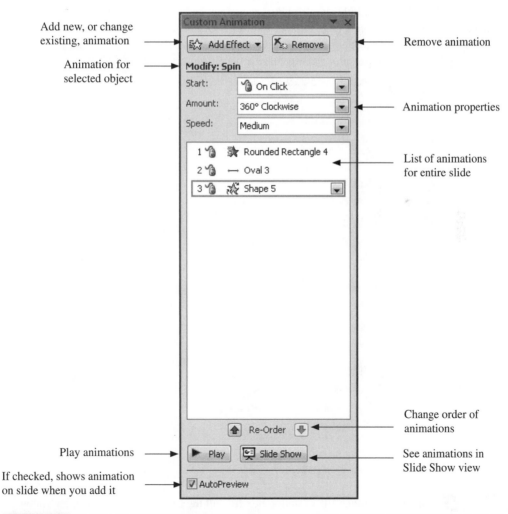

FIGURE 9-2   The Custom Animation task pane lets you create and manage animation.

You can choose from the following:

- **Entrance** Determines how the object appears on the slide.
- **Emphasis** Changes the object in some way to bring attention to it.
- **Exit** Determines how the object disappears from the slide.
- **Motion Paths** Moves the object along a preset or custom path.

As you pass your cursor over any of the four types of animation, a submenu appears listing commonly used animations. Each submenu also includes a More Effects (or More Motion Paths) item. Click this item to open a dialog box listing all of the animation effects available, as shown in Figure 9-3. Each listing includes basic, subtle, moderate, and exciting effects. Scroll down to see them all. Overall, you have a huge number of effects to choose from.

Motion Paths offer many opportunities for creativity. You can illustrate processes, progress, or the passage of time by moving objects from a start position to an end position. You can show

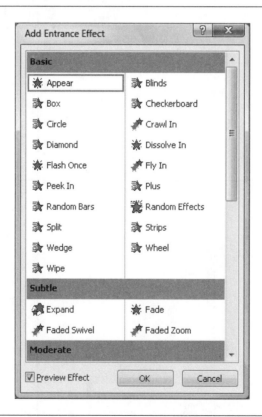

FIGURE 9-3   The Add Entrance Effect dialog box lists all the Entrance effects. Similar dialog boxes list Emphasis, Exit, and Motion Paths esffects.

changes in relationships by moving objects, or even pictures, from one location to another. Custom paths mean that you have total control of the movement of the object.

You can add more than one animation to an object. For example, you can fade an object in (Entrance effect), change its color (Emphasis effect), or move it along a path (Motion Paths effect), and then let it fly off the slide (Exit effect). You can also create a custom motion path by choosing Motion Paths | Draw Custom Path and then choosing Line, Curve, Freeform, or Scribble.

When Preview Effect is checked in any of the More Effects dialog boxes, you can select any object, click any effect, and see the effect on your slide. Move the dialog box to the side of the slide to see the effect clearly. To learn about the effects, try them all!

Once you have chosen an animation effect, click OK. You now see the effect listed in the Custom Animation task pane. Your slide also displays numbered tags next to each animated object to help you keep track of the order of animation, as shown here. These tags never show in Slide Show view and don't print. You see them only when the Custom Animation task pane is open.

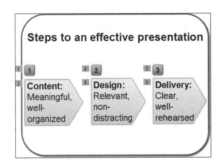

When you click Play to view an animation, you see a timeline that shows the seconds passing throughout the animation. This timeline helps you gauge the total time that your animation takes.

Choosing an animation effect is not always enough. You may need to refine the animation effect in many ways. You can do the following:

- Specify when the effect starts.
- Set the speed of the effect.
- Add a dimming effect after the main animation effect.
- Specify other properties particular to an effect. For example, for the Spin effect, you can specify how many degrees the object spins.

Specify How Custom Animation Starts

Choose when an animation effect starts from the Start drop-down list in the Custom Animation task pane. (Refer to Figure 9-2.) An animation effect can start in three ways. By default, animation starts only when you click the mouse. For example, if you animate bulleted text, you click the mouse to display each bullet of text. In this way, you control the timing of the animation.

 *To use the On Mouse Click setting, or the Hide on Next Mouse Click setting on the Effects tab (discussed in the next section), you must also have the On Mouse Click check box checked in the Transition To This Slide group of the Animations tab. (It's checked by default.) If On Mouse Click is not checked, your mouse click will have no effect when you run the presentation. Slide transitions are covered later in this chapter, in the "Choose the Ideal Transition Style" section.*

However, sometimes you want animation to start automatically, without requiring a mouse click. You can specify how animation starts from the Start drop-down list of the Custom Animation task pane:

- To start animation at the same time as the previous animation on the slide, choose With Previous. Use this option when you want two animations to occur simultaneously.

- To start animation after the previous animation, choose After Previous. Then you need to specify how many seconds to wait after the previous animation before the next animation starts. You do this by setting the timing of the effect. Use this option when you want the second animation to automatically follow the previous animation.

To set the timing of an effect, select the object whose timing you want to specify. You now see the effect also bordered in the animation listing in the Custom Animation task pane with a down arrow next to it. (Refer to Figure 9-2.) Click the down arrow to display the menu shown here:

Choose Timing to display the dialog box shown in Figure 9-4. The name of the dialog box varies according to the type of animation effect. Here you can set the following timing parameters:

- **Start** You can change when the animation starts. You have the same three options described previously.

- **Delay** Set the delay from the start. For example, if Start is set to After Previous and Delay is set to 2 seconds, then the animation automatically starts 2 seconds after the previous animation. (Adding a delay to the With Previous Start setting has the same effect.) You can add a delay to the On Click Start setting, in which case the animation starts the specified number of seconds after you click the mouse.

- **Speed** You can set the speed of the animation itself, from very slow to very fast.

If the preset speeds don't suit your needs, you can enter an exact number of seconds in the Speed text box. To specify parts of seconds in hundredths, add a period after the number of seconds. To specify timing in sixtieths of seconds, add a colon after the number of seconds.

■ **Repeat**   You can specify the number of repetitions. You can also choose to repeat the animation until the next mouse click or until the next slide. This setting creates a looping animation.

To return the object to its original condition or setting, check the Rewind When Done Playing check box.

To create a cascading effect of objects entering quickly one after another, use a Start setting of With Previous for all but the first object. Then, click the animation item's down arrow in the Custom Animation task pane, and choose Show Advanced Timeline. You now see orange rectangles representing the time covered by each animation. Starting from the second rectangle, drag each rectangle a little further to the right, so that each animation starts slightly after the previous one.

9

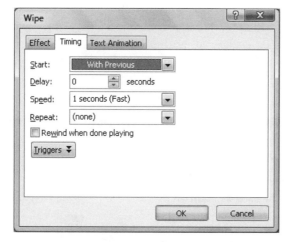

FIGURE 9-4   The Timing tab of the Wipe dialog box lets you set the timing of the Wipe animation effect. You use similar dialog boxes for other animation effects.

You can create a *trigger*, which means that when you click another object (the trigger), the animation starts. For example, you could click a circle to turn a star purple, using the Change Fill Color emphasis effect. This technique is great for creating games in PowerPoint.

To create a trigger object, click Triggers on the Timing tab of the dialog box and choose Start Effect on Click of. Then use the drop-down list to select one of the objects on your slide.

 Click OK when you have finished setting the timing. A triggered animation displays the icon shown here.

Add Effect Options

To specify settings for an animation not related to timing, select the animated object and click its drop-down arrow in the Custom Animation task pane's listing. Choose Effect Options to open the Effect tab of the dialog box for the particular animation you have applied, as shown in Figure 9-5.

The Settings section of the dialog box is available for only certain effects, and varies with the effect. As shown in Figure 9-5, the Spin animation effect offers you the opportunity to specify the amount of the spin and whether the spin is clockwise or counterclockwise. A number of animation effects let you create a smooth start and smooth end, by checking the appropriate check boxes in the dialog box. A smooth start slows the acceleration of the effect, and a smooth end slows its deceleration. Check Auto-reverse to play the effect backward after it has finished, doubling the total time of the effect.

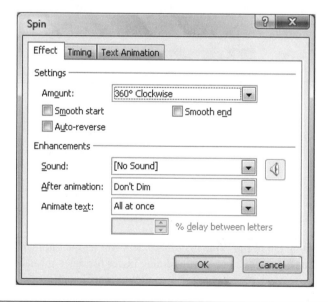

FIGURE 9-5 The Effect tab of the Spin dialog box lets you refine the Spin animation effect. Similar dialog boxes offer these settings for other animation effects.

The Enhancements section of the dialog box for each effect lets you do the following:

- Add sound effects (Chapter 10 explains how to add music, CD soundtracks, and narration to a presentation).
- Dim the object after animation.
- Animate text all at once, by word, or by letter.

PowerPoint comes with a few sound effects, such as applause, a drum roll, or a cash register. These sounds tend to have a humorous effect, which is fine if that's what you want. They're great for games created for children. For a presentation given by a real person to adults, sound effects tend to distract from the presenter. They can also be annoying. The first and last slides are two places where sound can be useful. For example, you might want music to be playing as the audience trickles in before the presentation or as they leave after the last slide (if you won't be taking questions). A drum roll on the first slide can get your audience's attention in a humorous way—but leave it at that. PowerPoint can play any WAV sound file (but no other type) attached to a transition or animation effect.

Use the Windows Search feature (Start | Search) to search for WAV files on your hard disk or network.

To add a sound to an animation, use the Sound drop-down list on the Effect tab of the animation dialog box (see Figure 9-5). Choose Other Sound to search for WAV sound files on your hard disk or network. When you have chosen a sound, click OK to close the animation dialog box.

Dim Objects

Dimming text after animation is especially effective in focusing your audience's attention on the current point. You can dim to a lighter color, hide the object completely immediately after the animation (which doesn't leave it on the screen for very long), or hide it on the next mouse click. Just as your audience can wander ahead of you when all the text is visible at once, your audience may start thinking about the points you just finished if they are still clearly visible on the slide. While bulleted text is most often dimmed, you can also dim other objects on a slide, such as shapes or text boxes.

Dim to a softer, lighter color to emphasize your current point so that the previous items are still visible enough to discuss if someone in the audience asks a question about a previous point. Don't dim when your slide contains an entire process that your audience needs to see as a whole. Audience members who want to look at all the items on a slide together may find dimming frustrating.

To dim an object, click the After Animation drop-down arrow on the Effect tab and use the menu shown here. Choose a dimming color or one of the Hide options—After Animation or On Next Mouse Click. Then click OK.

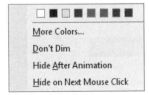

Figure 9-6 shows a slide that is animated with a dim to a lighter color. All the bulleted items are still visible, but the current item is much more obvious.

Set Text Animation Options

Finally, in the animation effect's dialog box (see Figure 9-5), you can specify how text is animated. From the Animate Text drop-down list, choose to animate text all at once (the entire paragraph), by word, or by letter. If you choose to animate by word or letter, specify the speed by setting the delay between words or letters. Animating text by letter gives the appearance of the text being typed, letter by letter.

When you are animating text, you can use the Text Animation tab in the animation effect dialog box, shown in Figure 9-7.

Use the Group Text drop-down list to specify how text is grouped when animated. For example, you can animate text As One Object (the entire text placeholder), By 1st Level

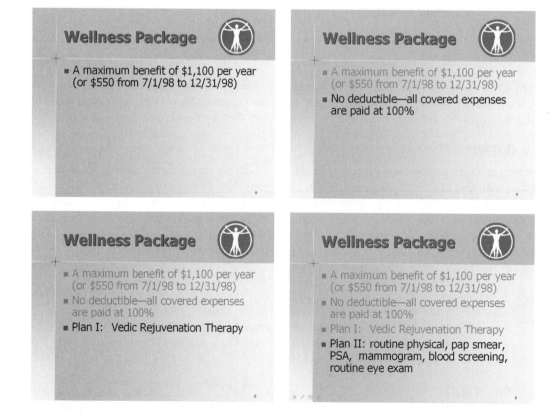

FIGURE 9-6 Dimming previously animated text helps to focus your audience's attention on the current point.

FIGURE 9-7 The Text Animation tab contains additional options for animating text.

Paragraphs (the most common choice), By 2nd Level Paragraphs, and so on. In addition, you can use the following settings:

- **Automatically After *x* Seconds** Set animation to occur automatically after the number of seconds you specify.
- **Animate Attached Shape** Animate the shape with the text if the text is in a shape and you select the shape when specifying the animation.
- **In Reverse Order** Animate the text from the bottom up.

When you're done with the settings, click OK to return to your slide.

Edit Animation

You may need to remove or change animation. When you are animating more than one object, you may also want to change the order of animation. You can perform any of the following tasks:

- **Remove animation** Select the animated object and click Remove in the Custom Animation task pane.
- **Change animation effect** Select the animation from the animation list in the Custom Animation task pane. (Do not select the object.) Click Change and choose a new animation.
- **Change animation timing or options** Select the animation from the animation list in the Custom Animation task pane. From the drop-down list, choose Timing or Effect Options and make the desired changes in the dialog box. Click OK.

- **Change animation order**   Select the animation from the animation list. Click the up or down Re-Order arrow that is beneath the animation list.

- **Edit animation path**   If you draw a custom path, you can edit it. Select the animation from the animation list in the Custom Animation task pane. From the Path drop-down list, choose Edit Points. You see small squares along the path, which you can drag to a new location. Right-click the path and choose Add Point to add a new point or choose Delete Point to delete a point. (See Chapter 6 for more information on editing points.)

Animation can be a major influence in a presentation that is not meant to tell a simple story but instead is used to create a visual impression. For example, some presentations are used as an impetus for a subsequent workshop or brainstorming session. In these cases, you want to excite or inspire your audience rather than systematically move from text item to item.

Figure 9-8 shows a presentation on one of Sharp Electronics' projectors. While it provides information, there is no bulleted text in the entire presentation. The word "introducing" flies in

FIGURE 9-8   Presentations can use animation to excite and inspire the audience. (Presentation courtesy of Gerry Ganguzza of Sharp Electronics Corporation, http://www.sharp-usa.com.)

from top left, "a compact projector" flies in from top right, "with a" flies in from bottom left, and "high IQ" flies in from bottom right. The purpose of the presentation is to excite potential customers about a new product. In other words, this is advertising. Although you can't see the actual animation in the figure, you can get an idea of how the first slide presents the material. This presentation is meant to run automatically, with preset timing.

Animate Charts and Diagrams

You can animate a chart created within PowerPoint or with Microsoft Excel. As with other objects, animating a chart can help to focus your audience's attention on a specific portion of the chart. Because charts often represent growth over time, building the chart over several steps is appropriate. You can animate a chart in the following ways (refer to the chart that follows the list), using the Chart Animation tab of the animation effect's dialog box:

- **All at Once**   The entire chart appears at once with the animation effect.
- **By Series**   For a chart with more than one series (for example, the chart following this list displays revenue for both sales and service), first one series appears, then the next, and so on, with the animation effect. All of the elements of the series (the breakdown by years) appear together as a group. Use this when you want to discuss each series separately.
- **By Category**   Each category (for example, each year is a category) appears together. Use this option when you want to discuss the chart year by year.
- **By Element in Series**   This option breaks down the animation by each element in each series.
- **By Element in Category**   The elements of each category appear in order.

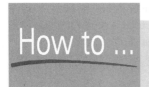
Animate Text on Top of Text

An interesting use of the Hide on Next Mouse Click feature, one of the After Animation options, is to enable you to cover a great deal of information on one slide. This technique lets you hide text and then display new text in the same location as the previous text, which is now invisible. You get to use the same "real estate" twice—or more.

Figure 9-9 shows a portion of a slide that uses this technique. The presenter wanted to discuss the products that his company offers, and wanted to add subtopics for each product. This slide includes some complex animation, in which major topics are animated on the presenter's mouse click and the subtopics are displayed automatically afterwards, and then hidden. See if you can follow the frames in Figure 9-9 to get a sense of the flow of the slide.

These options will not all be available if your chart doesn't contain all these features. For example, a simple pie chart will have only the All at Once and the By Category options.

If these options aren't enough for you and you must animate a chart in more detail, you can ungroup the chart. You can then animate each individual object as you wish. But beware, ungrouping a chart turns it into an Office drawing object, and it loses its connection with the underlying data. Also, any link to another file is severed. Another disadvantage is that you will probably end up with more objects than you want to deal with. But you can do it!

If you want to ungroup a chart, first duplicate the slide and hide it. (See the "Create Slide Show Variations" section in Chapter 14 for instructions on hiding a slide.) An alternative is to duplicate the chart itself and drag the original off the slide area. With these techniques, you still retain the original chart, in case you need to change it.

To animate a chart, follow these steps:

1. Select the chart.

2. On the Animations tab, click Custom Animations to open the Custom Animation task pane.

3. Click Add Effect and choose an animation effect. A typical choice would be Entrance | Wipe.

4. Choose the animation from the task pane's listing and choose Effect Options.

5. In the Direction section of the Effect tab, specify a direction. For example, you often want column charts to wipe from the bottom, so the column appears to grow up to its full height.

6. On the Chart Animation tab, choose an option from the Group Chart drop-down list. If you want each column to wipe up in order, try the By Element in Category option.

7. By default, the axes and background of the chart appear first, so that the columns (or other elements) have a context as they appear. Uncheck the Start Animation by Drawing Chart Background check box if you want the background of the chart to appear after the other elements.

8. Click OK.

9. Click Slide Show in the Custom Animation task pane and check out the animation. Make any adjustments you think are necessary. For example, you may want to change the speed of the animation from the Speed drop-down list in the task pane.

FIGURE 9-9   This slide uses the Hide on Next Mouse Click feature to display subtopics that would not otherwise fit on the slide.

You can animate other objects now. For example, in the chart shown in the previous illustration, after the columns appear with the Wipe Up effect, the arrow showing the percent increase wipes from the left. You can animate diagrams and organization charts like a chart. Instead of a Chart Animation tab in the dialog box (see Step 6 in the previous procedure), there is a SmartArt Animation tab.

 *When a composite object like multiline text, a chart, or a diagram is animated, the listing in the Custom Animation task pane is sometimes collapsed. Click the double down arrow below the list to expand the list and see all its components.*

Add Animated GIF Files

Animated GIF files are graphic files that include animation. You see them often on web sites. You can easily download them from many web sites that offer free web graphics. Try a search in your favorite search engine for "free animated GIF."

Among the more common animated GIFs are animated bullets. However, be aware that, like sound, the effect will usually be humorous. If you want to use animated GIFs in a business presentation, keep it low-key. You may be able to take an animated logo from your company's web site. Perhaps you could draw attention to one especially noteworthy or exciting item with an animated arrow. Too many animated GIFs make a presentation look like a cartoon.

You insert an animated GIF like any image. Follow these steps:

1. Display the slide to which you want to add the animated GIF.

2. To insert an animated GIF from a file, display the Insert tab and click the Picture button in the Illustrations group. Then navigate to the file, select it, and choose Open.

3. To insert an animated GIF from the Clip Gallery, click the Clip Art button in the same location. (For information on adding graphic files to the Clip Gallery, see Chapter 5.)

Animated GIFs move only in Slide Show view. In Normal or Slide Sorter view, they are frozen. You cannot edit an animated GIF image with the Picture toolbar in PowerPoint. To edit an animated GIF, you need an animated GIF-editing program.

Add Flash Animation to a Slide

Macromedia Flash is an animation program that is usually used on web sites. Flash's capabilities are far beyond PowerPoint's. You can add Flash animation to any slide fairly easily to create any sophisticated effect you wish. If you wish to learn an advanced technique for creating animation, try this one out.

First, you need to create the Flash movie using Flash. The file you create has an .fla extension. However, you need to publish the movie, using the Publish command in Flash. The result is a movie file with an extension of .swf. You use the SWF file in PowerPoint. (Perhaps someone else did this for you and you received only the SWF file.) To view the results, you need the Flash Player. You probably already have it on your computer, but, if not, it's a free download at http://www.adobe.com/shockwave/download/index.cgi?P1_Prod_Version=ShockwaveFlash. Here are the steps:

1. Write down the location of the SWF file you want to use. Ideally, it should be in the same folder as the presentation.

2. If the Developer tab is not available on the Ribbon, click the Office button and click PowerPoint Options. In the PowerPoint Options dialog box, choose the Popular category. On the Popular pane, check the Show Developer Tab in the Ribbon check box, and click OK.

3. On the Developer tab, click the More Controls button in the Control group.

4. Choose Shockwave Flash Object from the listing.

5. Drag a box across the screen to get the desired size and location. Don't cover the entire slide.

6. Right-click the box and choose Properties.

7. In the Properties window, click the top line, Custom. Then click the ellipsis at the right.

8. In the Movie URL text box of the Property Pages dialog box, type the location of the SWF file that you wrote down earlier, such as, c:\animation\animlogo.swf.

NOTE   *To make sure this works, I recommend saving the presentation first, putting the SWF in the same folder as the presentation, and entering the full path.*

9. Set the other parameters if you wish; for example, Quality: Best; Scale: Show All; Window: Window. Check Loop if you want the movie to continuously replay itself.

10. Click Embed Movie if you want to make sure the movie is always included with the PowerPoint presentation.

11. Click OK.

12. Close the Properties window using its Close button.

13. Choose Slide Show view to see the movie. If your movie didn't appear on the slide in Normal view, it will appear when you return to Normal view after running the slide show.

You cannot create the Flash movie the full size of the slide because PowerPoint doesn't recognize mouse clicks on top of the Flash movie. So, you need some blank space on the slide so that you can click to the next slide. You can match the movie background to the background of your PowerPoint slide. Use a one-color background on your PowerPoint slide. In Flash, choose Modify | Movie (or Document, depending on the version of Flash) to change the background before publishing your movie and choose the same color as your PowerPoint slide.

If the Flash movie doesn't play, open the Properties window again and look at the Playing property. If it says False, click Playing, click the down arrow, and change the Playing property to True. Flash movies placed on the slide master will play continuously from slide to slide to create an animated background. (But that can get distracting.)

There is a bug that automatically changes the Playing property to False if the Flash movie is not set to loop. In this situation, the Flash movie simply does not play. It may play each time you open the presentation, but does not play if you try to display the slide containing the animation twice in one showing. Two solutions are helpful:

■ **Save the presentation as a PowerPoint show**   Reset the Playing property of the SWF file(s) to True: select the Shockwave Flash object, right-click it, and choose Properties. Click the Playing row, then click the down arrow and choose True. Then choose File | Save As. From the Save as Type drop-down list, choose PowerPoint Show (*.ppsx). Keep the same file name and click Save. (A PowerPoint show automatically plays in Slide Show view when you open it by double-clicking the file in Windows Explorer.)

■ **Create Visual Basic for Applications (VBA) code to control the Playing property**   If necessary, display the Developer tab, as explained at the beginning of this section. On the Developer tab, in the Controls group, click the View Code button or press ALT-F11. The Microsoft Visual Basic window opens. Choose Insert | Module. In the main window, enter the following code, where the number after ActivePresentation Slides is the number of the slide containing the Flash movie. In the following example, the Flash movie is on slide 2. (The fourth and fifth lines are split here in the book, but you should type them on one line in the Visual Basic window.)

```
Sub PlayFlash()
   Dim obj As ShockwaveFlash

   On Error Resume Next

   Set obj = ActivePresentation.Slides(2).
      Shapes("ShockwaveFlash1").OLEFormat.Object
   obj.Playing = True
   obj.Rewind
   obj.Play

   Set obj = Nothing

End Sub
```

As you can see, the code simply sets the Playing property to True, rewinds the movie, and plays it. Now save the presentation. If the presentation doesn't have any other VBA code in it, you will be prompted to save it as a PowerPoint Macro-Enabled Presentation (*.pptm). In PowerPoint 2007, presentations with VBA code need to use this file type. (For more information, see Chapter 13.)

If you want more than one Flash movie in a presentation, you need to give additional movies unique shape names to replace ("ShockwaveFlash1") in the code. The second one could be "ShockwaveFlash2" for example. (You can find the name next to the Name property in the

Properties window. The previous code uses the default name given to the movie.) Then, in the Properties window, give the object the same name in the Name row (which is just under the Custom row).

Next, go to the slide containing the Flash movie. From the Insert tab, click the Shapes button and insert the blank action button. (I explain action buttons in detail in Chapter 11.) In the Action Settings dialog box that opens, choose the Run Macro option, choose the macro from the drop-down list ("Play Flash" in the previous example), and click OK. With the action button still selected, type some text on the button, such as "Play Movie" to label the button. Now, whenever you need to play the movie in Slide Show view, you can simply click the button.

Your macro security settings may stop the VBA code from running. I explain how to change these settings in Chapter 13.

NOTE   *For more information, see the following:*

- http://www.ellenfinkelstein.com/powerpoint_tip_putting_flash_in_powerpoint.html
- http://www.indezine.com/products/powerpoint/ppflash.html
- http://www.indezine.com/products/powerpoint/ppflash2.html

9

Transition from Slide to Slide

Another type of animation controls how each new slide appears. Because these effects control the transition from one slide to another, they are called *transitions*. While some of these effects have the same names as animations, they look quite different when applied to an entire slide.

Use Transitions Wisely

Transitions, like slide animation, need to be used with reserve. Many options are available, but that doesn't mean you should use them all in one presentation. One of the best solutions is to choose a simple transition and apply it to every slide in the presentation. If your presentation is divided into sections, you could use a second transition to introduce each new section.

Choose the Ideal Transition Style

The ideal transition style heightens your audience's attention without your audience noticing why. If the transition style is too active, your audience will get a headache looking at it. PowerPoint offers a transition style for every possible purpose.

You may want to set transitions in Slide Sorter view where you can get a sense of the flow of the entire presentation. PowerPoint places an Animation icon beneath each slide with a transition so that you can easily see which slides have transitions and which don't. However, you can add transitions in Normal view.

When you add a transition to a slide, the transition determines how that slide appears after the previous slide is removed from view.

To add a transition, follow these steps:

1. Select the slide or slides to which you want to add a transition.

2. Display the Animations tab. In the Transitions To This Slide group, click the More button to display the Transitions gallery, shown here:

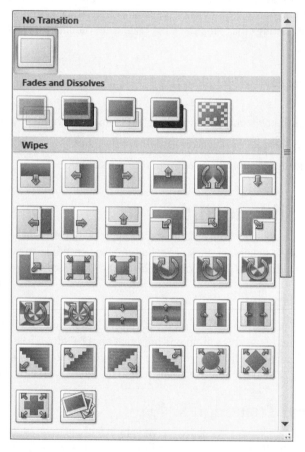

3. Choose a transition style from the gallery.

4. From the Transition Speed drop-down list, also in the Transitions To This Slide group, choose Fast, Medium, or Slow.

How to ...   Use Animations and Transitions Effectively

When presentation software programs introduced movement into their feature sets, it became the best of times and the worst of times. It's not enough to animate objects because you can; your audiences simply grow weary of the gratuitous use of any presentation element. The first time you animate some clip art, it gets a few oohs and aahs; the second and third time, some yawns. The flying objects appear to be nothing more than a multimedia shell game, causing audiences to wonder under which presentation component the real message resides.

That said, the proper use of movement can have a profoundly positive effect on how your audiences grasp, interpret, and retain your key messages. You can make a busy chart significantly easier to understand by introducing the content in animated stages. Mirroring how the presenter addresses the information (quarter by quarter or category by category) is essential in making the point.

Text-based information creates its own inherent challenges. When given a chance to read ahead, the audience is more likely to make quick judgments. By staging the bullets to enter on a mouse click, you get an opportunity to articulate the points before judgment is passed, providing the best chance of the audience staying with the flow of information.

The challenge in creating a quality presentation is to identify opportunities for making text-type information more graphical and introducing it in a way that best supports your needs. This could be processes, steps, chronologies, or other similar topics.

Transition effects fall into the same category. Presentation software provides many more options than will ever be appropriate. Look at transition effects as a tool for guiding the audience's eye or creating interest. For example, you could use a Wipe Up effect to guide the eye back to the top after each slide, or possibly a Wipe Left effect to reset the eye for more information. Pick a specific nondistracting transition and stick with it. Sort through the choices, eliminate those that fall into the cute category (audiences grow weary of "cute" very quickly), and throw in a change-up once in a while. Introducing a new topic in the presentation may be a time to use a different transition and then get back into your standard transition effect.

Let's face it: animations and transitions are just electronic effects. A wise presenter realizes that the stage lights don't make good presenters—compelling stories do.

Thanks to Jim Endicott, who is the owner/manager of Distinction, a business communications company that provides creative and consulting support services. He assists business professionals in enhancing the content, tools, and techniques of effective presenting. He can be reached at 503-554-1203 or jim.endicott@distinction-services.com.

9

5. From the Transition Sound drop-down list, choose a sound if you wish. If you want the sound to be continuous, choose Loop Until Next Sound.

Adding a sound to each slide transition can get very annoying. It might work for the beginning or end of a presentation.

6. Under the Advance Slide label, check the check boxes to choose whether you want slides to advance on a mouse click, automatically after a specified number of seconds, or both. If you want to use automatic timing, it's a good idea to keep the On Mouse Click option checked as well.

If On Mouse Click is not checked, your mouse will not work while you present! (You can still use the keyboard.) As a result, you should keep this box checked even if you also check the Automatically After check box.

7. Click Apply to All if you want to apply the transition to the entire presentation. Otherwise, the transition you chose (in Step 3) is applied only to selected slides.

You can view transitions in three ways:

- In Slide Sorter view, click the Animation icon. (You see animation for the slide as well as the transition.)
- Select a slide or slides and click Preview in the Preview group of the Animations tab. You see both animation and transition effects.
- In Slide Show view, view the presentation.

To remove a transition, select the slide or slides you want to work with and choose No Transition from the Slide Transition gallery. To remove a sound, choose No Sound in the Sound drop-down list in the Transition to This Slide group of the Animations tab.

Summary

In this chapter, you learned how to animate text and objects on a slide, both to help focus your audience's attention on what you're saying and to add interest and excitement to a presentation. Animation options include building text and applying various effects to objects, moving objects along a path, dimming or hiding objects after animation, and adding WAV sound effects. You can also add animated GIF files to a slide.

You can add transitions from slide to slide for a professional effect. PowerPoint offers many transition effects to choose from. For both animation and transitions, the main principle is to keep it simple.

In the next chapter, I explain how to add more sophisticated sounds as well as music to your presentation. In addition, I cover using a CD soundtrack, video clips, and narration.

Chapter 10

Use Multimedia

How to...

- ■ Add sounds and music
- ■ Use media clips
- ■ Play a CD soundtrack throughout a presentation
- ■ Show movies with video clips
- ■ Record narration

More and more, multimedia effects are showing up in PowerPoint. While PowerPoint does not yet offer the flexibility of creating a full-fledged video or movie, you can add some of the same features. You can add sounds, music, or CD soundtracks to your presentations. You can use short sounds with any presentation, but continuous music or soundtracks work best for unattended presentations, where the music doesn't compete with the presenter. For a self-running presentation, music can add a professional effect.

In addition, you can insert video clips onto a slide to be shown at any time during a presentation. They don't turn your presentation into a video but add the element of video where the static quality of a slide is not enough. These video clips are usually quite short, but they pack quite an impact.

For self-running presentations, you can record narration. Narration replaces what you would say if you were making the presentation and is appropriate whenever viewers see a presentation on their own. As with music, the effect of the narration can add a professional quality to your presentation.

Create a Mood with Sounds and Music

When you stand in front of an audience, you generally want the audience to pay attention to *you*. You talk, and that is probably the best sound effect your presentation can have. But when you create a self-running presentation for a kiosk or the floor of a trade show, you often need to replace your words with some type of sound, music, or narration. Music, especially, creates a mood that can add a lot to the overall impression of your presentation. You've probably heard of research done by retailers showing that music played in stores increases sales. Music can have a powerful effect on your presentation because music has an emotional effect on people. Of course, you need to choose appropriate music for your message. In this section, I explain how to add sound and music to a presentation. In the "Record Narration" section later in this chapter, I explain how to add narration to a presentation. (Chapter 14 explains how to create a self-running presentation.)

Insert Sound or Music Files

In Chapter 9, I explained how to add WAV sound files to animation and transitions. For more options, you can insert a music or sound file into your presentation. You have more file type options when you use this method. Table 10-1 lists the most commonly used sound formats that you can insert into a presentation.

Sound Format	Filename Extension	Description
Audio Interchange File Format	.aif, .aiff.	Developed by Apple, allowing for various sampling rates, sample size, and number of channels
Musical Instrument Digital Interface	.mid, .midi, .rmi	Primarily for musical instruments
Moving Picture Experts Group	.mp3	Can achieve high rates of compression without a noticeable decrease in quality
Windows WAVE	.wav	Specifies an arbitrary sampling rate, number of channels, and sample size and has many different compression formats
Windows Media Audio	.wma	Compressed using a Microsoft compression codec

TABLE 10-1   Common Sound File Types

When you insert a sound file, PowerPoint places an icon on the slide. The music or sound can be set to play automatically or only when you click its icon while you're in Slide Show view. (In Normal view, you can play the sound or music at any time by double-clicking the sound icon.)

CAUTION   *PowerPoint embeds most WAV files, but links to all other sound files and to large WAV files. Therefore, if you move the presentation, PowerPoint won't be able to find and play the sound. Before you insert a sound, you should move it to the same folder as your presentation. If you move the presentation, or give it to someone, be sure to include the sound file. In Chapter 14, I explain how to use the Package for CD feature, which helps ensure that a presentation includes all its linked files.*

Here's how to insert music or sound on a slide:

1. Display the slide you want to add the sound or music to.

 2. On the Insert tab, in the Media Clips group, click the Sound drop-down arrow.

3. On the submenu, choose either Sound from Clip Organizer or Sound from File. (If you simply click the Sounds button, you can immediately insert a sound from a file.)

▪ If you choose Sound from Clip Organizer, you see the Insert Clip Art task pane. You can choose from a category or type in a keyword to locate a sound on your system or from the Office Online collection. Click the sound to insert it on the slide. (See Chapter 5 for instruction on adding clips to the Clip Gallery. You add sounds in the same way.)

▪ If you choose Sound from File, locate the file, choose it, and click Open.

4. PowerPoint puts a sound icon on the slide.

5. A dialog box opens asking if you want the sound to play automatically or when you click it. Choose the option you want.

When you choose how you want to play the sound, PowerPoint creates an animation setting for the icon. You can change it by clicking the sound icon, and displaying the Options tab that appears on the ribbon. In the Sound Options group, use the Play Sound drop-down list to choose When Clicked, Automatically, or Play Across Slides. Another method is to display the Animations tab and click Custom Animation. In the Custom Animation task pane, in the Start drop-down list, choose On Click to play the sound only when you click its icon and choose After Previous to play the sound automatically as soon as you display the slide.

TIP   *If the sound is played automatically, you don't need the sound icon on the slide. Drag it off the slide so that it is invisible to your audience.*

Most music files come in MP3 format. Other sound files can be in any format. You can search for music or sounds in several places:

- Search your hard disk and network for audio files.
- The Windows\Media folder has additional sounds and music that you can use. Most are simple WAV sounds that Windows uses.
- The Office Online web site contains a large selection of sounds. From the Clip Art task pane, click Clip Art on Office Online. There you can search for sounds by keyword and download them.

Be especially careful when searching the Internet for music—much of it is copyrighted. You can insert more than one sound on a slide. Of course, check out the effect, as it could be confusing.

If you already have a sound icon on a slide, PowerPoint usually places a new sound icon on top of the previous one, making it hard to find. Just select it and drag it to a new location, and you immediately see that you have two sound icons on the slide.

Specify Play Settings

Once you have inserted a sound or music file, you can specify how it will play. These settings give you a great deal of control over the sound in your presentation. Here are your options:

- You can choose whether to play the music or sound automatically or when you click the mouse button.
- You can stop the sound or music after the current slide or after any number of slides that you specify. If you specify the last slide in the presentation, the sound or music plays to the end of the presentation.
- You can choose to start the sound or music file from the beginning again when it reaches the end, called *looping*.

- You can hide the sound icon before and after it plays.
- You can play the music or sound before or after other animation on the slide.

Somewhat confusingly, there are several places where you can set options for how your sound plays, as described in the following sections.

Use the Play Sound Dialog Box

To set the options for playing sound or music, select the sound icon. From the Animations tab, click Custom Animation to open the Custom Animation task pane. Click the drop-down arrow for the sound in the task pane listing and choose Effect Options to open the Play Sound dialog box, shown in Figure 10-1 with the Effect tab on top. Here you can decide where you want the sound to start (from the beginning, from where it left off the last time it was played, or after a specified number of seconds). You can also specify when the sound will stop playing. Finally, you can set the volume and hide the sound icon while it is not playing. Click OK when you're done.

Your decisions will depend on whether you are playing a short sound effect or a long piece of music. Is the sound or music appropriate for just this slide, or do you want to continue it throughout part or all of the presentation?

10

FIGURE 10-1   Use the Play Sound dialog box to specify when a sound starts and stops.

Use the Sound Options Dialog Box

How do you find out how long the sound or music will last? One way is to select the sound icon and click the Options tab that appears on the ribbon. Then click the dialog box launcher arrow in the Sound Options group to open the Sound Options dialog box, shown next. Notice that the playing time of the sound is displayed in the Information section of the dialog box. You now have the information you need to decide if you want to repeat the sound or music over and over. For example, if you want the music to play throughout the entire presentation, and the presentation will take longer than the sound, you may want to loop it. (Don't forget to check out the result to see how it sounds.) Check the Loop Until Stopped check box and click OK.

In the same place, you can also control the volume and hide the sound icon, just as you can in the Play Sound dialog box.

Another way to check the timing of a sound is to display the timeline. Choose any sound from the Custom Animation task pane's listing and click its drop-down arrow. Choose Show Advanced Timeline. Then click Play at the bottom of the taskbar and watch the timeline pass by, showing seconds as the sound plays.

Use the Options Tab

A third location to specify sound settings is on the Options tab, which appears on the ribbon when you select a sound icon. In the Sound Options group, you can do the following:

- Hide the icon during the show.
- Loop the sound until the presentation stops.
- Choose to play the sound when clicked or automatically when you display the slide.
- Set the maximum WAV sound file size that can be embedded. By default, this is 100KB and larger WAV sounds are linked.

TIP

You can set a WAV audio file (but no other file type) to play when you simply pass the mouse cursor over the icon—no mouse click. Instead of inserting the audio file as described previously, click the Insert tab and choose the Shapes button. In the Action Settings section, choose an Action Settings shape and place it on a slide. This automatically opens the Action Settings dialog box. (This dialog box is covered in detail in Chapter 11.) On the Mouse Over tab, check Play Sound. From the drop-down list, choose one of the sounds, or scroll down to Other Sounds and navigate to any WAV file. Instead of hiding the object while not playing it, you can format it with no outline or fill to make it invisible. Place it in one corner of your slide, so you know where it is. When you move the cursor to that corner, the sound will play, for no visible reason, and your audience will think you made magic!

NOTE

For a thorough discussion of PowerPoint and sound, go to http://www.indezine.com/ products/powerpoint/ppsound.html.

Add a CD Soundtrack

As you may know, you can play an audio CD in your CD-ROM drive. Just put the CD in the drive, and it should start playing automatically (or present a dialog box letting you choose to play it). The controls available depend on which software you have installed on your computer.

You can insert a CD audio track on a slide. The sound that you'll get will be superior to either WAV or MIDI files, for a more professional result. Like with other electronic files, be careful about copyright issues when using a CD audio track. Follow these steps:

1. Insert the CD into your CD-ROM drive.

2. Display the slide on which you want to place the CD audio track.

3. On the Insert tab, in the Media Clips group, click the Sound button's down arrow and choose Play CD Audio Track.

4. In the Insert CD Audio dialog box, shown here, set the options you want for playing the CD audio track. You can choose to loop the CD until it is stopped. You can also specify the exact tracks that you want to play, including the starting time of the first and last tracks (in minutes and seconds) in case you don't want to play all of the first and last tracks. You can generally find this information on the CD itself. Be sure to change the End Track setting. If you leave it at 1, PowerPoint stops and ends the play in the same place—that is, it doesn't play anything. To play the first track, start at track 1 and end at track 2. You can also set the volume and hide the CD icon. Click OK when you're done.

10

5. PowerPoint asks whether you want the CD to play automatically or when clicked when you display the slide. Choose the option you want.

PowerPoint places a CD icon on the slide. To listen to the CD audio track in Normal view, double-click the CD icon. Don't forget that you need to put the CD in your CD-ROM drive. If you are traveling, remember to take the CD with you! PowerPoint only remembers the track, not the actual CD. Therefore, if you set the options to play track 1, your presentation will play track 1 of whichever CD you place in your CD-ROM drive.

You can change the play settings for the CD icon in two ways:

- Select the CD icon and choose the Options tab that appears. In the Set Up group, you can change the tracks you want to play, the looping setting, when the CD plays (automatically or when clicked), and whether or not to hide the CD icon.

- To change when and how the music starts and stops, click the Animations tab and then click the Custom Animation button to open the Custom Animation task pane. Click the drop-down arrow for the sound object in the listing and choose Effect Options. The Play CD Audio dialog box opens, which, except for the title, is the same as the Play Sound dialog box shown in Figure 10-1.

Test your settings in Slide Show view to make sure you like the results.

Show Movies with Video Clips

You can also play video clips in your presentations. Video clips are usually AVI, WMV, or MPG (.mpeg, .mpe, or .mpg) files—electronic movies. They are usually videos of live scenes but can also be animated. Examples of videos you might use in a presentation are a short message from your CEO, a demonstration of a product, a screenshot of using a computer application, an example of how a product is produced, or a testimonial of a customer. Most videos should be custom-made to suit your needs. There are four ways to create a live video clip:

- Internet video-camera kits (web cams) let you record a video while sitting in front of your PC. They're intended mostly for sending videos of yourself while calling someone over the Internet or for creating web conferences. They include a small camera with a built-in microphone that you place on top of your monitor, facing you, and software to record the video into a digital file format. Prices range from under $100 to about $200.

- For screen captures, you can use TechSmith's SnagIt (in video capture mode) or, for more options, TechSmith's Camtasia Studio (http://www.techsmith.com).

- You can use a video capture device that captures analog videos created with a video camera or camcorder and converts them into digital format. You need both an analog capture card (hardware that you insert in your computer) and software to transfer the video onto your hard disk. The software also compresses the video files, which is generally important because they quickly grow to an unmanageable size.

■ You can create a video with a digital camcorder. Even some digital cameras can record video clips. Just make sure you can end up with AVI, WMV, or MPG format.

You may do none of the above and instead look for a professional service bureau that specializes in creating business or educational videos. To look on the Web, use a search engine to search for "digital video" and "service bureau." If you already have a video that you want to use, you can convert it yourself using one of the video capture devices or ask a service bureau to convert it for you. Be sure to explain that you want the video for insertion into a PowerPoint presentation, because PowerPoint doesn't accept all formats. Table 10-2 lists the formats that PowerPoint accepts.

Video capturing software transfers the video to your computer. Your video capture card may come with this software. Video editing software may include capturing features. You also use video editing software to edit the video, including trimming unnecessary frames or more elaborate effects. Finally, you export the files into a video format that PowerPoint can use (see Table 10-2). Windows includes the free Windows Movie Maker that can combine video and still images, add effects, and output a WMV video file.

Video clips are typically compressed because without compression, they are too large to store. There are many types of compression, called *codecs* (which stands for compression/ decompression). The beauty of codecs is that they decompress your video on the fly and then display it. Occasionally, a video file won't play because you don't have the codec it used. In that case, you need to try to find out the codec name and obtain it. (Many web sites offer free codec downloads.) Once you have the video, you can add it to the Clip Gallery. See Chapter 5 for instructions.

To insert a video on a slide, follow these steps:

1. Display the slide.

2. On the Insert tab, click Movie in the Media Clips group of the ribbon to insert a movie file. To insert a movie from the Clip Gallery, click the down arrow below the Movie button and choose Movie from Clip Organizer.

Video Format	Filename Extension	Description
Advanced Streaming Format	.asf	Can stream (deliver over time) video content
Audio Video Interleave	.avi	A common video format supported by many codecs
Moving Picture Experts Group	.mpg or .mpeg	Provides good file compression
Windows Media Video	.wmv	A compressed format for video

TABLE 10-2   Video File Types that PowerPoint Accepts

3. PowerPoint asks you if you want the movie to play automatically or when clicked. Choose the option you want.

4. You see the first frame of the video on your slide, as shown here. Once you have inserted the movie, you can watch it by double-clicking it.

Courtesy of Tom Carlisle, Maharishi Institute of Management.

You can change video playing options. To do so, select the video and click the Options tab that appears on the ribbon. In the Movie Options group, you can do the following:

- Change whether the video plays automatically or when you click it.

- Hide the video icon when it is not playing.

- Zoom the movie to full screen. Note that you generally lose resolution and the video can look grainy, unless your movie is already high resolution.

- Loop the movie to play it over and over.

- Rewind the video. This feature is useful if you might play it more than once during a presentation.

You can adjust the video clip for the resolution of your screen. This task is especially important if you are creating your presentation on a desktop computer with one resolution (such as 1280×800) but presenting it on a laptop with a lower resolution (such as 1024×768). Follow these steps:

1. Select the video object.

2. Click the Options tab that appears. In the Size group, click the dialog box launcher arrow to open the Size and Position dialog box. Choose the Size tab.

3. Check the Best Scale for Slide Show box. Then choose the resolution of the computer you'll be presenting from in the Resolution drop-down list. This feature scales any picture to the best scale for your screen's resolution.

4. Click OK.

Record Narration

For a presentation that will run unattended at a kiosk or trade show, or one that viewers will navigate by themselves, you may want to add narration to replace what you would say if you were there. PowerPoint lets you record narration that plays when you run the presentation.

Narration can add a professional touch. The problem is that poor narration is usually worse than no narration. Unless you can sound like those announcers on the radio, you should seriously think about hiring a professional to record the narration for your presentation. A professional likely has not only a better-sounding voice, but also the use of a sound studio, professional recording equipment, and the best sound-editing software. You can contact a sound studio yourself to make the arrangements, although your narrator probably has good contacts.

If you are looking for a professional narrator, you can try doing a search on the Web—use the keywords "professional," "narrator," and "announcer." A number of individual narrators have their own web sites. You may also want to consider a professional scriptwriter. An experienced outsider can often more easily envision the point of view of your intended audience and avoid technical language that you use every day, but your audience may not understand.

You should ask for the recording in digital WAV format, rather than on a cassette tape. (Otherwise, you need to digitize the tape yourself.) When you make arrangements for the narration, remember that you will eventually need a separate file for each slide. If necessary, you can divide the file yourself using sound-editing software. Most sound cards come with some sound-editing software.

10

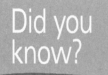

Online Video Resources

When you start to use video, you'll need to collect resources for video editing, compression, and conversion, especially if you want to create your own clips. Sources include the following:

- **Adobe Premiere Pro**   http://www.adobe.com/products/premiere/main.html
- **Pinnacle Studio**   http://www.pinnaclesys.com
- **Ulead VideoStudio**   http://www.ulead.com/vs/runme.htm
- **Autodesk Cleaner XL**   http://usa.autodesk.com/adsk/servlet/index?id=5562182&-siteID=123112

In addition, an excellent article on multimedia in PowerPoint is available at http://www.indezine.com/products/powerpoint/ppmultimedia.html.

While the exact steps depend on the software you are using, you can generally divide a file as follows:

1. Select part of the file and click Play. Do this, adjusting the amount you select, until you have the snippet you want.

2. Copy it to the clipboard.

3. Open a new file.

4. Paste the clipboard contents into the new file.

5. Save that file as slide 1, for example.

Once you have sound files for each file, you can attach them to the transition of each slide by displaying the Animations tab. In the Transition To This Slide group, click the Transition Sound drop-down list and choose Other Sound at the bottom of the list. In the Add Sound dialog box, locate and choose your WAV sound file and click OK. (Unfortunately, PowerPoint limits you to WAV files.) PowerPoint plays the slide file.

CAUTION *Windows Vista Sound Recorder now saves only in WMA format, which you can't attach to transitions. In Windows XP, Sound Recorder saves in WAV format, so you can use it to record your own sounds. To find Sound Recorder, choose Start | All Programs | Accessories | Entertainment | Sound Recorder. Illustrate's dBpowerAMP Music Converter (dMC) is a freeware program that you can use to convert between sound file types. Check it out at http://www.dbpoweramp.com/dmc.htm.*

If you do decide to record your own narration, here's the procedure:

1. Attach a microphone to the proper connector on your computer, generally the Mic In or Line In connector of the sound card. You may have to check your computer's manual.

NOTE *A good-quality microphone will provide better results than the cheap one that probably came with your computer. You can also purchase a good preamplifier that picks up less outside sound. Plug the microphone into the preamplifier and plug the preamplifier into the Line In connector. Find a quiet place to record and get close to the microphone, but not too close. Usually, if you put the microphone just below your mouth and a couple of inches away, you'll get good results.*

2. On the Slide Show tab, click Record Narration to open the Record Narration dialog box, shown in Figure 10-2. This dialog box displays the amount of free disk space and the number of minutes you can record before using up that space.

3. Click Change Quality to open the Sound Selection dialog box, shown here.

4. Choose a sound quality from the Attributes drop-down list. Then click OK. The higher the quality (CD quality is the best), the larger the file size.

5. For the first time you record, click Set Microphone Level in the Record Narration dialog box and follow the directions to set the proper microphone level for recording. Click OK.

6. If you want to link narration as a separate file, check Link Narrations In and click Browse to choose the desired folder. (The default location is the location of the current presentation file.) If you use separate files, you have greater control, especially if you want to make changes in the file. Otherwise, narration is inserted on your slides as OLE (embedded) objects. Click OK.

7. PowerPoint puts you into Slide Show view automatically. Start narrating. Move through the slide show, narrating on each slide as desired. Click to go to each following slide.

If you're not on the first slide, PowerPoint opens a dialog box allowing you to choose whether you want to start narrating from the current slide or the first slide.

8. When you reach the end of the presentation, PowerPoint asks you if you want to save the slide timings as well as the narration. If you save the timing, you can play the presentation automatically using the exact same timings for each slide. Click Save to save the timings. Click Don't Save to save only the narration. (You can set or change timing later. Setting the timing for a presentation is covered in Chapter 14.)

9. Run the presentation in Slide Show view again to listen to the narration. It's a lot of fun!

10

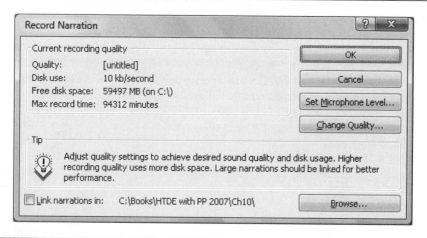

FIGURE 10-2   Start the narration process in the Record Narration dialog box.

 *In Chapter 14, I recommend recording narration as a practice technique when preparing for actual presentation. You can then sit back and listen to your presentation from the point of view of the audience.*

It's easy to make a mistake while narrating, and you might want to make changes, just as you make changes to any other part of your presentation. However, you wouldn't want to have to record the entire narration over from the beginning. Because the narration for each slide is separate, you can edit existing narration. You display the first slide that you want to edit and use the regular narration procedure for the slides you want to edit. Then advance to the next slide and press ESC.

Let's say you want to redo the narration for slides 2 and 3. Display slide 2. Start narrating using the steps just listed. Narrate for slides 2 and 3. When you get to slide 4, press ESC.

You have the option to run the presentation without the narration if you want. For example, you might want to record narration only as a backup (when you go on vacation) for a presentation that you usually present yourself. You might also have a presentation that is sometimes run automatically and sometimes given by a presenter. Or you might record narration as a practice to see how long the presentation will take and how it will sound. To run the slide show without the narration, choose the Slide Show tab and click Set Up Slide Show. Check Show Without Narration and click OK.

Summary

In this chapter, you learned how to include multimedia effects in a presentation by adding sounds, music, video, and narration. You can use PowerPoint's sound effects, sounds or music from files, or sounds or music from the Clip Gallery. The most common type of sound and music files are WAV, MIDI, and MP3 files. PowerPoint can play a CD soundtrack as well for a full-length, full-bodied sound.

You can show a video clip on a slide. The video clip is attached to an individual slide and plays when you display that slide. Video clips can add an extra dimension to a presentation, which is, in essence, mostly static.

You can record narration for all the slides in a presentation. Narration is usually used for self-running presentations. Your presentation will then play with that narration.

In the next chapter, I explain how to create hyperlinks, use action buttons to control your presentation, and move data in and out of PowerPoint.

Part III

Manage and Convey a Presentation

Chapter 11

Interact with Others

How to...

- Hyperlink to anywhere
- Create a web-style presentation
- Use action buttons to control your presentation
- Copy data from application to application
- Collaborate with others
- Let others view your presentation without PowerPoint

These days, the whole world is interconnected. A presentation can no longer stand isolated. A question from the audience can create the need to access data from another presentation, another application (such as a spreadsheet), or from your company's web site. If you're making a presentation to a customer, your customer might express an interest in any number of other products you sell, and you need to be ready to provide pertinent information at a moment's notice. However, you don't want to create a huge presentation with all the possibilities and make your customer sit through everything. In this chapter, you learn how to use hyperlinks and action buttons to create the ultimately flexible presentation. You also discover how to manage data from other presentations and applications.

Add Flexibility with Hyperlinks

A *hyperlink* is a command to go to another location. That other location can be another slide in the same presentation, a slide in another presentation, a file in another application, or a location on a web site or intranet. You can even go to an e-mail address. You attach a hyperlink to an existing object—text, shapes, a table, a chart, or a picture. In Slide Show view, click the hyperlink to go to the specified location. Hyperlinks are not active in Normal or Slide Sorter view.

 When you attach a hyperlink to text, PowerPoint underlines the text and displays it in the hyperlink color of the presentation's theme colors. When you click a text hyperlink, PowerPoint changes that text to the color designated in the theme colors for followed hyperlinks. Be sure to check out how these two colors look in your presentation. They may lack the necessary contrast to show up clearly. Chapter 6 explains how to change and customize theme colors. Note that when you attach a hyperlink to a text box or placeholder rather than to the text itself, PowerPoint does not underline the text or change its color.

One way to think of hyperlinks is as a way of providing supporting information for a presentation. In the days of paper presentations, you carried with you reams of additional data—perhaps sample swatches, price sheets, delivery schedules, and so on. Now you can include hyperlinks to the electronic versions (although nothing beats the feel of a real piece of carpet).

Moreover, you can include hyperlinks to various pages on your web site to add a truly unlimited potential for information.

Hyperlinks also add interactivity to presentations that viewers run themselves; for this reason they're great for educational projects and kiosks. Finally, a common use for hyperlinks is to let you quickly jump around in a complex presentation. You may be able to anticipate that your audience will have additional questions on a topic when you're done. On the last slide, for example, you can provide hyperlinks back to each major section of the presentation. In this scenario, hyperlinks create a navigational menu for your presentation.

Hyperlink to Another Slide in Your Presentation

To attach a hyperlink to an object that connects to a location in the current presentation, select the object to which you want to attach the hyperlink. You can choose any object or text on a slide. On the Insert tab, choose Hyperlink in the Links group (or press CTRL-K) to open the Insert Hyperlink dialog box. In the Link To bar on the left of the dialog box, click Place in This Document to display the options shown in Figure 11-1. Choose the location you want to hyperlink to and click OK. To create a ScreenTip that appears when you place the cursor over the hyperlink object, click ScreenTip and type the text you want.

You should now switch to Slide Show view and test the hyperlink. If you selected text to create the hyperlink, make sure it is still readable in its new color, both before and after you click it, as mentioned earlier. If necessary, change the hyperlink and followed hyperlink colors in the theme colors, as explained in Chapter 6.

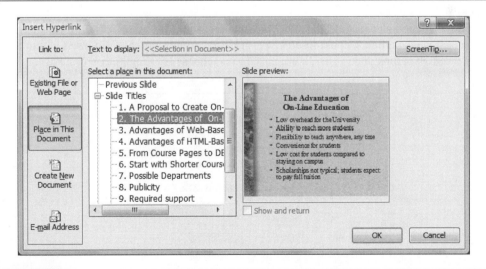

FIGURE 11-1   Use the Insert Hyperlink dialog box to create hyperlinks.

When you test the hyperlink, you will end up in the new location. You might wonder how you get back again. Usually you want to create a complementary hyperlink to bring you back to the original location.

There's an art to designing hyperlinks. You may want some hyperlinks to be obvious. You may wish others to be undetectable until you use them. (You may not want your potential client asking where each and every hyperlink goes to.) For example, you can place several obvious hyperlinks on a slide near the end of the presentation that simply says "Questions?" Here you pause and answer questions. You might have a series of text boxes, naming the topics you covered, hyperlinked back to those topics, as shown in Figure 11-2.

You should have hyperlinks on each of the slides to which you hyperlinked to bring you back to the Questions slide, but you wouldn't want them to be obvious, because they might be distracting during the main portion of the presentation. You could therefore attach those hyperlinks to graphic objects on the slide. During the presentation, your audience would have no clue that the slides were hyperlinked until you used the hyperlinks during the question-and-answer period. In the slide shown next, the hyperlink is added to the graphic of the dentist:

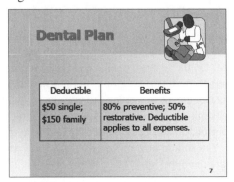

Hyperlink to a Slide in Another Presentation

You can create supporting presentations that contain information that you think you may need. You can then hyperlink to those presentations as long as they are available from the computer you are using.

To create a hyperlink to a slide in another presentation, select the text or object to which you want to attach the hyperlink. Choose Insert Hyperlink (in the Links group of the Insert tab) to open the Insert Hyperlink dialog box. In the Link To bar, choose Existing File or Web Page.

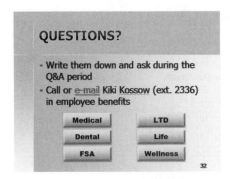

FIGURE 11-2   You can hyperlink to any slide in your presentation.

Choose the presentation you want to link to and click Bookmark. PowerPoint opens the Select Place in Document dialog box, shown here. (If the Bookmark button returns an error message, see the tip in the next session.)

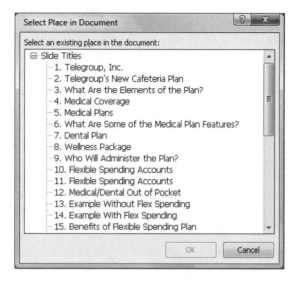

Choose the slide you want to hyperlink to and click OK. PowerPoint identifies the slides by their number and title. If your slides don't have titles, you'll need to know the slide number.

Switch to Slide Show view to test out the hyperlink. When you click the hyperlink, PowerPoint sends you to the specified slide in the other presentation. Press ESC to automatically return to your original point.

When you hyperlink to another presentation, you can display as many slides in the presentation as you wish. Pressing ESC always brings you back to your original point in the first presentation.

Hyperlink to Another File or a Web Page

You can hyperlink to any other file, even in another application. For example, you can hyperlink to a word processing document, a spreadsheet, or a CAD drawing that might contain additional details your audience may be interested in. You can also hyperlink to a web page, which is, after all, just another file.

Hyperlinking to another file or web page is similar to hyperlinking to another slide in a presentation. Follow these steps:

1. Select the object to which you want to attach the hyperlink.

2. On the Insert tab, choose Hyperlink in the Links group. (Refer to Figure 11-1 for the Insert Hyperlink dialog box.)

3. In the Link To bar, choose Existing File or Web Page.

4. To link to a file, type the filename and path in the Address box, choose it from the list, or use the Look In drop-down list to navigate to the file. To link to a web page URL, enter the URL in the Address box. You can also click the Browse the Web button to browse to the web page. If you click Browse the Web, make sure you are connected to the Internet. PowerPoint opens your browser. In your browser, locate the web page you want by typing the URL, using the Favorites/Bookmark feature, or using the list of recently visited web sites. Then switch back to PowerPoint by choosing your presentation's button on the Windows taskbar or by closing your browser. The URL is now displayed in the Address text box.

5. Click Bookmark to choose a named location in the file to which you are hyperlinking.

*The Bookmark feature does not always work. An effective workaround is to type the pound (#) character and the bookmark name after the address in the Insert Hyperlink dialog box. For example, if you have a bookmark in a Word document called "prices," link to the document and type **#prices** after the address. This technique also works for a named range in an Excel spreadsheet.*

6. Click ScreenTip to enter a label that will be displayed when you place the mouse cursor over the hyperlink. Without a ScreenTip, PowerPoint uses the path of the file or the URL of the web page.

7. Click OK when you're done.

As with all hyperlinks, you should go into Slide Show view and test the hyperlink. PowerPoint opens the file or opens your browser and links you to the URL. You can close your browser or the application to return to your presentation or use the Windows taskbar button.

Hyperlink to a New File

You can also use a hyperlink to open a new file. You might want to open a new file if your presentation is part of an in-house working session and you want to have a place to enter ideas as they come up. Your audience will appreciate seeing their ideas appear on the screen as you enter them. Here's how it works:

1. Select an object for the hyperlink.

2. On the Insert tab, in the Links group, choose Hyperlink.

3. In the Link To bar, choose Create New Document. In the Name of New Document text box, type the name of the file you want to create. You determine the type of document by the filename extension. For example, if you name the file **New Ideas.docx**, then you will create a Microsoft Word 2007 document. To change the location from the path listed, click Change. You can then find a new location and type a name for the file in a dialog box, as well as select a file type.

4. In the When to Edit section, choose when to edit the file. If you choose to edit the file now, PowerPoint opens the file. You can create a framework for inserting those new ideas, for example, such as headings of your major topics. Save the file and close it. When you show the presentation, your hyperlink will open the file again as you saved it. If you choose to edit the document later, PowerPoint will open it the first time you try out the hyperlink in Slide Show view—which should be before you actually give the final presentation.

If you are opening a new PowerPoint presentation, choose to edit the slide now. If you try to edit it later in Slide Show view, PowerPoint creates a new presentation with no slides and immediately returns you to your original presentation.

5. Click OK when you're done.

Once you create the new document, the hyperlink is connected to it. You can open the file any time you use the hyperlink. If you use the Windows taskbar to return to your presentation, be sure to choose the taskbar button that says PowerPoint Slide Show, not the button that says Microsoft PowerPoint, which returns you to Normal view or the view you last used.

Create an E-mail from a Slide

You have probably seen web sites that let you instantly e-mail the sponsoring company. You click a link on the web page, and your e-mail software opens with the correct e-mail address already in the message window. You can do the same on a PowerPoint slide. You can use this technique for self-running presentations when you want potential customers or other viewers to e-mail you with questions or for further information. Be sure to check that this system works properly. Obviously, you need an e-mail program and an active Internet connection. Once you get it working, this strategy is a great tool for creating an interactive presentation.

You can easily set up this kind of system over a company intranet. For example, you may have a networked computer set up with presentations on various topics for employees to view. Or you can place the presentations on an employees-only area of your company's web site or intranet. One could be a presentation on the new employee benefits plan—employees could e-mail their questions. Another presentation might present the employee suggestion program and ask employees to e-mail their suggestions. The possibilities are endless.

Here are the steps:

1. Select any object on a slide. Label it clearly—for example, "Click here to e-mail us your questions."

2. On the Insert tab, in the Links group, click Hyperlink.

3. In the Insert Hyperlink dialog box, choose E-mail Address from the Link To bar. In the E-mail Address text box, type the e-mail address you want the e-mail to go to.

4. In the Subject text box, type a subject. You can insert a general subject that will let you know which presentation the e-mail came from so that you can distinguish it from other e-mail you receive.

11

5. If you wish, choose ScreenTip and type a ScreenTip to appear when you place the mouse cursor over the hyperlink. Otherwise, PowerPoint uses the e-mail address and subject.

6. Click OK.

Look back to Figure 11-2 for an example of a slide with an e-mail link. Employees viewing the presentation on their own can click to e-mail the appropriate person in the Human Resources department.

Edit Hyperlinks

You sometimes need to edit a hyperlink. You can change any of the settings that you created. To edit a hyperlink, right-click it and choose Edit Hyperlink. PowerPoint opens the Edit Hyperlink dialog box, which is the same as the Insert Hyperlink dialog box. Make any desired changes and click OK. To remove a hyperlink, right-click it and choose Remove Hyperlink.

You can play a sound or highlight a hyperlink to draw attention to its action. The next section explains how to attach actions to a hyperlink.

Use Action Buttons to Control Navigation

Action buttons are graphics on a slide that control actions you specify. You can use them to create hyperlinks, to play movies or sounds, or to open applications. Action buttons have the following advantages:

■ They include familiar graphic symbols from web sites for going back, forward, to the first slide (home), and so on. Action buttons are therefore ideal for self-running presentations at a kiosk or on a web site because their controls are familiar to users. As mentioned earlier, the blank action button is useful when you need to add your own label.

■ They often look more professional than graphics you would create yourself. When they are used during a presentation, they appear to be depressed, similar to buttons that have been clicked on web sites.

■ You can play a sound while executing an action.

■ You can use action buttons to run movies or play music.

■ You can use action buttons to run macros or programs.

■ You can choose whether clicking the button or passing the mouse cursor over it executes the action.

Navigate Within a Presentation

Action buttons don't need to be limited to self-running presentations. You can also use them for presentations that you deliver. The buttons are cute but professional looking. Whenever you want

How to ...   Create a Web-Style Presentation

Most presentations are *linear*; they start at the beginning, end at the end, and give viewers no choice about what they see. When you deliver a presentation, you control what your audience sees. However, from experience viewing web sites, people are accustomed to choosing what they see from an array of hierarchically arranged information. You can create a presentation that functions like a web site. This style is ideal for presentations to small groups of clients—you can let them choose which information they want to see. Based on questions, you can access additional content that you have included. You can also use this type of organization for a presentation shown at a kiosk, or whenever the viewer is controlling the navigation. It's great for educational purposes; students love clicking the buttons and going to more in-depth resources, either within the presentation or on the Internet.

If you wish, start with a title page; in web jargon, this is called a *splash page*. Then create a home page with your logo, a brief explanation of what you are offering your audience, and a menu. Turn each menu item into a hyperlink to other slides.

To create the hierarchical structure, create a menu on each of the second-tier slides and link to yet more slides. These slides contain the information you want to present. Finally, create links on each of the slides to return to the tier above and to the home page, just like on a web site.

On the Insert tab, click Shapes in the Illustrations group to display the Shapes gallery and choose from the Action Buttons section to insert premade web-style buttons on your slides, such as the house icon, to go to your home page. The blank action button is ideal when you want to add your own labels.

When you give your presentation, present your home page and use the menu to explain the information available. If your prospective clients indicate an interest, go that way. If not, you can use the links to direct the presentation yourself.

Why not just present your company's web site? There are many reasons not to:

- The web site probably doesn't contain all the specialized information you want to present and probably contains lots of information your audience doesn't need.

- Getting a fast, reliable Internet connection is tricky. You don't want prospects to have to wait for pages to download (or worse, not download at all).

- Web sites may limit graphics to improve downloading speed and provide consistency over various platforms and browsers. In PowerPoint, you can create the compelling look you want.

- You have easier animation options in PowerPoint. On a web site, you would have to use third-party software to animate your content.

Hierarchical presentations take some getting used to for both the presenter and the audience, but you'll soon find that they offer incredible flexibility and power.

11

navigation in a presentation to be obvious, you can use an action button. Here's how to add an action button:

1. Display the slide where you want to place the action button.

2. On the Insert tab, click the Shapes button in the Illustrations group. From the Action Buttons section, shown here, choose one of the buttons. Each button has a ScreenTip so you can tell its intended purpose.

3. To insert the button in the default size, click the slide. Otherwise, drag the shape to the desired size. You can adjust the size and shape later. You may want to change the color as well. (The default color depends on the theme colors.)

4. PowerPoint opens the Mouse Click tab of the Action Settings dialog box, shown in Figure 11-3, with a suggested hyperlink based on the action button you inserted. If necessary, click the Hyperlink To drop-down list and choose another option from the drop-down list. Click OK.

5. When you use the Hyperlink To drop-down list, not only can you choose another slide option, but you also have all the options you would have if you attached a hyperlink to an existing object, as described in the "Create Hyperlinks" section earlier in this chapter:

   ■ **Slide**   Choose any slide in the presentation by its number and title

   ■ **URL**   Type a URL

   ■ **Other PowerPoint Presentation**   Locate any other presentation and then choose any slide from that presentation

   ■ **Other File**   Choose any file you have access to

As with regular hyperlinks, you should always go to Slide Show view and test how the hyperlink works and how to get back to your presentation or original slide. Here you see a slide with a set of action buttons along the right side:

FIGURE 11-3   You can specify a hyperlink in the Action Settings dialog box.

By default, the Action Settings dialog box opens with the Mouse Click tab on top. You activate the hyperlink you create by clicking it with the mouse. The Action Settings dialog box also has a Mouse Over tab, which is identical to the Mouse Click tab except that it creates actions that you activate by passing the mouse cursor over the action button.

Most of the time, you'll use the Mouse Click tab. You certainly don't want to accidentally move elsewhere in a presentation because you (or someone else, if you have a self-running presentation) happen to move the mouse over the action button.

A good use for the Mouse Over tab might be to play a sound file that says, "We need your comment" or something similar.

At the same time that the action button executes a hyperlink, it can play a sound. While you can attach only one action to an object, playing a sound is an exception. To make an action button play a sound, check Play Sound on either the Mouse Click or the Mouse Over tab. Then choose a sound from the drop-down list. Choose Other Sound at the bottom of the list to locate any sound file on your system. A typical use for a sound would be to add a clicking sound to an action button to simulate the clicking of a button.

Use Action Settings

You can use the Action Settings dialog box for hyperlinks that you create with the Insert Hyperlink dialog box. Select the hyperlinked object and display the Insert tab of the ribbon.

Click the Action button in the Links group to open the Action Settings dialog box. You can then add a sound, for example.

You can run a macro by clicking or passing the mouse cursor over an object. Using an object or an action button to run a macro lets you execute complex actions with a click of a button. To do this procedure, you first need to create the macro. For more about macros, see Chapter 13.

Here's how to use action settings to run a macro:

1. Select the text or object you want to use.
2. On the Insert tab, click Action in the Links group.
3. Choose Run Macro on either the Mouse Click or Mouse Over tab.
4. From the drop-down list, choose the macro you want to use.
5. Play a sound if you wish.
6. Click OK.

Test the macro in Slide Show view. Note that some macros do not work in Slide Show view. For example, macros that edit a slide will not work in Slide Show view because you cannot edit in that view.

You can also use action settings to run a program. This technique simply opens another application—you can't open a specific file. Follow these steps:

1. Select an object.
2. Click Action in the Links group of the Insert slide.
3. Choose Run a Program.
4. Click Browse.
5. Choose the executable file (for example, winword.exe for Microsoft Word) in the Select a Program to Run dialog box.
6. Click OK.

When you click the object in Slide Show view, PowerPoint opens the application. You can then use that application in any way you want. For example, you could record data in a spreadsheet file. Save the file and close the program to return to where you left off in your PowerPoint presentation.

Copy Data

When you create a presentation, you often use data from other applications. You can copy data from other documents and paste it into PowerPoint, or you can drag-and-drop it. You can also import and export entire files. Another way to use data from other applications is to embed an object, such as a spreadsheet, into a presentation. Finally, you may want to investigate linking data from another document, so that it is always updated as the other document changes. Linking is especially valuable for price lists that change regularly.

Use the Clipboard and Drag-and-Drop

The Windows and Office clipboards let you copy data from place to place, whether within a presentation, from one presentation to another, or from one application to another. (See Chapter 3 for more about the Windows and Office clipboards.)

While I have already covered using the clipboard within PowerPoint, I have not talked much about using it to insert data from other applications. In order to decide how to best bring data into your presentation, you should understand how PowerPoint formats it.

When you paste data from another application via the clipboard, it becomes part of your presentation. PowerPoint creates PowerPoint objects. For example, if you paste data from an Excel spreadsheet, PowerPoint creates a table. You can then format it as you would any other table.

When pasting in text from a word processing document, keep in mind that you can't fit very much text on a single slide. Remember that spreadsheet and word processing documents almost always contain text that is too small for a slide—you'll need to enlarge the text once you paste it into your presentation.

You'll have different considerations when pasting in graphics. You often can't determine the size the graphic will be until it's pasted into PowerPoint. Enlarging a small bitmap graphic may make it grainy. Sometimes there will be a background that you don't want. You may need to make the background transparent. See Chapter 5 for more details on editing graphics for PowerPoint.

Drag-and-drop works just like the clipboard. You can select data, text, or a graphic from one application, drag it down to the Windows taskbar onto your presentation's taskbar button, and your presentation will open. Continue to drag the data onto the slide and release the mouse button.

You can drag-and-drop an entire file onto a PowerPoint slide from Windows Explorer. Locate the file in Windows Explorer and size the window so that you can see both your slide and the icon for the file. Then drag the file onto your slide. This technique works well for graphic files.

11

Import and Export Files

A different way of sharing information is to import and export files. For example, you might need to import a presentation created in another presentation program. You might also need to export a PowerPoint presentation into another format.

Import Files

You can create a PowerPoint presentation by simply opening a file from another application. This method doesn't provide satisfactory results in many cases, but occasionally, it will be just what you need to start you off on a presentation. For example, you can open a Microsoft Word document in PowerPoint, and PowerPoint converts it to a presentation. When looking for the Word document, don't forget to change the Files of Type drop-down list to All Files in the Open dialog box.

PowerPoint uses file converters to accomplish this conversion, and the converters are not all installed automatically. You may see a message offering to install the converter. Insert your Microsoft Office CD and click Yes. PowerPoint installs the converter and converts the file.

If you have a presentation created in another program, you probably have to convert the text and the graphics separately. You can probably save the presentation as a text (.txt) or Rich Text

Format (.rtf) file. Generally, you can save each slide as an image file, which you can then insert into PowerPoint.

PowerPoint can directly import the following graphic types:

- Enhanced Metafile (.emf)
- Windows Metafile (.wmf)
- Graphics Interchange Format (.gif)
- Joint Photographic Experts Group (.jpg or .jpeg)
- Portable Network Graphics (.png)
- Windows Bitmap (.bmp)
- Tagged Image File Format (.tif)

In addition, PowerPoint can open some of these file types in their compressed formats.

PowerPoint can also open graphic files in the following formats, but these require a special graphics filter. These are generally not installed automatically. When you try to open them, PowerPoint usually displays a message offering to install the filter. If not, you can start Setup from the Office CD-ROM and install the filter yourself.

- Computer Graphics Metafile (.cgm)
- FlashPix (.fpx and .mix)
- Kodak Photo CD (.pcd)
- Macintosh PICT (.pict or .pct)
- WordPerfect graphic (.wpg)

PowerPoint 2007 is more integrated, so it can import any charts that Excel can work with. If you don't have Excel, it can import the following file types as charts. For more information on importing charts, see Chapter 8.

- Delimited text—text separated by tab characters, commas, or spaces (.txt, .csv)
- Lotus 1-2-3 (.wks, .wk1)
- Microsoft Excel worksheet or workbook (.xlsx or .xls)
- Microsoft Excel—versions 5.0 or earlier (.xlw, .xlc)

Export Files

PowerPoint can also export to different file types. You have the following options when exporting to different file types:

- Web page (HTML)—for more information, see Chapter 12.

- A 97-2003 version of PowerPoint so you can give your presentations to users who don't have the latest version.

- Several graphic formats: GIF, JPEG, PNG, TIFF, TGA, WMF, EMF. After you click Save in the Save As dialog box, PowerPoint asks if you want to save the entire presentation or only the current slide. Whichever you choose, PowerPoint creates a graphic file from an entire slide. If you save the entire presentation, PowerPoint automatically creates a subfolder with the same name as your presentation and places the graphic files in the subfolder.

- Rich Text Format (RTF). Saves only the text but preserves some of the text formatting.

These options are described in more detail in Chapter 1, Table 1-1.

Insert OLE Objects

An OLE (Object Linking and Embedding) object is a "piece" of data from another software application. When you insert an OLE object into PowerPoint, you are embedding the object. In some instances, the object, while part of your presentation, retains an "awareness" of its original application. When you double-click the object, the original application opens within PowerPoint and you use the menus and toolbars of that application to edit the object. To return to PowerPoint menus, click anywhere outside the object. For example, if you embed a Microsoft Equation document in PowerPoint, when you double-click the equation, you see Equation tools. On the other hand, if you embed a WordPad document, PowerPoint treats it as part of PowerPoint, and you use PowerPoint's tools to edit it. Embed an object when you don't need to update the data from the original source document.

There are three main ways of embedding an object:

- On the Insert tab, choose Object in the Text group. In the Insert Object dialog box, either choose Create New to create a new object and choose the type of object you want to create, or choose Create from File to embed an existing file and choose an existing file (using the Browse button). Click OK.

- Double-click a placeholder on a slide—chart, organization chart, media clip, or object.

- Go to the source document, select the data you want to embed, and copy it to the clipboard. Return to PowerPoint and, on the Home tab, in the Clipboard group, choose Paste Special from the Paste button's drop-down list. In the Paste Special dialog box, choose Paste. In the As box, choose the type of object you want to create. Click OK. Use this method to create an object from part of a file.

Inserting objects has been discussed in several chapters in this book. For example, Chapter 8 discussed inserting chart objects, and Chapter 10 covered inserting media clip objects.

Link Objects

If you need to update data from its original source, you should link an object. Linked data is not actually part of your presentation. Instead, PowerPoint stores the location of the data and only displays it. Linked objects can help reduce the size of a file, but the main reason to link is to keep your data current. Each time you open the presentation, PowerPoint reloads the file from the source, giving you the most current data. Also, if the source changes while the presentation is open, PowerPoint updates the data on the spot. There are two ways to insert a linked object:

- On the Insert tab, choose Object. In the Insert Object dialog box, choose Create from File to embed an existing file and choose an existing file (using the Browse button). Check the Link check box, and click OK.

- Go to the source document, select the data you want to embed, and copy it to the clipboard. Return to PowerPoint and, on the Home tab, in the Clipboard group, choose Paste Special from the Paste button's drop-down list. In the Paste Special dialog box, choose Paste Link. In the As box, choose the type of object you want to create. Click OK. Use this method to create an object from part of a file.

Links need to be well taken care of. Because PowerPoint stores the location of the source file, if that source file is moved, PowerPoint cannot maintain the link. If your slide doesn't properly display a linked object, or you get a message that PowerPoint cannot find the object, you have a broken link. Click the Office button and choose Finish I Edit Links to Files. (This item only appears if you have a link in the presentation.) Use the Links dialog box, shown in Figure 11-4, to reconnect the linked object. You can choose to update the link automatically or manually. If necessary, choose Change Source to reconnect a link to a file that you have moved. You can also break a link that you no longer require.

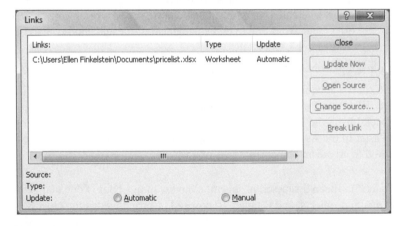

FIGURE 11-4   Use the Links dialog box to manage links to other files.

Manage Files

When you create presentations, you often collect numerous supporting files as well, especially graphic files. Managing your files is an important part of creating a presentation. Chapter 1 contains some tips for saving files so you can easily find them again. In Windows Vista, you can also search for files within PowerPoint using the Open dialog box (click the Office button and choose Open). In the Open dialog box, enter the search text in the Search box at the upper-right corner and then press ENTER to immediately search in the folder displayed in the address window at the top of the dialog box.

To search further afield, you can click the down arrow to the right of the address window to choose other recently used locations or type a location, such as c:\presentations. Windows Vista also has its own Search feature. Click the Start button and click Search.

To open a presentation from the resulting list, double-click it.

Collaborate with Others

Whether you are creating a presentation for your company or for a client, you usually need to collaborate with others and share your ideas before the presentation is finalized. The old-fashioned way of collaborating involved printing out the presentation, mailing it to everyone, getting their feedback via return mail or phone, and making the necessary changes. Nowadays, you can collaborate online via a network or the Internet. These options make it easier to control the flow of comments. Collaborating online also allows you to keep up with the fast pace of today's electronically enabled businesses.

How you collaborate with others will depend largely on the systems you have where you work. In this section, I review some of the options you have to enable you to work with colleagues, managers, and clients on a presentation.

Share and Send a Presentation

Windows contains a built-in feature that lets you give others on a network access to files on your hard disk. It's called *file sharing*, and it creates a special shared folder. The steps vary depending on your version of Windows and the type of network you have. For instructions, ask your system administrator or check Help for your operating system.

NOTE

Windows Vista has a special folder, called the Public folder, which is especially for sharing files with others.

You will often want to send a presentation via e-mail. You simply attach a presentation file to an e-mail message. You can also send a presentation via e-mail directly from within PowerPoint. This method also sends the presentation as an attachment.

To e-mail a presentation from within PowerPoint, you need Microsoft Outlook or a MAPI-compliant e-mail program (MAPI is a common mail interface standard). This method also works with e-mail programs that are compliant with Lotus cc:Mail or VIM (another mail interface standard).

To mail an entire presentation as an e-mail attachment, follow these steps:

1. Open the presentation and click the Office button. Choose Send | E-mail.
2. PowerPoint opens a new message window. Complete the names in the To and Cc boxes.
3. If you wish, select the name of your presentation in the Subject box and type a new subject.
4. Click Send to send the e-mail.

Fax a Presentation

You can fax a presentation (and other Microsoft Office files) using an Internet-based fax service. You must have installed Outlook and Word on your computer to use this feature. Sent faxes are stored in Outlook like e-mails. Note that faxes are always in grayscale. Before sending a fax using this method, you need to sign up for an Internet-based fax service. To sign up, click the Office button and choose Send | Internet Fax, as you would if you were sending an actual fax. Click OK at the message to go to a web page on Microsoft's site where you can choose a provider. Follow the instructions to sign up. Several providers provide a free trial period.

To send a presentation by fax, follow these steps:

1. With the presentation open, click the Office button and choose Send | Internet Fax. A new e-mail message opens in Outlook. Your presentation is already attached as a multipage TIF file. (TIF is a bitmap image format). The Microsoft Office Document Imaging program that comes with Microsoft Office supports viewing the multipage TIF format. You can also use IrfanView (http://www.irfanview.com). The message itself has a Preview button that you can click to preview the pages of the fax.

You can right-click the attachment and choose Save As to save the multipage TIF file. You can then e-mail it or use another method of delivery.

2. In the To field, enter a name. You can click the To button and choose a name that has an associated fax number.
3. Complete the Subject field. You can also type a message, which becomes a cover sheet.
4. Click Send. The e-mail is sent and the fax service takes care of sending the fax for you.

NOTE *If you have fax software (many modems come with fax software), you may be able to use it to send a presentation by fax using your modem. Usually, you choose Print from the Office button menu and choose your fax print driver to open the software and send the fax.*

Let Non-PowerPoint Users View Your Presentation

You may need to send your presentation to someone who does not have PowerPoint. For you to be able to collaborate with clients, managers, or colleagues who do not have PowerPoint, they need the PowerPoint Viewer, a free program for viewing PowerPoint presentations. You can send the viewer to them or direct them to where they can download it. A new viewer for PowerPoint 2007 is available.

PowerPoint Viewer is automatically installed with PowerPoint. You can find it at c:\Program Files\Microsoft Office\Office12\pptview.exe if you installed PowerPoint in the default location. PowerPoint Viewer is also available from Microsoft's web site. A special update site—http://office.microsoft.com/downloads/—lists updates. Choose PowerPoint as the product and 2007 as the version. Find the listing for the PowerPoint viewer and click Download Now to download the viewer. Once installed, PowerPoint Viewer can be easily loaded and any PowerPoint presentation viewed. (Chapter 14 covers PowerPoint Viewer in more detail.)

NOTE   *If you're on a Mac or any other non-PC platform, you can use Tonic Systems' TonicPoint Viewer, http://www.tonicsystems.com/products/viewer.*

Review a Presentation

Many presentations are collaborative efforts or need approval before being finalized. What do you do with a presentation when you need to review it? You can edit the presentation directly or add comments. Unfortunately, you cannot show revision marks the way you can in a Word document.

Instead, you can add comments. Anyone can add comments to a presentation. Each comment contains the name of its author, so you'll always know who made the comment. To insert a comment, display the Review tab and choose New Comment in the Comments group. A comments box opens where you can type your comment.

To work with comments, use the Review tab, shown next. The Comments group lets you easily add comments, show/hide comments (the Show Markup button), delete comments, and move from comment to comment throughout a presentation. Spelling and language tools are also on this tab. After you have added comments, return the presentation back to the original sender.

11

Protect a Presentation

When you're done with your presentation, there are several steps that you can take to protect it. Usually, you use these options when you are about to send the presentation to someone else. Click the Office button and choose Prepare to display the menu shown here:

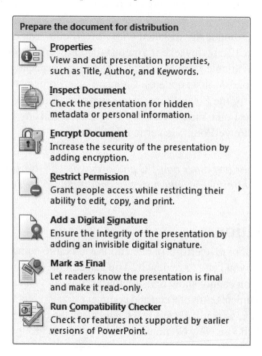

You can choose any of the following:

- **Properties** Opens the Document Information pane. Here you can add keywords to the file. To add more properties, click the Document Properties button and choose Advanced Properties.

- **Inspect Document** Opens the Document Inspector dialog box, shown in Figure 11-5. The Document Inspector allows you to inspect the presentation file for various kinds of data, such as comments and notes, that you might want to remove before sending it out. To inspect the presentation, click the Inspect button. You get a report like the one you see here. You can click the Remove All button to remove the items or go back to your presentation and make changes.

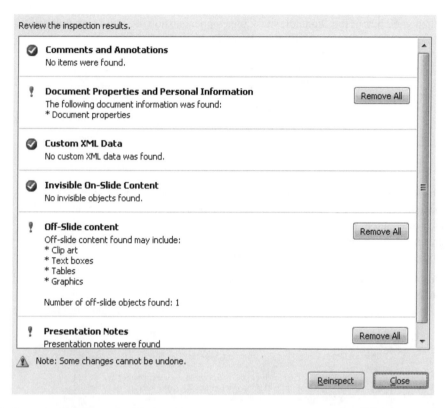

■ **Encrypt Document**   Allows you to add a password to the presentation file so that it cannot be re-opened without the password. Enter a password in the Encrypt Document dialog box and click OK. After this list, I explain another way to add a password to a presentation file.

■ **Restrict Permission**   Offers an Information Rights Management service that verifies the identity of people who receive documents that are set to have restricted permission. These people connect to a server that verifies that they can open the document. Microsoft has set up a trial service that you can sign up for.

■ **Add a Digital Signature**   A digital signature ensures that a file has not been changed. If you send a presentation to someone and get it back with the digital signature still valid, you know that the presentation hasn't been changed. When you choose this option, you can click a button to go to a web site listing several companies that offer digital signature services. You can also click OK and create your own digital signature, which is valid only on your own computer. When you do so, after completing some information, you see the Signature Confirmation message shown next. At this point, you can no longer change your presentation unless you remove the digital signature! After you create the digital signature, a new item, View Digital Signatures, appears on the Office I Prepare menu.

When you click it, the Signatures task pane appears, showing valid signatures with the name of the person who signed the document.

■ **Mark As Final**   When you mark a presentation as final, it notifies people that they shouldn't change it. Typing, editing, and proofing commands are turned off for the presentation. However, this feature does not make it impossible to change the presentation; anyone can simply turn off this feature by choosing the Mark As Final item from the Prepare menu. In other words, this item is a toggle to turn final status on and off.

■ **Run Compatibility Checker**   If you need to share presentations with people who have earlier versions of PowerPoint, you should check backward compatibility. PowerPoint lets you know if any text will not be editable or if any effect won't display, as you see here:

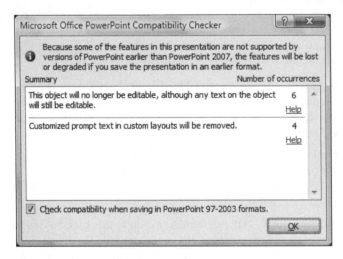

The Encrypt Document item on the Prepare menu, mentioned in the previous list, allows you to add a password to a presentation, but another method offers more options. You can require a user to enter the password to open it or to edit it, or both. To add a password, follow these steps:

1. Click the Office button and choose Save As.

2. In the Save As dialog box, choose Tools | General Options. The General Options dialog box opens:

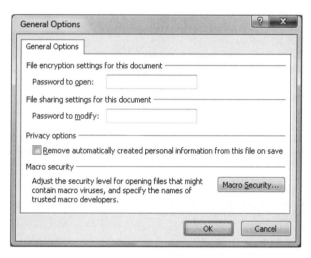

3. In the Password to Open text box, enter the password that you want to use for people to open the presentation.

4. If you want people to use a password to edit the presentation, add it in the Password to Modify text box.

5. Click OK.

6. In the Confirm Password dialog box, re-enter your password or passwords and click OK.

7. Back in the Save As dialog box, click Save. This saves the password or passwords with your presentation.

8. When prompted (if you've already saved the presentation once), click Yes to replace the original presentation.

Remember to write down that password or save an unencrypted version of the presentation for yourself! You won't be able to open the presentation file without that password. Also, people using PowerPoint 2000 or earlier will not be able to open or edit your password-protected presentation, even if you give them the password. You can save the presentation in an earlier version's format, but then you cannot add a password.

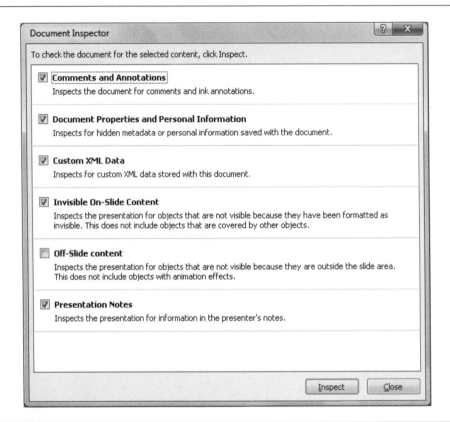

FIGURE 11-5 The Document Inspector looks for the type of data that you might not want in a presentation that you are ready to send to someone else.

Summary

In this chapter, you learned how to create hyperlinks to other slides, other presentations, other files, or the Web. You can even create a hyperlink that opens a new e-mail message. Action buttons provide a professional way to display hyperlinks as well as other actions, such as opening a program, playing a macro, or playing a sound.

Part of managing the relationship between your presentation and the rest of the world is knowing how to copy and move data in and out of files. You can use the clipboard or drag-and-drop to paste in data. You can embed objects with or without a link to the source document.

Use the Search feature to find files. Set file properties using the Properties feature to help you find files more easily in the future.

Collaboration is often as simple as e-mailing a presentation to others. You can e-mail a presentation to others for review. If you need to collaborate with someone who doesn't have PowerPoint, you can include PowerPoint Viewer along with the presentation. It can be downloaded free from Microsoft's web site. You can also fax a presentation.

You can add comments to a presentation. If you send your presentation to others, they can add comments to your presentation. When you get the presentation back, you can incorporate the suggestions in the comments.

You can protect a presentation by adding a password, using a digital signature, and with several other features. You can also run the compatibility checker to see what features, if any, will be affected if the presentation is saved in an earlier version.

The next chapter covers the process of publishing a presentation on the Internet.

11

Chapter 12

Display a Presentation on a Web Site

How to...

- Create a presentation for a web site
- Publish a presentation on the Internet
- Save a presentation for a web page

You can save a presentation in HTML format, the format used on the Web, and then open it in PowerPoint like any other presentation for further editing. Viewers can see your presentation on your web site, in some cases with all the animation and special effects intact. This chapter describes these features as well as some of their limitations.

The HTML features have not been updated for PowerPoint 2007. Therefore, new features that you use may not appear properly in a browser. Furthermore, as of this writing, presentations did not display well in Mozilla Firefox 2.0 and sometimes omitted images in Microsoft Internet Explorer 7.0.

Show Presentations on the Web

You can use PowerPoint to create web pages. In this situation, you are not creating a presentation at all; rather, you are using PowerPoint's ability to create fully graphic slides as a tool to design a web page. You must take into account the usual design features of a web site, such as a heading, links to other pages, more (and smaller) text, and so on.

You can also add a presentation to an existing web site. In this case, you want your audience to be able to run the slide show self-sufficiently while browsing the web site. You create a typical presentation, although you may add special design elements because it is shown on the web site. Also, due to the fact that no one is personally delivering the presentation, you often need to change the way you express the content.

Use PowerPoint to Create Web Pages

When you use PowerPoint to create a web page, you are using PowerPoint as your design tool. You then save the presentation in Hypertext Markup Language (HTML) format. *HTML* is a format that browsers can read.

Although designing web pages is beyond the scope of this book, here are a few simple guidelines:

- *Format the page's text and graphics appropriately.* Most web pages include graphics. However, too many large graphics make a web page slow to download. Text for a web site can be smaller than for an onscreen slide show.

- *Provide links on each page to go to other pages.* Figure 12-1 shows an example of a web page for a Human Resources department web site. Most pages should also have a link to your home (main) page. Create consistent navigational tools throughout the web site pages using action buttons or shapes. Chapter 11 explains how to create hyperlinks in your presentation.

- *Keep the colors simple.* The rich, dark colors appropriate for an onscreen presentation are often overwhelming on a web site.

- *Include a way to contact the Webmaster and the organization that created the web site.* Add an e-mail link to the Webmaster on the first page. See the "Create an E-mail from a Slide" section in Chapter 11 for instructions on creating an e-mail link.

- *Before publishing your web pages, open them in your browser and check out all the links and graphics.* Once you send the web pages to your server or web site host, check them out again. Professional web designers test web pages on major browsers, earlier versions of browsers, various platforms (PC and Mac), and at varying screen resolutions.

You can include all the pages of the web site in one presentation using each slide in the presentation as a web page. You can also create a different presentation for each web page; you may end up with a large number of files, but each file is smaller and loads faster.

Note that many programs are specifically designed for creating web pages, and they offer more features and control than PowerPoint. Microsoft FrontPage and Adobe Dreamweaver are two examples.

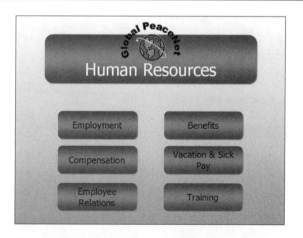

FIGURE 12-1   When you design a web site using PowerPoint, provide hyperlinks on each page to navigate to other pages.

Before saving your presentation in HTML format, you can preview it as a web page. However, this command is hard to find and you need to add it to your Quick Access toolbar first. Click the Office button and then click the PowerPoint Options button. Choose the Customize category. In the Choose Commands From drop-down list, choose Commands Not in the Ribbon. From the list below, choose Web Page Preview and click Add. Then click OK. PowerPoint adds the Web Page Preview command to your Quick Access toolbar. When you click this button, PowerPoint opens your default web browser and displays the first slide in the presentation. Figure 12-2 shows a slide viewed in Internet Explorer. Using this preview, you can test all the links that don't require Internet access, such as links within the presentation.

Create a Viewer-Controlled Presentation for the Web

You can publish a presentation to a web site so that others can view the presentation. When you publish to the Web, the presentation appears in the browser with navigational tools so that users can view the presentation.

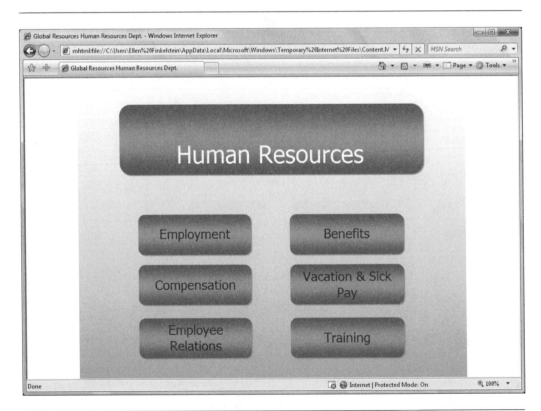

FIGURE 12-2   A slide previewed in Internet Explorer.

Create a viewer-controlled presentation when you want to simply place your presentation on a web site and let viewers decide when they will view it. A presentation can be part of a larger web site. You may have seen web sites that include PowerPoint presentations.

When you publish the presentation to the Web, as explained in the next section, PowerPoint automatically creates the navigational tools your viewers need. (You can turn off the navigational tools, but you shouldn't do so for a presentation designed to be controlled by your viewers.) You can create a timed presentation that moves from slide to slide automatically, but viewers may find this frustrating, especially if they need to interrupt their session. (Their phone may ring, for example.) Chapter 9 explains how to create a timed presentation.

Figure 12-3 shows the first slide of a presentation as it appears in a browser.

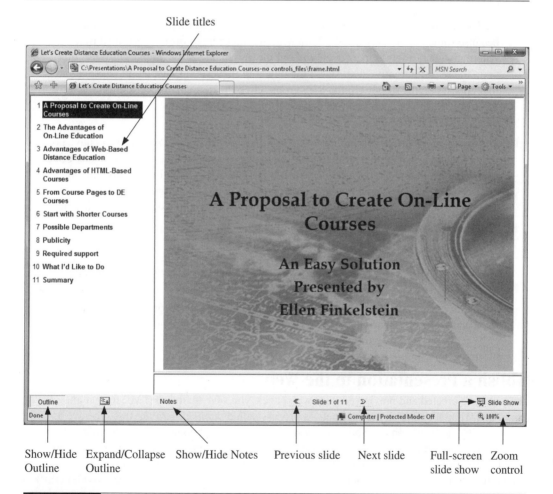

FIGURE 12-3   A presentation on a web site contains navigational tools so your viewers can move from slide to slide and decide which slides they want to see.

Remember that viewers may need instructions to get the most out of the presentation. The navigational controls at the bottom are not large, and some viewers may miss them. Viewers can click to move from slide to slide, but they may not know that. One solution is to include instructions for using the controls on the first slide.

If you include a video file, it may need to be double-clicked to run. Viewers will not know this, so you could include a text box on the slide containing the video with instructions to this effect.

You need to pay special attention when designing a presentation that is viewed on a web page. Here are some pointers:

- *Make sure that each slide has a meaningful slide title.* On a web site, these titles appear in a frame at the left side, listing each slide's title. Viewers can click any slide's title to go to that slide.

- *Add alternative text for graphics.* Browsers use this text while pictures are loading because some people may use the Web with graphics turned off to speed load time. Alternative text offers impact even without the graphics. Search engines also use this text. To create alternative text, select the object in PowerPoint, display the Format tab that appears on the ribbon. In the Size group, click the dialog launcher button (next to the word "Size") to open the Size and Position dialog box. On the Web tab, type the text. Click OK.

- *Don't use builds or other animation that requires a mouse click.* Your viewers have no way of knowing about this animation. If you want to use animation, set automatic timing. (See Chapter 14 for details.) Even with automatic timing, animation (builds) may be confusing to viewers because they have no control over the timing. Dimming does not work well because viewers may not have finished reading a line of text before it dims.

- *Expand text to be self-explanatory.* Succinct, bulleted text that you may use when delivering a presentation may not be clear when read by a viewer alone. Similarly, relationships between images and text that require explanation may be confusing on a web site. Make sure that the presentation makes sense on its own. As I explain in the next section, you can include notes when you publish a presentation to the web; your notes can supplement the content on the slides. Another alternative is to record your talk and add it as sound to the presentation. Chapter 10 explains how to add sound to a presentation.

Publish a Presentation to the Web

Once you have created and previewed your web pages, you save them in HTML format and save them to their final location on the Internet—a process called *publishing to the Web*. To save a presentation to the Web, you need access to a server, with a direct connection to the Internet. You can also save a presentation to an intranet server within your company. If you are saving to an intranet, your company's system administrator has the information you need to save files to the intranet. If you are saving to the Internet, you usually do so via an Internet service provider (ISP) and web host, who can give you the information you need.

When you save a presentation for viewing in a browser, PowerPoint offers two formats:

■ **Single File Web Page format (.mht or .mhtml extension)**   Lets you save all the components of a web site into one file. (This format is also available for other Office applications.) Working with one file makes it easier to upload, send as an e-mail attachment, and store.

> **CAUTION** *This format works with Internet Explorer 4.0 or later, but is not supported by most other browsers. Also, some people have had problems using the MHT format when the presentation contains sound and video. You can convert an MHT file to an HTML file in Internet Explorer—choose File | Save As and choose one of the HTML options.*

■ **Web Page format (.htm or .html extension)**   Creates many supporting files, including separate files for each slide, for graphic files, and for the navigational tools your viewers use to browse through the presentation. PowerPoint creates a new folder and places all the new files in that folder. One presentation creates an array of GIF and HTM files. You may also have WAV, AVI, JPG, and other types of files. Use this format for browsers or servers that do not accept the single file web page format, or if you want access to the individual components of a presentation.

> **NOTE** *A third option is to use a third-party program to convert the PowerPoint presentation to Flash movie (SWF) format. The SWF format is small, fast to load, compatible with most, if not all, browsers, and secure. For two excellent lists of conversion programs, see http://www.indezine.com/products/powerpoint/ppflash.html and http://www .masternewmedia.org/2004/04/14/powerpoint_to_flash_conversion_tools.htm.*

The procedure for publishing to the Web is the same whether you are using PowerPoint to create a web site or using the Web to present your slide show. Follow these steps:

1. Choose File | Save As. PowerPoint opens the Save As dialog box. From the Save as Type drop-down list, choose Single File Web Page (*.mht, *.mhtl) or Web Page (*.htm, *.html).

2. In the File Name text box, type a name for the web page. By default, PowerPoint uses the name of the presentation.

3. The Save As dialog box now has two additional buttons, as shown in Figure 12-4. Click the Change Title button to change the text that appears in the title bar of your web browser. (The page title also appears in the browser's History and Favorites lists.) Make this title descriptive, because many search engines use this title. In the Page Title box, type the new title and click OK.

4. In the address box at the top of the dialog box, choose a location for the web page. If you usually save to a web site using an FTP program, you can save to your hard disk now and use the FTP program afterwards. If you are saving directly to the Internet, you should ask

12

your ISP or your company's network/web administrator for this location, as well as how supporting files (such as graphics) should be organized.

5. Click Publish. PowerPoint opens the Publish as Web Page dialog box, shown in Figure 12-5. It has the following options:

   ■ In the Publish What? section, specify whether you want to publish the entire presentation, certain slides, or a custom show, if available. (I discuss custom shows in Chapter 14.)

   ■ Uncheck Display Speaker Notes if you don't want your viewers to automatically see your notes. Leave this option checked if you are publishing the presentation for others to review or if you have used the Notes pane to provide additional information that you want your viewers to see. For example, you can place the words you speak in the Notes pane to give viewers a more complete idea of a presentation that you delivered.

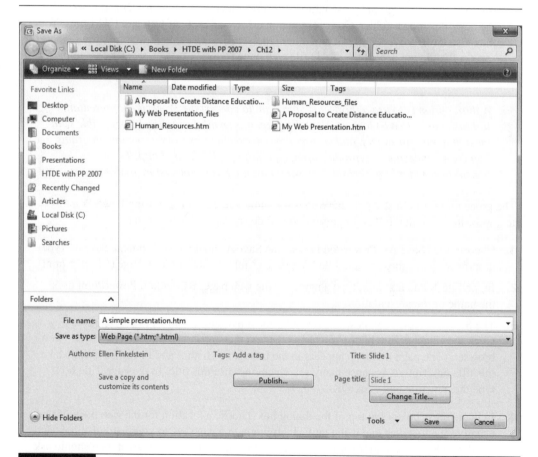

FIGURE 12-4 When you choose the Single File Web Page or Web Page file type, the Save As dialog box has special options for publishing a presentation to the Web.

If you include navigation controls (see the explanation of the General tab of the Web Options dialog box, next), viewers can choose to display notes. Therefore, you should not include notes that you don't want viewers to see.

6. Click Web Options to open the Web Options dialog box, shown in Figure 12-6. Here's how to use the tabs on the Web Options dialog box:

■ **General tab**   You can check Add Slide Navigation Controls (it's on by default) to include the Outline and Notes panes, as well as the navigational arrows at the bottom of the screen. (The Notes pane will not automatically appear if you unchecked Display Speaker Notes, as explained in Step 5.) Viewers can use the Outline pane to navigate around your presentation by clicking on any slide listed in the outline—just as you do in Normal view. PowerPoint gives you some color options in the Colors drop-down list. For example, you can use presentation colors, black on white, white on black, or your default browser colors. You can disable slide animation (builds). You can also disable the automatic resizing of graphics to fit the browser window.

■ **Browsers tab**   You can make choices about the browsers that will be used to view the presentation and how graphic elements are handled. For more information, see the "Did You Know?" box.

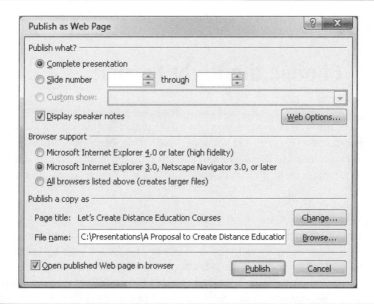

FIGURE 12-5   Use the Publish as Web Page dialog box to specify how you want to publish your presentation.

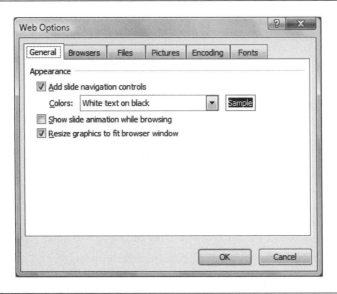

FIGURE 12-6   The Web Options dialog box lets you specify the details about your published presentation.

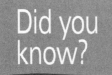

Choose the Right Format

The Browsers tab of the Web Options dialog box offers several format choices that are optimized for various browser types and versions. Predictably, Microsoft offers more support for Internet Explorer, so if you want to support other browsers, you should test the resulting web presentation in those browsers. Each format has its advantages and disadvantages:

- **Microsoft Internet Explorer 3.0, Netscape Navigator 3.0, or Later**   This option loses many of your special effects. You still get a good basic presentation, and people with older browsers can view it. It works best for a simple text presentation, but might be the best option if you want people in other browsers to be able to view your presentation. You cannot open and edit this format in PowerPoint. Therefore, if you edit your presentation, you need to resave it using this HTML format.

■ **Microsoft Internet Explorer 4.0, Netscape Navigator 4.0, or Later**   This option retains almost all of the features of a presentation, including transitions, animations (builds), sounds, and video clips. Viewers can see your presentation in full-screen mode, which makes it look like a real presentation rather than just a presentation inside a browser. When you save a presentation in this format, you can open and edit it in PowerPoint like a regular presentation. When you choose this option, PowerPoint automatically checks the Save an Additional Version of the Presentation for Older Browsers check box. This procedure creates more files, but is insurance for more situations; those with older browsers see a basic version of your presentation without animation or other special effects.

■ **Microsoft Internet Explorer 4.0 or Later**   This option is like the previous one but automatically checks the Save New Web Pages as Single File Web Pages option.

■ **Microsoft Internet Explorer 5.0 or Later**   This option allows you to check the Rely on VML for Displaying Graphics in Browsers check box. (VML, or Vector Markup Language, is an older graphics standard for specifying vector-based graphics in XML format. Only Internet Explorer 5.0 or later supports this standard, which has been mostly supplanted by a newer format, called SVG.)

■ **Microsoft Internet Explorer 6.0 or Later**   This option allows you to check the Allow PNG as a Graphics Format check box. PNG files are now commonly used on web sites because they support transparency, allow a large number of colors, and are fairly small.

The Options section lets you allow PNG as a graphics format. When you choose this option, PowerPoint automatically changes the browser choice to Microsoft Internet Explorer 6.0 or Later. Another option, which requires Internet Explorer 5.0 or 6.0, is to rely on VML for displaying graphics in browsers. Finally, you can specify that you want to save new web pages as single file web pages (MHT files); this option requires one of the 4.0 browser version options.

 *MHT files are problematic because most browsers (other than Internet Explorer) don't support it. If you don't want to save in MHT format, be sure to uncheck this check box.*

■ **Files tab**   You can change the names and location of the files that PowerPoint creates. For example, you can disable the feature that puts in a separate folder all the files of a presentation published to the Web. You should disable this feature only if instructed by your ISP or web administrator, because PowerPoint creates a large number of files for each presentation.

12

- **Pictures tab** You can specify the screen resolution. If you are publishing to an intranet and know the screen resolution of your viewers' monitors, you should set it here. If you are publishing to the Web for anyone to view, you should try different resolutions and view them with different browsers to see the results. The default is 800 × 600 which works fine for the majority of web users.

- **Encoding tab** You can save your presentation in various language formats. Use these options if text and symbols are not properly readable from your browser.

- **Fonts tab** Choose the character set that you want to include with your presentation.

7. When you're done setting the web options, click OK to return to the Publish as Web Page dialog box.

8. In the Browser Support section, choose the type of web format you want to create. (See the descriptions of the different HTML formats earlier in this section.)

9. In the Publish a Copy As section, you have another opportunity to change the filename and text title. Click Change to change the title text. Click Browse to navigate to a new location.

10. Check Open Published Web Page in Browser to open the presentation in your default browser immediately after publishing it.

11. Click Publish. PowerPoint works for a couple of seconds to create the new files.

If you checked Open Published Web Page in Browser, your browser opens and displays the presentation. Otherwise, you can open your browser and access the presentation that you saved as you normally would access files on your hard drive, network, or the Web.

Internet Explorer 7.0, by default, blocks certain content and you may have to click the Information bar at the top to allow the blocked content and then click Yes in the Security Warning dialog box that follows.

If you usually upload web files using an FTP program, use that program now to upload the presentation to the web site. Don't forget to recreate there any folders that PowerPoint made in your presentation's folder structure.

In Internet Explorer 7.0, to open a local file, press ALT-F to display the File menu. Then choose Open.

Test Your Web Site

Once you have published your web site, you should access it as your viewers would and test it out. Here are some things to test for:

- *Test any links that connect to sites outside your web site.* You may have forgotten to save supporting files to the Web, such as text files containing additional data.

■ *Test any multimedia objects, such as sounds and video clips.* First and foremost, do they work? Then, are the means to open these objects clear to your viewer? If not, add instructions such as "Double-click to see the video."

■ *Test any action buttons that you created.* These may have hyperlinks, may open programs, or may play a sound, for example.

■ *If you added animated GIFs, make sure they work.* Check if you get any warning messages in your browser.

An excellent precaution is to view your web site using multiple browsers (at least Microsoft Internet Explorer and Mozilla Firefox), perhaps with previous versions as well as the current ones, at varying screen resolutions and with varying numbers of screen colors. These factors can affect how your web site appears.

Summary

In this chapter, you learned about creating a presentation for a web site. You can use PowerPoint to create a web site or you can place a presentation on a web site so that people can view it in a web browser. When you publish your presentation to the Web, PowerPoint creates the HTML and other files for you.

In the next chapter, you learn about customizing PowerPoint.

12

Chapter 13

Customize PowerPoint

How to...

- ■ Set PowerPoint's options to suit your needs
- ■ Customize the Quick Access toolbar
- ■ Use an add-in
- ■ Create and use a macro
- ■ Start programming PowerPoint

Most of the customization you do in PowerPoint is not visible in your final presentation; rather, it helps you work more quickly and easily. Having the options settings that work for you is a great boon to efficiency. If you create a macro, you can automate some of your editing and turn a long task into a short one. But you can also create macros and Visual Basic for Applications (VBA) programs that change how your presentation appears or works—and the results are readily visible to your viewers.

Customization offers you great power to control PowerPoint. This chapter explains what you can accomplish without being a programmer and introduces you to the advanced capabilities of customization.

Customize PowerPoint's Options

One of the most basic ways to customize PowerPoint is to use the PowerPoint Options dialog box. To get there, click the Office button and click the PowerPoint Options button. Here, in one place, you can specify many of PowerPoint's features. Some people use PowerPoint for months, being frustrated with one feature or another, before discovering that they can change the way the feature works.

The PowerPoint Options dialog box has several panes, which are discussed in the next few sections.

Set Popular Options

The Popular pane of the PowerPoint Options dialog box, shown in Figure 13-1, enables you to customize the most often-used features of PowerPoint and add your personal information.

Here are the options you can choose:

- ■ **Show Mini Toolbar on Selection**   Displays the Mini toolbar when you select text. The Mini toolbar allows you to quickly specify commonly used text formatting. This option is on by default. I cover the Mini toolbar in Chapter 3.

- ■ **Enable Live Preview**   Displays the effect of a gallery choice before you click, so you can quickly see if you like the result. This option is selected by default. It's a great option; disable it only if it slows down your computer too much.

- ■ **Show Developer Tab in the Ribbon**   Displays the Developer tab (off by default), shown in Figure 13-2, which contains tools relating to macros, VBA code, and the Document panel. This chapter covers the Developer tab.

- **Color Scheme** Lets you choose among three colors schemes for PowerPoint's interface: blue, silver, and black. For example, your choice affects the background of the ribbon and the slide pane.

- **ScreenTip Scheme** Allows you to choose whether you see ScreenTips when you hover the mouse over a button on the ribbon. The default option is to show ScreenTips that include both the button's name and a brief description of what it does. Once you're familiar with the buttons, you can choose Don't Show Feature Descriptions in ScreenTips, which displays just the button's name, or you can turn off ScreenTips completely.

- **User Name and Initials** Allows you to enter your name and initials as you want them to appear in dialog boxes that use them, such as the Properties dialog box.

- **Language Settings** Enables you to change the language that you use with all of Microsoft Office.

When you're done with these settings, click OK or choose another pane.

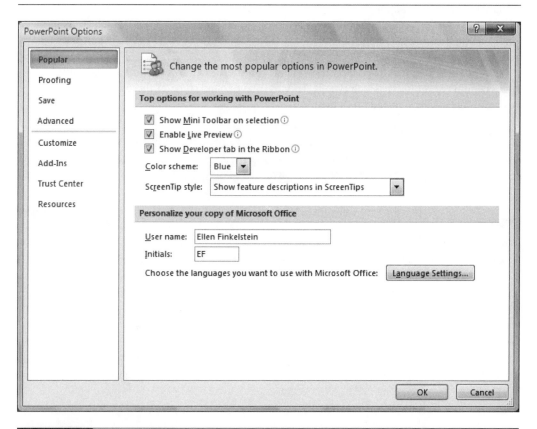

FIGURE 13-1 Use the Popular pane of the PowerPoint Options dialog box to customize often-used features and add your name and initials.

FIGURE 13-2 You need to display the Developer tab if you want to work with macros or VBA—which you can do by checking the appropriate option in the Popular pane of the PowerPoint Options dialog box.

Set Spelling and AutoCorrect Options

The Proofing pane, shown in Figure 13-3, lets you specify how the spell check features work and lets you set AutoCorrect options.

Click the AutoCorrect Options button to open the AutoCorrect dialog box, which contains settings relating to automatic adjustments to text. The AutoCorrect and Smart Tags tabs are covered in Chapter 3.

The AutoFormat As You Type tab, shown here, specifies how PowerPoint automatically changes certain types of text as you type it. You may have found some of these settings to be annoying—here's where you can turn them off.

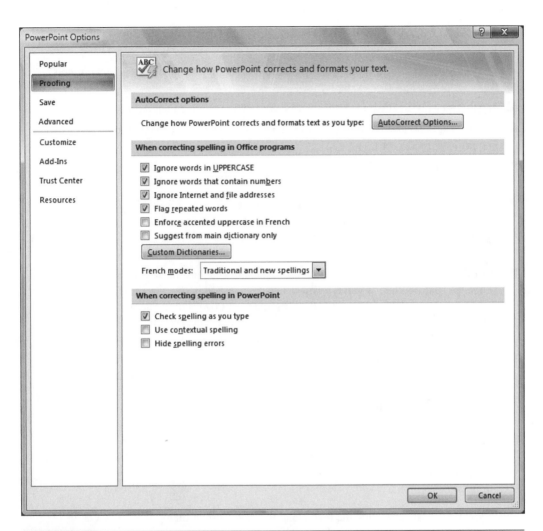

On the Proofing pane, you control the spell check and AutoCorrect features.

The options are the following:

■ **"Straight Quotes" with "Smart Quotes"**   Automatically changes a double quotation mark to a curved quotation mark. If you type a pair of quotation marks (around a word or phrase), the quotation marks automatically curve toward each other. The same goes for apostrophes. Uncheck this option if you need to use apostrophes and quotation marks as primes and double primes (to indicate feet and inches measurement).

■ **Fractions (1/2) with Fraction Character (½)**   Replaces a typed fraction with a built fraction.

■ **Ordinals (1st) with Superscript**   Replaces ordinal numbers that you type with their superscript versions (for example, 1st).

■ **Hyphens (--) with Dash (—)**   Replaces two hyphens with an em dash.

■ **Smiley Faces :-) and Arrows (==>) with Special Symbols**   Creates smiley faces (☺) and arrow symbols (➔).

■ **Internet and Network Paths with Hyperlinks**   Creates a hyperlink when you type an Internet URL or network path.

■ **Automatic Bulleted and Numbered Lists**   Starts a bulleted list when you type an asterisk (*) or dash and then a space or tab, and starts a numbered list when you type a number, a period, and then a space or tab. If you find this feature annoying, here's where you turn it off.

■ **AutoFit Title Text to Placeholder**   Automatically changes the size of slide title text to fit the text placeholder. If you type more text than can fit in the placeholder, PowerPoint makes the text smaller. If you then delete some text, PowerPoint enlarges the text again. Uncheck this option if you want all your text to be the same size (for greater consistency) and prefer instead to move some text to another slide or shorten your text.

■ **AutoFit Body Text to Placeholder**   Automatically changes the size of body text to fit the text placeholder. This is on by default, and is the cause of your text automatically getting smaller when you type too much text to fit in a body text placeholder. If this feature frustrates you, uncheck the check box.

If you like the AutoFit Body Text to Placeholder feature but want to turn it off sometimes, you can. When you want to turn off the text resizing after you type some text, click the AutoFit Options button and choose Stop Fitting Text to This Placeholder or one of the other options.

When you have finished setting the features in the AutoCorrect dialog box, click OK to return to the PowerPoint Options dialog box's Proofing pane.

The second section of this pane holds options that apply to correcting spelling in all Office programs. By default, the spell check feature ignores words in uppercase, words that contain numbers, and Internet and file addresses. Repeated words are underlined with the wavy red underline. You can choose to enforce accented uppercase letters to show their accent marks in French. Finally, you can limit spelling suggestions to the main dictionary only, ignoring custom dictionaries. You create a custom dictionary item when you right-click a word and choose Add from the shortcut menu. If you click the Custom Dictionaries button, you can add a custom dictionary and edit the list of words in the dictionary. Some people have separate dictionaries for each language that they work in. A drop-down list lets you choose if you want to allow new spellings in French.

The last section of the Proofing pane is more basic. By default, PowerPoint checks spelling as you type, inserting a wavy red line under words not in the dictionary.

A new item, Use Contextual Spelling, uses grammar to check spelling. For example, if you type, "I want to go their," this feature will mark "their" as misspelled, because it's wrong in the context. This is a great idea to improve spell checking; unfortunately, as you can see in the slide here, it doesn't work very well. All the items on the slide have a misspelled word, but PowerPoint caught only two of them. So, use Contextual Spelling, but don't get complacent!

NOTE *Contextual Spelling uses a lot of memory resources, so it might slow your system down.*

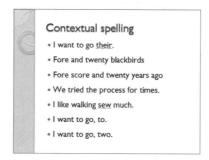

Check the Hide Spelling Errors check box if you don't want to see those wavy red lines. You can always check spelling when you're done, by clicking the Spelling button on the Review tab.

Specify Save Options

The Save pane, shown in Figure 13-4, offers options related to saving presentations. Here are the options for this pane:

- **Save Files in This Format** You can automatically save presentations in the normal PowerPoint 2007 format (.pptx), in the macro-enabled format (.pptm), or in PowerPoint 97-2003 format. Use the 97-2003 format if you regularly exchange presentations with people who don't have PowerPoint 2007. (You can always change the format for individual presentations when you save them.) I discuss the various formats in Chapter 1.

- **Save AutoRecover Information Every *x* Minutes** Check this box to make sure that recovery information is saved regularly. The default time is 10 minutes. If your electrical supply is often cut off or you want to avoid doing even 10 minutes of work again, reduce the time.

- **Default File Location** You can specify the default location where PowerPoint saves files.

- **Save Checked Out Files To** Specifies where to save documents that you check out from a server location. You can also specify a location for draft documents.

13

■ **Embed Fonts in the File**   Embeds TrueType fonts so that people on other computers
can see the original fonts, even if the fonts are not installed. Otherwise, PowerPoint
substitutes similar installed fonts. To avoid making the presentation too large, you can
embed only those characters actually used. However, if someone else will be editing the
file, embed all the characters, in case that person uses a new character. Use this feature if
you use unusual fonts that didn't come with Windows.

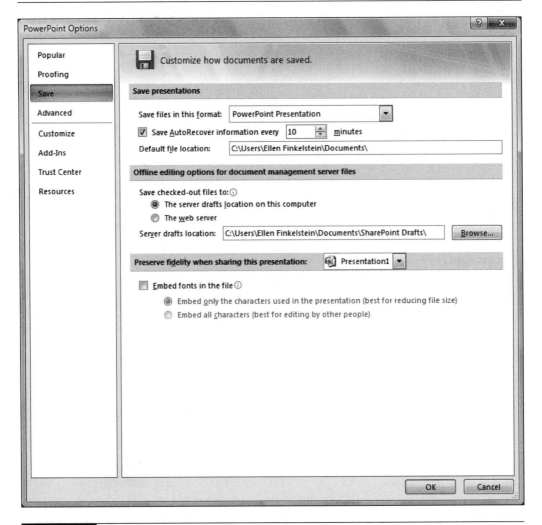

FIGURE 13-4   Use the Save pane of the PowerPoint Options dialog box to make sure you
don't lose your work.

When you're done with the Save pane, click OK to close the PowerPoint Options dialog box, or choose another pane.

Set Advanced Options

The Advanced pane, shown in Figure 13-5, is a misnomer; it contains many important and basic settings. The Editing Options section allows you to choose whether you want to automatically select entire words only when you drag across text to select it. This option is off by default, which is probably good; when this option is on, it's difficult to select part of a word.

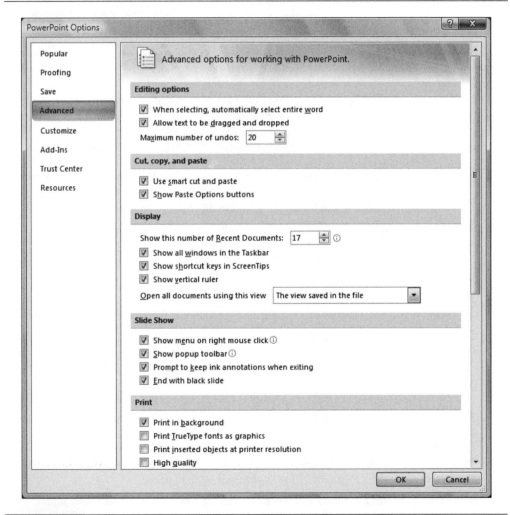

FIGURE 13-5   The Advanced pane contains many basic settings that you should know about.

 *If you want to select one entire word, double-click it.*

By default, you can drag and drop text, but you can turn off this feature in this section. Uncheck this box if you want dragging to extend text selection instead.

You can also control the maximum number of undos that PowerPoint remembers. The default is 20. You could reduce the number to use less memory resources on your computer.

The Cut, Copy, and Paste section controls smart cut and paste, which automatically adds or deletes spaces before and after pasted text when appropriate. You can also decide if you want to see a Paste Options button when you paste data—a small drop-down list next to the pasted material, as shown here. This list lets you decide how you want the pasted material formatted. For example, if you are pasting text, you can keep the source formatting, use the destination theme, or paste only plain text.

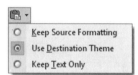

The Display section controls how PowerPoint displays certain features. For example, you can customize the number of recently used presentations listed when you click the Office button. You now have a maximum of 50, much more than the previous limit of nine presentations.

The other settings in this section are as follows:

- **Show All Windows in the Taskbar** Displays in the Windows taskbar a button for each open presentation. If you uncheck this option, you can switch between presentations on the View tab, using the Switch Windows button in the Window group.

- **Show Shortcut Keys in ScreenTips** By default, when you hover the mouse over a button that has a keyboard shortcut, you see the shortcut, as shown here. If you don't want to see the shortcuts (perhaps you know them all already), uncheck this option.

- **Show Vertical Ruler** Displays the vertical ruler at the left of each slide. You can uncheck this option if you don't use the ruler. The ruler is a valuable layout tool, but is probably not used by most people.

- **Open All Documents Using This View** By default, when you open a presentation, you see the last view you were using, but you can choose to always open in Normal view (in fact, you can choose which panes are displayed) or some other view.

The Slide Show section controls what you see in Slide Show view. I discuss this view further in Chapter 15. The following are the settings:

- **Show Menu on Right Mouse Click** Displays a shortcut menu when you right-click in Slide Show view. This menu offers navigation and other options.

- **Show Popup Toolbar** Shows a subtle toolbar at the lower-left corner of your screen in Slide Show view, which offers similar options to the shortcut menu.

■ **Prompt to Keep Ink Annotations When Exiting** As I explain in Chapter 15, you can temporarily draw on a slide to emphasize certain points. For example, you can circle some text. This option prompts you to keep this annotation when you leave Slide Show view, in case you want to save it.

■ **End with Black Slide** Ends a presentation with a black slide. The black slide helps you avoid returning to Normal view, thus showing the audience the authoring side of PowerPoint.

The Print section lets you turn background printing on and off. Background printing makes it easier to do something else while you are printing. You can also print TrueType fonts as graphics (to make sure they will display as they look on all computers) and print inserted objects at your printer's resolution.

I discuss the Customization and Add-Ins panes later in this chapter.

Set Security Options

The Trust Center pane seems to offer only links about privacy, the Customer Improvement Program, and the Windows Security Center, but there's a Trust Center Settings button that hides many options, including translation options, add-in settings, and macro settings—all of which you may need to change. The warning on this pane, that suggests that you don't change these settings, may seem daunting, but you just need to know what you're doing and you'll be all right.

When you click the Trust Center Settings button, the Trust Center dialog box opens, shown in Figure 13-6 with the Privacy Options pane displayed.

The Trusted Publishers pane lists publishers of macros that PowerPoint will open without question. I discuss trusted publishers later in this chapter when I talk about macros.

The Trusted Locations pane lists locations that are considered safe. Certain locations are automatically considered trusted because they are sources for opening files, such as themes and templates. You can add your own locations, such as folders on your hard drive where you store presentations. Click the Add New Location button, browse to the folder, and click OK.

The Add-Ins pane contains settings for PowerPoint add-ins, which are programs that you can integrate with (add in to) PowerPoint. This pane allows you to require that the source of the add-in be listed on the Trusted Publishers pane. You can also disable add-ins. Of course, that means that add-ins won't work, which is not very helpful, but it helps to ensure that no add-ins are installed without your knowledge. I discuss add-ins later in this chapter.

ActiveX controls are outside objects that use code to function within PowerPoint. For example, when you insert a Flash movie into PowerPoint, you are using an ActiveX control. (I explain how to insert a Flash movie in Chapter 9.) The ActiveX Settings pane allows you to choose the level of access you give to ActiveX controls. The default setting, Prompt Me Before Enabling All Controls with Minimal Restrictions, allows the ActiveX controls to run only if you explicitly choose to enable the content when you see a Security Alert similar to the one shown here. This may not look good during the delivery of your presentation, so you may want to change the setting just during the time of your presentation.

13

I discuss the Macro Settings pane later in this chapter, when I discuss macros.

In the Message Bar pane, you specify whether or not you want to see a message when content or code has been blocked, as shown here. You can then choose to enable the content or open the Trust Center to change your settings. Again, this might be annoying while you are delivering a presentation, but is useful otherwise.

The Privacy Options pane, shown in Figure 13-6, contains information about your privacy, as well as research and translation options. Regarding privacy, you can disable features that connect with the Internet, including Microsoft Office Online Help. The translation options involve features that translate text from one language to another. The research options determine where PowerPoint looks when you look for a definition or synonym.

When you're done with the Trust Center dialog box, click OK to return to the PowerPoint Options dialog box.

Find Resources

The Resources pane of the PowerPoint Options dialog box offers resources for updating Microsoft Office, diagnosing and repairing problems, contacting Microsoft, activating the product, registering for online services, and obtaining general information about the product.

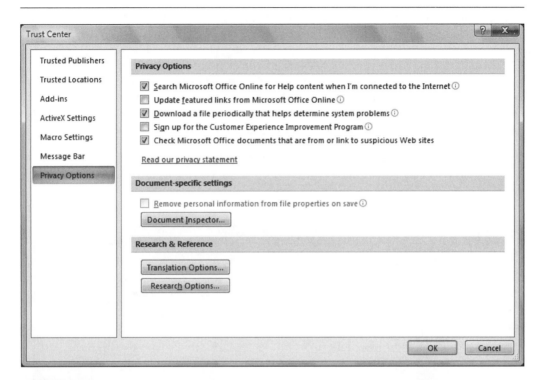

FIGURE 13-6   The Trust Center dialog box offers many settings relating to security, privacy, and translation.

When you're done with the PowerPoint Options dialog box, click OK to return to your presentation.

Customize the Quick Access Toolbar

The PowerPoint 2007 interface does not include the many toolbars of previous versions. However, the Quick Access toolbar, at the top-left corner of the application window, is customizable. The value of the Quick Access toolbar is that its buttons are always visible; to access buttons on a ribbon tab, you first have to click the tab. Moreover, some commands are available only by adding them to this toolbar, shown here:

To customize this toolbar, click the arrow at its right side. To move the toolbar beneath the ribbon, choose Show Below the Ribbon. The reason to do this would be to provide room for more buttons.

When you click the arrow, you can choose from a quick list of commonly-used commands. However, you can add any command to the toolbar. You can also change the order of the commands. To do so, choose More Commands. This opens the Customization pane of the PowerPoint Options dialog box, shown in Figure 13-7. You can also click the Office button, click the PowerPoint Options button, and choose Customization to get to the same place.

SHORTCUT *To add any command from the ribbon to the Quick Access toolbar, right-click any button on any tab of the ribbon and choose Add to Quick Access Toolbar.*

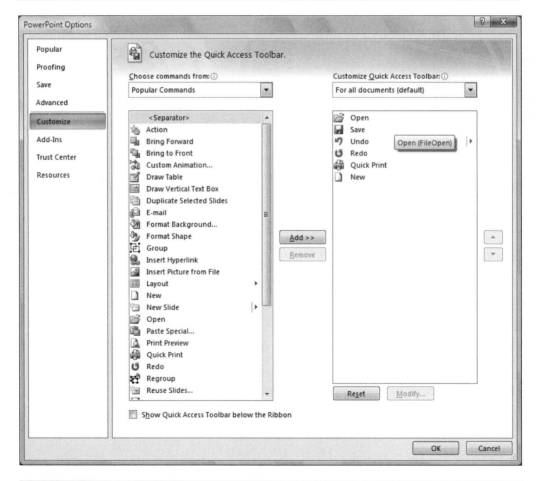

FIGURE 13-7 The Customization pane of the PowerPoint Options dialog box is the place to find commands to put on the Quick Access toolbar.

To add a command, choose a category from the Choose Commands From drop-down list. Then click a command and click the Add button. On the right side of the dialog box, you can choose to apply the changes to all documents (the default) or only to the active presentation. You can also reorder a button by selecting it and clicking the Up or Down arrow.

TIP   *An especially useful category on the Choose Commands From drop-down list is Commands Not in the Ribbon. Here you'll see some hard-to-find treasures, such as Redo, Web Page Preview, Close, Promote, Demote, Send to Microsoft Word, Add-Ins, and Toggle Case.*

When you're done customizing the Quick Access toolbar, click OK to close the PowerPoint Options dialog box.

Did you know?

Using Add-Ins

Add-ins are programs (written by a programmer) that add a feature to PowerPoint. You install an add-in and then load it into PowerPoint. PowerPoint add-ins are files with the filename extension .ppam.

Microsoft's web site has several add-ins that you can download and try out. Go to http://office.microsoft.com/downloads/ and choose PowerPoint as the product. Among the available PowerPoint downloads are the add-ins. Microsoft provides self-extracting .exe files. Double-click the file to install the add-in. Follow the simple instructions to complete installation.

For other add-ins, make sure you know the location of the .ppam file (or .ppa if it's from an older PowerPoint version) because you'll need it when you add it. However, Microsoft has a default location for add-ins and it's convenient to use this folder. In Windows Vista, it's in the Users\[username]\AppData\roaming\Microsoft\AddIns folder. To load the add-in, follow these steps:

1. Click the Office button and then click PowerPoint Options.
2. Choose the Add-Ins category to display the Add-Ins pane.
3. From the Manage drop-down list, choose PowerPoint Add-Ins and click Go.
4. In the Add-Ins dialog box, choose Add New.
5. In the Add New PowerPoint Add-In dialog box, choose the add-in that you want and click OK. Click Close.
6. If you see a message about a potential security concern, choose Enable Macros if you want the add-in to work.

(continued)

13

Of course, how you use an add-in depends on the add-in. Most add-ins come with a text file or some other method to provide you with instructions. (You may see instructions at the web site that you can print.) Generally, the add-in places a button on the Add-Ins tab of the ribbon that you click to execute the feature.

You can also unload an add-in when you are finished using it. From the same Add-In pane, choose PowerPoint Add-Ins from the Manage drop-down list and click Go. Choose the add-in from the Add-Ins dialog box. Click Unload to remove it from memory but retain the availability to load it again. Click Remove to remove the add-in completely.

If you have some VBA code, you can save it as an add-in. Type the code in the Visual Basic Editor (discussed later in this chapter in the section "Program with VBA"). You can use any presentation to do this. Close the Visual Basic Editor and then choose Save As from PowerPoint's Office menu. In the Save as Type drop-down list, choose PowerPoint Add-In (*.ppam). Type a name in the File Name text box and click Save.

When you save your presentation as an add-in, be sure to save it as a .pptm (macro-enabled) file and do not delete this presentation file. You'll need the file if you ever need to edit your add-in.

You can require add-ins to be *trusted*, or disable all add-ins. Click the Office button and click PowerPoint Options. Choose the Trust Center category and click the Trust Center Settings button. Click the Add-Ins category, choose one of the options, and click OK twice to return to your presentation. By default, the standard folder for add-ins is a trusted location.

Work with Macros

A *macro* is a series of PowerPoint commands that you save. You can then run the macro and execute all the commands in the macro. A macro can save you hours of time doing repetitive tasks. All macros are written in Visual Basic for Applications (VBA).

Unfortunately, you no longer can record macros in PowerPoint. All macros need to be written in VBA.

In this section, I explain how to run macros. I also provide an introduction to writing VBA macros, with the assumption that you are not a programmer. You'd be surprised what a nonprogrammer can do with a few VBA phrases. If you are a programmer, this section will provide you with an introduction to the programming tools available in PowerPoint 2007.

Understand the Object Model

VBA uses a hierarchy of objects to enable you to specify an object. In this way, you can distinguish text in a text placeholder from shapes or pictures. To get information on any object, you use the Object Model Reference, which you can display by following these steps:

1. If necessary, display the Developer tab. On the Office menu, click PowerPoint options. On the Popular pane, check the Show Developer Tab in the Ribbon check box and click OK.

2. On the Developer tab, click the Visual Basic button in the Code group to open the Microsoft Visual Basic editor, shown in Figure 13-8 after choosing Insert | Module to open a window where you can type VBA code.

3. On the Visual Basic Editor Standard toolbar, choose Help | Microsoft Visual Basic Help.

4. On the PowerPoint Developer page that appears, choose PowerPoint Object Model Reference (Figure 13-9).

5. Click any object listed here to get further help on that object.

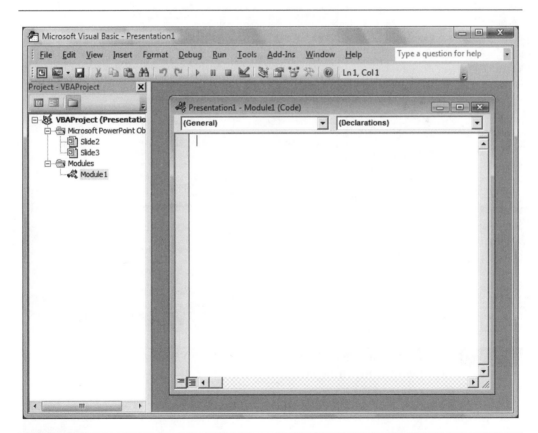

FIGURE 13-8   Use the Visual Basic editor to write VBA code for PowerPoint.

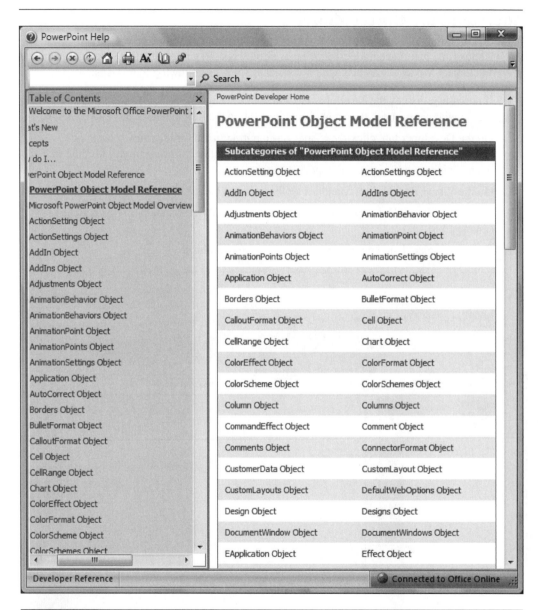

FIGURE 13-9 The PowerPoint Object Model displays available VBA objects and links to more information on each one.

Another way to get information on VBA objects and their place in the hierarchy is to use the Object Browser, shown in Figure 13-10. Here, objects are called *classes.* Classes have *members,* which can be other objects. To open and use the Object Browser, follow these steps:

1. Click the Object Browser button on the toolbar, shown here, or press F2 to open the Object Browser.

2. From the Object Browser's Project/Library drop-down list, choose PowerPoint.

3. Select any PowerPoint object from the list (or enter the name of an object in the Search text box, just below the Project/Library drop-down list, and press ENTER).

4. Click the Help button inside the Object Browser window.

For example, if you want to find out about the ActiveWindow object, you can type **ActiveWindow** in the Search text box and press ENTER. The results are displayed in the Search Results window. (If you get more than one result, click the item you want.) Click Help to get information on that term.

Use Methods and Properties

It's not enough to specify objects—you need to do something with them. In VBA, objects have methods and properties. A *method* is an action that you perform on an object or an action that an object can perform itself. A *property* is an attribute of an object, such as the fill color of an object or the font of text. After looking up any object, you can find its methods and properties. The Help page usually also provides some examples of code using that object. In Figure 13-11, you see the Help page for the ShapeRange object.

When you choose an object on the left side of the Object Browser, the right side shows its members, which can be subobjects, methods, or properties. For example, when you click ShapeRange on the left and then Fill on the right, you can click Help in the Object Browser window to view Help for the Fill property.

All VBA code uses this structure of the object hierarchy and accomplishes tasks by means of methods and properties. You can also use built-in functions, such as If, For Each, or For...Next.

You can create dialog boxes that appear when you run a macro. This topic is more involved, but to start, choose Insert | UserForm from the Visual Basic for Applications menu. A *UserForm* is the raw material for a dialog box. The toolbox appears, letting you draw in the dialog box typical controls such as buttons and text boxes. You can double-click any control on the UserForm to write code that specifies how the control functions.

To create a form in a presentation that viewers can use in Slide Show view, display the Developer tab and choose a control from the Controls group. Then drag it onto a slide.

13

Search text box   Project/Library list   Object Browser Help

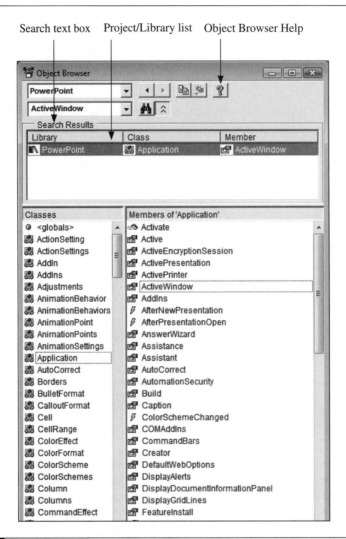

FIGURE 13-10   The Object Browser helps you find out about PowerPoint objects.

Use VBA in Your Presentations

Programming in PowerPoint with VBA first appeared in PowerPoint 97. However, programming PowerPoint has proved a challenge for both PowerPoint experts and VBA programmers. While programming Excel or Word is fairly straightforward, writing VBA for PowerPoint programming requires not only programming knowledge, but also an understanding of the graphical nature of PowerPoint.

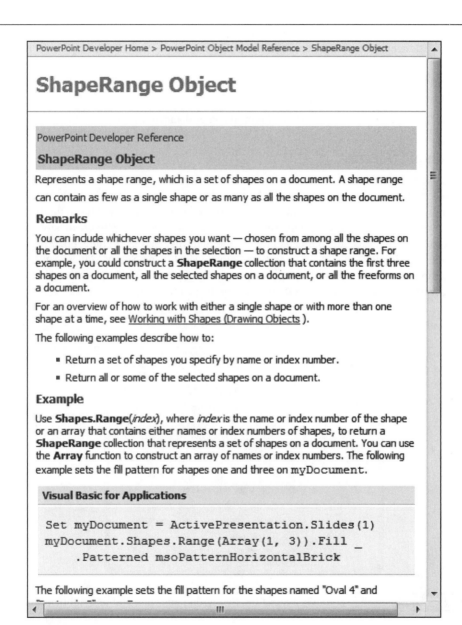

PowerPoint Developer Home > PowerPoint Object Model Reference > ShapeRange Object

ShapeRange Object

PowerPoint Developer Reference

ShapeRange Object

Represents a shape range, which is a set of shapes on a document. A shape range can contain as few as a single shape or as many as all the shapes on the document.

Remarks

You can include whichever shapes you want — chosen from among all the shapes on the document or all the shapes in the selection — to construct a shape range. For example, you could construct a **ShapeRange** collection that contains the first three shapes on a document, all the selected shapes on a document, or all the freeforms on a document.

For an overview of how to work with either a single shape or with more than one shape at a time, see Working with Shapes (Drawing Objects).

The following examples describe how to:

- Return a set of shapes you specify by name or index number.
- Return all or some of the selected shapes on a document.

Example

Use **Shapes.Range**(*index*), where *index* is the name or index number of the shape or an array that contains either names or index numbers of shapes, to return a **ShapeRange** collection that represents a set of shapes on a document. You can use the **Array** function to construct an array of names or index numbers. The following example sets the fill pattern for shapes one and three on `myDocument`.

Visual Basic for Applications

```
Set myDocument = ActivePresentation.Slides(1)
myDocument.Shapes.Range(Array(1, 3)).Fill _
    .Patterned msoPatternHorizontalBrick
```

The following example sets the fill pattern for the shapes named "Oval 4" and

13

FIGURE 13-11   The Help page for the ShapeRange object provides a description and code examples.

This section discusses three real-world examples of what VBA can accomplish in PowerPoint. These examples facilitate three types of processes in PowerPoint:

- Create simple quizzes
- Speed up routine production tasks
- Add interactive capability to PowerPoint to gather data from viewers

Create Simple Quizzes

Without being a programmer, you can use some simple VBA code to create multiple-choice quizzes. When the user chooses an answer, a message box pops up, explaining if the answer is right or wrong. When the answer is right, the code moves the user to the next question. If the answer is wrong, the user must try again. You can use the instructions here to create any quiz you want. You can also find this quiz online at http://www.ellenfinkelstein.com/htde_pp2007.html.

In Figure 13-12 you see a slide of a safety quiz that a Health and Safety Manager might create for employees. Only one of the three answers is right, of course. The three possible answers are simply shapes with text on them. You can format the shapes in any way you want.

Each slide contains a question, two wrong answers, and one right answer.

To create the quiz, you would create all the questions, one on each slide, with the answers. Then it's time to create the VBA code. Follow these steps:

1. If the Developer tab is not available, click the Office menu and choose PowerPoint Options. On the Popular pane, check the Show the Developer Tab in the Ribbon check box and click OK.

2. On the Developer tab, click the Visual Basic button in the Code group to open the Microsoft Visual Basic editor.

3. Choose Insert | Module to open a window where you can type VBA code.

4. In the window, type the code shown in Figure 13-13. (You don't need to type the horizontal lines; they will appear automatically.) You are typing three separate macros, as follows:

   ■ **Wrong**   Displays a message box that says, "Sorry, that's not right. Please try again."

   ■ **Right**   Displays a message box that says, "That's right!" This macro also displays the next slide containing the next question.

   ■ **RightLast**   Also displays a message box that says, "That's right!" However, this macro doesn't display the next slide, because it's used only for the last question of the quiz.

5. Click the Save button on the Standard toolbar of the Visual Basic editor and use the Windows taskbar to return to your PowerPoint presentation.

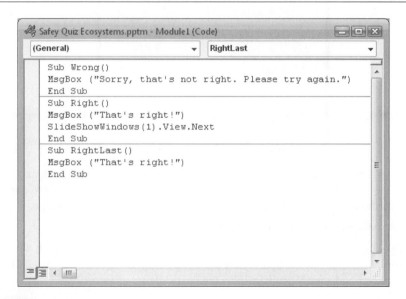

FIGURE 13-13   The VBA code for the right and wrong answers

6. On the first question slide, select one of the shapes containing a wrong answer. If the border on the selected shape is dashed, click the shape again to display a solid border. (This ensures that the macro will be attached to the entire shape, not just the text on the shape.)

7. On the Insert tab, click Action in the Links group.

8. In the Action Settings dialog box, choose Run Macro on the Mouse Click tab, and choose Wrong from the drop-down list. Notice that the three macros you wrote are on the list. Click OK.

9. To make sure that your macro settings don't interfere with the VBA code, click the Office button and then click PowerPoint Options. Click the Trust Center category and then click the Trust Center Settings button. Click the Macro Settings category. In the Macro Settings section, choose the Enable All Macros option.

   *This is not an ideal setting to keep, but it is helpful for testing VBA code. For a more permanent option, read the How To box, "Sign Your Macros," later in this chapter.*

10. To check that the macro works, save the presentation as a macro-enabled presentation (.pptm) and enter Slide Show view. Display the slide that you worked on and click the wrong answer. You should see a message box appear telling you to try again, as shown here:

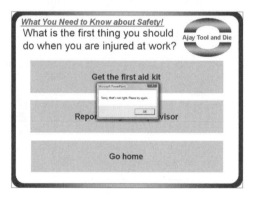

11. Assuming that the macro works, return to Normal view. (If it doesn't, you may need to check the VBA code or your macro settings.) Choose the other wrong answer and use the same method you used in Steps 6-8 to assign the Wrong macro to the shape.

12. Use the same method to assign the Right macro to the correct answer.

13. Save your presentation and check out the macros in Slide Show view. Both wrong answers should display the appropriate message box. The right answer should display its message box and automatically display the next slide.

14. If everything works, continue to assign the macros to every answer in the presentation. On the last slide, assign the RightLast macro to the right answer on the last slide.

You're done! Check all the answers to make sure that you assigned the right macro to each answer.

 Macro security settings can affect whether the macros work. Be sure to save and close the presentation, reopen it, and test the macros again. Also see the How To box, "Sign Your Macros." You may have to close and open PowerPoint after you change the settings.

Accelerate Routine Production Tasks

Many routine production tasks take a lot of time or are just not straightforward in PowerPoint. For example, presentation designers often need to keep track of the filename and where that presentation is located during and after the production process. Users have often asked for a way to include the path and filename of a presentation on draft printouts.

You could type the filename and the path into the footer, but that information is not updated if you change the filename or the location of the presentation. A simple VBA routine can help you accomplish this goal quickly and dynamically. You can go to http://www.ellenfinkelstein.com/htde_pp2007.html to download an add-in that toggles between showing and not showing a complete path and filename in the footer. You can use this macro to print presentations for draft purposes (with path and filename). You can then turn it off for either the final presentation or printouts. See the How To box, "Using Add-Ins" for instructions. When you click the menu item Do Everything | Toggle Path on the Add-Ins tab, PowerPoint displays the presentation's path and filename as a footnote in the slide master. Click again, and the footnote disappears.

Similarly, you can improve other time-consuming, repetitive, or error-prone tasks with a VBA tool created and customized for your own specific needs.

Add Interactive Data-Gathering Capability to a Presentation

Suppose you are at a trade show and have set up a presentation to show in kiosk mode. You want to make it easy for someone to give you information or request to be added to your mailing list. Create the entry form on a PowerPoint slide and export the information from that slide into an Excel workbook. This example both controls Excel from within PowerPoint and uses PowerPoint as a way to capture and store information. The user never sees Excel. PowerPoint opens Excel in the background, captures the data supplied by the viewer, and tells Excel to place those values into an Excel worksheet. PowerPoint then tells Excel to save that file and wait for the next viewer's input.

To use this code, you need two files, Join Our Mailing List.pptm and Submit to Mailing List. xlsx. The presentation contains the VBA code for this example. After you download the files from http://www.ellenfinkelstein.com/htde_pp2007.html, place them in the same folder. Open the presentation and switch to Slide Show view. Follow the instructions on the slide to enter the requested information. You can try typing in several names and addresses. Then open the Excel worksheet, and voilà!—you see the data on the spreadsheet.

*Thanks to Brian Reilly, a Microsoft PowerPoint MVP and owner of Reillyand, Inc.,
a consulting firm that specializes in automating MS Office applications, for much of the information
in this section and for the original VBA code. He can be reached at brian@reillyand.com.*

NOTE *You can find more VBA resources on Steve Rindsberg's web site, http://www.rdpslides.
com. Steve is another Microsoft PowerPoint MVP and coauthors the popular PPTools
(available at www.pptools.com) with Brian Reilly. Steve also updated Brian's code for
PowerPoint 2007.*

Use a Macro

You can obtain macros from third-party developers or try your hand at writing your own. If you
have a macro that runs in Normal view, follow these steps to run it:

1. On the Developer tab, click Macro in the Code group to open the Macro dialog box,
   shown in Figure 13-14.

2. Choose the macro from the list.

3. Click Run.

FIGURE 13-14 You can choose a macro to run in the Macro dialog box.

If the Run option is not enabled when you try to run your macro, unsigned macros may be disabled. I explain how to sign macros later in this chapter, in the "Sign Your Macros" How To box.

If you use a macro often in Normal view, you can put it on the Quick Access toolbar. Choose Macros from the Choose Commands From drop-down list. I explain how to customize the Quick Access toolbar earlier in this chapter.

In Slide Show view, the only way to run a macro is to attach it to an object. For details on attaching a macro to an object, see the section "Use Action Settings" in Chapter 11.

Manage Macros

The more you understand about how VBA code works, the more easily you can manage your macros. You should know how to specify macro settings. Also, you often need to edit or copy macros; this section explains how.

Specify Macro Settings

The macro settings in the Trust Center determine whether or not your macros run or whether they run with notification. Ideally, you should leave the default setting unchanged and sign or trust your macros instead. (I explain how to sign or trust macros in the upcoming sidebar, "Sign Your Macros.") However, if you want to run a macro during a presentation, you may want to temporarily change the macro setting to avoid seeing a notification during the slide show. To specify macro settings, follow these steps:

1. Click the Office button and choose PowerPoint Options.

2. Click the Trust Center option and then click the Trust Center Settings button.

3. In the Trust Center dialog box, choose Macro Settings to display the Macro Settings pane, shown here:

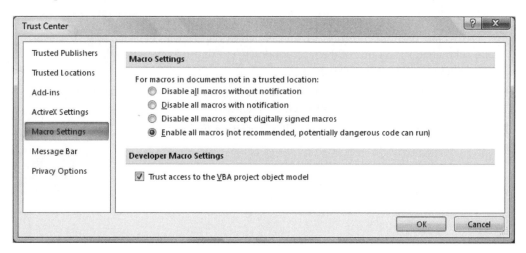

13

4. Choose one of the following options and click OK twice:

■ **Disable All Macros Without Notification** This option disables all macros except those in a trusted location. I explain trusted locations in the "Set Security Options" section earlier in this chapter.

■ **Disable All Macros with Notification** This option, the default, disables macros but notifies you and gives you the opportunity to enable them, as shown here. This is an excellent option for working in Normal and Slide Sorter view, but looks awkward in Slide Show view in front of an audience.

■ **Disable All Macros Except Digitally Signed Macros** This option has three levels. If the macro is not signed, it is disabled without notification. If it is signed, but not by a trusted publisher, you are notified so you can enable the macro. If it is signed by a trusted publisher, it runs without notification.

■ **Enable All Macros** This option, which comes with the warning "not recommended, potentially dangerous code can run," is the most liberal. It's helpful to use temporarily while you're working on your code.

Edit Macros

To edit a macro and view the code, choose View Code in the Controls group. You can also choose Macro in the Code group, choose the macro you want to edit, and click Edit. You are now in the Visual Basic editor. Figure 13-15 shows a macro.

The editor window contains a *code module,* which stores VBA code. You can have several code modules in a *project,* which contains all the pieces necessary for a VBA program.

Here's how this simple macro works:

■ The first line starts the macro. A VBA macro always opens with the word *Sub*. (It stands for subroutine.) The name of the macro follows. The line always ends with a set of parentheses, in this case, empty.

■ The next line is the actual code. It uses the selected text on the active slide and changes its font color to blue, using the RGB color system.

■ The last line ends the subroutine, with the expression *End Sub.*

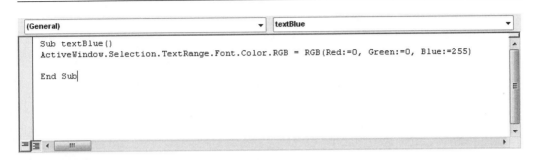

| (General) | ▼ | textBlue | ▼ |

```
Sub textBlue()
ActiveWindow.Selection.TextRange.Font.Color.RGB = RGB(Red:=0, Green:=0, Blue:=255)

End Sub
```

FIGURE 13-15 A simple macro in the Visual Basic editor.

You can see that you could easily change the color if you knew its red-green-blue numbers. For example, you could edit the macro to change text to red. If you edit a macro, click Save on the Visual Basic Editor toolbar to save your changes. To close the Visual Basic Editor, click its Close button.

Copy Macros

You can create a duplicate of a macro by copying and pasting. You can then edit the new macro to create a different macro, instead of creating it from scratch. To create a duplicate, open the Visual Basic editor to display the macro. Select all the text and copy it to the clipboard. Then choose Insert | Module to create a new code module window. Paste the macro into the new window and edit it. You can also paste the text at the bottom of the same window to create a new macro.

You can use the Project Explorer (the top-left window of the Visual Basic editor in Figure 13-8) to copy a macro module to another presentation. Open both presentations. If necessary, click the plus (+) sign next to the presentation to display its modules. Then drag a module from one

How to ... **Sign Your Macros**

The best way to run macros is to sign them. Then you *trust* them, which means assigning them a trusted status. This process allows you to run your own macros without lowering the security level. To run your own macros while using high security, you must sign and trust them. Microsoft Office comes with a self-signing certificate feature that you can use for your own VBA programs. Follow the steps described next, to use this feature.

(continued)

13

1. In Windows (XP or Vista), click Start | All Programs | Microsoft Office | Microsoft Office Tools | Digital Certificate for VBA Projects to open the Create Digital Certificate dialog box, shown here:

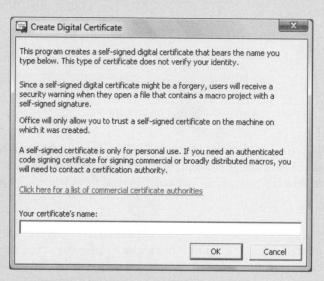

2. In the Your Certificate's Name text box, enter a name for the certificate and click OK. You see the message shown here. Click OK again. You're now ready to sign a VBA macro project.

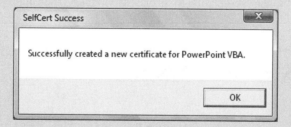

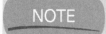 *You can see the certificate in Internet Explorer. Choose Tools | Internet Options. Choose the Content tab and click the Certificates button. Look on the Personal tab.*

3. In the PowerPoint presentation that contains the macro, display the Developer tab. In the Code group, click Visual Basic to open the Visual Basic editor.

4. In the Project Explorer window, double-click the module that contains the code you want to sign. If you have created a project (which may contain more than one module), select that.

5. In the Visual Basic editor, choose Tools | Digital Signature. If a digital certificate is listed and you want to use it, click OK. Otherwise, click the Choose button, choose the certificate in the Select Certificate dialog box, and click OK twice.

6. To assign trusted status to VBA code that you create—or to other VBA publishers— reopen the presentation. You'll see the Security Alert below the ribbon, notifying you that macros were disabled, as shown here:

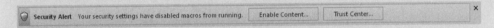

7. Click Enable Content to open the Trust In Office dialog box. Choose Trust All Documents from This Publisher and click OK.

> **NOTE** *You can now find your certificate listed as a trusted publisher by clicking the Office button, choosing PowerPoint Options, then choosing Trust Center. Click the Trust Center Settings button and choose Trusted Publishers to display the Trusted Publishers pane, shown here:*

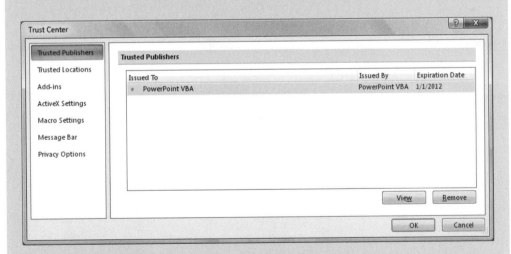

Now your macro will run without any notification, even though you still have a high level of security.

presentation to the other, all within the Project Explorer. If the Project Explorer isn't visible, you can open it by choosing View | Project Explorer.

Summary

In this chapter, you saw how to set PowerPoint's options to suit your needs. You can customize the Quick Access toolbar by adding buttons to it. This chapter also explained how to use add-ins. The second part of the chapter explained how to create and use a macro, and then introduced you to programming in Visual Basic for Applications (VBA).

In the next chapter, you prepare to deliver your presentation.

Chapter 14

Prepare to Deliver Your Presentation

How to...

- Decide on the best slide format
- Choose the right equipment
- Create a timed presentation
- Set slide show parameters
- Rehearse, rehearse, rehearse
- Create slide show variations

You have completed your presentation. Now is not the time to run out and deliver it. Now is the time to prepare. You need to decide on some of the mechanical aspects of your presentation, such as which type of slide format and projector you will use. Will you manually forward each slide or let PowerPoint do it for you? Then it's time to rehearse until you are thoroughly familiar with your presentation. Finally, you may want to create custom shows so that you can vary your presentation based on your audience's reactions.

Decide on the Best Slide Format

Your first decision is how you will present your slide show. Your decision should be based on the equipment you have available, what type of impression you want to give, and the venue of the presentation.

 *It's best to decide on the slide format before you start creating your slides. If you change the size and proportion of slides, your objects may get distorted.*

Print Handouts

If you want or need a low-tech method, you can print handouts from your presentation and give them to your audience. You don't need any equipment (or even any electricity). You should consider this method if you will present outdoors or in a country where you can't count on electricity. However, in all other situations, your audience probably expects you to take advantage of the electricity!

Of course, handouts are a great aid to your audience members, helping them remember what you said after they have gone home. In most cases, use handouts as an addition to your presentation. Research shows that handouts increase the effectiveness of a presentation in a sales situation. In Chapter 15, I explain more about printing handouts and using them during your presentation.

Use 35mm Slides

You can send your presentation to a slide bureau to have 35mm slides made and show the slides from a slide projector. Using 35mm slides has two advantages:

- They generally provide the clearest, sharpest picture, with very bright colors.

- A 35mm slide projector is inexpensive and easy to use.

If you have only a 35mm slide projector, you may want to go this route. Of course, remember that 35mm slides are static; you lose all your animation and transitions. You also lose any video, sounds, or music.

To create 35mm slides, before starting the presentation, display the Design tab and click the Page Setup button to open the Page Setup dialog box. In the Slides Sized For drop-down list, choose 35mm Slides, as shown in Figure 14-1. PowerPoint sizes your slides appropriately for 35mm slides.

Once you have completed your presentation, you send it to a service bureau that makes the actual slides. Look in the Yellow Pages for "Photographic Color Prints and Transparencies" or "Slides and Filmstrips." Otherwise, search for "35mm slides" using any Internet search engine. Don't hesitate to ask your colleagues for referrals. You should check the following about the service bureau:

- Do they use Macs or PCs, and does their platform match yours?

- Can you send them your PowerPoint 2007 presentation as is, or do you have to convert it? If you have to convert it to a previous version, you will lose new features.

- Can you e-mail them your presentation?

- How quickly will they send your 35mm slides back to you? (Expect to pay more for rush service.)

Use Overhead Transparencies

You can make overhead transparencies from your slide show and project them with an overhead projector. Overhead projectors are much less expensive than LCD or DLP projectors. (Projector terms are explained in Table 14-1.) You are more likely to find an overhead projector in an educational setting. Overhead projectors usually need dimmed lights to work well, especially in larger groups.

14

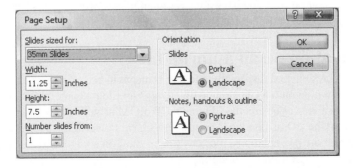

FIGURE 14-1   Use the Page Setup dialog box to set the size of your slides.

Overheads are easy to create. Many printers can print directly onto a special transparency acetate that stops the ink from creating puddles. If you do not have this special transparency acetate, you can also print onto paper and use a photocopier to copy onto acetate. Of course, you would ideally use a color printer or copier to make the transparencies. Service bureaus can also create transparencies for you.

Generally, overhead backgrounds should be light. You can even create overheads with no background at all. Remember, all the color on the slide needs to be printed onto the acetate. To create a quick, inexpensive color background, you can buy colored acetate that acts like the background.

To create overheads, before starting your presentation, open the Page Setup dialog box (previously shown in Figure 14-1). In the Slides Sized For drop-down list, choose Overhead. While 35mm slides and onscreen presentations almost always use a landscape orientation, overhead transparencies often use a portrait orientation. In the Page Setup dialog box, choose the orientation you want. PowerPoint then sizes your slides appropriately for overhead transparencies.

Overheads are a great backup for an onscreen presentation; you can use them if your projector or computer dies. Of course, like with 35mm slides, you lose any animation, video, or sound when you print to overheads.

Present Directly from a Computer

Nowadays, most presenters show presentations directly from a computer using an LCD or DLP projector. The general term is a *data projector* because it transmits data from your computer onto a screen. You could possibly use an LCD panel over an overhead projector, but LCD panels are rarely used any more—they are not bright enough for most situations.

For very small groups (1–5 people), you can present directly from a laptop with no projector. If you use a large monitor, you can show a presentation to a group of 15 or so. You could do a new employee orientation like this. You can also buy very large display systems, such as 80-inch televisions and plasma screens, that will present to larger groups—but they are quite expensive. For most groups, you need a projector and a screen. For more information on choosing a projector, see the section, "Choose the Best Equipment."

The default setting in the Page Setup dialog box (see Figure 14-1) is for an onscreen show with a 4:3 width-to-height ratio. If you have a wide-screen monitor (or your projector supports wide-screen format), you can choose a 16:9 or 16:10 format.

Run a Presentation on an Autorun CD

One way to deliver a presentation, especially one that is meant to be self-run, is on a CD. You can copy a presentation onto a CD along with an *autorun* file that automatically starts the presentation when a viewer inserts the CD into a CD-ROM drive. You can also include PowerPoint Viewer on the CD in case the viewer doesn't have PowerPoint. This feature enables you to include one or more presentations, plus any linked files, on a CD-ROM. As an alternative, you can copy all the files you need to a folder.

To create a CD, you need a CD burner with the appropriate software and a blank CD. Follow these steps:

1. Click the Office button and choose Publish I Package for CD. The Package for CD dialog box, shown here, opens.

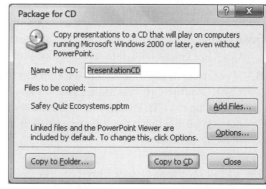

2. Type a name for the CD in the Name the CD text box.

3. The dialog box lists the active presentation. To add other presentations or other files, click Add Files, choose the files, and click Add. Any linked files and PowerPoint Viewer are included by default. (See Chapter 15 for more information about PowerPoint Viewer.) If you add files, they're listed in the dialog box and you can change their play order by selecting a file and clicking the Up and Down arrows that appear.

4. To specify whether to include PowerPoint Viewer, linked files, and embedded TrueType fonts, click Options to open the Options dialog box, shown here. Choose which types of files you want. To choose how your presentations play (automatically or not), choose one of the options from the Select How Presentations Will Play in the Viewer drop-down list. You can also password protect presentations. When you are done, click OK.

NOTE   *A common problem occurs when movies and sounds don't play once the presentation is on a CD. Make sure you place all of the movies and sounds in the same folder as your presentation before inserting them into the saved presentation.*

14

> NOTE
>
> *To make sure that you always have the latest version of PowerPoint Viewer, go to http://office.microsoft.com/downloads. Choose Downloads for Office 2007 and then choose PowerPoint as the product and click the Viewers link. Follow the instructions to download and install it.*

5. If you want to copy the files to a folder (instead of to a CD), click Copy to Folder. In the Copy to Folder dialog box, choose a location and name the new folder.

6. If you want to copy the files to a CD, insert a blank CD-ROM (CD-R or CD-RW) in your CD-ROM drive. (If you use a CD-RW that contains files, PowerPoint overwrites them.) Click Copy to CD. PowerPoint immediately copies the files to the CD and creates the autorun.inf file that causes the presentation to run automatically when the CD is inserted in a CD-ROM drive.

> NOTE
>
> *If you choose to include linked content (the default), you'll see a message warning you that linked content can be used by hackers to invade your privacy and lure you into running malicious code. Click Yes to include the linked content. If you choose No, links won't work. You may see a second message letting you know that macros, links, and embedded objects won't work in PowerPoint Viewer. Click Continue.*

7. If you have created an autorun CD, eject and reinsert the CD, and your PowerPoint presentation should start! (If you have disabled the CD autorun feature in Windows, you need to start the CD manually.)

Choose the Best Equipment

LCD and DLP projectors are quite complex. To buy one, look under "Projection Apparatus" in the Yellow Pages. In the past, projectors were rarely sold in computer stores, but that is changing as prices come down. Before you buy a projector, you need to understand the terminology involved, as explained in Table 14-1.

Using a projector is generally simple: you connect its cable to the external display port of a laptop or computer and plug it into an outlet. A projector will come with a manual to help you adjust color, focus, and so forth. You may need to read your computer's documentation for details on displaying the picture both through the projector and on the computer's monitor at the same time. Most laptops have a keyboard key or keyboard combination (often labeled CRT/LCD) that you press to toggle displaying on the laptop's screen, through the projector, or both. Usually you want to see the presentation on both the laptop and through the projector.

If your presentation includes sound, you need to connect speakers to the projector, which you do with the cables that are generally included with the projector. Most projectors come with a remote controller so that you can move around the room as you control the presentation. If yours doesn't have one, you can probably buy a remote controller separately.

Projectors have a *native* resolution, a resolution that is built into the projector. If your computer screen uses the same resolution, no adjustments are necessary. Many projectors automatically adjust for differences in resolution. As I explain in the "Set Slide Show Parameters" section later in this chapter, you can adjust the resolution of the presentation.

 ## Reuse a Presentation in Another Format

Most presentations contain content that you can reuse, either in new presentations or as e-mail or in other software formats. Chapter 12 explains how to export a presentation to HTML to display it on a web site or intranet. For more options, try PPT2HTML, developed by Steve Rindsberg (http://www.rdpslides.com/pptools). You'll have more control over how your presentation appears in various browsers.

Several programs convert PowerPoint presentations into Macromedia (Adobe) Flash SWF format. Flash is a program for creating web-based animation. These programs are server-based or desktop-based. Two desktop-based options are PointeCast (http://www .pointecast.com) and PowerCONVERTER (http://www.presentationpro.com/products/ powerconverter.asp).

Impatica for PowerPoint (http://www.impatica.com/imp4ppt/) converts PowerPoint files into Java presentations with faithful rendition of most transitions, animation, sound, and narration. Viewers may need to download Sun Microsystems' Java Virtual Machine to view the presentation (http://java.com/en/download/index.jsp). Impatica even includes an option that allows you to run your presentation from a BlackBerry phone.

Another possibility is to capture a presentation as it runs in a movie format. TechSmith's Camtasia Studio (http://www.techsmith.com/camtasia.asp) and Hyperionics Technologies' HyperCam (http://www.hyperionics.com/hc) can accomplish this task so that you can play a presentation as RealMedia or Windows Media content. You can also convert these presentations to video CDs or DVDs for display on a television screen.

As discussed in Chapter 1, you can save a PowerPoint file in Adobe Acrobat PDF format. The PDF is a static format, and you lose all animation and transitions. While PDF is generally a static format, the newest version, 5.0, does the best job of including hyperlinks and some slide transitions. For another option, try Prep4PDF (http://www.rdpslides.com/ pptools/prep4pdf/index.html) from PPTools, which works with Adobe Acrobat.

Perhaps you *really* present on the run and would like to have your presentation on your handheld PC or PDA. Windows Mobile, which offers versions of software that run on mobile devices, includes a Pocket PowerPoint version. There are third-party companies that have offered slide show options for hand-held devices, but as of this writing, their compatibility with PowerPoint 2007 hasn't been confirmed. For more information, use your favorite search engine to search the Web for "PowerPoint handheld" or "PDA."

Thanks to Geetesh Bajaj, PowerPoint MVP and the technical editor of this book, for some of this information.

14

Term	Definition
LCD projector	LCD stands for *Liquid Crystal Display*. An LCD projector electronically takes the data from your presentation and displays it on a screen.
DLP projector	DLP stands for *Digital Light Processing*. Developed by Texas Instruments, a DLP projector uses a technology involving over a million micromirrors. Micromotors move the mirrors to help focus the image. DLP projectors generally produce a brighter, smoother image and are especially valued for video and photographs.
LCD panel	An LCD panel fits on top of an overhead projector. The overhead projector provides the light, optics, and focus, and the LCD panel reads the data from your computer. LCD panels are less expensive than projectors.
Projector	A projector includes a light source and lens, and the ability to read data from your computer. Most include speakers.
Overhead projector	Overheads are mostly used for transparencies, with no computer involved. You can combine an LCD panel with an overhead projector to project a PowerPoint presentation.
Passive LCD	Passive LCD is the oldest technology for projectors. It is lower in cost, but the color contrast is unsuitable for video clips.
Active LCD	This is the current technology for LCD projectors, providing higher color contrast. Suitable for video.
Resolution	This is the number of horizontal × vertical pixels displayable on a screen. There are three major types: SVGA (800 × 600), XGA (1024 × 768), and SXGA (1280 × 1024).
Lumen	This is a measure of the brightness of light.

TABLE 14-1   Projector Terminology

When buying a projector, which is an expensive piece of equipment, it pays to do some homework before and during the process. Be sure to look for reviews online. Then, consider these points:

- *How much can you afford?* Prices have come down recently, but you'll still find that the newest lightweight ultraportables cost a little more. Of course, you'll have to pay a higher price for more performance, features, or brightness. You can often find refurbished rental-return units and closeout models at a significant discount, some with respectable warranties.

- *How will you use the projector?* If you expect to carry it around every day, the weight of the projector is a very important issue. But if you're not going to lug it around very often, the weight isn't as crucial. A sturdier, heavier projector with more features will work perfectly well—and you can get it for the same price or less. You'd be surprised how many features you can get by adding a few more pounds.

■ *Where will you put the projector and what size screen will you use?* These questions are important because there is no universal standard for projector placement and image size. Some projectors are designed to be used close to the screen, and others come with a wide-ranging zoom lens so that you have the option of being either close to the screen or farther away. You also need to consider *keystoning,* the image distortion caused by projecting at an angle that the projector wasn't designed for—you see an image that is wider on the top than on the bottom. Most projectors offer "keystone correction."

■ *How bright should the projector be?* Of course, you want to have the brightest image possible. However, there's a catch—the size of the image a projector is displaying greatly affects your perception of its brightness. A 600-lumen projector looks great on a 60-inch screen (measured diagonally), but the same projector looks quite dim when you need to fill a 120-inch screen, because it has four times the area. You may find hundreds of lumens of difference between the claims of the manufacturer for the model line and the actual brightness of individual projectors in that model line. Look for a reputable, trustworthy salesperson who is honest with you about these discrepancies.

■ *How long will the lamp last and how much does it cost?* Generally, the lamp is your projector's light source—and burns out just like any lightbulb. Replacement bulbs can be expensive (often over $300!) and are a hidden cost of owning a projector. Find out how often you'll need to replace a bulb and consider that answer in your buying decision. You may find that buying a more expensive projector with a longer lamp life is less expensive in the long run than buying a cheaper projector that burns bulbs faster. Ask three questions: How many hours of use can you expect to get from the lamp? How bright will the projector be after the lamp has been run for several hundred hours (it often dims dramatically)? And how bright will it be near the end of its life? Don't forget to ask about the lamp's rated power in watts. Let's say you're trying to decide between two projectors with similar lumens of brightness, but one uses a 500-watt lamp to produce its light and the other uses only a 100-watt lamp. In that case, you should choose the 100-watt lamp projector—it will stay bright longer, produce less heat, require a less noisy cooling fan, use less energy, and last longer because it is inherently more efficient.

■ *What is the projector's resolution?* A projector's resolution is a key factor in a projector's price. As described in Table 14-1, there are three options: SVGA (800 × 600), XGA (1024 × 768), and SXGA (1280 × 1024 or higher). Before you start shopping, know which resolution you need. You probably don't need the highest resolution if you're going to use your projector just for simple, bulleted-text PowerPoint slides. SVGA may be fine. On the other hand, you'll need the highest resolution possible— SXGA or better—if you will be presenting a circuit design you created on a workstation. Find out from your salesperson the projector's native resolution. Most new projectors can shrink or expand a computer's image to fill the fixed matrix of pixels of the projector. With most images, when this resizing is accomplished skillfully, you will have a hard time discerning the projector's exact native resolution. But if you try to project a detailed CAD drawing on that same SVGA projector in full SXGA resolution, some of the lines

14

will be missing and other lines will be blurry. These resizing problems will not occur if you project the same image with a projector that has a native SXGA resolution.

- *What are the lens specifications?* Besides knowing whether you need a motorized zoom lens (only a few projectors are zoomless these days), what else is there to know? Besides the *zoom range* (the amount of change you can get in image size), look for a lens with all-glass elements. To save weight, many projector lenses are made of plastic or of a plastic composite, but the onscreen image from a good glass lens cannot be beaten; it will be sharp and in focus, even in the corners. If you are buying a projector for a conference room, an optional projection lens is important to consider. To allow projectors much greater flexibility to "throw" images farther and wider, many manufacturers are starting to offer a range of lens options. If the projector's manufacturer doesn't provide them, a third-party lens company such as Navitar (http://presentation.navitar.com) probably does.

- *What contrast and color saturation do you need?* Most projectors have more than enough contrast for the majority of situations. Contrast shouldn't be much of an issue unless you're very picky about video quality, which looks better with lower black levels. For today's projectors, a three-panel LCD projector or a three-chip DLP projector provides the best color saturation, compared to a one-panel LCD or one-chip DLP projector. CRT projectors deliver a level of color saturation somewhere between the three-panel and one-panel projectors. The big light-valve projectors are close behind the LCD and DLP units but show more color variation across their images. Check color intensity under various lighting conditions to get an idea of the projector's performance in the real world.

- *What is the projector's weight and what are its other features?* To start with, find out how many inputs, outputs, and onboard speakers the projector has. Other capabilities, such as a motorized zoom, focus, and lens shift, should be added to the list. Additional features are related to ease of use: easily operated elevator feet, handles that are comfortable and sturdy, easy-to-use onscreen menus, and a lightweight carrying case for portables and ultraportables. If weight is important, you need to consider the total carrying weight of the unit, case, and accessories. When you add in all the required cables and accessories, you'd be surprised how much different projectors' carrying weights are equalized. Besides the weight of the carrying case, the signal cables and remote-control unit usually add about two pounds to a projector's overall heft.

- *What should you expect from the warranty and service?* Let's say you're out in the field and the projector suddenly quits on you. What now? Now your warranty kicks in—and you'd better make sure you have one. The good news is that, because the overall quality of projectors is now so good, many manufacturers are competing to offer the best warranty and service options. Some manufacturers now even offer free overnight replacement of a dead unit, no questions asked. If you're a road warrior, that's the kind of service you need. Otherwise, warranties of one, two, or three years are the rule. Still, you should read the fine print carefully, because there is a wide range of service plans to choose from, depending on the manufacturer and dealer. In particular, check out how long the lamp is covered under the warranty; it may be for only a few months. As always, get everything in writing, and keep a file with your warranty and other projector-related materials in it. When you need to use that warranty, you'll know where it is.

The best way to learn about a projector is to see it perform. So ask for a demo—or better yet, a number of demos. To judge a full range of image-quality parameters, bring a disk of professional test patterns and images, such as DisplayMate (http://www.displaymate.com). If you don't have a professional test pattern available, just use a disk of your favorite images and see what that new projector can do. A great way to decide between two competing models is to ask your salesperson to arrange a "shootout," so you can view both projectors with the same image at the same time. Practically every projector looks good by itself; but make a direct comparison, and all its warts appear.

Thanks to William Bohannon, chief scientist at Manx Research (760-735-9678), for the material on evaluating a projector.

Time Your Presentation

When giving a presentation, you can manually control the timing of each slide by clicking the mouse, or you can set timing and let PowerPoint forward each slide for you. Usually, timed slides are used when your presentation will run unattended at a conference or kiosk. However, if you are presenting, you can always pause a presentation that has timed slides, to maintain full control. Timing was more important before the days of ubiquitous remote controllers. In that case, automatic timing freed the presenter from being tied to the computer. Nowadays, with a remote mouse, you can control the computer and still walk around the room without restriction.

Timing slides can be used as a technique for rehearsal. When you rehearse timings, PowerPoint lets you know the length of the entire presentation, which is extremely useful information. You also learn how long you are spending on each slide. From this data, you might decide to divide a slide into two, to break up the message into smaller bites. On the other hand, you might realize that two slides should be combined.

Set the Timing

There are two ways to set timing for a presentation. When you use the first method, you run through your presentation as a rehearsal and time the slides based on your rehearsal. In the second method, you directly assign a number of seconds to each slide. If your presentation is designed to run unattended, you can still use the rehearsal method to get an idea of how many seconds to assign to each slide. Then you can assign timings directly.

Rehearse Timings

Before rehearsing timings, especially if you will be presenting your slide show, gather together any notes you might need so that you are ready to present. You are about to rehearse your entire presentation for the first time! Follow the steps described next.

1. Open your presentation and make sure that the first slide is displayed.

2. On the Slide Show tab, click Rehearse Timings in the Set Up group. PowerPoint switches you to Slide Show view and opens the Rehearsal toolbar, shown here:

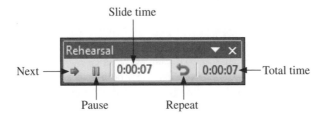

3. Start talking! Present your slide show like you plan to when you are actually presenting.

4. When you are finished with the first slide, click as usual to go to the next slide.

5. Continue until you have finished the last slide.

6. After the last slide, PowerPoint displays the time of the entire presentation and asks if you want to record the timing and use it when you view the slide show, as shown here. If you do, click Yes. PowerPoint switches you to your previous view and ends the rehearsal.

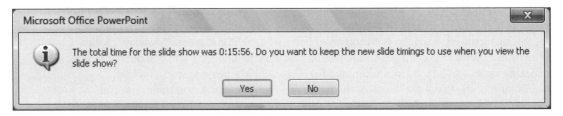

While timing a presentation, you have two other options on the Rehearsal toolbar. To pause the timing process, click Pause. Click Pause again to continue timing the slide. If you make a mistake and want to start a slide over, click Repeat.

After you have recorded the timings, you can see the time beneath each slide in Slide Show view, as shown here:

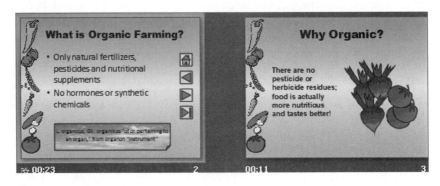

Assign Timing to Slides

You can directly assign timing to slides without going through the rehearsal process just described. You can also rehearse the presentation and then use the timings you obtain as a guideline for assigning your own timings. To assign timing to the slides in your presentation, follow these steps:

1. Switch to Slide Sorter view.

2. Select the first slide. If you want other slides to have the same timing, select them as well.

3. Display the Animations tab. In the Transitions To This Slide group, check Automatically After. Then use the text box or the arrows to set the number of seconds you want the slide(s) displayed. You can set timing to the hundredth of a second. The timing is applied to the active slide.

4. To apply the slide timing to all the slides in the presentation, click Apply to All.

Continue to set timing for other slides if necessary, using the same procedure.

CAUTION *When you set up a presentation to use automatic timings, don't include animation that requires a mouse click. The audience won't know that they need to click, and the slide will advance before the animation takes effect. Instead, set automatic timings for the animation as well. See Chapter 9 for more information on animation and timing. Another option is to show the presentation without the animation, as I explain in the next section.*

Use Timing When You Present

To automatically advance slides with the timing you set, you should make sure that the slide show is set up to use the timings. To do so, display the Slide Show tab. In the Set Up group, check the Use Rehearsed Timings check box. In addition, on the Animations tab, make sure that the Automatically After check box is checked.

Now, when you run your presentation in Slide Show view, PowerPoint uses your timings. You can go back and uncheck the Rehearsed Timings check box if you decide not to use the timings you have set.

NOTE *You can also choose Manually or Using Timings, If Present in the Set Up Show dialog box, discussed next and shown in Figure 14-2.*

14

FIGURE 14-2 Use the Set Up Show dialog box to specify how your presentation runs.

Set Slide Show Parameters

Before running a slide show, you can set a number of parameters that determine how your presentation runs. These settings give you last-minute control over your presentation. To set these parameters, display the Slide Show tab and click Set Up Show. The Set Up Show dialog box, shown in Figure 14-2, opens.

The Show Type section of the dialog box determines the type of show you want to present. By default, your presentation is shown full screen. However, if the presentation will be browsed by an individual at a kiosk or computer station, you can choose one of the following:

- **Browsed by an Individual (Window)** The presentation runs in a window and can include a scroll bar that people can use to run through the presentation at their own pace.

- **Browsed at a Kiosk (Full Screen)** The presentation runs full screen, which is a good option if your presentation will use automatic timings.

NOTE *If you chose the kiosk option, mouse clicks do not work. If you want to allow viewers control over the presentation, you must either include a scroll bar or add hyperlinks or action buttons that move the presentation to the next slide.*

For self-running presentations at trade shows and conferences, check Loop Continuously Until 'Esc' in the Show Options section of the dialog box. As soon as the presentation ends, PowerPoint starts the presentation from the beginning again. If you chose Browsed at a Kiosk (Full Screen), the presentation is automatically looped.

Check Show without Narration if you have recorded narration but don't want to use it. This is a great option for presentations that are sometimes run without a presenter and sometimes with one. You can also record narration for practice purposes and then check this box when you are ready to give the presentation.

Check Show without Animation to show the presentation at the end of any animation on each slide. Use this option when you want to allow individuals to browse the presentation themselves. Because they are not familiar with the animation, they could find it confusing to have to click several times before going to the next slide. Worse, if you have automatic timings, they won't click and the slide will advance before they see all the text!

In the Show Slides section, you can choose to display all the slides or only a group of slides. Specify which slides you want to display. If you have created a custom show (covered in the "Create a Custom Show" section later in this chapter), you can choose it here.

You can use multiple monitors to display a presentation. In the Multiple Monitors section, choose which monitor displays the slide show. The other monitor can display the next slide or speaker's notes for your own private viewing during the slide show. This feature is available only if you have multiple monitors. Most laptops support multiple monitors—the laptop's own screen and a projector, for example.

If your computer supports multiple monitors, you can use Presenter view, which lets you see a special view on one monitor while the audience sees the Slide Show view of the presentation. Presenter view, shown in Figure 14-3, includes tools to let you navigate to, and display for the audience, any slide so that you can customize the order of the slides.

To set up Presenter view, connect your second monitor (or a projector), if you haven't already done so, and check the Show Presenter View check box in the Set Up Show dialog box. A message may open offering to check whether your computer supports two monitors; if so, click the Check button. The Display Settings dialog box opens, as shown in Figure 14-4.

NOTE   *You can also access the Display Settings dialog box by right-clicking the Desktop and choosing Personalize. (Alternatively, click Start on the Windows taskbar and choose Control Panel. Double-click the Personalization category.) Then choose the Display Settings option.*

14

In the Display Settings dialog box, click the Identify Monitors button to display large numbers showing you which monitor is which. Then drag the rectangles, which represent monitors, so that they're in the same position as your real monitors. For example, if your monitor #2 is on the left, drag rectangle #2 to the left; this helps avoid confusion.

From the drop-down list, choose the Multiple Monitors option. If necessary, you can switch which monitor is the main monitor. Click the #2 monitor and check the This Is My Main Monitor check box.

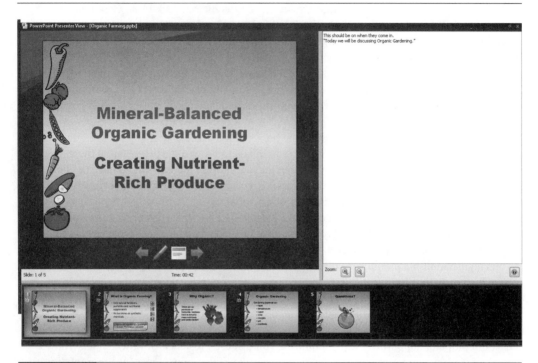

FIGURE 14-3 Presenter view gives you tools to control the slide show while the audience sees Slide Show view.

You want your main monitor (#1) to be the monitor that will show Slide Show view. You want your secondary monitor (#2) to be the monitor that will show Presenter view—the monitor that you will look at. On a laptop, therefore, the secondary monitor should be the laptop's own screen.

To turn on the multiple monitor support, select the second monitor and check the Extend the Desktop onto This Monitor check box, as shown in Figure 14-4. Conversely, unchecking this checkbox turns off multiple monitor support.

When you're done with the settings, click Apply. You then have to confirm the settings. If you got them right, click OK to close the dialog box.

In the Performance section of the Set Up Show dialog box, you can choose to use the capabilities of graphics acceleration if your video card offers this feature. You can also choose the resolution of the slide show. Usually, you can use the Use Current Resolution setting; however, if you don't like the result, you can change it.

Click OK when you are done.

FIGURE 14-4   The Display Settings dialog box enables you to specify dual monitor settings.

Prepare Your Notes

It's now time to think about what you will say when you stand up in front of your audience. If you haven't already done so, before going any further, research your audience. How much do they know about the topic? What do they want to get from your presentation? Even if the slides are the same, your explanation of the slides will change for varying audiences. Always get as much information about your audience as you can.

> **NOTE**   *The best time to research your audience is before you start writing your presentation, so you can design the content around your audience's needs and level of knowledge.*

As a last resort, if you can't get any information in advance, you may be able to ask questions of your audience just before you start presenting. You may need to make some quick changes to your planned talk based on the answers you receive.

If you will work from notes, print them out and use them when you rehearse. If you didn't create notes as you worked, now is the time to go back and add presentation notes for each slide.

14

To print notes from the Notes pane in your presentation, click the Office button and choose Print to open the Print dialog box. From the Print What drop-down list, choose Notes Pages and click OK.

> **TIP** *Notes pages make great handouts, because they show the slides plus what you said about each slide. Notes pages are especially useful when you need to send the presentation to people who missed your talk. If they view just your slides, misunderstandings can occur, but with the notes pages, they get a more complete message. I talk more about handouts in Chapter 15.*

Practice live in front of a person. Others can pick up potential problems more easily than you can. A useful technique is to leave out your overview and summary slides and see what the person remembers as your main points. Ask your test audience what was interesting, appealing, or confusing.

Before you actually deliver your presentation, prepare a backup plan. Every presenter has experienced or heard stories about equipment catastrophes. Practicing with your equipment not only benefits you, but it tests your equipment. Then think what you would do if your computer died, your projector conked out, or your remote controller stopped working. Practice your backup plan, too. Here are some musts:

- Always have printed handouts or overhead transparencies for the worst-case scenario— no electricity, a dead computer, and so on.
- Make sure you have a regular mouse if your remote controller doesn't work or gets lost.
- Always carry at least one spare bulb for your projector.
- If you are traveling, call ahead to see which equipment is available locally.

Create Slide Show Variations

Sometimes you want to vary a presentation. If you present a slide show more than once for different audiences, you can hide a slide in your presentation that isn't suitable for a specific situation. You must hide the slide in advance, so you need to think ahead.

To hide a slide, select the slide you want to hide and display the Slide Show tab. Click Hide Slide in the Set Up group. You can do this in Normal or Slide Sorter view.

Create a Custom Show

You can create a presentation that includes slides for more than one situation. You can then specify which slides you will use for one situation and which ones you will use for another. These variations are called *custom shows*. Let's say you are giving a presentation on a new employee benefit package but the packages vary slightly for two different groups of employees. You can create slides appropriate for each group and include them all in the presentation. Then you create custom shows that present only the slides you need.

Often, you start with a set of slides that is common to both groups. When the presentation must diverge, you jump to the custom show.

Did you know?

The Three Stages of Rehearsing

Before you present, you need to rehearse your presentation until you are thoroughly familiar with it. You should know your presentation so well that you almost have it memorized, but not well enough that you can repeat it by rote.

Practice delivering your presentation in three stages. The first stage is to talk through the presentation in front of your computer. You can look directly at your slides, which is okay for a first run. Repeat this step a couple of times. Next, attach your mike to your computer and use PowerPoint's narration feature to record what you have practiced saying, going through the entire presentation. (See Chapter 10 for details.) Now, sit back and run through the presentation again, just listening to the presentation. How was the tone? Did you speak too fast or slow? Were you clear? You are sure to find room for improvement. Make adjustments and go through the cycle of practicing, recording, and listening until you are happy with the results.

The second stage is to run through the presentation using the equipment (laptop, projector, and so on) you will use when you actually deliver the slide show. New elements to focus on at this stage are becoming comfortable with the equipment, talking without looking directly at the slides for more than a second, and standing up, even walking around a bit, while you talk. You should practice your opening remarks, when you will turn the lights up and down (if at all), how you will start and end the presentation (for example, opening and closing remarks; ending with a final slide or black screen), answering questions, and so on. If possible, rehearse in front of a real person to get feedback. If you can videotape yourself, do so. Just like narration lets you listen to how you sound, video lets you see how you look as you present.

The final stage is to run through your presentation in the actual physical environment you plan to use, if possible. (If you are presenting in-house, you can combine stages two and three.) If you will use a projector and screen, set them up and use them. Where will you stand? Check out the view from the last seat. Can you read the smallest text? Learn everything you can about the room—where the lights and thermostat are, where to get more chairs, where the outlets are, and so on.

Once you have completed these steps, you will be well rehearsed and ready for anything! The confidence you have gained from being prepared will shine through.

14

Another use for a custom show is to allow for more than one possible response from your audience. You could include some slides with more details if you find out at the last minute that your audience is more sophisticated than you expected.

To create a custom show, you must first create all the possible slides you will need. The variations should be together in a group so that you jump around as little as possible.

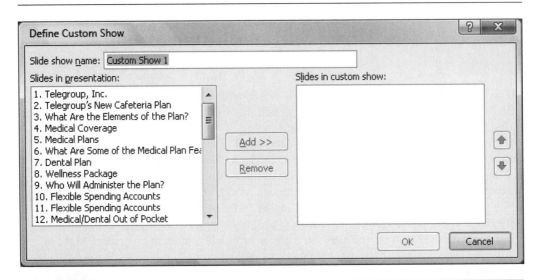

FIGURE 14-5 In the Define Custom Show dialog box, specify which slides go in the custom show.

On the Slide Show tab, click Custom Slide Show | Custom Shows. In the Custom Shows dialog box that opens, click New to open the Define Custom Show dialog box, shown in Figure 14-5. In the Slide Show Name text box, name the custom show.

Select the slides for the custom show from the Slides in Presentation list and click Add to move them to the Slides in Custom Show list. To select a contiguous group of slides, click the first slide in the group, press SHIFT, and click the last group. To select a noncontiguous group of slides, click the first slide in the group, press CTRL, and then select each additional slide. Click OK to create the custom show. PowerPoint now displays the Custom Shows dialog box with your new custom show listed. To preview the custom show, select it from the list and click Show.

Edit a Custom Show

To modify a custom show, on the Slide Show tab, click Custom Slide Show | Custom Shows. Select the show you want to edit. Click Edit. PowerPoint opens the same Define Custom Show dialog box you used to create the custom show originally. Use the same tools to add or remove slides or to move them around in the custom show.

To delete a custom show entirely, select the show you want to delete in the Define Custom Show dialog box and click Remove. Note that the slides are not deleted from the presentation.

Use a Custom Show

In most cases, you want to display slides not in the custom show with the option of using the custom show slides when you choose to. Using a custom show is like hyperlinking. There are three ways to jump to a custom show during a presentation:

■ Select an object on the slide where you want to create the option to jump to the custom show. (The object can be a text placeholder.) On the Insert tab, click the Action button in the Links group. On either tab of the Action Settings dialog box, choose Hyperlink To. From the drop-down list, choose Custom Show. PowerPoint opens the Link To Custom Show dialog box, shown here. Now choose the custom show you want. If you want to return to the same slide after displaying the custom show slides, check Show and Return. (Otherwise, PowerPoint displays the custom show and ends the presentation.) Click OK.

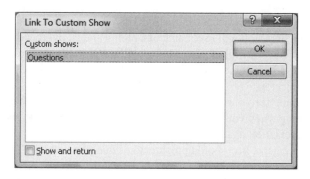

■ Select an object on the slide where you want to create the option to jump to the custom show. On the Insert tab, click Hyperlink in the Links group. In the Insert Hyperlink dialog box, click Place in This Document. Under Custom Shows, choose the custom show you want. If you want to return to the same slide after displaying the custom show slides, check Show and Return. Click OK.

■ In Slide Show view, right-click, choose Custom Show, and choose the custom show you want. When you use this method, you can't return to the current slide.

You can create several custom shows if you wish, but be careful not to make your navigation possibilities too complex. It's easy to get confused during your presentation!

NOTE   *In Chapter 11, in the "Create a Web-Style Presentation" sidebar, I explain how to create a nonlinear presentation. This technique is another way to create options to jump to different slides.*

14

To print a custom show, follow these steps:

1. Click the Office button and choose Print.

2. In the Print Range section of the Print dialog box, choose your custom show from the Custom Show drop-down list.

3. Click OK.

To set up your presentation so that PowerPoint displays *only* the slides in the custom show, display the Slide Show tab and choose Set Up Show. In the Set Up Show dialog box, choose Custom Show in the Show Slides section. This option is available only if the presentation includes a custom show. If you have more than one custom show, choose the one you want from the drop-down list. Then click OK. Now, when you start your presentation in Slide Show view, only the slides in the custom show are displayed. To display all the slides of the presentation again, open the Set Up Show dialog box again and choose All in the Show Slides section.

Summary

In this chapter, you reviewed all the necessary steps involved in preparing for a presentation. You need to decide which medium you will use: handouts, 35mm slides, overhead transparencies, or onscreen projection. You can copy all of your files to a CD-ROM, either to transport them or to create a presentation that runs automatically from a CD. The chapter covered information about choosing and using a projector.

You can rehearse timing for your presentation or directly assign timing. You can choose whether to use your timing when you actually present. You can specify slide show parameters, such as displaying a presentation at a kiosk or using two monitors.

Before you start to rehearse, you should prepare notes that you will use. Then rehearse, rehearse, rehearse!

To create variations on your presentation, you can hide slides or create a custom show. If you create a custom show, you can choose when delivering your slide show whether or not to use the custom show.

The next chapter covers the process of delivering a slide show.

Chapter 15

Present Your Slide Show

How to...

- Print and use handouts
- Use PowerPoint Viewer
- Practice professional presentation skills
- Control your slide show
- Let your slide show run itself

The time is at hand! You have completed your presentation, you've practiced and timed it, and now you're finally ready to present it to an audience. You need to decide if you want to print handouts. You may want to work on your presenting skills. Think about what will happen during the presentation—how will you control your presentation? Will you want to mark up slides to emphasize certain points? This chapter discusses these issues and more.

Print and Use Handouts

Of course, handouts are a great memory aid for your audience members, helping them remember what you said after the presentation is over. In most cases, you want to provide handouts after the presentation because people will tend to read them while you're speaking. However, if you have a great deal of technical content, a handout is easier for people to follow than lots of small text and numbers on a slide. This type of handout covers a limited amount of data-heavy content rather than the entire presentation.

If you are going to make your presentation using only printed handouts, you don't need any equipment except a printer, which you almost certainly already have. You should invest in a good color printer if you don't already have one. It's a shame to create color slides in PowerPoint and then print them in black and white.

Even if you want to give handouts to your audience only as take-home material, make them look as professional as possible. Your handouts will be sitting on their desks long after your voice has faded. Don't forget to package the handouts. Provide a pocket or binder folder at the very least. Make sure to include your business card or contact information if appropriate.

PowerPoint lets you print your presentation to use as handouts. When you print handouts for your audience, you are simply giving them a copy of your presentation, minus the animation and transition effects. You may also want to print handouts simply to show your colleagues and supervisors. To format your handouts, use the handout master. Don't forget that you can add a logo or other graphics to the handout master. (See Chapter 7 for an explanation of the handout master.)

Once you have formatted your handouts, click the Close Master View button on the Handout Master tab. You are now ready to print. Follow these steps:

1. If you wish to change the orientation of the page for printing, click the Design tab and click the Page Setup button in the Page Setup group. Under Notes, Handouts & Outline, choose Landscape or Portrait. Click OK.

2. From the Office button's menu, choose Print to open the Print dialog box.

3. In the Print What drop-down list, choose Handouts.

4. If you created a handout master, PowerPoint sets the Slides per Page drop-down list accordingly, but if you change your mind, you can change the setting here. You can print up to nine slides per page.

5. If you choose four or more slides per page, choose Horizontal or Vertical to specify the order in which PowerPoint places the slides on the page. The Print dialog box provides a diagram to show you the results of your choice, as shown in Figure 15-1.

6. If you don't want the border around the slides, uncheck Frame Slides. (The dialog box diagram does not display the result of this choice.)

7. Click Preview to see what the handouts will look like. To return to the Print dialog box, click the Print button in the Preview window.

8. Click OK to print.

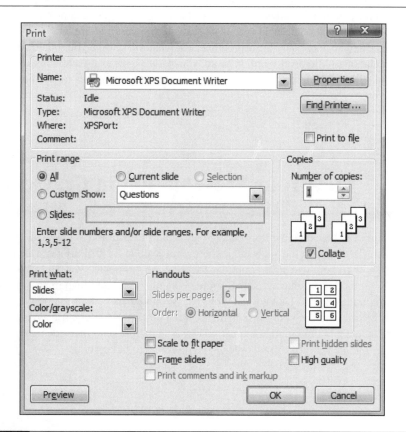

15

Use the Print dialog box to print handouts.

You can also make the presentation or handouts available to people for download from a web site. Chapter 12 explains how to display a presentation on a web site. You can record what you said using the narration feature, as explained in Chapter 14, so that people viewing the slide hear the full value of the presentation. Also, many people create handouts using the Adobe Acrobat Reader PDF format. Chapter 1 and Chapter 14 have more information about saving presentations and handouts in PDF format. For more information on handouts, go to http://www.indezine.com/products/powerpoint/pphandout.html.

If you need to send the presentation to people who missed your delivery, remember that the standard handouts do not include what you said. A better idea may be to enter what you plan to say in the Notes pane and use notes pages instead.

Send the Presentation to Microsoft Word

You may feel that printing handouts does not provide you with enough options. Perhaps you want to provide more information than you can fit using the handout master. For example, you may want to add supporting documentation or include references to the sources of your material. Perhaps you want your audience to take home only the text outline. For whatever reason, you should consider sending the presentation to Microsoft Word. In Word, you can make changes, additions, or deletions. You can also format the text differently. PowerPoint offers a number of options for sending your presentation to Word.

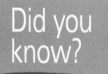

View Your Presentation in Grayscale

If you need to print in black and white, you can view your presentation in grayscale to see how it will look. To do so, on the View tab, choose Grayscale in the Color/Grayscale group. You then see a new ribbon with several options to refine the grayscale view. Unfortunately, if you use the common technique of using a template that includes a bitmap image or if you insert a bitmap image onto the background, your background does not appear, making it hard to judge the final look of your presentation. On the other hand, if you use a template that does not include any bitmap images or if you insert a picture onto the slide master (and send the image to the back of the draw order), you do see your background.

Here's how to send your presentation to Word:

1. Click the Office button and then choose Publish I Create Handouts in Microsoft Office Word. PowerPoint opens the Send To Microsoft Office Word dialog box, shown in Figure 15-2.

2. Choose one of the options. The options that include notes with the slides print the contents of your Notes pane. If most of your notes are for your eyes only, remember that you can change the contents of these notes once you have sent them to Word. For example, you could replace your notes with supporting information you would like your audience to take home, or with the text of your speech.

3. At the bottom of the dialog box, choose either Paste or Paste Link. If you paste link the slides, the Word document is updated whenever you make changes in your presentation and then open the Word document. If you are sending your presentation to Word to print handouts for a one-time presentation, you don't need to link the slides.

4. Click OK.

Wait while Microsoft Word opens with your presentation in the format you specified. It's a good idea to save the document before making further changes.

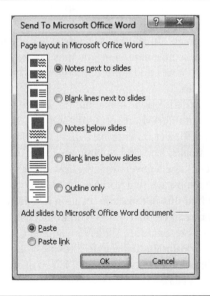

FIGURE 15-2   You can choose the layout when you send a presentation to Microsoft Word.

15

Once you have created your file in Word, you can use Word's more advanced features to edit the text as you wish. Here are some ideas for additions to your handouts:

- Thank your audience for attending.
- Tell your audience how they can contact you if they have any questions or want further information.
- Offer access information for web sites and other resources where audience members can obtain further information.
- Add supporting data such as a price list, delivery schedule, your resume, your company's history and accomplishments, and so on.
- Offer your audience a means of providing feedback on your presentation.

As you can see, this feature provides a great deal of flexibility, letting you design the most effective handout possible.

Use PowerPoint Viewer

PowerPoint Viewer is a program that can run a slide show on a computer that doesn't have PowerPoint. PowerPoint Viewer is an essential part of the road warrior's equipment. While you are on the road, your computer's hard disk may crash. If you have your presentation and PowerPoint Viewer on a removable storage medium (such as a CD), you can still show your presentation on any available computer. In another scenario, your client might have told you in advance that there is no time for a presentation or you may not be planning to show a slide show at all. However, if you have Viewer and a presentation with you, you can still show your presentation if the opportunity arises.

The main PowerPoint Viewer file is pptview.exe, but it requires several other files as well. You should have it in your Program Files\Microsoft Office\Office12 folder, but your location may be different. If you can't find Viewer on your hard disk, you can download the file from http://office.microsoft.com/downloads. Look for downloads for Office 2007 and then choose PowerPoint as the product and click the Viewers link. Follow the instructions to download and install it. Also, you may see a message that you need to download a converter to view PowerPoint 2007 files; you can find this in the same location on Microsoft's web site.

PowerPoint Viewer is free and can be distributed with no license required. For example, you can send it to a client along with a presentation. With Viewer, you can view not only PowerPoint 2007 presentations, but also PowerPoint 2000 through 2003 presentations. It also works with presentations created on a Macintosh (but viewed on a PC). You need Windows XP with Service Pack 2 or later (such as Windows Vista).

Present a Slide Show with PowerPoint Viewer

The easiest way to use PowerPoint Viewer is to use the Package for CD feature, as explained in Chapter 14, saving either to a folder or a CD. If you don't choose the CD and automatic start options, you need to start PowerPoint Viewer. To start PowerPoint Viewer, locate pptview.exe on your hard drive or on the CD and double-click the file to start Viewer, shown in Figure 15-3. Choose the presentation you want to play and click Open.

CAUTION *PowerPoint Viewer does not support multiple monitors, VBA (programming), ActiveX (certain objects from other applications), pen annotation, or navigation to a custom show.*

When you use the Package for CD feature and choose more than one presentation to include, viewers do not automatically see all the presentations if they start PowerPoint Viewer by double-clicking pptview.exe. Instead, they see the dialog box shown in Figure 15-3, where they can choose which presentation they want to view. This might occur if viewers have disabled the autorun feature in Windows or use Windows Explorer to browse the CD-ROM.

If you think you may show your presentation using PowerPoint Viewer, practice presenting using the program. Make sure you can easily open Viewer—you don't want to have to fuss to find it in front of your audience. You may want to put a shortcut to the file on your desktop. Check that the closing of your slide show is smooth and professional so that your audience doesn't see the mechanics behind the message.

NOTE *If you want to play more than one presentation at a time automatically, use the Package to CD feature.*

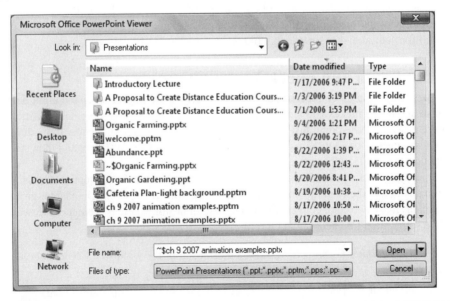

FIGURE 15-3 PowerPoint Viewer opens and displays PowerPoint files.

15

Practice Professional Presentation Skills

Most of the skills required for an effective delivery apply whether you use PowerPoint, paper handouts, or no visual aids at all. These skills are based on the relationship you create with your audience. A successful presentation includes the following characteristics:

- The audience has a need—for information, for a product, for training, and so on.
- Your presentation meets the audience's need.
- The audience understands and appreciates how your presentation meets its need.

As you can see, to create an effective presentation, you need to know what your audience needs. You also need to meet that need in a way that your audience can understand and appreciate.

Sometimes, you are the one who determines your audience's needs. If you are a sales manager presenting your company's latest products to your sales representatives, you have decided that your audience needs to know your company's latest products. All you need to do is present in a way that your sales representatives can understand and appreciate. The information you present in a clear manner provides the understanding. The excitement you generate helps your audience appreciate your message. If you are a teacher, giving a lecture to your students, you probably determine the content based on your syllabus.

In many instances, however, you need to do some research to determine your audience's needs and level of understanding. If you are speaking to a large group, you should try to find out from the group's organizers something about the audience members. How much do they already know about the topic? What is their level of education and expertise? Why are they attending? The answers to these questions can help you avoid a presentation that is either too simplistic or too advanced for your audience, or one that misses the mark entirely.

Set up the Room and Check Your Equipment

One of the best ways to prepare for a presentation is to get a good night's sleep the night before. Feeling fresh and rested makes you feel and appear brighter, happier, and more enthusiastic.

If you're nervous, settle down just before your presentation. If you know how to meditate, do so. If not, sit quietly for a few minutes with your eyes closed. Get up slowly and then start moving about and making preparations to gear up for the presentation.

Sometimes, you have no control over a room. If you are presenting in a potential client's office, you are probably not at liberty to move the furniture. When you are presenting in a larger group situation, such as in a classroom, convention center, or auditorium, you may have more leeway.

Here are some ideas for checking out a room:

- *Do you feel too hot or too cold?* Find the thermostat or the windows. Cooler is better than hotter.
- *Does the air smell stuffy?* Open the windows. Leave the doors open until your presentation starts.

- *Do you have enough chairs?* Are they comfortable? If necessary, get more chairs or move existing chairs farther apart. Hopefully, you won't have to replace all of the chairs, but an uncomfortable audience has a hard time appreciating anything.

- *Can people get to the chairs?* Perhaps the rows are too close together. A center aisle can help if the rows are too long. Depending on the number of people attending, you may want to set up the chairs all facing front or in a U shape. A U shape is more conducive to interaction, especially among the participants.

- *Does everyone have an unobstructed view of your screen?* If the room has columns, move the chairs that are behind them.

- *Will latecomers have to pass between you and your audience?* Perhaps you can create an aisle going toward the back of the room.

- *If you will use a microphone, is it working?* How do you turn it on and off? Can you remove it from the podium or its stand if you want to walk around? Try it out before the audience arrives to make sure it doesn't squeal. If you have a pin-on mike, make sure you can put it on and take it off easily.

- *Where are the lights?* If you need to turn down the lights to start your slide show, can you do so without walking to the back of the room or asking an audience member to do it for you? (A well-designed presentation room should have light controls at the podium, but you might not be in a well-designed presentation room.)

- *Where are the electrical outlets?* Are there enough of them? Do you need extension cords? If you have to run extension cords across the room, it is a good idea to tape them down with duct tape.

- *Where are the restrooms?* You should know the answer in case anyone asks.

Once you have checked out the room, set up your equipment. Set up your slide show as you want it to appear when your audience walks in. If you want to speak a while before turning on the slide show, open the presentation and simply turn off the projector or toggle off its image. Then you can start your slide show with one simple motion.

Now, with the slide show displayed, make sure the slide looks straight and centered on the screen. Decide where you will stand and where you will walk.

Finally, run through your presentation. Practice going back one slide and using your hyperlinks and action buttons. If you are using equipment provided by the facility, find out where the spare bulbs and batteries are kept, who can replace them, and how you can contact that person at a moment's notice.

When you are done, you can heave a sigh of relief. While the unexpected can always happen, at least you did everything you could to ensure a problem-free presentation.

Speak in Front of a Group

Many people are afraid of speaking in front of a group. While being 150 percent prepared helps, the truth is that once you strike up a relationship with your audience, much of your fear will dissipate.

15

An actor cannot create a relationship with his or her audience in advance because the requirement of acting is to stay in character, but you have a lot more control over the situation when you present. Here are some tips:

- *Chat with audience members as they come into the room.* Smile and introduce yourself. If they traveled, ask them how their trip was. Say anything to start up a brief conversation. You may even be able to use this opportunity to find out more about your audience.

- *Start your presentation with some humor, a quotation, or a personal experience.* This personal touch creates a pleasant relationship between you and your audience immediately (unless your jokes aren't funny or are in bad taste).

- *Dress conservatively.* You can never go wrong and you'll feel more comfortable.

- *Don't hide behind a podium or your computer.* If you are going to turn down the lights, start talking before you do so to let the audience see your face and get to know you.

- *Look at your audience.* Don't look at the slides on the screen for more than a second. If you need to look at a slide, it's better to look down at your laptop, because that way you don't need to turn away from your audience. When you speak, establish eye contact with as many members of the audience as possible.

- *Look at one or two individuals in more detail.* Pick a person to talk to, then another, and so on, so that you can focus on something. You will also get some feedback during your presentation—such as someone sleeping! You should be able to give your presentation with only occasional glances at your slides or notes.

- *Don't mumble.* Project your voice and feel free to use gestures and facial expressions. Express your enthusiasm for your topic. It's infectious.

Remember, your audience members are just people, like you. They probably empathize with you. They want you to succeed because they want to learn something. So they're with you, not against you. Just start!

Cope with Disasters

Sometimes a disaster occurs. Your computer crashes or the projector dies. You leave your projector on the plane. You rip your sleeve. Well, anything *can* happen.

For technological mishaps, always come with an alternative—overhead transparencies if you will have an overhead projector available, or simple paper handouts. Bring a change of clothes. Make sure you have with you a comb and any other personal articles that you might need. A bottle of room-temperature water is useful in case your throat needs clearing or you start to cough. Oh, and always use the bathroom before you start your presentation.

The Internet offers a number of useful web sites for presenters. These sites offer tips and advice for everything from organizing your presentation text to standing up in front of an audience. The following are some Internet resources for presenters that include information on the delivery process.

- **EllenFinkelstein.com**   My own site contains many tips on PowerPoint, including a section on delivery. You can also sign up for the free, monthly PowerPoint Tips Newsletter or visit the PowerPoint Tips Blog. http://www.ellenfinkelstein.com

- **Indezine**   Includes articles about PowerPoint and presenting from Geetesh Bajaj, the technical reviewer of this book and a PowerPoint MVP. A very wide-ranging site. http://www.indezine.com

- **Presenters Online**   Offers loads of articles and tips for presenters. http://www.presentersonline.com

- **3M Meeting Network**   Includes articles and advice on delivering presentations. Although run by 3M, there's lots of general information here. http://www.3m.com/meetingnetwork/presentations/index.html

- **Wilder Presentations**   Includes lots of visual examples and tips for your presentations. You can sign up for a monthly newsletter that includes ideas and tips for designers and presenters. http://www.wilderpresentations.com

- **SpeakerNet News**   Contains lots of helpful information for those who stand up in front of audiences. A weekly e-mail newsletter for professional speakers. http://www.speakernetnews.com

- **Presenters University**   Includes loads of articles on every aspect of presenting. An excellent site. http://www.presentersuniversity.com

- **Toastmasters International**   While not about PowerPoint, Toastmasters is a club that you can join to practice becoming a better speaker. Find the local chapter near you. http://www.toastmasters.org

Be Prepared When Using Computer Projection

Projectors paired with laptop computers have undeniably changed the way presentations are delivered. They encourage the use of color, photography, animation, and even 3-D effects. The portable and ultraportable models have led on-the-go presenters to take along their own equipment for assurance that proper equipment will be available and for ease of familiarity no matter what far-flung outpost they are visiting.

If you've recently adopted such technology, you're likely to read at least part of the user's manual to learn how to configure and adjust the system. Once you've mastered the physical connections and the software, remember to go these extra ten steps to make presenting with computer projection smooth and comfortable for both you and your viewing audience:

15

1. *Check colors for accuracy.* Colors vary among the desktop on which you design the presentation, the laptop screen, and the projection screen. If an exact color is important (for example, in a company logo), test and adjust the color in its final projection form ahead of time.

2. *Keep the colors and special effects simple.* Use no more than six colors on each slide. Use slide transitions and builds to entertain without detracting from your message.

3. *Test your slides for size and readability*. Stand six feet away from your computer monitor. If you can read the monitor, your audience will likely be able to read the screen.

4. *Turn off all screen savers*. Remember to disable the screen savers on your computer— any that are part of the computer software, plus the one that comes with the laptop. You would be embarrassed if you were talking about important points on the screen only to realize that your audience is staring at flying toasters. It would be even worse should your energy-saver kick in and shut down the whole presentation, so check the hibernation and power-saving settings.

5. *Learn how to use the toggle switch*. Find the switch that shows the image on both the computer and projection screens. Often the toggle is a function key; it controls whether your laptop, your projector, or both are on (showing an image). You want both to be on so you can look at the laptop while the audience watches the same image behind you on the screen.

6. *Arrive early and test everything*. Reread this line—again!

7. *Stand on the left as the audience sees you*. Because in English we read from left to right, if you stand to the audience members' left, they can look at you, follow your gestures to the screen—read left to right—and return their eyes to you. If you present in Hebrew or Arabic, reverse the approach.

8. *You are the show*. Too many people hide in the dark behind the laptop. You should stand away from the computer and in the light. Use a remote mouse so you can walk away from the computer. Arrange the lighting in the room so you are in the light while the screen is dark. You might even need to unscrew some of the lightbulbs.

9. *Motion attracts people's eyes*. Gesture to the screen when you want audience members to look there. Use moving text to grab their attention. Stand still when you want them to focus on the screen. Then move when you want to capture their attention again.

10. *Murphy's law applies to technology*. Any little thing might go wrong, so be ready to give your presentation without the hardware. If your presentation absolutely must be given by computer projection, have a backup system. Be prepared with backup files, a power source for the laptop and projector, and batteries for your remote mouse.

Thanks to George Torok, host of the weekly radio show Business in Motion *for this information on working with computer projectors. He specializes in helping sales and marketing people present themselves effectively. He can be reached at http://www.torok.com.*

Control Your Presentation

As mentioned earlier, you should display the first slide on the screen in Slide Show view before your audience arrives. You can turn off the projector or the switch that projects to the screen before you start, if you wish. If you cannot set up in advance, like when you present in someone else's office, you can open the presentation and switch to Slide Show view before turning the monitor around for others to see. The general guideline is to create a clean start.

Once you start, simply click the remote mouse to move from slide to slide. If you're working from your laptop, just click.

For more controls, you use the Slide Show View menu. As you move the mouse around, the menu bar, shown here, appears at the lower-left corner of the screen. The menu bar contains four buttons:

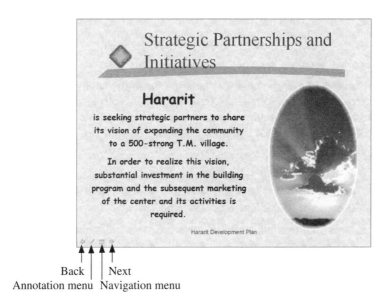

Back | | Next
Annotation menu Navigation menu

- **Back**   Goes to the previous slide or animation step on a slide.

- **Annotation menu**   Contains options for annotating your slides. You can also access these options by right-clicking and choosing Pointer Options. See the next section, "Mark Slides as You Present."

- **Navigation menu**   Contains options for navigating throughout your presentation. You can also access these options by right-clicking to display the shortcut menu.

- **Next**   Goes to the next slide or animation step on a slide.

Right-click anywhere on the screen to open the Slide Show shortcut menu.

15

You should be very familiar with this menu so that you can quickly navigate anywhere in your slide show. Here are some of your options on this menu:

- **Next** Moves you to the next slide or the next animation step.
- **Previous** Moves you to the previous slide or the previous animation step, if any.
- **Go to Slide** Opens a submenu that lists all the slides in your presentation.
- **Custom Show** Lists custom shows. (See Chapter 14 for details on creating a custom show.)
- **Screen** Provides options that control how your screen looks and functions:
    - **Black Screen** Displays a black screen. If you don't want to leave the last slide on the screen at the end of your slide show, a black screen is an alternative to returning to the PowerPoint screen. Returning to your application looks unprofessional because your audience sees the nuts and bolts behind the presentation.
    - **White Screen** Displays a white screen.
    - **Switch Programs** Displays the Windows taskbar (usually at the bottom of your screen) and the Microsoft Office Shortcut bar (if you have it open) so you can switch to a different program while still in Slide Show view.
- **Pointer Options** Offers options for the cursor arrow and for annotating slides. See Figure 15-4 in the next section for an example of an annotated slide.
    - **Arrow** Changes the cursor from a pen back to the default arrow.
    - **Ballpoint Pen** Changes the cursor to one of the three annotation modes. The ballpoint pen draws the thinnest line.
    - **Felt Tip Pen** Changes the cursor to one of the three annotation modes. The ballpoint pen draws a midweight line.
    - **Highlighter** Changes the cursor to one of the three annotation modes. The ballpoint pen draws a wide translucent line that looks like a highlighter.
    - **Ink Color** Opens a color palette where you can choose the color for one of the annotation modes.
    - **Eraser** Changes the cursor to an eraser. Drag the eraser over any annotation to erase it.
    - **Erase All Ink on Slide** Erases all annotation on the slide.
    - **Arrow Options** Sets the way that the arrow functions. Automatic, the default, displays the arrow but hides it if you don't move the mouse for three seconds. Moving the mouse redisplays the arrow. Visible displays the arrow all the time. Hidden hides the mouse all the time.

NOTE *Hiding the arrow removes any distraction for your audience. All they see is your slide show. On the other hand, you may want to use the arrow to point to objects on the slide. To use the Slide Show shortcut menu with the pointer hidden, you need to right-click. (The cursor reappears on the menu so you can choose menu items.)*

■ **Help**   Provides help, which hopefully you won't need during a slide show. After all, you are supposed to come across as knowledgeable about PowerPoint. However, this option can be a lifesaver if your remote mouse dies. PowerPoint displays a list of keyboard shortcuts (see Table 15-1) that you can use to navigate through your presentation. Click OK to close the Help screen.

■ **Pause**   Pauses a slide show that is running automatically using slide timings. (See the "Time Your Presentation" section in Chapter 14.)

■ **End Show**   Immediately ends the show. You can also press ESC.

Table 15-1 lists the many keyboard shortcuts that you can use if your mouse fails or if you like to use the keyboard.

Mark Slides as You Present

As a presenter, you have several techniques for focusing the audience on a specific item. The simplest is to use words; for example, "Look at the sales in the Northeast Division for last year." However, can you be sure that everyone in your audience has found the correct bar in your chart?

Many presenters use a pointer—either the old-fashioned wooden kind or an up-to-date laser one. A laser pointer is a necessity, of course, if you can't reach the screen.

PowerPoint offers the ability to annotate a slide directly. For example, you can circle a word or draw an arrow to that bar on your chart. The advantage of using annotation is that the audience can't miss it. The results are striking and immediate. The disadvantage is that annotation sometimes looks messy; with a mouse, you don't have much control over your circles and arrows. Figure 15-4 shows an example of the three annotation modes.

To annotate a slide, you need to change the pointer from its default arrow to a pen. If you are close enough to the keyboard, press CTRL-P because it is less distracting to your audience. Otherwise, right-click to open the Slide Show menu, choose Pointer Options, and then choose one of the options.

FIGURE 15-4   It's hard to keep the lines straight, but annotation can draw your audience's attention to a point on your slide.

The cursor now looks like a pen. To draw, move the cursor to where you want to start and hold down the mouse button as you move the mouse. Release the mouse button to stop drawing.

> **TIP**
>
> *If you plan to annotate a slide, practice beforehand. If necessary, change the color so that the annotation is visible. You can reset the pen color before starting your slide show. On the Slide Show tab, choose Set Up Slide Show. From the Pen Color drop-down list, choose the color you want to use. Choose More Colors to open the Colors dialog box for a wider range of color choices. Click OK.*

Shortcut	Result
N, ENTER, PAGE DOWN, RIGHT ARROW, DOWN ARROW, or SPACEBAR	Advance to the next slide or perform the next animation build.
P, PAGE UP, LEFT ARROW, UP ARROW, or BACKSPACE	Return to the previous slide or perform the previous animation build.
Any slide number-ENTER	Go to that slide number.
B or .	Display a black screen or return to the slide show from a black screen.
W or ,	Display a white screen or return to the slide show from a white screen.
S or +	Pause or restart an automatic slide show.
ESC, CTRL-BREAK, or -	End a slide show.
E	Erase existing annotations.
H	Go to the next hidden slide.
T	Set new timings (use while rehearsing).
O	Use original timings (use while rehearsing).
Both mouse buttons for two seconds	Return to the first slide.
CTRL-P	Redisplay hidden pointer; change the pointer to a pen.
CTRL-A	Redisplay hidden pointer; change the pointer to an arrow.
CTRL-H	Hide the pointer and menu icon immediately.
CTRL-U	Hide the pointer and menu icon in 15 seconds (or less).
SHIFT-F10 (or right-click)	Display the shortcut menu.
TAB	Go to the first or next hyperlink on a slide.
SHIFT-TAB	Go to the last or previous hyperlink on a slide.
ENTER while a hyperlink is selected	Perform the mouse click action of the hyperlink.
SHIFT-ENTER while a hyperlink is selected	Perform the mouse over action of the hyperlink.

TABLE 15-1 Keyboard Shortcuts to Use When Delivering Your Presentation

You can't leave the mouse cursor as a pen if you want to use the mouse to navigate through your slide show. If you try to click the mouse button, you just keep getting little dots on your screen! To change the cursor back to an arrow, choose Pointer Options | Arrow or press CTRL-A. If you want to keep the pen and can use the keyboard, you can use N, ENTER, PAGE DOWN, or one of the other keyboard shortcuts to navigate through your slide show.

As mentioned earlier, you can hide the mouse cursor, whether it is an arrow or a pen. From the shortcut menu, choose Pointer Options | Arrow Options | Hidden.

When you leave Slide Show view, you see a message, shown here, asking if you want to keep your annotations. Click keep to turn them into PowerPoint drawing objects that you can edit and save in your presentation.

Use Hyperlinks and Action Buttons

If you have created hyperlinks and action buttons to help you navigate through a presentation, now is the time to use them. While most hyperlinks and action buttons work with a mouse click, some may be set to work when you pass the mouse cursor over them. Watch out that you don't end up somewhere unplanned by mistake!

You also need to be careful that you don't get lost! It can be embarrassing if you go from slide to slide and forget how to return.

What you need is a compass. As discussed in Chapter 11, each hyperlink and action button should provide a return trip mechanism, but you need to make sure you know what it is, because not all hyperlinks and action buttons are obvious. In addition, you can forget that an object on your screen is a hyperlink or action button, especially if you have camouflaged it.

Create a list of hyperlinks to help you out or include the information in your speaker notes. List the location of the hyperlink or action button, what it looks like (if necessary), where it goes to, and how to get back. If you have action buttons that use a mouse over effect, be sure to note it. Make sure to take the list with you when you present, but, just as important, become very familiar with the list so that you don't need to refer to it except in a rare lapse of memory. The more complex your slide show, the more you need to know its myriad paths.

15

Summary

In this chapter, you saw how to create and use handouts for maximum effect with your presentation. This chapter also explained how to present a slide show using PowerPoint Viewer. A good part of this chapter covered the basics of professional presentation skills—you can use these skills whether or not you are showing a PowerPoint presentation.

Once you start presenting, PowerPoint offers a number of controls that let you navigate wherever your presentation might lead—even if off the beaten, linear track. You can also use any hyperlinks or action buttons that you have created.

You now have the knowledge you need to create and give professional presentations. I wish you all success. Enjoy!

Index

A

action buttons, 320, 322–324, 423
    navigation with, 320, 322–323
action settings, 323–324
ActiveWindow, 371
ActiveX, 363
    PowerPoint Viewer and, 413
adding slides, 39, 63–64, 97
add-ins, 367–368
Adobe Flash, 391
    animation with, 290–293
    in slides, 290–293
    Visual Basic and, 292
Adobe Photoshop, 158–159
Adobe Photoshop Elements, 159
alignment
    horizontal, 121–122
    of objects, 175–176
    of text, 120–122
    vertical, 122
animation, 96
    adding, 66
    charts and, 287–290
    creating, 274–275
    custom, 276–285
    diagrams and, 287–290
    dimming objects and, 283–284, *284*
    editing, 285–287
    emphasis, 278
    entrance, 278
    exit, 278
    fade, 275, *276*
    Flash, 290–293
    fly in, 275
    GIF files and, 290
    motion paths, 278–279
    objects, 274–275
    preset, 275–276
    repeating, 281–282
    slide master and, 224–225
    SmartArt and, 290
    sound and, 282–283
    start of, 279–280
    Task Pane for, 277–280
    text and, 274–275, 284–285, 288
    triggers for, 282
    using effectively, 295
    wipe, 275
arrows, 162, 164–165
AutoCorrect, 59, 87
    dialog boxes for, *81, 82, 84*
    options for, 356–359
    smart tags and, *84*
    using, 80–83

autoformat, 59, 356
AutoRecover, 359

B

Back Up Files Wizard, 10
background, 31
    changing, 185, 187–188
    colors of, 180
    creating, 188–197
    fills and, 201–202
    gradient, 188–192
    image, 192–195
    slide master and, 222–223
    solid, 18
    style, 35–36
    texture, 195–197
bevel, 92
    3-d effect for, 211–213
bitmap, *25,* 136, 326
blank presentation, 36
BMP. *See* bitmap
borders (outlines), 198–199
bulleted lists
    alternatives to, 117–118
    bullet color for, 106–107
    bullet size for, 106–107
    bullet type for, 104–106
    images as bullets for, 107–110
    indenting and, 115–116
    slide masters and, 223–224

C

callouts, 52, 168
CD
    add sound from, 303–304
    autorun, 388–390
charts
    adding, 64–65
    animating, 287–290
    area, 245–246
    bar, 245
    bubble, 248
    choosing, *242,* 242–249
    clear, 263
    column, 243
    doughnut, 248
    elements of, *253,* 255–260
    Excel and, 251, 262
    flow, 165–166
    formatting, 252–262
    inserting, 241, 262
    layout of, 254
    line, 243–244

charts (*Cont.*)
    linking to, 251–252
    organization, 272
    pie, 244
    presentation and, 64–65, 241–249,
        252–263, 262, 272, 287–290
    radar, 249
    saving, 261–262
    scatter, 246
    stock, 246–247
    style of, 254
    text in, 260–261
clarity, 70
classes, 371
clearing formatting, 86, 94
clip art
    collections of, 132–134
    online sources of, 136–138
    Task Pane for, 131–134
    using, 131–134
Clip Organizer, 134–135, 137–138
    drawing objects in, 168–169
clipboard, 72
    copying data with, 325
    importing slides with, 98–99
collaborating, 329–331
color
    background of, 180
    effect of, 186
    of fills, 200
    font, 95
    of gradients, 190
    re, 150–151, 180–185
    transport, 153
color scheme, 182, 355. *See also* themes
columns, 122
comments, adding, 331
communication, 4–5
    elements of, 5
Compatibility Checker, 334
Compatibility Mode, 10, 13, 26
compress images, 26, 154
connectors, 165
content, 5
contrast, selective, 186
Corel Paint Shop Pro, 159
Corel Painter, 159
CorelDRAW, 159
cropping images, 144
custom show, 402–406

D

data
    copying, 324–327
    interactive gathering of, 377–378
    presenting, 240–241, 262–267
    spreadsheets and, 249–251
    in table, 262–267
delete
    objects, 142–143
    placeholders, 75
    text, 74

default file location, 11
default file format, 27
delivery, 5
demote text, 42
design, 5, 34
    tips on, 176–178
Developer tab, 354, *356,* 369
diagrams, 267–271
    animating, 287–290
    formatting, 270–271
    process, 165–166
    SmartArt, 267–271
dialog boxes. *See also* Task Panes
    Action Settings, 323–324
    Add Clips to Organizer, 108
    AutoCorrect, *81, 82, 84*
    Document Inspector, 332, *333, 336*
    font, 94–95, 97
    Format Shape, 156–158
    Header and Footer, 225, *226*
    Insert Outline, 74
    Links, 328
    New Presentation, 30
    open, 8–10
    Picture Bullet, 107–108
    Play Sound, 301
    Publish as Web Page, 347–350
    Record Narration, *309*
    Save As, 22, *23*
    Sound Options, 302
    Spelling, 58
    symbols, *80*
    Wipe, *281*
digital certificates, 382
digital signatures, 333–334
dimming objects, 283–284, *284*
disasters, coping with, 416–417
Display Settings, 399–401
document management, 8
    saving and, 26
drawing objects, 141, 160. *See also* shapes
    arrows, 162
    curves, 162
    formatting, 163–165
    lines, 161–164
    saving, 168–169
duplicate
    slide, 98
    objects, 142

E

editing, 70–71
effects, *See* special effects
e-mail
    sending presentations with, 329–330
    from slides, 319–320
EMF. *See* Enhanced Metafile
Enhanced Metafile (EMF), 326
Equation Editor, 80
equipment
    checking, 414–415, 417–418
    choosing, 390, 392–395

F

fade, 275, *276*
files, 4–5, 25–27
    back up wizard for, 10
    default location of, 11, *12*
    encrypting, 333–335
    exporting, 326–327
    formats of, 22–23, *24–25*
    importing, 325–326
    managing, 329
    presentation, 4–5
    saving, 22–27
    sound, *299*
    video, *305*
    for web publication, 345
fills
    background-matching, 201–202
    color of, 200
    transparent, 201–202
    working with, 199–202
find, 76–77
Flash animation, 290–293
FlashPix, 326
flipping, 146
flowcharts, 165–166
fly in, 275
fonts, 80
    changing, 85–86
    choosing, 176
    color of, 95
    dialogue box for, 94–95, 97
    embedding, 360
    size of, 86–87
    spacing of, 87
    styles for, 87–94
    types of, 85
    x-height of, 176
footer, 225–227
Format Painter, 97
formatting
    auto, 59, 356
    diagrams, 270–271
    drawing objects, 163–165
    images, 155–158
    lines, 163–164
    paragraphs, 112–113
    removing, 86, 94
    slide master, 218–219
    SmartArt, 270–271
    tables, 265–267
Free form, 162

G

GIF. *See* Graphics Interchange Format
glow, 91, 203
gradients, 182
    for backgrounds, 188–192
    choosing stop position of, 190–192
    color of, 190
    types of, 190

graphics
    adjusting contrast and brightness of, 152–153
    content and, 178
    cropping, 144
    editing, 158–160
    impact of, 130–131
    recoloring, 150–151
    setting transparent color of, 153
Graphics Interchange Format (GIF), *25,* 136, 326
    animated, 290
graphs. *See* charts
grayscale, 410
grid
    custom, 173
    snap to, 172–173
group and ungroup objects, 146–148
group speaking, 415–416
guides, 171–172

H

handles, 49
handout master, 230–232, 410
    customizing, 232–233
handouts
    Microsoft Word for, 410
    print, 386
    printing, 408–410
    using, 408–410
headers, slide master and, 225–227
headings, 223–224
help, 20–21, *21*
Hide on Next Mouse Click, 288, *289*
hide slide, 402
HTML, 10, *24,* 340
HyperCam, 391
hyperlinks, 80, 314–315, 423. *See also* action buttons
    colors of, 180
    editing, 320
    to files, 317–319
    slide-to-slide, 315–317
    to web pages, 317–318
hypertext markup language (HTML)

I

images, 159, 187. *See also* graphics; stock photography
    alternative text for, 155
    backgrounds of, 192–195
    bullets with, 107–110
    compressing, 26, 154
    cropping, 144
    deleting, 142–143
    duplicating, 142
    editing, 141
    flipping, 146
    formatting, 155–158
    inserting, 138–139
    managing, 153–155
    moving, 142
    in presentation, 130–131
    resizing, 143–144

images (*Cont.*)
    rotating, 144–146
    saving cas picture, 109, 169
    selecting, 141–142
    substituting, 149–150
Impatica, 391
import
    outlines, 47, 74
    slides 98–100
    Spreadsheet data files, 325–326
    Picture files, 138
indenting, 113
    bulleted lists and, 115–116
    ruler and, 114–115
    text, 115–117
Internet, *See* web
isolation effect, 186

J

Joint Photographic Experts Group (JPEG), *25,* 136, 326
JPEG. *See* Joint Photographic Experts Group

K

kerning, 87
keystoning, 393
Kodak PhotoCD, 326

L

layout gallery, *37,* 37–39
layouts, 37
    of charts, 254
    Comparison, 45
    Content with Caption, 52
    custom, 229–230
    guides and, 171–172
    Picture with Caption, 52
    rulers and, 171
    tips on, 176–178
    Title Slide, 44
    tools for, 171–176
    Two Content, 45
lighting, 183
line(s)
    drawing, 161–163
    formatting, 163–164
    style of, 163, *164*
line spacing, 122
linking, 328
lists
    bulleted, 104–110, 115–118, 223–224
    numbered, 110–111
Live Preview, 354

M

Macro-enabled presentation file, 292
Macromedia Dreamweaver, 341
Macromedia Flash. *See* Adobe Flash

macros
    copying, 381
    editing, 380–381
    managing, 378–381
    settings for, 378–380
    signing, 381–383
    using, 378
    working with, 368–378
margin, 112
    changing, 118, *119*
Mayer, Richard, 178
method, 371
MHT. *See* Single File Web Page
MHTML. *See* Single File Web Page
Microsoft Digital Image, 159
Microsoft Excel, 64, 67
    charting in, 251, 262
    entering data in, 249–251
Microsoft FrontPage, 341
Microsoft Graph, 64
Microsoft Internet Explorer, 348–349
Microsoft Office Online, 31, 32
    clip art and, 136–137
Microsoft Office SharePoint Server, 101
Microsoft Outlook, 84
    sending presentations with, 330
Microsoft Paint, 159
Microsoft Visual Basic. *See also*
  Visual Basic for Applications
    editing, 369, 375–376
    Flash and, 292
Microsoft Visual Basic Editor, 375
    Project Explorer in, 381, 383
Microsoft Word, *48*
    sending presentations to, 410–412
Mini toolbar, 73
monitors, multiple, 399–401
mood, 183
motion paths, 278–279
move objects, 142, 171–176
movies. *See* video clips
multimedia
    definition of, 5
    impact of, 6
Multimedia Learning (Mayer), 178
music
    from CD, 303–304
    inserting, 298–300
    play settings for, 300–303

N

narration, recording, 307–310
navigation, 20, 320, 322–323, 419
Netscape Navigator, 348
Normal view, 16–17
Notes Master, 233–234
Notes Page view, 19, *19*
notes, preparing, 401–402
numbered lists, 110–111

O

Object Browser, 371, *372*
Object Linking and Embedding (OLE), 327
Object Model Reference, 369
objects
    distributing, 175–176
    drawing, 141, 160–165, 168–169
    methods and, 371
    properties of, 371
    ShapeRange, 371, *373*
Office button, 13, *14*, 15–16, 332
OLE. *See* Object Linking and Embedding
open dialog box, 8, *9*
    options for, 9–10
options, setup, 354–364
organization charts, 267, 270, 272
outlines, 76
    as borders, 198–199
    developing, 46
    importing, 47
    inserting, 74
    of text objects, 56
    preparing, 47
    structuring presentations from, 40–45, 47–48
    using, 47–48, *49*
overhead transparencies, 387–388

P

page size, 234–235
Paint, 159–160
paragraphs
    formatting of, 112–113
    spacing between, 124
    spacing within, 123
    working with, 111–112
password, 26, 334–335
PDF, 23, 391
photo album, 139–140
Picture Correction Options, 152–153
Picture Styles, 155–156
pictures *See* images
placeholders, 39
    content, 49
    duplicating, 76
    editing text in, 72–76
    OLE objects in, 327
    text, 49–51, *50, 51*, 72–76, 118, *119*
    working with, 75–76
PNG. *See* Portable Network Graphics
point, 86
Portable Network Graphics (PNG), *25*, 136, 326, 349
PowerCONVERTER, 391
PowerPoint
    add-ins for, 367–368
    color schemes for, 355
    customizing, 354
    earlier versions of, 10, 25–26
    files of, 4–5, 22–23, *24–25*, 25–27
    integration of, 326
    language settings in, 355
    object model of, 369, *370*

overview of, 4–5
screen elements of, 13, *14*, 15
setting popular options in, 354–355, *355*
starting, 6
web page creation in, 340–342
PowerPoint Object Model, 369, *370*
PowerPoint Options dialog box, 354–367
PowerPoint Viewer, 331
    presenting with, 412–413
    using, 412
PPT2HTML, 391
Prep4PDF, 391
presentation
    audience relationship and, 415–416
    on Autorun CD, 388–390
    backing up, 27
    being prepared for, 417–418
    blank, 36
    controlling, 418–423
    creating new, 6–8, *7*
    data in, 240–241, 262–267
    design of, 178
    directly from computer, 388
    disasters and, 416–417
    elements of, 5
    encrypting, 333–335
    from existing, 36–37
    faxing, 330
    file containing, 4–5
    framework for, 60–62
    keyboard shortcuts for, *422*
    linear, 321
    macro-enabled, 292
    Microsoft Word and, 410–412
    objective of, 46
    OLE objects in, 327
    opening, 6–12
    from outline, 40–45, 47–48
    outlining, 46
    permission restrictions for, 333
    protecting, 332–336
    purpose of, 5, 183
    reformatting, 391
    rehearsing, 395–396, 403
    reusing, 391
    reviewing, 331
    rhythm of, 177
    room characteristics and, 183
    saving, 22–27
    self-running, 399
    sending, 329–330
    setting up for, 414–415
    sharing, 329–330
    skills for, 414–418
    sound in, 298–304
    structure of, 40, 46
    timing, 395–397
    VBA in, 372, 374–378
    viewing, 13–15
    web pages from, 340–342
    web publication of, 344–350
    web versions of, 342–344
    web-style, 321

Presenter view, 399
Print handouts, 386, 408–409
process diagrams, 165–166
Project Explorer, 381, 383
projectors, 387–388
    brightness of, 393
    checking, 417–418
    choosing, 392–395
    LCD/DLP, 387–388, 390
    lenses of, 394
    overhead, 387–388
    resolution of, 390, 393
    terminology for, *392*
    35mm slide, 386–387
Promote text, 41
proofreading, 59
properties, 371

Q

Quick Access toolbar, 13, *14,* 16
    customizing, 365–368
QuickStyles, 88
quizzes, creating, 374–377

R

readability, 96
recolor graphics, 150
reflection, 91, 202–203
rehearsing, 394–396, 403
rename objects, 142
reorder objects, 148
replace, 76–77
resize objects, 143–144
return character, 111
Ribbon, 13, *14,* 15, 366
    Design tab of, 34, *34*
    Developer tab in, 354, *356*
    grayscale view on, 410
    Slide Master view and, *220*
Rich Text Format (RTF), *25*
rotating, objects, 144–146, 209–210
routine tasks, accelerating, 377
RTF. *See* Rich Text Format
ruler
    options for, 362
    slide layout and, 171
    using, 114–115

S

Save As dialog box, 22, *23*
saving, 22–27
    as picture, 109, 169
    default location for, 26–27
    document management and, 26
    file formats for, 22–23, *24–25,* 25–26
    options for, 26, 359–361
scale, 143
ScreenTips, 355, 362
scribble, 162

security options, 363–364
selecting objects 141–142
selection and visibility task pane, 142, 148
setup, 398–400, 414–415
shadow copies, 10
shadows, 89–91, 96
    3-d, 205–208
shape styles, 197
ShapeRange, 371, *373*
shapes
    closing, 162
    constraining, 174
    editing, 169–170
    fill options for, 157
    freeform, 162
    gallery of, 160, *161*
    inserting, 166–168
    substituting, 149–150
    text in, 53, *54,* 62, 77–78
    3-D, 208–211
    uses for, 79
Show Type, 398
Single File Web Page (MHT/MHTML), 345, 349
slide library, 101
slide master, 31, 61, *221, 224*
    animation and, 224–225
    applying, 229
    background and, 222–223
    bulleted text and, 223–224
    formatting, 218–219
    headers/footers and, 225–227
    headings and, 223–224
    making exceptions to, 228–229
    managing, 220–222
    repeating objects and, 224–225
    themes and, 222–223
    Title, 44
Slide Master view, 219, *220*
slide show
    creating variations of, 402–406
    custom, 402–406
    parameters of, 398–400
Slide Show view, 18, *18,* 67
Slide Sorter view, *17,* 17–18, 65
    working in, 97–98
slides, *4,* 4–5
    adding, 39, 63–64, 97
    Adobe Flash in, 290–293
    automatic advancement of, 397
    copying, 97
    creating e-mail from, 319–320
    deleting, 97
    duplicating, 98
    expanding, 75
    formats of, 386–390
    graphs in, 241
    hiding, 402
    importing, 98–100
    laying out, 37–39, *38*
    marking, 421–423
    moving, 65, 97
    presentation made up of, *4,* 4–5

rearranging, 97
reusing, 99, *100*
size, 234–235
35mm, 386–387
timing assigned to, 397
web pages from, 340–342
web publication of, 344–350
web versions of, 342–344
Smart Tags
AutoCorrect and, *84*
options for, 83
using, 84
SmartArt, 165
animation and, 290
diagrams, 267–271
formatting, 270–271
snap to grid, 172–173
snap to object, 172–173
soft edges, 204
sound
animation and, 282–283
file types for, *299*
inserting, 296, 298–300, 323–324
play settings for, 300–303
recording narration, 307–310
spacing
font, 87
line, 122
between paragraphs, 124
within paragraphs, 123
special effects, 202–204
glow, 91, 203
reflection, 91, 202–203
soft edges, 204
spelling
checking, 58–59
options for, 356–359
splash page, 321
spreadsheets
entering data in, 249–251
inserting, 252
stock photography, 138
substitute objects, 149
symbols, 79–80, *80*

T

tables
creating, 263–264
data in, 262–267
formatting, 265–267
importing, 264–265
tabs, setting, 119–120
Tagged Image File Format (TIFF), *25,* 136, 326
Task Panes
Clip Art, 131–134
Custom Animation, 277–280
Document recovery, 22
Reuse slide, 99–100
Selection and visibility, 142
TechSmith Camtasia Studio, 391

templates, 7–8
choosing, 30–32
creating, 236
finding, 236
themes vs., 219
text. *See also* WordArt
adding, 48–52, 56
aligning, 120–122
alternative, 155
animating, 274–275, 284–285, 288
bevel effect for, 92
body, 40–41
bulleted, 223–224
case of, 77
in charts, 260–261
color of, 180
copying, 71–72
direction, 78
effects, 56
finding and replacing, 76–77
glow effect for, 91
images and, 155
indenting, 115–117
levels of, 40
moving, 71–72
other effects for, 97
placeholders for, 49–51, *50, 51,* 72–76,
118, *119*
readability of, 96, 176
reflection effect for, 91
shadows effect for, 89–91
in shapes, 53, *54,* 62, 77–78
style of, 85–97
3-D rotation effect for,
92–93
transform effect for, 93–94
text boxes, *52,* 52–53, 77–78
uses for, 79
textures, 195–197
themes, 8
choosing, 31, 33–35
colors and, 180–185
creating, 182, 184
custom, 235–236
slide master and, 222–223
visual, 177
themes vs., 219
thesaurus, 59, *60*
35mm slides, 386–387
3-D effects, 205–215
beveled edges, 211–213
depth and contours, 213
lighting for, 213–215
material for, 213–215
rotation in, 92–93, 209–211
shadows, 205–208
shapes, 208–211
TIFF. *See* Tagged Image File Format
Title Master. *See* slide master
timing, 395–397
TonicPoint Viewer, 331

toolbars. *See also* Quick Access toolbar
    Mini, 73, 354
    Visual Basic Editor Standard, 369
transform, 93–94
transitions, 66, 274, 293–296
    choosing, 293–294, 296
    styles of, *294*
    using, 293
    using effectively, 295
transparency, 153, 160
triggers, 282

U

Ulead PhotoImpact, 159
undo, options for, 362
usability, 177
UserForm, 371

V

VBA. *See* Visual Basic for Applications
vector art, 148
Vector Markup Language (VML), 136, 349
video clips, 304–306
    file types for, *305*
    software tools for, 307
viewer, 412–413
views
    Handout Master, 231
    navigation and, 20
    Normal, 16–17
    Notes Master, 233
    Notes Page, 19, *19*
    Slide Master, 219, *220*
    Slide Show, 18, *18*, 67
    Slide Sorter, *17*, 17–18, 65, 97–98
    using, 16–20
visibility, 142

Visual Basic for Applications (VBA), 368
    code structure of, 371
    creating quizzes in, 374–377
    interactive data gathering with, 377–378
    macros in, 368, 380–381
    methods and, 371
    object model of, 369–371
    objects and, 371
    PowerPoint Viewer and, 413
    in presentations, 372, 374–378
    routing tasks and, 377
VML. *See* Vector Markup Language
von Restorff effect, 186

W

web browsers, 348–349
web pages, 340–342
Windows bitmap. *See* bitmap
Windows Metafile Format (WMF), *25*, 136, 326
Windows Mobile, 391
Windows Vista, 383
    file sharing with, 329
    open dialog box in, 8, *9*
Windows XP, 383
    open dialog box in, 8
wipe, 275, *281*
wizards, back up files, 10
WMF. *See* Windows Metafile Format
WordArt, 55–56, *57*, 62, 67, 88
    editing, 56, 79
    effects, 56, *57*
    Styles for, 89
    uses for, 79
WordPad, 327

X

XPS, 23